Once Upon a Time

J. RANDY TARABORRELLI is the author of ten books, including the bestsellers *Madonna: An Intimate Biography*, *Call Her Miss Ross*, *Michael Jackson: The Magic and the Madness*, *Sinatra: The Man and the Myth* and *Jackie, Ethel and Joan: Women of Camelot*.

J. Randy Taraborrelli lives in Los Angeles.

J. RANDY TARABORRELLI

Once Upon a Time

The Story of Princess Grace, Prince Rainier and their Family

PAN BOOKS

First published in Great Britain 2003 by Sidgwick & Jackson
and simultaneously in New York by Warner Books, Inc.

This edition published 2004 by Pan Books
an imprint of Pan Macmillan Ltd
Pan Macmillan, 20 New Wharf Road, London N1 9RR
Basingstoke and Oxford
Associated companies throughout the world
www.panmacmillan.com

This edition published by arrangement with Warner Books, Inc., New York,
New York, USA. All rights reserved

ISBN 0 330 41832 7

Copyright © Rose Books, Inc. 2003

The right of J. Randy Taraborrelli to be identified as the
author of this work has been asserted by him in accordance
with the Copyright, Designs and Patents Act 1988.

1 3 5 7 9 8 6 4 2

A CIP catalogue record for this book is available from
the British Library.

Printed and bound in Great Britain by
Mackays of Chatham plc, Chatham, Kent

All Pan Macmillan titles are available from
www.panmacmillan.com
or from Bookpost by telephoning 01624 677237

For my mother, Rose Marie Taraborrelli

A Word from the Author

If you could talk to the person you were twenty years ago, what would you say? Would you advise your younger self to forge a new and different path? Or do you think that the person you've become, the place in which you find yourself today, is exactly as you had planned?

When I began writing this book, I set out to tell the story of two people from disparate backgrounds brought together by a strange twist of fate to then share a life that was, I thought, as close to a true fairy tale as anyone could imagine: A famous actress, Grace Kelly of Philadelphia, gives up a successful career for the man of her dreams, Prince Rainier III of Monaco, to live royally at his side, as his Princess. Obviously, I was aware that the story would have a tragic ending because of Grace's untimely death. However, as I dug deeper, I found the tale to be far more complex than what first meets the eye. I discovered that it is also about choices, consequences, regrets, and, ultimately, acceptance.

Grace Kelly, at the top of her profession, was a woman ahead of her time, a person accustomed to blazing her own path, making important decisions about her life, refusing to become stuck in any circumstance—whether romantic or career-related. When this particular Cinderella was presented a glass slipper by her Prince Charming, she did what many women would do: She stepped into it, eagerly . . . and into his world. It was a perfect fit, or so they both thought. However, once the Princess got to the Palace, she was in for a big surprise. The illusion of perfection that surrounded her life in Monaco hid certain harsh realities: her imperfect marriage, her imperfect husband, and, eventually, her imperfect children.

For reasons explained in this book, Grace found herself trapped, unable to make a hasty exit as she had always done in the past when dissatisfied with a choice. Rather, she was caught in a strange place thousands of miles away from friends and family, and far from her career. The world she once knew and loved was gone forever, a casualty of her failed attempt to meld fantasy and reality.

Captive in a fairy tale of her own making, Grace felt she had ruined her life. It was only with the help of Rainier that she would then make some important and tough choices. She would learn that love is more than just a passion. It is an obligation. It is a commitment. While her world would still not be perfect—whose is?—she and her husband would bravely face future challenges, make the best of them, and have twenty-six years of marriage to show for their efforts, for better or worse.

While Princess Grace's circumstances are obviously extreme, her story is universal. Sometimes, the real challenge of living has to do with making a life that seems to no longer work . . . *work*. All of us have had hope that was, over time, transformed into regret. The secret is to not succumb to those regrets, but to rise above them, and then get on with things . . . just as Princess Grace did and, as you'll learn here, Prince Rainier continues to do, to this day.

It is my hope that, through the pages of this book, you will step into their world and get to know Grace and Rainier as real people, not only as royalty but as a man and woman courageous enough to face their demons, admit their shortcomings, and come to terms with their choices. She transformed a lost and lonely prince, product of a cold and loveless bloodline, into a kind and gentle leader. He helped the woman he loved find a way to say good-bye to the past and feel at home in the present. Together, they faced the future, raising three children who will, one day, continue their dynasty.

The story of Grace and Rainier begins as many fairy tales do: two young people drawn to each other, unaware of what awaits them, filled only with hope for the future . . . once upon a time.

J. Randy Taraborrelli
Los Angeles
March 2003

Contents

Once Upon a Time

When love beckons to you follow him . . . though his voice may shatter your dreams as the north wind lays waste the garden. . . . Even as he is for your growth so is he for your pruning.

—KAHLIL GIBRAN

PART ONE

Courtship

The Kellys

Grace Patricia Kelly was born in Philadelphia, Pennsylvania, on November 12, 1929, the third of four children to John—better known as Jack—Brendan Kelly and Margaret Majer Kelly. It is not difficult even today to come across Philadelphians who have fond memories and fascinating anecdotes about local legend Jack, recently described by a journalist there as "one of the greatest characters in the history of the City of Brotherly Love." The son of an immigrant farm boy from County Mayo, Ireland, Jack promoted the myth that he had started out as a poor bricklayer, quit high school to help his parents and nine siblings, started his own company, and then worked his way up the ladder of "hard knocks" until finally becoming a millionaire. In truth, Jack *did* quit high school, but only in order to have more time to practice sculling on the Schuylkill River, not to support his family. He did, eventually, lay bricks, but not on his own, at least not at first. He actually worked for two older brothers, Patrick and Charles, who had already established their own successful construction company. When the ambitious Jack later started his own company, "Kelly for Brickwork," he did so in competition with those brothers. Eventually Charles went to work for Jack, alienating Patrick and causing a huge family rift.

Jack Kelly was a man to whom image was paramount. He realized that his rags-to-riches story had great appeal, especially in 1935 when, at the age of forty-five, he was the Democratic candidate for mayor of Philadelphia. Although he lost that election—the Republicans had held the office for the previous sixty years—he garnered more votes than had any Democrat before him. He was a popular, formidable man in Philadelphia, and would remain so for decades.

While most of the Kellys simply accepted Jack's fibs as an element of his image-making mentality, George Kelly was always the one dissenting voice, the brother eager to set the record straight. An award-winning playwright, his successes included *The Torch-Bearers* (his first Broadway hit in 1922), *The Show-Off*, and *Craig's Wife* (for which he won a Pulitzer Prize). Jack's stories of an impoverished background were completely at odds with George's version of his own childhood. In truth, George could be as pretentious as his brother, but in his own way. For instance, he fabricated the story that he had been privately tutored; he had actually attended public school like the rest of his family. Though fastidious, a man of impeccable manners with an obsession for the proper serving of high tea, George couldn't escape his and Jack's background: They were middle-class, at best.

What needs no embellishing, however, is that Jack Kelly was dedicated and persistent enough in his practicing to finally win a gold medal in sculling in the 1920 Olympic Games, after having been previously excluded from competition at Henley. His medal, his ready wit, and his good looks would take him far. When he wanted to start his own business, he did not have to scramble for seed money. Instead, his brothers supplied the funds, George as well as Walter, a noted vaudevillian performer. (There had also been a sister, Grace, who had show business aspirations and for whom Grace Kelly would be named. Sadly, she died at the age of twenty-three of a heart attack while ice skating.)

Though the Kelly family was wealthy, because theirs was "new money," it denied them certain status. Jack and Margaret longed for acceptance into the ranks of Philadelphia's elite, but they would never achieve it, no matter the balance of their checking accounts. The highest stratum of Philadelphia society at the time consisted of White Anglo-Saxon Protestants—WASPs—and that was it: No other ethnic group was allowed entrée. Working against the Kellys was the unavoidable fact that Jack was son of an Irish immigrant. At the time, Irish Catholics were thought of as the "working class," looked down upon, regarded as inferior by the snobbish Philadelphia high society—and nothing galled Jack and Margaret more than the inequity of such a caste system. (It is ironic that in Grace's last film, *High Society*—a remake of *The Philadelphia Story*—her character, Tracy Lord, is a member of the same social circle that considered her to be invisible when she was growing up.)

Though not accepted in the "inner" circle of Philadelphia society, Jack Kelly was a true bon vivant and raconteur, a man brimming with clever anecdotes, everyone's best friend, the life of any party. Tall, muscular, and strikingly handsome, with receding dark, wavy hair and penetrating, aquamarine eyes, Jack always wore custom-fitted suits made for him by the best tailors in the business; he wouldn't even put his car keys in his pockets for fear of ruining the contours. Though about as nearsighted as a person could be, he refused to wear prescription glasses because he felt he looked better without them. Passionate about politics, Jack was an early supporter of Democrat Franklin D. Roosevelt—who had once described Kelly as "the handsomest man in America"—and campaigned for him in Philadelphia, where Republicans outnumbered Democrats ten to one. After he was elected President, Roosevelt remembered Kelly's support by making certain that the Public Works Administration offered work to Jack's Kelly for Brickwork company, which soon became one of the largest construction companies on the East Coast. Jack was also a close friend of George J. Earl, Pennsylvania's first Democratic governor in fifty years, elected in large part because of Jack's having stumped for him.

Margaret Majer Kelly, Grace's mother (called "Ma" in the family, short for Margaret and not a diminutive of "Mother"), was also an intriguing person, with noblemen in her German ancestry who could be traced back to Württemberg in the sixteenth century. The Majers had lived at Schloss Helmsdorf by Lake Constance before emigrating to Philadelphia. In 1914, when she was fourteen, Margaret met Jack Kelly at the Turngemeide swimming pool, a German club located at Broad Street and Columbus Avenue in Philadelphia, while the two enjoyed a recreational swim. Jack, a member of the swim team at Turngemeide, was ten years Margaret's senior.

Athletic, eye-catching, and full of life, the fair-haired Margaret held the distinction of becoming the first female athletic coach for coeds to be hired at the University of Pennsylvania. Also a local swimming champion, she went on to teach athletics to students at the Women's Medical College. Margaret also enjoyed a modestly successful career as a model, though it was not a vocation to which she was devoted, preferring instead to set her sights on traditional family goals. She married Jack Kelly on January 30, 1924, nearly ten years after first meeting him, at which point she converted from Protestant to Catholic. Margaret and Jack went on to make a formidable team: passionate, ambitious, determined—and both image-conscious, sometimes to the point of distraction, at least according to their friends and relatives.

In Margaret's view, Jack was the most fascinating, best-looking man in the Philadelphia metropolitan area, and no one would dare hint otherwise to her. Never, say those closest to her, did she think anything less of him, even though he was known to enjoy the occasional extramarital dalliance. However, "naive" would not have been a word to describe this strong-minded woman. She was well aware that her husband was unfaithful to her. "He's the kind of man women tell their secrets to," she once confided, "and, then, the girl wants him, he wants her, and that's that." As long as her husband was home when she needed him to be there, she would ignore his outside romantic entanglements, continuing to love and admire him. Anyway, divorce created scandal, and Margaret would have none of that. In situations such as hers, financial security was the supreme reward for feigning ignorance. If she ever challenged Jack about any of his consorts, the argument stayed strictly between them; no one close to the family seems to have any memory of open marital discord between the Kellys. Perhaps it was because she could not control her husband that she then tried to exert so much power over her offspring. The couple had four children in nine years: Margaret (Peggy) in September 1925; Jack Jr. (Kell) in May 1927; Grace on November 12, 1929; and Elizabeth Anne (Lizanne) in June 1933.

Margaret had her life just as she chose to live it . . . but at what cost? Though she acted the part well, she wasn't always the happy woman she presented to the world. The knowledge that she wasn't enough for Jack would eat away at her self-esteem, cause her to become brittle and, with the passing of time, unable to access honest, heartfelt emotions. Few knew the full extent of the emotional wounds beneath the surface of her sociable, polished persona. How would it look to outsiders if they were to discover the truth about her, about her marriage? Therefore she would never allow herself to lose control and would always keep others at a distance.

Still, Margaret was a woman with impeccable taste—and there was a great deal to be said for such an attribute if one hoped to move smoothly in society circles. Her table was always beautifully appointed with fine china, the food always delicious, exotic, and elaborately served. The consummate hostess, she was hospitable, personable, chatty, and witty. Servants at her parties were instructed to casually meander about in order to create an easy atmosphere. "I don't want my guests to think they [her employees] are afraid of me," she explained to a relative at a holiday party one year. "Though, in truth, they had damn well better be," she concluded with a wink.

Jack and Margaret's colonial manse at 3901 Henry Avenue, in the East Falls section of Philadelphia across the Schuylkill River from the Main Line, was built brick by brick by Jack's company, Kelly for Brickwork. Boasting seventeen opulently appointed rooms, the house sat on parklike, beautifully manicured grounds, along with a tennis court, a game room, and garage space for expensive antique automobiles. It was a showplace, an estate to which the four Kelly children could proudly invite friends for extravagant parties, a place where all were encouraged to engage in athletics.

Jack, always the competitive "man's man," was a strong believer in physical fitness.* He had hopes that his brood would be the most athletic on the block, and three of his offspring were qualified for that challenge. Grace, though, was a disappointment. Eventually,

---

*In March 1956, Jack Kelly wrote an article, "Are We Becoming a Nation of Weaklings?" for *American,* later reprinted in *Reader's Digest.* In it he complained, "American youngsters today are weaker and flabbier than those in many other countries, and they are growing softer every year. Their physical fitness or lack of it constitutes one of our gravest problems. If parents and teachers fail to wake up to the alarming trend, we shall become a nation of weaklings."

when she got older, she would become a fairly good swimmer and tennis player, but mostly in an unsuccessful bid to please her father. As a young girl Grace lacked the self-assuredness that was one of the defining characteristics of the rest of the Kelly family. She was the child who would trip on her own feet while running up the stairs, bloodying her chin in the process. She was the needy girl with the runny nose who never seemed quite healthy; she had a cold for what seemed like ten years. She was the scared kid who hid behind Mommy's skirt as Daddy begged her to "at least try" to dive into the deep end of the swimming pool. More than once Jack demanded to know, "What's Grace sniveling about now?" It was as if the family had a secret meeting, took a vote, and decided that Grace was the odd one out.

This family dynamic led Grace to retreat within herself as a child and create a rich world of fantasy. The reality that she was an unwelcome guest in her own home would inspire her to dream of a different life, a life in which she was the center, where she was noticed, where she mattered. However, all the childhood reverie couldn't change the circumstances of her early youth: Grace grew up lonely, timid, and feeling like an ugly duckling in a family of swans.

A Complex Family

Past accounts of Grace Kelly's life have suggested that she was unloved by her parents. While there is no doubt that Grace had a difficult childhood, family interactions are far too complicated to be painted with broad strokes of the brush. Whether trying to understand the Kellys of suburban Philadelphia, the Grimaldis of

Monaco, or any familial unit anywhere, a family's internal dynamics are difficult for spectators to fully understand.

Actually, Jack and Margaret loved all of their children. However, as often happens in families, they had their favorites, and Grace didn't place on top of either preferred list, most especially her father's. Because she was such an anomaly in the family, Jack barely knew what to do with her, how to handle her. He was even a bit fearful of her. In his view, she was so fragile that "if you look at her the wrong way, she'll probably start bawling," as he once put it. No doubt, there were times when young Grace felt unappreciated in her family, even disregarded and unloved—but they were her family members nonetheless, and she never ceased to adore them unconditionally.

Grace would always have a complex relationship with her mother, to whom she gravitated as a result of her father's disaffection. However, as much as Margaret cared for her daughter, it was difficult for her to be demonstrative emotionally, not only to Grace but to all her children. Margaret was reserved and detached, almost to the point of frostiness. She was fine as long as one didn't expect her to give much of herself. If one did, she would close up like a clam under attack. Also, like her husband, Margaret was rigid, tough-minded, principled, and determined to instill a sense of propriety in her offspring, often at the expense of tenderness and understanding. However, she and young Grace would often be seen walking on the beach at the family's Ocean City, New Jersey, summer home, immersed in long conversations. Family photos show them looking as if they adore one another. Of course, when someone on the other side of a camera says, "Smile," people usually do just that. Still, while other accounts of Grace's life have portrayed Margaret as being an unfeeling mother, a more accurate version would present a trait that Grace and her mother shared. Each of these women, in their own right, had an emotional intuition; an ability to see both the joys and injustices handed them. Sadly, the injustices far outweighed the joys: Margaret, an unhappy spouse married to a man who needed more than she was able to give, and Grace, a lackluster child, living in the shadow of overachieving siblings. While these women had the same knack for emotional understanding, they wouldn't speak of their deep pains. Such discussion would have been considered self-pitying—and more was expected of them than that.

It had always been the eldest daughter who filled Jack and Margaret's world with sunshine. Grace's sister Margaret, born in June 1925, was known as Peggy, although to her adoring father she was always "Baba." Peggy was tough, she was smart, she never cried (or certainly not in front of Jack, anyway). Mention Grace to Jack, and he would inevitably find a way to turn the conversation around to Peggy, the pretty one, the funny one, the one who would go on to make him proud. She actually was quite a woman, well-known among friends for her splendid Irish sense of humor, her disarming charm. As a young woman, Peggy was a prize-winning amateur artist; her father marveled at her talent. Jack had great expectations for Peggy, and could hardly imagine Grace doing anything worthwhile with her life. Grace was "a good girl," "a nice girl," "a pretty girl" . . . and whatever she would do with her life would probably, at least in her father's view, not be anything that would shake up the world. She'd probably marry someone who didn't have much going for him, Jack reasoned. They'd have a few kids, and then, if they were lucky, maybe one of *those* children would amount to something, but not Grace.

Peggy and Grace had their places in the pecking order of the family, as did Lizanne, born Elizabeth Anne, in June 1933 (and sometimes also known as Lizzie). Though not as funny or as athletic as Peggy, Lizanne was the more personable sister, or at least that was the opinion of most adults who visited the family's home. She too dabbled in acting, appearing in a few theatrical productions in the Philadelphia area, though she never took it seriously. She was an observer, a girl with uncommon common sense. From an early age, she had a deep, intuitive understanding of the family's dynamics. "I knew Peggy was the favorite and Grace was the one trying to win favor," she now says. "I fell in the middle of the girls somewhere, mostly as a witness to all of the drama. I was the one who sat back and tried to figure it out, rather than be too affected by it."

Once, when Lizanne was five, she got so angry with Grace that she locked her in a cupboard. "I hoped she'd start kicking and screaming, just lose her composure. But hours went by with no sound. In exasperation I unlocked the door. Grace didn't even look up. She just said, 'Hi, Lizzie.' She had been playing with her toys for all that time. She seemed to have been born with a serenity the rest of us didn't have."

No matter what little sibling rivalries occurred among them, the four impeccably behaved Kelly children were always close, and would remain so throughout their lives. They rarely exhibited any jealousy of one another. Rather, they were protective of each other, sometimes even forming secret alliances of understanding against their parents, as children of complex families often do.

Outside the family, Grace seemed fun-loving and giggly to a small number of friends, but her shyness made her appear cold and aloof to those who did not know her well, especially to her peers in junior and senior high school. By the time she was about twelve, she began wearing glasses for nearsightedness, an eye condition she shared with her father. Small, thin, shy, and bespectacled, she certainly wasn't one of those girls found in the popular clique at school. "Grace was an ugly duckling when you consider how damned good-looking the rest of the family was," said Jane Wooster Scott, who was a childhood friend of Lizanne's and later became friendly with Grace in New York. "She was the plainest of them all. Her brother was drop-dead gorgeous! Actually, they all were."

Grace became interested in acting around her twelfth year. In 1942, she appeared in *Don't Feed the Animals*, staged by the Old Academy Players, a small theater group near the family home in East Falls. Though Jack and Margaret were impressed by Grace's natural ability, they were also certain that she was going through a phase, one that she would, hopefully, soon outgrow. Jack couldn't find the time to pay much attention to Grace's acting anyway. His focus, when not on Peggy, was on the tall, rugged, and handsome "Kell," born John Brendan, Jr., in May 1927, the golden son destined to balance the scales of history for the Kelly family.

As it happened, Jack had never gotten over his exclusion from the Diamond Sculls at Henley in 1920 by an interpretation of nine-teenth-century rules (which have since been changed) whereby a man who performed manual labor—and Jack was considered a bricklayer—was thought of as having an unfair advantage in strength over "better-bred" English entrants, or "gentlemen."[*]

Later that year, he took his revenge at the subsequent Olympics by beating his English rival and then triumphantly sending his row-ing cap to Buckingham Palace. However, that victory was not ret-ribution enough for him. He insisted that Kell take up rowing, even though the boy didn't much like the sport at first, preferring foot-ball. Father personally began training son when he was seven years old, intent on turning the youngster into a personal instrument of vengeance aimed at winning at Henley. Kell was constantly en-couraged to excel in sculling, at the expense of any other hobbies, or friends—or anything else—in his young life.

After coming in second in his first race, Kell would eventually win the Diamond Sculls Regatta at Henley in England, which would certainly make his father proud even if it would do little to enhance their relationship. (Kell would also go on to win a bronze medal in the 1956 Olympic Games.) "The old man pushed the hell out of me," Kell once recalled.

Meanwhile, Grace had attended the Ravenhill Convent School for nine years, beginning in 1934, until transferring to Stevens High School ("wonderful and terrible years") in nearby German-town, Pennsylvania. She graduated in May 1947. In the fall of that year, she enrolled at the American Academy of Dramatic Arts in New York, almost by chance. Grace's parents had been so immersed in Kell's regatta efforts that—no surprise—they ignored the fact that she was due to enter college later that same year. At the time, universities were crowded with returning veterans attending on the GI Bill, and so, with her late application, Grace could not enroll at Bennington, a women's college in Vermont, her first choice. Through the intercession of Marie Magee, Ma Kelly's friend, who

---

[*]Another version of this story has it that what actually occurred at Henley was a disagreement be-tween Jack's sponsor and Henley stewards, and had nothing to do with Jack having been a manual laborer.

invoked the name of George Kelly, Grace was finally accepted at the Academy. Grace's sister Lizanne has recalled that her parents expected Grace to last no more than a month in New York, agreeing that she should probably go "just to get it out of her system."

Usually in the narrative of celebrity biographies, the child with an interest in show business is at cross-purposes with parents who have more "realistic" goals in mind for their offspring. The child then has to convince Mom or Dad that being a doctor or being an attorney is not what he or she wants to do, and then plead for the chance to try show business. That is not Grace Kelly's story. Her parents really had not yet thought of her as doing anything specific with her life, in terms of a career, so she wasn't letting them down in her ambition to be an actress. Whatever she chose to do would have been more than what they expected of her.

However, Jack recognized that show business was a tough game, and that if his daughter was to become a player, she should be prepared. "It's a dangerous profession before and after you reach the top," he told Grace, according to his later recollection. "If you go into this, you must dedicate yourself to it. You can't be halfway about it. There will be sacrifices. Once you reach the top, you become public property. There will be no privacy. The public will make great demands on you." It's interesting that in trying to scare her with the worst, Jack was actually predicting for Grace what would have to be the best possible scenario for any actress: enormous success and worldwide acclaim. Finally, according to what he would remember, he asked his young daughter the big question: "Are you ready to pay the price?"

The answer to that question was simple for a buoyant Grace Kelly in 1947: a quick, resounding "Yes!"

"Okay, then," said Jack. "See you later, alligator."

"In a while, crocodile," Grace said, finishing their good-bye in the Kelly family tradition.

After the chat with her dad, Grace felt ready to meet an uncertain future. She had boundless energy, even if she didn't have enthusiastic parental approval. At least there was an understanding between father and daughter that she should try her hand at acting.

Whereas her siblings pretty much did what their parents wanted them to do, Grace was as much the rebel in the family as she was the runt of the litter. Off to New York she went. Lizanne recalled Margaret telling Jack, "Look, it's not as if she's going off to California, right? She'll be back."

Once there, Grace became fascinated by New York. In recent years, she had bonded with her Uncle George—also an outcast in the family because of his chosen profession and apparent (but discreet) homosexuality—and had felt inspired and emboldened by his achievements. George was a worldly, vivacious man whose stories were the stuff of show business legend. Lizanne recalls that she and Peggy were "bored to tears by George's endless anecdotes, but Grace savored every one of them." George encouraged her in her New York dreams, visited her regularly (he lived in Pennsylvania), and assisted her in making contact with certain influential showbiz folk who could, hopefully, one day help her.*

In New York, Grace Kelly lived at the strict and conservative Barbizon Hotel for Women, located at Lexington Avenue and 63rd Street.† While there, she met people who would become lifelong friends, including roommates (at different times) Prudy Wise, Carolyn Scott, and Sally Parrish. However, there were also some who remembered her as chilly and remote, a "big snob," as one woman called her.

Much like her mother, Grace was not an easy woman to know, not emotionally accessible to others. Grace had her own reasons for being remote and unreachable. For years, she had felt emotionally beaten down, treated by her father as if she weren't destined to amount to much, held by her mother at a careful arm's length.

---

*Grace was ahead of her time in her tolerance of alternative lifestyles. Unlike her parents, particularly her mother, who had no time for George because of what she presumed to be his sexual orientation, Grace was open-minded when it came to homosexuality. For instance, in a letter to her friend Prudy Wise in early 1953, she chastised Prudy for having mocked a gay friend of theirs. "He's very sensitive and I'm sure he must have been hurt by that," Grace wrote. "You must be so careful around him, talking about queers. If he has those tendencies, you shouldn't criticize. It is so easy to become mean without realizing it."

†In 1981 the hotel changed its name to simply the Barbizon, opening its doors to men as well as women.

Though she loved her siblings, and they returned her affection, she didn't really relate to them when she was younger. It was as if she had no real place in their world. Who were these people with whom she had spent her childhood, anyway? Surely, as she once recalled having thought, she must have been adopted. Her *real* family was no doubt a dreamy bunch who detested sports and spent quality time huddled in front of a roaring fire. It's no wonder Grace was reserved, protective, sometimes mistrustful. Like many adults who are regarded as aloof and distant, she was actually still the hurt, damaged, and easily intimidated girl of her youth—especially cowed by people who seemed confident and secure, those who glided easily through life, fitting comfortably into the scheme of things as square pegs do in square holes, round pegs in round ones.

Grace enjoyed the quickened pace of life of Manhattan, as well as the challenges offered her by the Academy. Although she hoped to become a stage actress, she first became successful as a print model. Not only did she appear on the covers of *Redbook*, *Cosmopolitan*, *True Romance*, and *True Story*, but she also was in Old Gold cigarette ads and was a candidate for Miss Rheingold, a modeling competition sponsored by Rheingold beer, the winner awarded a year-long contract to appear in the brewer's ad campaign. She found that her wholesome yet glamorous appearance was perfect for a variety of television advertising campaigns for toothpastes, soaps, and detergents. She also made many guest appearances on TV dramas.

Such work wasn't easy for her, as anyone who knew her well would later recall. It was because of the persistent encouragement of several people close to her, trusted friends whom she met at school as well as professors who believed in her, that Grace Kelly was able to muster the courage she needed in order to go on auditions. She didn't feel like a beauty on the inside, even though she most certainly was one on the outside. Only a person raised as she had been, or who knew the specifics of her story, would be able to recognize the courage it took for Grace to persevere, especially on those days when she would be rejected for a role simply because she "wasn't right" for it. She confided in some friends that on audition days she experienced a knot in her stomach from the moment she awakened until the moment she went back to bed. To have to act as if she were a self-confident performer, a woman who believed in who she was as well as in her ability to "be" someone else—to occupy any personality or identity—was often a more challenging job than the one for which she was auditioning.

"Still, she was determined, a trait I guess she got from her father," said her friend Sally Parrish. "If she didn't get much else from him, she got that. Plus, of course, she had 'it'—whatever 'it' is. It didn't take years for her to build her confidence. That was Grace. 'You just do it,' was her motto. I guess she got that from Jack, too."

Concurs popular writer Dominick Dunne, "Oh, she was fabulous. I stage managed her on television shows in the early fifties. She was the only unknown actress I ever knew who wore a mink coat to rehearsal. Sometimes, if you looked at her closely when she wasn't aware, you sensed that it was all an act, that she was on the edge of losing it. But she never did."

Ever the practical Kelly daughter, Grace used the money she made while modeling and making TV commercials to pay for her tuition at the Academy, and for her room at the Barbizon. Somehow, it seems poetic justice that she didn't require, or desire, her parents' financial assistance. Even though she would always look to her family, especially her father, for approval, paying her own bills was a major step toward independence from them. Would her eventual success as an actress change anything, though? Would it magically transform her father's opinion about her, making him suddenly realize that he had been wrong about her, that she had always possessed the potential to do something wonderful with her life?

Actually, Grace's Hollywood triumph would come as a complete surprise to Jack Kelly—or at least he would always act as if it had. Even after she was an acclaimed actress, well loved by the world and respected by her peers, he withheld his support of her. He rarely treated her in a way that would have made her feel that he was proud of her accomplishments. Even as he got older, Jack would remain a real "character" to whom people gravitated—always the funny one, the back-slapping one with the best jokes. Surely he viewed it as much more interesting for him to act astonished by Grace's success than to play the role of the encouraging, pleased father. As years went by, it became his shtick: Peggy was the favored daughter, not Grace. That's the way it was, and the way it would always be for Jack—even when it didn't really make much sense anymore.

For instance, when Grace later won her Oscar for *The Country Girl*, Jack expressed bewilderment by her achievement. "I thought it would be Peggy," he told the press. "Anything that Grace could do, Peggy could always do better. I simply can't believe Grace won. Of the four children, she's the last one I'd expect to support me in my old age. How do you figure these things?"

Though comments like that hurt Grace deeply, she, like most children in such situations, understood her parent better than the outsiders to whom such insults were made. Often she would explain away her father's insensitivity to concerned friends by saying, "Well, that's just Daddy being Daddy." If pushed about his thoughtlessness, Jack would bluster, "Oh, come on! You know I don't mean it. That's just the way I am."

Luckily for Jack Kelly, Grace decided to hide from the world the personal disappointment his jibing caused her. She made a valiant effort to appear the easygoing daughter of a good-humored Irishman. Yet the years of constant ribbing affected Grace, and led her on a hopeless quest to win the approbation of her father. It turned out that some of her choices, as a means to that end, would prove to be more than a bit startling.

Actress

In 1947, at the age of eighteen, Grace Kelly left Philadelphia for New York to attend the American Academy of Dramatic Arts. During her second (and final) term, just before she turned nineteen, she met Don Richardson (né Melvin Schwartz), thirty, a former student at the Academy, and now a teacher of acting. A professional director as well as a teacher, he had most recently worked with Richard Burton on Broadway. He was separated from his wife. Years later, Don said that his relationship with Grace became intimate the evening he first met her at the Academy, and then continued surreptitiously, lest he find himself in hot water as a faculty member.

Since her departure for Manhattan, it had become traditional for Grace to return to Philadelphia once a month to visit her parents. It probably spoke to her growing affection for Don that—after he directed her in *The Philadelphia Story* at the Academy in the spring of 1949, she decided to introduce him to her family. She did not hide from her parents the fact that Don was Jewish and older, and decided that their "concern" about both matters was something that would alleviate itself in time. She felt, as she later explained it, that when they had the opportunity to meet Don, they would more readily accept him in her life. However, she did conceal his marital status, probably realizing that this detail was one Margaret and Jack would never be able to overlook. How would it appear, after all, if Grace was involved with a married man?

Though Grace told Don that she was certain her parents would be accepting of him, his instincts told him otherwise. When Grace brought Don to Henry Avenue, her parents and brother didn't waste much time before treating him disrespectfully. It didn't matter that he was making a name for himself in theater. The big headline was that he was Jewish, and that was the fact upon which the Kellys focused their disapproval. "They mocked me," he recalled years later, "with what they thought were funny Jewish accents and Jewish jokes. It was unpleasant."

When they treated the young couple to a meal at the country club to which they belonged, Jack and Margaret were as critical of Grace as they were of Don. Years later, in an interview, Don remembered details of the uncomfortable dinner conversation. He said that the Kelly parents mocked his enthusiasm for Grace's ambition to be an actress, telling him he "must be joking" when he said that she could be a star, that such a thing could never happen. The next day, however, Grace continued to insist to Don that her parents were fair and level-headed, and that he would agree with her about that once he got to know them better. "She seemed to be in a state of denial where they were concerned," he said.

A turning point came when Don and Grace went to visit George Kelly in Germantown. Margaret took advantage of the opportunity to rifle through Don's belongings. In his suitcase, she found a letter from his attorney pertaining to his pending divorce. As if that weren't surprise enough, she also found condoms that Don had brought with him in case he and Grace had the opportunity to be intimate. Margaret now realized that her nineteen-year-old Catholic daughter was probably having sexual relations with a married man. In all fairness to Margaret Kelly, her concern was understandable. After all, this *was* 1949. It's likely that many parents would be rattled about such a scenario today, more than fifty years later.

When Don and Grace returned home, Margaret ordered her daughter up to her room, and Don out of the house. Once upstairs, Don realized that the contents of his suitcase had been disturbed; it wasn't as if Margaret had attempted to camouflage what she had done, nor would she later apologize for it. In an hour, Don was on a train headed back to New York. He wasn't permitted to say good-bye to Grace, who was sequestered in her bedroom and crying her eyes out. In a subsequent confrontation with her parents, Grace was told that she would have to leave school and return home, that she was "out of control" and would need to be looked after until she "learned to behave." Luckily for Grace, it was the end of the term, so she was able to leave school without interrupting her studies. She had hoped to stay on at the Barbizon while she pursued her acting career in New York, but that was now out of the question.

On April 13, 1949, Grace tearfully evacuated her Barbizon quarters, where she had experienced so much freedom and happiness, and so much—but certainly not enough, in her view—of what New York had to offer her. During the two-hour train ride back to Philadelphia, she took out pen and paper and wrote a lengthy, emotional letter to her roommate, Prudy Wise, to explain what had occurred. She wrote that Don's visit had been "gruesome," that the family had treated him terribly. She recalled that, after Don left the house, she was told by her parents that the time had come for some "straight talk" (which apparently in the Kelly household meant disciplinary action). She wrote that "the fact I could fall in love with a Jew was just beyond them," and that the ensuing argument with her parents about Don had so drained her that she could barely recall its details. Moreover, Grace wrote, when she finally confessed to them that she knew that Don was married, her father "blew a fuse." She continued by saying that she had cried so much over the weekend's occurrences, "hell can't be much worse." She added that the worst part of what had happened, along with having to end it with Don, was that she would now have to interrupt her career pursuits and endanger the opportunities she probably would have found in Manhattan if allowed to stay. She had made so many contacts in such a short time, she wrote—"that kind of luck doesn't come unless some kind of miracle happens." Her mother had made the concession, Grace wrote, that, in time, she could resume her life in New York, for a couple of days a week—though she would have to commute from Henry Avenue. With typical humor, even in what seemed to her at the time to be some of the darkest days of her youth, Grace concluded her emotional missive by writing, "Don't dare let your friends know that your celebrity roommate is anything but a celebrity." Then she asked Prudy to destroy the letter, lest anyone ever read it.*

In the weeks to come, even from Philadelphia as home base, Grace Kelly would continue to forge ahead with her career. Through a contact of Don's she signed with MCA for acting representation. Then, in the spring of 1949, she asked her Uncle George to talk to Broadway producer Theron Bamburger, director of the Bucks County Playhouse, about the possibility of auditioning for that prestigious theater stock company in New Hope, Pennsylvania, and appearing in their summer productions. She auditioned, was easily accepted, and was soon onstage in George's own *The Torch-Bearers* (1922), a satire on amateur dramatics.

Allen Kramer, technical director and assistant stage manager of the Bucks County Playhouse, befriended Grace while she was in New Hope. He recalled, "She was modest and sweet, with no great confidence in herself. She was a good amateur actress who tried hard. You sensed that there was strong family neglect there. To my memory, no one in her family ever came to any of the shows we did at Bucks County."

In the fall of 1949, Grace Kelly was hired for a role in *The Father* on Broadway, obviously a big break for her. It was at that time that she convinced her parents to allow her to move back to New York, where she settled in an apartment on East 66th Street. She was only permitted to go, however, as long as she promised her parents that she would not see Don Richardson. However, on her first night in Manhattan, the temptation to see Don was too strong; she broke her promise and spent the night with him.

When Jack learned that Grace was once again seeing Don, he showed up unannounced at the front door of Don's Manhattan apartment. He offered Grace's suitor a Jaguar automobile, in exchange for his promise to end it with Grace. Don refused the bribe. In weeks to come, he would receive a number of threatening telephone calls from Jack and Kell, guaranteeing him physical harm

---

*Forty-four years later, in 1994, this letter, and more than a hundred like it from Grace to Prudy Wise, were sold in a Butterfield & Butterfield auction.

unless he stopped dating Grace. When told about them, Grace acted perplexed and said that she was certain Don was mistaken— or that the threats weren't really coming from her family members but rather from crank callers.

Meanwhile, on November 16, 1949, Grace Kelly made her Broadway debut in *The Father*, playing the daughter of Raymond Massey and Mady Christians in a revival of the August Strindberg tragedy. Present and sitting close to the stage on opening night were Margaret and Jack, much to Grace's exaltation. Backstage after the performance, Jack ran into Raymond Massey, an old friend. "What are you doing here, Kelly?" Raymond asked. "Why, my daughter Grace is in your play," Jack said. Raymond was surprised; Grace had never mentioned the identity of her father. When Massey then began to praise Grace's debut Broadway performance, Jack fell back into his shtick. "So, listen," he said, "did you know that Kell won at the Henley Regatta?"

Though the *New York Times* drama critic Brooks Atkinson gave the play—which ran for sixty-nine performances at the Cort Theatre—a mixed review, his comments about Grace were anything but: "Grace Kelly gives a charming, pliable performance of the beautiful and broken-hearted daughter."

If Grace needed validation of her acting skills, with reviews like that one (and several others), she certainly had it. Though her professional career was on an upswing, her private life with Don Richardson was in rapid deterioration. Then, much to his surprise, Don discovered that there were other men in Grace's life.

It may have been the clandestine nature of his and Grace's courtship that made it easier for her to juggle more than a few gentlemen during their relationship. It seemed she compartmentalized her life while she was involved with Richardson, which made the guilt she felt for betraying her father's wishes more bearable. She knew their union could never lead to marriage, so Grace tried to view the time she spent with Don as stolen moments. While they may have been filled with romance and passion, those moments had to be clearly defined by her as unimportant. What better way to dilute Don's significance than to date other men? As it turned out, there were many of them. A litany of unfamiliar names, men with whom Grace Kelly became romantically involved during these early years—before and during her time with Don Richardson—has been outlined numerous times in biographies about her. However, today such detail about fleeting romances and youthful indiscretions probably serves little purpose. Suffice it to say that Grace Kelly was a young woman who enjoyed dating and, arguably unusual for the times and especially so for a Catholic, felt liberated enough to conduct her private life as she saw fit, in her own way. She also apparently had sex—and she had it often.

Years later, in 1971, Grace told writer Curtis Bill Pepper, "When I was younger I was always falling in love with someone who gave more to me than I gave back. I knew I was immature and incomplete as a person, that I was really taking and absorbing more than I was giving. But I think that's true with all young people. In the selfishness of youth, we need to feed our psyches and our souls by taking from others."

When Don learned that Grace was dating the popular and controversial playboy Aly Khan, he was unhappy about it. Apparently, Khan had gifted Grace with an expensive emerald bracelet, which Grace displayed to Don one evening after a night out with him. Why would she have done such a thing? Only Grace would have known the answer, but it certainly seemed as if she were looking for a way out of her romance with Don. If she was trying to force his hand, it worked. Don snatched the bracelet from her, dropped it into the fish tank, and bolted from the apartment. "I was as finished with her as she was with me," he recalled.

After *The Father*, Grace's career began to change dramatically, taking an upward trajectory into the motion picture business with a small part in a well-made little gem of a film from 20th Century-Fox, *Fourteen Hours*. Grace wrote to Prudy Wise that, as a result of the movie, someone in Oregon actually formed a Grace Kelly fan club, a clear indication of her growing popularity. She explained that she was thunderstruck by so many letters from new fans, and felt that she was truly beginning to make an impact on show business. Also, she was now able to afford the services of a maid—

which no doubt made her feel as if she were living a life at least comparable to what she had had at her parents' home.*

After *Fourteen Hours*, Grace Kelly returned to the Bucks County Playhouse for another play (*Accent on Youth*), and then on to Colorado, where she was scheduled to appear in a series of weekly productions with the prestigious Elitch Gardens stock company in Denver. Then, in 1952, she had her first major cinematic success in Fred Zinnemann's *High Noon*, starring Gary Cooper (in what would be an Oscar-winning performance for him).

Produced by Stanley Kramer, *High Noon* tells the story of small-town sheriff Will Kane (Cooper), who searches desperately, but ultimately in vain, for support among the locals when he gets word that a vengeful gang of outlaws is coming to town for a showdown. Arrival time: high noon. As Cooper's wife, Grace is resolute and stalwart. Though this western is a symbolic, suspenseful black-and-white film that would go on to become a classic of its genre, Grace felt she did a dreadful job in it. Or, as she said years later, in 1975, "After I saw *High Noon*, I thought, God! This poor girl may not make it unless she does something very quickly. I was horrified. I was miserable."

Star

The early word from Hollywood after Grace Kelly's first two features was loud and clear: Not only had a star been born, but a seemingly flawless one at that. Grace had the kind of face the camera

---

*Grace was always kind to her maid, Nellie. In one letter to Prudy Wise, she expressed concern that the mother of their friend Sally Parrish had been unkind to the servant. "Who the hell does she think she is that she can say anything to our maid?" Grace fumed. "Nellie is none of her goddamn business. I wish she would stay the hell out of the apartment."

loved: porcelain complexion; high cheekbones above rounded cheeks; a full, wide mouth; Wedgwood-blue eyes; flowing blonde hair; skin that glowed with vitality. Enviably thin—115 pounds at about five foot seven—she stood on long, shapely legs. The classic 1950s beauty if ever there was one, she was exquisite; no other word described her. At the time, her logical show business peers were Elizabeth Taylor, Ava Gardner, Sophia Loren, and Marilyn Monroe. She was definitely playing in the big leagues.

At least where her professional life was concerned, Grace had made the right choices. The architect of her own career and image, she had the resolve, stamina, and dedication to become a successful actress—even without the full support of her parents. Though she found the business behind the show distasteful, she still loved the show itself. Acting was her passion.

Her next movie, released in 1953, was *Mogambo*, with Clark Gable and Ava Gardner. The film was a remake of the successful 1932 melodrama *Red Dust*, which had also starred Gable (with Jean Harlow). In the new movie, Grace portrayed Linda Nordley, a proper Englishwoman and wife of an engineer who finds herself entangled in a romantic complication with a white hunter (Gable) and a sexy showgirl (Gardner). Grace had recently signed a seven-year contract with MGM; this was her first motion picture under that agreement.

For this new version, MGM moved the setting of the film from an Indo-Chinese rubber plantation to an African game preserve. The film received a first-class production, typical of the studio that boasted having "more stars than there are in the heavens." Though some of that production budget might have been better spent on a decent screenplay, the film proved to be a success thanks to the star power of Gable, Gardner, and Kelly. Despite the studio's push for the musical *Lili* at Oscar time, both Ava and Grace received Academy Award nominations, for Best Actress and Best Supporting Actress, respectively.

After *Mogambo*, Grace would appear in Alfred Hitchcock's *Dial M for Murder*.

Hitchcock's utter fascination—almost an obsession, really—with stylish, intelligent leading ladies reached its apogee with Grace Kelly (loaned out by MGM to Warner Bros. for this movie). Her predecessors in this mold included Madeleine Carroll, Joan Fontaine, Carole Lombard, Ingrid Bergman, Jean Arthur, Jane Wyman, Marlene Dietrich, and Anne Baxter. Though there would be others after Grace—Doris Day, Vera Miles, Kim Novak, Eva Marie Saint, Janet Leigh, and Tippi Hedren—none of these ladies quite fulfilled the Hitchcock ideal (although Hedren came closest).

This Hitchcock ideal woman was almost always some shade of blonde, beautiful, sexy, and indomitable—a woman who is resolute, gutsy, cool, and calm under fire. Think Janet Leigh (*Psycho*) as she matter-of-factly rips off her boss's receipts and, guiltless, falls into bed with John Gavin for an afternoon of steamy sex. Think Doris Day, her young son in grave danger, after having been kidnapped and sequestered by terrorists, singing "Que Sera, Sera" in *The Man Who Knew Too Much*. Or Ingrid Bergman (*Notorious*), nerves as cold and as hard as steel, becoming Cary Grant's informant, even marrying Claude Rains, to get the goods on the Nazis. All are examples of Hitchcock's ideal woman.

The Hitchcock-Kelly three-picture collaboration would be the most rewarding for the portly director, both personally and professionally. *Dial M for Murder*, an adaptation of the stage play by British playwright Frederick Knott, was the first of two back-to-back films Grace would make with him in 1954 (the other being *Rear Window*); later she would make *To Catch a Thief*.

In *Dial M for Murder*, Tony Wendice (Milland) discovers that his wife, Margo (Kelly), is having an affair with mystery writer Mark Halliday (Robert Cummings). During one of Mark's visits to London, Tony hatches a plan to have Margo murdered. The plan goes awry when Margo kills her would-be murderer. What follows is a game of cat and mouse.

Dial M for Murder was shot in 3-D ("Too much goddamn trouble," Grace wrote of the technique to Prudy Wise), but by its release date the novelty had lost its momentum, and the movie was never shown in that format. Grace would go on to receive the New

York Film Critics Award in the Best Actress category for her role in this movie.

In Grace's follow-up Hitchcock film, *Rear Window,* she costarred with Jimmy Stewart. The film is pure entertainment—a thriller, a mystery, a romance, and, at times, a comedy of manners. Grace is stunning to look at and her acting shows a range not seen in her earlier films. *Rear Window* was the third highest grossing film of the year and received three Oscar nominations, including one for Hitchcock, his fourth. Like with all the others, he would go unrewarded this time too.

After *Rear Window* Grace filmed an adaptation of James Michener's bestselling Korean War story *The Bridges at Toko-Ri,* costarring William Holden. Actually, Grace has little to do in this movie except keep a stiff upper lip and the home fires burning when her husband (Holden) goes off to war. There's not much more to say about *The Bridges at Toki-Ri,* other than that, in Grace's filmography, it precedes *The Country Girl,* which also starred Bing Crosby, and in which she would be reunited with William Holden.

Adapted from a play by Group Theatre cofounder Clifford Odets, *The Country Girl* tells the dark, downbeat story of a washed-up actor/singer (Crosby), a neurotic alcoholic who wallows in self-pity. He is given a chance for a comeback when a director (Holden) offers to cast him in his new musical. Crosby welcomes this opportunity as a new lease on life, only to struggle under the pressure and return to the bottle. A completely deglamorized Grace Kelly, as Crosby's wife, navigates the waters between anger and pity as she tries to get her husband to confront his demons.

Although *The Country Girl* does not hold up as well as some of the other films released in 1954 (such as Judy Garland's *A Star Is Born* or Marlon Brando's *On the Waterfront*), in the year of its release it was one of Paramount's biggest hits. MGM loaned Grace to Paramount for this film. It received seven Academy Award nominations, including Best Picture, which it lost to *Waterfront.*

However, it was for this movie that Grace would take home the Oscar as Best Actress, beating out such heavy favorites as Garland and Audrey Hepburn. For the young girl from Philadelphia who knew that her parents never thought she would amount to much, certainly not a great actress, winning the film industry's highest honor was a huge accomplishment. "If she was the kind of woman who would have been surprised by winning, I'm not sure she would have been the kind of woman who would have ever gone ahead and become an actress," says Virginia Darcy, Grace's MGM hairdresser. "She always believed that she would be good at what she wanted to do. It took courage for her to do it but, ultimately, she did believe in herself. Films, they were easy. It was in her personal life, all of those bad relationships, where she faced her biggest challenge."

For her fourth film of the year, Grace Kelly returned to her home studio, MGM, to do *Green Fire*, which had previously been turned down by Lana Turner. Judging by the script, Grace should have followed Lana out the door. In this one, Grace plays a coffee plantation owner in Colombia pitted against a mining engineer (Stewart Granger) who is looking for emeralds—the "green fire" of the title. Grace wrote to Prudy Wise that *Green Fire* had provided a wretched experience for her: "Everyone knew it was an awful picture, and it dragged on in all the heat and dust because nobody had any idea how to save it." After *Green Fire*, Grace began turning down scripts from MGM that she judged to be inferior, resulting in a suspension from the studio that would take about a year to reconcile before her next film could be made.

A Fateful Telephone Call

Only Grace Kelly could have created Grace Kelly," producer John Foreman, who knew Grace for most of her life, once told Gwen Robyns, her good friend and loyal biographer. "It must have been a concept in her head," he said. "No one else did. No manager, no agent, no producer, not even her family."

Perhaps one of the most enduring fantasies ever spun by the Hollywood image-making studio system of the 1950s was MGM's take on Grace Kelly, whom it portrayed as a prim-and-proper, pristinely mannered, white-gloved ingénue, above reproach. Actually, it wasn't all smoke and mirrors. Grace *was* raised, first and foremost, to be a lady. Her sophistication was intrinsic, not artificial. For instance, she wore gloves—at Margaret Kelly's insistence, all three of her daughters wore them—long before they became integral to her image. She could be chilly and remote, and often was to people she didn't know well.

Ironically, her upbringing left her somewhat isolated in early adulthood. Grace impressed people as a self-sufficient, confident powerhouse of a woman. This image was both a blessing and a curse. While she had respect and admiration heaped upon her, she was less likely to receive simpler expressions of social contact. She appeared to much of the world as a finished product, a woman rarely in need of a heartfelt compliment, a word of advice, even an occasional hug. She might have wrinkled her nose at the suggestion that she sacrificed common courtesies in order to create the star she became, but it was true. Many people just didn't realize that there was more to Grace than her image of aristocratic, patrician beauty. The Hollywood image she created was at odds with her true sense of humor and warmth, her sensitivity, her need to be cared for, her craving for approval.

For her, the work of fine-tuning the public persona she shared with Hollywood came easily. And, yes, there was work to be done. For instance, she had possessed a reedy and nasal voice, partly the result of her suburban Philadelphia environment, partly a consequence of sinus problems that had plagued her in her youth. She also had difficulties with vocal delivery and stage projection, and was told by her instructors that she would face serious challenges if she were ever to perform in a large theater, such as those found on Broadway. With typical determination, Grace enrolled in a number of speech courses, during which she worked to acquire the seemingly British mode of speaking that became so much a part of her fame and mystique. Her parents called it "Gracie's new voice"— and teased her about it. However, she knew what she was doing when she developed that sound of well-bred vulnerability. All of those hours with a clothespin on the end of her nose (to lower the register of her voice) while doing voice exercises would surely pay off.

By the beginning of 1955, twenty-six year-old Grace Kelly might have felt as if she had it all. She was a world-famous, Academy Award–winning actress. Not only was she adored by her fans, but she enjoyed the love of friends and even the respect of former paramours. Unbeknownst to her, what lay ahead in the next year would change everything . . . her entire world as she knew it.

It was in March 1955 when *Look* magazine's West Coast editor, Rupert M. Allan, Jr., telephoned her in Manhattan to ask if she would like to attend the Cannes Film Festival that spring.

"Oh, darling, I don't want to go," Grace told him. In the background, as she spoke, a legion of workers slogged away on her new, luxury apartment. Painters, carpenters, and wallpaper-hangers took orders from an impatient male decorator who spoke in a loud, barking voice.

"Oh, but you must, Grace," Rupert insisted, according to his memory. "You'll be so glad you did."

Grace and Rupert had known each other for two years, since becoming friendly at a party in Ava Gardner's apartment in England. A Rhodes Scholar, Allan was soft-spoken and polite, unlike many of the journalists Grace had to endure. Bright and witty, he was the kind of man whose company she enjoyed. He was also the Cannes Film Festival's unofficial liaison with Hollywood. (Plus, he had written three cover stories on her in just two years, which guaranteed him at least some loyalty.)

Desperate for American movie stars to attend the upcoming festival in May, the organizers had asked Rupert to invite any he could persuade. Most specifically, they wanted Grace Kelly to be present because of her increasing popularity in France. It had been decided that *The Country Girl*—for which she had won an Oscar—would be screened at the prestigious festival.

Frustrated by the hammering noises in the room, Grace told Rupert that she couldn't "hear myself think," and asked if she could call him back at another time. After she hung up, as she would later recall it, she never gave his offer a second thought.

Ever the persistent reporter, Rupert rang Grace up again the next day to ask if she had made a decision. The actress then began ticking off her reasons for turning him down. She was emotionally and physically exhausted "after making six major films in just a year and a half," she said, "and you know that's a lot on a girl, Rupert!" She was also in the middle of supervising the remodeling of her new apartment. The incessant clatter in the background again on this day testified to the work being done there. "And, I tell you, it is driving me mad," she concluded. "But I love it and I'm not leaving."

Rupert would not take no for an answer. He continued to try to persuade her, telling her that she would be provided with a round-trip, first-class ticket, one that would be open-ended and allow her to spend as much time in Europe as she liked. "Why sit around and fret about your apartment, Grace?" he asked. "It's spring. Get out. Live!"

"Oh, for goodness' sake! I'll call you tomorrow," she said before clicking off.

The next day, Grace did call Rupert as promised and said that she had decided to accept his offer. She added that he would have to accompany her to the festival, however, and deal with matters concerning press and publicity, "because you know how much I hate doing those things."

Rupert happily agreed.

"Well then, fine," Grace concluded. "Maybe I am meant to go to France. Why fight it?"

After arriving in France on April 4, 1955, Grace Kelly and her traveling partner, Baroness Gladys de Segonzac (wardrobe mistress on *To Catch a Thief*), journeyed on the overnight *Train Bleu* from Paris to Cannes. It was on this part of the trip that luck, happenstance, fortuity—or whatever unexplainable force that serves to put things in their natural order—would begin to shape the circumstances of Grace Kelly's life. During her railroad journey, Grace happened upon actress Olivia de Havilland and her husband, journalist Pierre Galante, also on their way to the festival. The next morning, they all had breakfast together. "So what is the festival like?" Grace asked. "What will be expected of me?"

Pierre explained that the festival's schedule of press conferences and screenings would probably make for an exhausting itinerary, no surprise to Grace. It might be a good idea, he suggested, if she took some time away from the events to visit Monaco.

After the Vatican City, Monaco is the smallest independent state in the world, located approximately eleven miles east of Nice on the French Riviera, close to the Italian border. It's astonishingly small, considering how much attention it has gotten over the last fifty years: 485 acres along 2.5 miles of Riviera coastline. Its weather mild and its scenery breathtaking, it is a constitutional monarchy headed by His Serene Highness, Rainier Louis Henri Maxence Bertrand de Grimaldi, a.k.a. Prince Rainier III.

Pierre suggested that Grace plan to visit the Prince's Palace there (called Palais Princier on local maps of Monaco), and if so, perhaps the editors of *Paris Match* would be interested in featuring her on the cover of their annual issue devoted to the festival. It might even be interesting, Pierre further proffered, if they put their heads together and came up with an imaginative angle, perhaps along the lines of a photo session featuring her with Monaco's Prince Rainier Grimaldi—a movie Princess meets a true Prince. Grimaldi was sure to cooperate, Pierre theorized, if only to promote the tourist trade in the principality.

To some observers, Pierre Galante's ingenuity may have seemed too convenient. In truth, the photo idea of pairing Grace with Rainier hadn't popped into Pierre's head while he, his wife, and his new friends chugged along the Mediterranean seaboard. Actually, the *Paris Match* editors had, earlier in the week, conjured up the notion of Grace meeting Prince Rainier for a layout, and had wondered how they might go about arranging such a photo session.

Imagine Pierre Galante's astonishment, then, when he happened upon Grace Kelly on the train and found himself in a position to suggest to her that she go to Monaco and be photographed with Rainier Grimaldi! However, those who knew the enterprising writer theorized that it wouldn't have been so far-fetched to wonder if he hadn't somehow orchestrated the entire scenario, maybe even having gone so far as to learn which train Grace would be taking to Cannes and then booking the same one for him and his wife. Whatever the case, unbeknownst to Grace, the stage had been set for her to meet her moment in history. Like Rupert Allan before him, Pierre wouldn't accept no for an answer. He would push forward with his idea for Grace, a Palace performance that would change the life of both its major players. It would take some doing for the curtain to go up on this show, because Grace wasn't even sure she wanted to meet the Prince. However, considering his hidden agenda, Pierre must have been heartened by Grace's ambivalence—at least she hadn't declined. During a platform stop, he got on the telephone and started making quick arrangements with his magazine editors and with the Palace.

A couple of hours later that morning, Pierre gave Grace the "good news." The Prince had agreed to meet her and have his photo taken with her . . . on the next day, Friday, April 6, at 4 P.M. Grace became flustered. "But my goodness," she fretted, "I didn't say yes."

"But you also did not say no."

"Oh, I don't know," Grace said. "In fact," she concluded, probably scrambling for a way out, "I just now remembered that I can't make it." She had to attend a reception for the American delegation in Cannes at 5:30, she explained. She was the hostess, so she couldn't back out of that obligation. How could she meet the Prince at four o'clock in Monaco and be back in Cannes by five-thirty? It seemed impossible. Pierre said he would try to work out the details for her. Instead, Grace suggested that he "please cancel the whole thing."

About an hour later, Grace received more "good news" from Pierre. The Prince's secretary had informed him that Rainier had agreed to move the meeting with Grace up to 3 P.M. Though he would be entertaining friends at his villa in Beaulieu prior to that time, he would do his best to be back at the Palace by three. Now Grace would have time to meet him, and also to attend the reception for the delegation.

That evening over dinner at the Carlton Hotel, where Grace was staying, she spoke to Rupert Allan about the matter of the Prince, wondering aloud how she had ever gotten herself into what she called "such a pickle." She said that she now felt it would seem impolite to suddenly cancel the meeting, since the Prince had gone through the trouble of altering his princely schedule in order to accommodate hers. No, Grace decided, she would simply have to go.

A Comedy of Errors

Not that Grace ever would have thought to prepare for such a thing—who would have?—but during the evening of April 5, 1955, after she went to bed, French labor unions called a national strike. The next morning, after Grace arose, showered, and shampooed her hair, she plugged in her hair dryer only to find that it did not work. She plugged it into another outlet. No power. She went to turn on the lights in her room. Nothing. It was only upon telephoning the front desk in exasperation that she learned that the electricity had been turned off all over France, a consequence of the strike. Not only that, but she was told that the photographers from *Paris Match* were in the lobby, probably waiting for her to make an appearance befitting an Academy Award–winning actress. It would be hours before the power would be restored.

As Grace wrapped her head in a towel, the chambermaid arrived to iron the rose-and-beige tea dress intended for the day's events. Of course, without electricity, the servant's duty was impossible. Frantic, Grace summoned Gladys. "Look, I'm in trouble up here," she told her friend. Gladys arrived within moments.

Fifteen minutes later, Rupert Allan showed up in Grace's room to find her pacing the floor wearing her tortoiseshell glasses, a large terry-cloth bathrobe . . . and elegant black satin pumps. In her arms she held a black dress that Gladys had extracted from a suitcase because it seemed to need no pressing. As he examined the dress, Rupert told Grace that she would look fine in it. (Later he would admit that "it was an awful dress, but we had to get this show on the road, didn't we?")

"Oh my God, this is the worst day," Grace said as she rushed into the bathroom. "Why, it's a comedy of errors!"

Fifteen minutes later, Grace emerged wearing the boat-necked, longsleeved dress, with a tight-fitting, long-waisted bodice and a voluminous skirt. It boasted a loud floral-printed design of red-and-green cabbage roses. With every step she took, the taffeta fabric rustled noisily. She didn't look happy, let alone glamorous, while lamenting that she couldn't possibly "meet a Prince in this awful thing."

Her still-wet hair parted in the middle, Grace brushed it in swift, even strokes and then began patting it dry with a towel. Frustrated, she pulled it into a chignon and hoped that it would dry in the car. "Other than that, I simply don't know what to do with it," she observed. She stopped and studied herself in the mirror. "Darling, look at me," she said, turning to Rupert. "I look a fright."

Rupert stood behind her and, examining her reflection, told her that she was "an absolute vision." It was probably true; even in the worst of circumstances, Grace Kelly was alarmingly beautiful.

Unconvinced, Grace leaned closer to the mirror, grimaced, and then wondered aloud why she hadn't just rejected the idea when

Pierre Galante first mentioned a Palace visit to her. "When will I ever learn?" she asked.

When Grace and Rupert got down to the lobby, they were greeted by a large contingent of fans and photographers who had heard she was staying at the Carlton. Waiting for her at the Peugeot automobile were Pierre Galante, two photographers from *Paris Match*, Gladys de Segonzac, and two MGM publicists.

"Grace, you look wonderful," Pierre said happily. However, he hastened to add that she would need a hat, explaining that she could not meet the Prince without wearing one. Worried glances were exchanged all around. A hat? One more request of her, and surely Grace would call the whole thing off. She didn't have a hat, she said anxiously, and hadn't even thought to bring one. Perhaps they would have to purchase one on the way? However, true to the day's calamitous nature, it was one-thirty in the afternoon and the middle of southern France's daily two-hour lunch break. All of the shops were closed. "Then, fine, we won't go," Grace decided finally. Her tone was sharp; she had reached her breaking point.

Just then, Gladys remembered a headband of artificial flowers that Grace had packed in her suitcase. She and Grace dashed to the elevator. Five minutes later, when the pair emerged in the lobby, Grace wore what appeared to be a tiara of flowers—the headband stretched into something that appeared to be a hat, yet wasn't one. "It is rather pretty, isn't it?" Grace said of the floral arrangement on her head. She seemed to feel a bit better about things. "So who has a ciggie?" she asked. After Rupert gave her a cigarette, she lit it and said, cheerily, "Let's go then, shall we?" (Grace seldom smoked, only if she was particularly nervous, and even then it was unusual for her.)

After it was decided that Rupert Allan would stay behind at the hotel, Grace, Pierre, and Gladys piled into the backseat of the car. One of the MGM publicists drove, and the other also sat in the front seat. The contingent then sped off in their Peugeot to begin the nearly two-hour journey to Monaco, followed by the *Paris Match* staff in its automobile. The publicist, so determined to be on time for the Monte Carlo appointment, drove at an alarmingly high rate of speed. On a road outside the city, she stopped short in order to avoid a taxicab and ended up slamming instead into the back of a Studebaker. The damage was minimal, but everyone was rattled just the same.

Grace had always been afraid of automobiles, whether she was driving or being driven. When in New York, she was fortunate enough to be able to take taxicabs. During her times in Los Angeles making movies, she would rent a car and drive as slowly as possible, or the studio would arrange for a driver. Even a "fender bender," such as the one she'd just been in, was upsetting to her. The day had not started out well and seemed to worsen with each passing moment, as if some force of nature was doing everything in its power to prevent Grace from meeting the Prince.

The Palace

Who would dare drive these roads?"

That was the question Grace Kelly asked after nearly two hours of enduring the most frightening of narrow, snaking roadways to Monaco, along perilous cliffs far below which could be seen ocean waves smashing into jagged rocks. The driver slowly negotiated each turn. Still, it was unnerving to the passengers as they looked out the windows and realized how narrow the two-lane highway upon which they were driving seemed. "I'm scared to death back here," Grace said, clutching Gladys de Segonzac's arm.

"It's pretty bad," Pierre Galante agreed.

"My God," Grace said. "I would never drive this route. Forget it. I would go right over the side, I'm sure of it."

Pierre later recalled that "everybody just sat tight" as they waited for the journey to end. Finally, the Prince's large pink Palace was visible, gleaming in the distance atop what appeared to be a small mountain. Then more snaking roads, more terrifying curves . . . until finally, at about 3 P.M., the Kelly contingent arrived at the Palace of Monaco. "Thank God," Grace said, according to Pierre Galante's memory. "I am absolutely carsick," she added, alluding to the twisting drive.

The automobile stopped at a gate and was approached by two stern-looking uniformed Palace guards. After some brief conversation with the driver, one of the guards waved Kelly and company onward, through the Great Portal and into the Court of Honor, from which Grace got her first good look at the Palace.

What a place. It actually looked like a storybook castle right out of a fairy tale, with its many majestic peaks and grand turrets. One couldn't help but be impressed by such grandiosity. As Grace looked up at it, the construction might have seemed to her like an ornate Hollywood set for a grand-scale, epic film. She'd certainly never seen a palace up close. How many people have? However, this was no Hollywood façade; it was the real thing. Everyone gazed up in wonderment.

The first stones of the Palace of Monaco were laid in 1215. It was originally built as a fortress to guard the harbor below. Back then, as people made their way up the winding road, they could be spotted by guards in the watchtower. Any marauders who continued onto the wide ramp could easily be turned back at the arch that led to the Place du Palais (where Grace and her party had first been stopped), the outer courtyard with its old cannons, a reminder of its earlier duty as a fort.

Now out of the car, Grace stood silently and looked around her at all of the royal surroundings. Meanwhile, people scurried about with worried looks on their faces. Grace Kelly knew all too well what such anxious scattering by handlers meant: Something had not occurred as it was supposed to occur, and she was about to be given news that would inconvenience her. Finally, Pierre Galante approached her.

"Gracie, the Prince isn't exactly . . . here," he said, according to his memory.

"Surely you're joking," Grace said.

He wasn't

As it happened, Rainier had been delayed at his prior commit-ment in Beaulieu. He would arrive soon—hopefully.

An aide-de-camp quickly stepped forward and offered to take Grace and her party on a tour of the Palace, perhaps in an effort to calm the star down, maybe kill some time. It wouldn't have served anyone if she were unhappy when she finally met the Prince. So, the tour was on; Grace and her party climbed the horseshoe-shaped staircase, thirty white steps made of Carrara marble.

At the top of the gracious stairway was the Gallery of Hercules, a long and brilliantly lit veranda with its renowned fresco ceilings. Despite certain modifications carried out over the years, this is con-sidered the oldest, most central part of the original fortress built at the beginning of the thirteenth century. A half dozen maids in black dresses and crisp white aprons scattered when Grace's party approached. "Must be cleaning day," she said, laughing. Grace ad-mired the golden wall sconces and wondered, "Where else but in a palace would a person find such beautiful things?"

Then it was on to the Hall of Mirrors, where the mirrors on fac-ing walls seem to reflect into infinity. Then there was the Throne Room, with its deep-red walls, blue and violet velvet hangings, and crystal chandeliers. Here, important matters of state took place. The Prince's gilded throne, with its red velvet cushions, sat be-neath a gold-embroidered canopy of the same fabric. (The Throne Room, now open to the public during tours of the Palace, is still re-markable.)

Each room was more spectacular looking than the one before it. As Grace's group took its private tour, the aide explained, in per-fect English, the historical relevance of each opulently appointed location. Most of the interior of the Palace was painted in shades of white and gold. Chandeliers hung all about, each dripping with crystal pendants. Plaster moldings on the ceilings were tastefully and delicately overlaid with gold-leaf patterns. Rich velvet drapes— some blue, some red, some white—hung heavily in front of large, ornate windows. Tall French doors opened out onto semicircular balconies. Elegant white-and-gold French antique furniture was positioned in such a way that no matter where a person stood, he or she would be framed by history, the subject of a memorable picture. Because the Grimaldis had occupied this Palace since the early thirteenth century, walking through it was like passing through the threshold of a time machine. There was family history on display everywhere, including marble busts and family portraits. Strikingly beautiful paintings were also featured throughout, some by great masters.

After the Palace had been looted during the French Revolution, as Grace's guide explained, it was restored in an even more opulent style than before. Indeed, it was spectacular, but such a blur in its enormity . . . so much to see. However, if one stopped for a moment and actually studied some of its details, the Palace was actually like a once-rich dowager—magnificent in her prime, but showing some of the ravages of age.

After the end of the Second World War in 1945, few people could afford the excesses of Monaco. By the late forties, the casino was operating at a loss and the Palace was in desperate need of repairs. Rainier's father, Prince Pierre, had neglected it terribly, spending most of his time in Paris. By the mid-fifties, there was still a shortage of income, not only for the citizens but also for their Prince. Though obviously a beautiful place, this was a Palace—and a principality—in need of both a moral and a financial boost.

Nearly an hour after her arrival, Grace had viewed more sweeping staircases, graceful wings, and impressive galleries than most people would see in a lifetime, yet Prince Rainier had still not arrived. By now Grace's patience was exhausted. After all, as stunning as the Palace was to see, the day had still been a dreadful one for her. "Really," she whispered to Pierre Galante, "this is outrageous." She said that she found it "rude" of the Prince to keep her waiting. "Let's get out of here," she decided finally.

The Grimaldis

The first of the Grimaldis arrived in Monaco on January 8, 1297, when a small group of men led by Francesco Grimaldi, disguised as a monk, scaled the escarpment cliffs to reach the top of the Rock, the high plateau that overlooks the Mediterranean. Once there, he knocked on the gate of the yet-unfinished Genoese castle being erected on that spot. When the door opened, Francesco and his followers forced their way inside, killed the soldiers who had been guarding the fortress, and took over as the new rulers. Their reign was interrupted in 1793 when French revolutionaries took possession of the territory and the Grimaldi rulers were imprisoned. When Napoleon came to power, the Monegasques (as the people of Monaco are known) hoped things would improve, but they did not. However, once Napoleon was defeated in 1814 and Louis XVIII came to the throne, the Principality of Monaco was restored and a Grimaldi was once again upon the throne.

Wars, the ever-changing politics of Europe, and a series of inept and uncaring Grimaldi rulers damaged Monaco and its people. Things improved in the 1860s when a road from Nice and a casino arrived. As soon as the railroad line from southern France to Italy established a stop in Monaco, the building boom began. Soon the casino at Monte Carlo and its luxurious hotels would attract high-living, party-loving, glamorous people from around the world.

At the end of World War I, however, the French consummated an unusual treaty with Prince Albert, Rainier's great-grandfather. Since an aggressive German family, the d'Urachs, had placed a mysterious claim on Monaco, the French granted Albert a treaty recognizing the principality as an independent sovereignty, one that could not be relinquished to any foreign power except France.

However, according to the treaty, if the throne were vacant for even a day, Monaco would be returned to France.

At the age of eighteen, Prince Albert joined the Spanish navy and became known as Albert the Navigator. He was a lieutenant when, in 1869, at age twenty-one, he resigned to take an English bride, Lady Mary Douglas-Hamilton, daughter of the eleventh Duke of Hamilton and Brandon. After she bore him a son, Prince Louis II, Mary became so distressed by her marriage that she suddenly fled. She left the country and took their son with her.

When his first marriage was declared void, Albert married the widowed Duchess of Richelieu, the exotic and popular Alice Heine, a native of New Orleans. Alice, who had left New Orleans when she was a small child and only returned twice in her lifetime, was actually the first American Princess of Monaco.

Albert re-joined the Spanish navy and is credited with setting up the Oceanographic Institute and Museum in Monaco at the turn of the century. (A few years later, he founded the Institute of Oceanography, headquartered in Paris.) The cultured Princess Alice brought concerts, ballet, and opera to the principality. However, her marriage only lasted twelve years before it ended after Albert learned she had been unfaithful to him. (He slapped her face in public at the opening of opera when he realized that her lover was also present!) Alice was then banished from Monaco—forever, as it turned out.

Meanwhile, Lady Mary raised her son, Prince Louis II, into a fine young man who, after joining the French army, fell for a lovely laundress, Juliette Louvet. Some Monegasques like to believe that Louis and Juliette married, but historical purists insist that they did not actually wed. Rather, they had an affair, and from it was produced a baby girl in 1898, Charlotte Louise Juliette—Prince Rainier's mother.

Charlotte was raised in France until she was a teenager, when she was called back to Monaco by her grandfather. The time had come for her to learn the protocol required in order that she take on her role as heiress to the throne. Charlotte went on to marry the handsome French aristocrat Comte Pierre de Polignac, retitled Prince

Pierre after the union. They had two children, Princess Antoinette on December 28, 1920, and Prince Rainier on May 31, 1923.

In 1929, when Rainier was six, the arranged and unhappy marriage between Charlotte and Pierre ended in divorce. Pierre was banished from Monaco at that time and would not return to Monte Carlo until after World War II, when Rainier ascended the throne. Meanwhile, when her marriage ended, Charlotte renounced the throne and went off to live in the French countryside.

Rainier and his sister, Princess Antoinette, had an unpredictable and, from all accounts, mostly unloved and unhappy childhood. With their father banished and their mother in self-imposed exile, their grandfather, Louis, took over much of their upbringing, often with dire results. Overweight and spoiled, Rainier was sent to two different boarding schools in England: Summerfields in St. Leonard's-on-Sea near Hastings, and Stowe in Buckinghamshire, where he was taunted terribly because he was the only foreigner enrolled there, and was Catholic in an Anglican country. Some of the other students called him "Fat Little Monaco," and forced him to do menial tasks for them (called "fagging"). Self-conscious and miserable, he ran away from school, making headlines in newspapers in England and France. "It turned out be much easier than I thought it would be," he later recalled. "I left the grounds and headed for the railway station. My plan was to buy myself a ticket to London and then make my way home from there." Rainier's plan was thwarted, however, when the police were notified by school authorities, and he was then spotted by an officer waiting for a train. He was returned to Stowe.

Things became much better for Rainier later, when he attended the Château de Rosey in Switzerland, also known as Le Rosey, at the age of fourteen. The curriculum at Le Rosey (sometimes called "The School of Kings" since so many future monarchs were educated there) was not as strict as it had been at Stowe; students were permitted to choose their subjects as long as certain educational requirements were met. "The students were much friendlier because they were from such diverse, international backgrounds," he recalled. "I felt, for once in my childhood, that I could take a breath."

When Rainier graduated from Le Rosey three years later (in the summer of 1939), he continued his studies at Montpellier University, where he obtained a bachelor of arts degree, followed by studies in Paris at the Ecole Libre des Sciences Politiques (School of Political Sciences). He then enlisted in the Free French army in September 1944, where he saw action fighting the Nazis and was eventually promoted to lieutenant. Two years later, he became a captain, and then later, colonel.

Louis made Rainier official heir to the throne on June 2, 1944, shortly after his twenty-first birthday. The title carried no official duties, just social ones such as ribbon cutting and attending certain galas. It wasn't until Louis became ill in April 1949 that he allowed Rainier to take over the responsibilities of governing.

Louis died on May 9, 1949, three weeks before Rainier turned twenty-six. At his official coronation, April 11, 1950, Rainier Louis Henri Maxence Bertrand de Grimaldi was crowned *Son Altese Serenissime* (His Serene Highness) in a royal and official day of ceremony that culminated with the new Prince watching as his own standard was raised on the Palace's flagpole amid the jubilant flourish of trumpets.

Two questions often posed about Rainier and Monaco are, "Why is Rainier not a King?" and "Why isn't Monaco a kingdom?" At the risk of seeming simplistic, they can both be answered succinctly: "Because Rainier is a Prince," and "Because Monaco is a principality." Like Liechtenstein, which is also a principality (and not a kingdom) and ruled by a Prince (and not a King), Monaco never had status as an independent country—monarchy or otherwise—and looked to France (which was once a monarchy and ruled by a king) for its survival. Modern Monaco, since 1911, has been a constitutional monarchy (which is descriptive of its form of government, not its status within the world community of nations). Luxembourg, like Liechtenstein and Monaco, is another of those "not-quite" countries, in its case a grand duchy, with an archduke (Jean de Luxembourg) as its titular ruler. It is very difficult to be simplistic about the whys and why-nots of the royal countries and principalities. We have to take it as an act of faith that Monaco and

Liechtenstein are principalities and Luxembourg is a grand duchy, and leave it at that.

Also, in a kingdom (such as Holland, Denmark, or Great Britain), the King or Queen is known as "Your Majesty." However, in a principality (such as Monaco) ruled by a Prince and not a King, that ruler is known as "Your Serene Highness," even though he is an absolute monarch—thus Prince Rainier's title as ruler of the Principality of Monaco.

Rainier

In the 1950s, Prince Rainier III of Monaco was considered one of the world's most eligible bachelors. In April 1955—when Grace Kelly came into his life—he was about to turn thirty-two. The so-called absolute monarch of a principality and scion of the oldest ruling family in Europe, he was the subject of great scrutiny by the international press, which was always fascinated by projections of his personal life—such as who he was dating, and whether or not he would soon wed and produce an heir. A charming, charismatic, and fairly good-looking young man, he enjoyed practical jokes, sports, boating, and deep-sea diving. He also had a bit of the daredevil in him and took pleasure in fast boats, fast cars (that is, until a 1953 accident scared him away from that hobby), and—from time to time, in a discreet fashion—fast women as well, though he knew that the woman he ended up with would never be one who wasn't virtuous. He needed a Princess, and he needed one soon . . . someone to bear him a child to whom he could hand over the sovereignty.

Since his mother, Princess Charlotte, had relinquished to him her right to the throne in 1944, and in 1951 his sister, Princess Antoinette, had also renounced all claims on behalf of herself and her children, only a child of Rainier's could succeed. The terms of the 1918 treaty between Monaco and France were clear: The country would revert to French control should Rainier die without an heir.

By the early fifties, the slightly faded Monte Carlo casino still pumped out sufficient revenue that none of Rainier's 20,000 subjects had to pay any personal income taxes. However, under the terms of the 1918 treaty, if the Monegasques became citizens of France, they—or their sons and daughters—would most certainly find themselves paying French taxes. This, as well as the forfeiture of other privileges to which they had always been entitled, was unthinkable. Therefore, the subject of Rainier's future, his potential Princess, and their heir was a constant matter of discussion between him and his family, as well as his advisers. There seemed to be no end to the parade of women who came through the Palace, dispatched by well-meaning friends and relatives who hoped that one would interest the Prince enough to merit a position by his side at the throne.

In recent years, Rainier Grimaldi had been primarily involved with actress Gisele Pascal in a relationship that seemed to be going nowhere for either of them. None of his family or friends took her seriously as a potential Princess—she'd been around for years, and she still hadn't excited the Prince enough for him to ask for her hand in marriage. It seemed to most people as if it would never happen and, at least as far as his family was concerned, Rainier should just cut his losses and continue his search.

The gamine-faced Gisele Pascal was born Gisele Tallone in Cannes to a French mother and an Italian father. Rainier met her in Monaco in 1942, when the nineteen-year-old was home during a month off from his schooling in Montpellier. Gisele, who was a couple of years older than Rainier (though she insisted she was younger), was appearing at the time in the comedy *Vive le théâtre*, which Rainier attended.

Focused on her career ambitions at the time, after just having appeared in her first starring film role in *L'Arlesienne*, Gisele was newly divorced and not interested in a new relationship. Still,

Rainier was enchanted by her. When he returned to Montpellier, he began a lengthy letter correspondence with Pascal in Paris. In the summer of 1943, after earning his B.A., Rainier enrolled at the Ecole Libre des Sciences Politiques in Paris and, while there, finally began dating Gisele. With her career on hold as a result of the war, she began to return his interest.

Later, in 1948, Gisele appeared in two romantic comedies, *Après l'amour* and *Mademoiselle s'amuse*, both of which were considered to be somewhat risqué for the times. As a result of her work in those films, certain members of Rainier's family—including and especially his sister, Antoinette—developed an animus toward Gisele, which would only become stronger with the passing of time. At this same period, there was also a significant amount of infighting in the Grimaldi family, as the aggressive and ambitious Antoinette began plotting with her husband to seize control of Monaco by putting her son on the throne. Since his own sister seemed so intent on stabbing him in the back, Rainier understandably had little interest in anything she had to say about Gisele Pascal.

It wasn't his family's disapproval of Gisele that concerned Rainier. Rather, it was her career: He didn't want her to have one. However, Gisele was headstrong and independent—which was one of the reasons the Prince was drawn to her. Though he didn't admire weak women, he wanted it both ways: He wanted her to be a strong person, but also subservient when it came to her relationship with him.

Over the next two years, Gisele continued making movies, appearing in *La Femme nue*, *La Chocolatière*, *Veronique*, and *Bel amour*. Not only did Rainier find this work unbecoming, he disliked her show business friends. He did what he could to convince her to abandon her career. Finally, she granted him his wish and made no movies for about three years. However, she was miserable during that time. "I must act," she said when she returned to her profession. "It's what I do. Why, it's *all* I do!" If Gisele wanted so badly to act, then she would have to do so without Rainier's approval—and with the knowledge that she would probably never be his Princess.

The principality was too important to Rainier to have a wife at his side who might court controversy with her career.

When Rainier Grimaldi became Prince, he took a more active role in Monaco's affairs than had any Prince since Honoré II in the seventeenth century.

Monaco had changed little since the end of the First World War. Rainier's intention was to modernize the principality and, hopefully, transform it into an international cultural and recreational center by building hotels and beach resorts to attract tourists from around the globe. Whereas his grandfather had been cautious and conservative in his thinking—probably due to the war and the Great Depression—Rainier hoped to increase employment opportunities on every level. He was thought of by the Monegasques as a renegade Prince because, for him, the status quo was not enough: He wanted more and better for Monaco.

In a 1999 interview, he explained, "When I was young, I got tired of hearing that the principality made its money from gambling losses. I remember seeing a cartoon showing people with 'Monaco' labels stuck on their backs, collecting money from unlucky gamblers who were throwing themselves out of hotel windows. That image made a big impact on me, it's why my goal during the first years of my reign was to make the rest of the world take us seriously. I didn't want to be sovereign of a state that was caricatured in any way."

Rainier was a busy man, a person with great aspirations—and little time for romance. Early on, Gisele Pascal began to feel left out of his life. Not only was his time for her limited, but Rainier was disenchanted with her because of her ongoing career aspirations. He would not let her take part in the business of the principality because there was too much at stake, in his view, to allow her to be perceived as the principality's hostess as long as she was an actress. Gisele was in love with Rainier, however, and was hoping things might change. However, if his family had anything to say about it, matters for her would only get worse.

Rainier's sister, Antoinette, was determined to get Gisele out of the royal picture. In her bid to end the romance, she began spreading stories about Gisele's "lowly" background, implying that she wasn't worthy of the throne. Actually, Antoinette's and Rainier's personal history was even more checkered than Gisele's: Their mother had been illegitimate, their grandmother a dancer, and their great-grandmother a laundress. Still, Antoinette was adamant that the actress Gisele was not good enough for the Grimaldis. Plus, Antoinette was usually the high-profile woman at Rainier's side at most official functions, and she wasn't about to give up that honored position without a fight.

Though Rainier confronted Antoinette about her campaign against Gisele on a number of occasions, demanding that she stop spreading rumors, his protestations did nothing to discourage her. She wanted Gisele out of the way, and would stop at nothing to achieve her goal, even if that meant spreading stories that she had been intimate with Rainier's friends.

Gisele Pascal didn't need the proverbial brick to fall on her head—even though it did take the poor girl more than five years to come to her senses that she was better off without the Grimaldis. Her romance with the Prince was not going to have a happy ending, and she would simply have to accept as much. "I waited," Gisele observed years later, "hoping that everything would work out, but it didn't. It is only in fairy tales that the prince and princess live happily ever after."

When Gisele accepted a role opposite the young Italian actor Raymond Pellegrin in *Marchands d'illusion*, she found herself drawn to him and, eventually, began an affair with him. With her many years of misery with Rainier now a lukewarm memory, Gisele was ready for true passion, which she found with Pellegrin. Then, seemingly a woman on a mission, she found it again with actor Gary Cooper, whom she met at the Cannes Film Festival in 1951. Within weeks, she was back with Pellegrin, the man she finally ended up marrying.

Prince Rainier was flummoxed by the way his relationship with Gisele Pascal had ended. After all, he hadn't been the one to break it off with her—though official Monaco history has it that he did. *She* ended it, which was a surprise to him. Perplexed by the whole matter—How dare she leave him! That had been *his* intention!—he swore off women ("for a while," as he said at the time), and instead devoted his energy to the building of an exotic zoo on the Palace grounds.

What now?

Grace Meets Rainier

It must have seemed to Grace Kelly, a woman whose belief in the mystical was well-known to most of her friends, that every contrary force in the universe had conspired to prevent her from meeting Prince Rainier Grimaldi III of Monaco. After having gone to great lengths to get to his Palace, she found that the Prince was not on the premises. Grace paced the floor of a grand chamber that looked out over all of Monaco. Her escorts would assure her from time to time that Rainier was certain to be along in short order; he was not one to miss a social obligation. Finally, Grace had had enough. She announced that she would have to meet His Highness on her next visit to France. "Maybe it's all for the best," she explained. "I'll pack a proper hat next time."

As she turned to head for the door, a servant rushed in. He informed her that the man of the hour had just driven his sports Lancia into the courtyard. Suddenly, as she recalled it, Grace felt a pang of apprehension. With all that had occurred on this day, she'd had scarcely a moment to compose herself in order to prepare for the unusual meeting. Now that the time was upon her, it was accompanied by a flash of intense panic. "How old is this Prince?" she wanted to know, perhaps suddenly realizing that she didn't know a thing about him. "Is he handsome? What will he be like?" she asked. "Why," she continued while inspecting her reflection in her compact, "I don't even know how to address him. Shall I call him Prince?"

"Yes," Pierre Galante told her, she should call him "Prince" or, perhaps "Your Highness." She should also curtsy. "Oh my," Grace said nervously. "I haven't done that in a while."

She broke away from the group and found a quiet corner. With her back to the room, she subtly practiced her curtsy. Unbeknownst to her, the rest of the attendants stiffened as Prince Rainier III entered. All eyes were on His Serene Highness as he took in the show that Grace was putting on. He smiled curiously as he watched the beautiful movie star sway to one side and dip—clearly mouthing her pretend greeting to the gilded wall she faced. Finally, pleased with her rehearsal, Grace shifted her gaze to a massive mirror before her to examine her makeup. As she wiped some lipstick from a corner of her mouth, she froze. A moment hung as she composed herself. She then spun around, with little more than a hint of embarrassment, and approached the Prince, treating him to a flawless curtsy.

Years later, Rainier Grimaldi would recall, "I knew, of course, that this was a promotion. I didn't mind. I knew that Miss Kelly was famous and I was even prepared to offer her a cup of tea, or some other light refreshment."

"How do you do?" Rainier asked. Old-world charm was immediately evident despite his youthful appearance and boyish smile. He wore a superbly tailored navy blue, two-button suit. Squarely built at just five feet six inches, he did not appear in stature the way one might imagine a royal. However, his facial features were clean-cut and well-defined: cheekbones, high; cleft chin, resolute; eyes, sapphire blue; hair and mustache, inky black. His was an assemblage of features that came together to create a face that was, at least to Grace's eyes, unusually attractive. Later, Grace would recall that Rainier appeared much younger than she had imagined him to be and, in her opinion, better-looking than she had expected. (He had turned thirty-two years old on May 31, 1955, making him six years older than Grace.)

"I'm so sorry to be late," he said, giving Grace a comprehensive once-over. "Please forgive me."

Grace would later say she was surprised that Rainier spoke perfect, unaccented, upper-class English. She couldn't have known at the time that he'd had an English nanny and had been educated in English schools. Perhaps she was nervous, or maybe surprised by his apologetic demeanor, because she said nothing upon meeting him. She simply smiled graciously.

When Rainier offered to show the group the Palace, Grace finally spoke, telling him that they'd already received the grand tour. He then suggested that they tour his private zoo. He was fond of the animals, he said, and wanted Grace to see them.

While the Prince and his visitor walked to the zoo, they were trailed by the photographers and the rest of the small entourage. As Rainier introduced Grace to two young lions, several monkeys, and a baby Asian tiger (given him by Emperor Bao Dai of Vietnam), she was wide-eyed. Standing a safe distance from the cage, Grace watched nervously as the Prince slipped his hand between the metal bars. Gently he petted the tiger, caressing the beast's neck and speaking in a soft, soothing voice, as would a father to his beloved. Later, the Prince would say that the tiger "didn't seem to please Grace all that much. I think she was more used to poodles."*

"It was all very formal," recalled Rainier. "The photographer posed the pictures, and every now and again he would tell me, 'Point over there,' as we walked around. I was amused."

With a smile, Rainier then offered to take Grace on a tour of the gardens, a delight for a woman who loved flowers and surrounded herself with them whenever possible. Even when she was traveling, her hotel suites would be filled with vases of fresh blossoms. If it

---

*Here Rainier was referring to Grace's cherished miniature black poodle, Oliver, a gift from Cary Grant and his wife, actress Betsy Drake. Grace had even set up a small checking account for the dog, though no one ever understood her reasoning for that.

weren't for her busy life, Grace often said, she would be an enthusiastic gardener.

May is always one of the most beautiful times of the year in Monaco, with primulas circling every tree and plumes of mimosa covering the Palace's towering walls. As Grace and Rainier strolled through the vibrant surroundings, multicolored roses, snapdragons, daffodils, carnations, and tulips seemed to dance all about them in a soft breeze. The air smelled of salt and sea.

The others held back, not wanting to intrude on the couple's privacy. However, even from a distance, it was obvious that movie star and Prince were enjoying their time together. "Grace's complexion seemed to acquire a new glow as they walked silently ahead," Pierre Galante once recalled.

Prince Rainier then led Grace to one of the terraces. She floated out onto the deck like a soap bubble on a warm breeze, confident, self-possessed, ever the movie star.

Rainier made a sweeping gesture with his arm. Beneath them lay the blue Mediterranean, its waves slamming against ancient stone. Geysers of water sprayed into the air. White yachts bobbed in the harbor. From that vantage point, one could see Rainier's entire country, all 485 acres, less than a square mile. The Prince explained to Grace that Monaco is comprised of four districts. The capital is Old Monaco, or Monaco-Ville, atop Le Rocher (the Rock), the soaring peninsula jutting out onto the sea, upon which they were standing at that moment. A short distance away, opposite Le Rocher, could be seen Monte Carlo, a busy metropolis sitting atop a smaller promontory. There one would find the famous Casino, the Opera House and Sporting Club, and many exclusive hotels. Monte Carlo is, of course, a spectacular place, the heart and soul of Monaco, one of Europe's most decadently luxurious attractions for more than a century.

The nearby seaport is known as La Condamine. Finally, the industrial and residential region is known as Fontvieille. We'll never know, however, just how much of this expansive vista Grace actually saw, because ladies in the fifties believed in Dorothy Parker's dictum: "Men seldom make passes/At girls who wear glasses." Poor

Grace left hers in her purse, even though she was profoundly myopic.

Rainier's manner was efficient; there was a certain hardness about him that suggested a military background. However, he soon relaxed in Grace's presence, his interest in her growing with each passing minute—especially as he realized the effect he was having upon her. What more could a man ask for—even if he is a prince—than an attractive woman who seems to return his interest? After all, Grace Kelly was an Academy Award–winning movie star, one of the world's most famous women. She was also beautiful, exuding enormous self-assurance. Quiet-mannered, she was a woman of taste and refinement, yet also sexy—none of which was lost on the Prince. Rainier would later confide to one associate that it was Grace's mouth that had truly intrigued him, from the perfect shape of her lips to the way they parted and moved when she spoke.

Years later, Rainier would also reveal that, as they were being photographed, Grace had confided that she had not wanted to visit him at the Palace at all. It was nothing personal, she had explained, but simply that she'd felt so harried: It would have been so much easier if she hadn't had the additional commitment on her schedule. Rainier told her that he too had not been eager for the photo session when it was first suggested to him. They then shared a conspiratorial laugh about their mutual dilemma: to be somewhat forced to do what was expected of them. Perhaps they also realized that as different as they may have been as people, they were actually very much alike: Both were public figures often coerced to do that which they really did not want to do, for purposes of career and publicity, and often to the benefit of others.

Because Prince Rainier had not yet visited the United States, his moments with Grace were the first he had ever spent with an American woman of note. He was surprised, he would say, "because I supposed I had been influenced by what I saw on the films and read about, and this was nothing like what I had expected. The fact that she spoke clear English and was calm, agreeable to talk to, was a pleasant revelation."

Those who were present recall seeing a side of Grace emerge that day that had previously gone undiscovered. She had a peaceful ease about her, a calm that seemed genuine. She was not just a portrayal of serene contentment but, rather, the embodiment of it.

Forty-five minutes later, the photographers, who had never stopped clicking away in the background, were finished with their work. It was time to go. However, now Grace didn't want this meeting, the idea of which had earlier been such a nuisance in her life, to end. Rainier had put her so at ease that she probably could have stayed much longer. The Prince actually had a refreshment buffet planned for them in another part of the Palace, though he never told them about it. Indeed, if Grace didn't take her leave immediately, she would be late for her next commitment, the reception.

Rainier smiled through his disappointment and bid Grace a fond farewell. He grasped her slim wrist and pulled it toward him. She watched as the Prince gently kissed her hand, then carefully returned her arm to her side. The two stood there a moment.

"Well, I simply must go," Grace announced, as she moved toward the waiting entourage. Rainier called after her and mentioned that he would be in the United States in the near future. Perhaps, he said, he could make an attempt to visit her while he was there. He had recently committed to an appearance at a charity ball in Manhattan—"A Night in Monte Carlo"—to be held on January 6, 1956. "Why, that would be wonderful," Grace said enthusiastically.

Grace kissed the tips of her fingers and waved one final good-bye as she made her exit. She joined the group and started toward the car.

"So? What did you think of him?" Pierre Galante asked.

"He's charming," Grace said, smiling. "So charming."

Home-Wrecker?

Today, many people think of Grace Kelly as a woman who had affairs with all of her leading men, mostly due to the "yellow" journalism that hinted at such affairs during her movie star heyday, and then, many years later, with the publication of biographies about her. "Grace had more lovers in a month than I did in a lifetime," says Zsa Zsa Gabor. While Zsa Zsa is perhaps not the most reliable source for such information, since she is a renowned exaggerator, her succinct observation does provide a good example of the kinds of things Grace's peers say about her.

A careful examination of the facts, however, reveals that she did not have romances with *all* of her costars—though she did become involved with two of them: Ray Milland (*Dial M for Murder*) and William Holden (*The Bridges of Toko-Ri* and *The Country Girl*.)

There are some interesting parallels between the two men, both older than Grace (Milland was forty-nine, Holden thirty-six), both long married, and both apparently deceptive, since they indicated to her that their marriages were either in trouble or over. Both were also known in Hollywood as being unrepentant Lotharios. Lizanne LeVine has confirmed in numerous interviews over the years that her sister had affairs with these actors, that they were "out of their minds" with passion over Grace, and that both times the relationships were serious enough for marriage to be a strong consideration. However, maybe these gentlemen compared notes because they both followed the same course of action: When the going got tough (that is, they realized how much money they would have to forfeit in divorces), they went crawling back to their long-suffering wives—only to later have affairs with other women, and probably hand them the same line they handed Grace about impending divorce.

The publicity Grace Kelly received at the time of these two extramarital affairs cemented an "other woman" reputation for her, one that was—and still is—so tantalizingly in contrast to her ice-princess persona that it has become apocryphal. The affair with Ray Milland in particular was a major public relations catastrophe for Grace. Milland's angry wife went to gossip columnist Louella Parsons and complained that Grace was a "home-wrecker" who had stolen her husband. Back in the fifties—even today!—that is not the kind of publicity any star wants to generate.

Grace was heartbroken and disillusioned by the end of the affair with Ray Milland, swearing never to do it again. She had risked her reputation for little in return, other than rejection, a loss of dignity, and a great deal of nasty press. She confided in friends and family members that she was embarrassed by the way she'd lost herself in that relationship, calling it "a big mistake" when speaking to her sister Lizanne about it. Then, as sometimes happens in life, she made the same "big mistake" again with William Holden—and that was the last time she ever went down that particular road. (The fact is that she'd had relationships with men who were still married—though separated—before she was a star: Don Richardson comes to mind.)

Contrary to the countless reports over the years of Grace's romantic encounters with her remaining costars, there is no uncontested evidence to support such affairs. If Grace was actually bedding all of her leading men, certainly Frank Sinatra, one of the great playboys of his time, would have made the list when they filmed *High Society*. However, it never happened. (He did try, but Grace told him she wouldn't be intimate with him unless he was "the last man on earth," adding, "and even then I wouldn't do it." Also, Grace and Ava Gardner, Frank's on-again/off-again wife at the time, were good friends.)

Bing Crosby, Grace's costar in *The Country Girl*, also became enamored of her. He was widowed at the time and, according to Lizanne, asked Grace to marry him. As much as Grace admired him, his strong feelings for her were not reciprocated; she turned down his proposal. They remained friends, however, and went on to make *High Society* together.

There was also a painful time in Grace's youth concerning Clark Gable. During production of *Mogambo* in 1952, she became infatuated with him. At fifty-one, he was twenty-eight years her senior, and he was not interested in her as a romantic partner. Still, when Margaret Kelly heard about her daughter's fascination, she was worried enough to fly to London to chaperone Grace during the film's final month of production there. If Grace had ever hoped to change Clark's mind about her, Margaret's presence in England put the kibosh on that notion. After four marriages, Clark Gable was too old, experienced, and impatient to tolerate anyone's meddling mother. Anyway, he hoped Grace would get past her infatuation and see him as a friend, a peer. Alas, it was too late: She had truly become attached to him, viewing him perhaps as a father figure, but also, it seemed, much more. When Clark finally leveled with her and told her that he didn't want her "in that way," Grace was hurt. His rejection filled her with intense feelings of inferiority.

"I'm not speaking to Clark these days," she wrote in a letter home to Prudy Wise. "But don't tell anyone that."

Of the other logical romantic contenders for Grace's affection in terms of costars, she most certainly did not become involved with Jimmy Stewart, Cary Grant, or Alec Guinness, with whom she costarred in *Rear Window, To Catch a Thief*, and *The Swan*, respectively. While there have always been rumblings of something torrid having occurred with Grant during *To Catch a Thief*, Grace was close to Cary and his wife, Betsy, and no such romance ever happened.

A year before her death, Grace would say, "As an unmarried woman, I was thought to be a danger. Other women looked on me as a rival and it pained me a great deal. The worst was when the Hollywood gossip columnist Hedda Hopper started to persecute me with her hatred. She turned all producers, directors, and actors against me. Bing Crosby told me that Hedda had described me as a nymphomaniac!" Grace, who must also have reserved a modicum of distaste for Louella Parsons for publicizing her affair with Ray Milland, concluded, "I hated Hollywood. It's a town without pity."

Oleg Cassini

The most important man in Grace Kelly's life prior to her marriage to Prince Rainer of Monaco was not one with whom she starred in movies. Rather, he was fashion designer Oleg Cassini.

Oleg Loiewski-Cassini, born in Paris and raised in Florence, was one of two sons of Alexander Loiewski, a Russian diplomatic attaché, and Countess Marguerite Cassini, daughter of Czar Nicholas II's ambassador to the United States. At forty, he was twice divorced, from heiress Merry Fahrney and actress Gene Tierney. A personable and handsome Russian Jew, Oleg first met Grace in a French restaurant in New York City and immediately determined that he had to have her. He proceeded to charm his way into her heart over a months-long campaign until, finally, she saw him in something other than a platonic light. After ending it with Ray Milland, Grace sent Oleg a postcard and suggested he meet her in Paris, where she was about to begin filming *To Catch a Thief*. She wrote, "Those who love me, follow me."

To Catch a Thief was Grace's ninth movie and the final film in the Kelly-Hitchcock collaborative trilogy. Filmed on location on the French Riviera, the film, billed as a comedy/mystery, details the efforts of a reformed and retired cat burglar (Grant) to uncover the identity of a jewel thief who mimics his modus operandi in a series of new burglaries. In so doing, he hopes to deflect suspicion away from himself and prove his innocence. Along the way he enlists the help of a beautiful American heiress (Kelly), in the south of France on holiday with her mother (Jessie Royce Landis).

During a break in filming, Grace and Oleg shared a romantic meal at a quiet bistro just outside of Paris. Grace looked at Oleg dreamily and said, "Well, here we are, Mr. Cassini. You've been following me all over the world," she said. "So what do you have to say for yourself?"

"The depth of my feelings should be clear," he told her, according to his recollection. "I would be happy to continue as we are now, or to take this in any direction you want, including marriage. What do you wish, my dear?"

"I want to make my life with you," she said quietly. "I want to be your wife." Being swept off her feet seemed to be the one thing Grace Kelly could never resist. It didn't take much for her to lose herself in romance—and, it would seem, with little recuperative time between difficult relationships.

When Oleg and Grace returned to the States, she hoped her parents would accept him and not give her too much trouble. She wanted nothing more, she said, than to be his wife. That she ever thought the Kellys would warm to the idea of Oleg Cassini— older and divorced—demonstrates how deluded Grace was about what she was up against and how blind she was to her parents' wishes. Or, maybe for Grace Kelly, hope really did spring eternal. Over lunch with Grace and Oleg, however, Margaret Kelly dashed all hope for all concerned. She made it clear to Oleg that he was wrong for Grace. He was a playboy, in her view, and a divorced one at that. She demanded a "six-month moratorium" on the relationship.

Oleg refused to be cowed. He'd been down this road before. More than a decade earlier, he had become involved with actress Gene Tierney, whose father threatened to have her declared mentally unstable if she married him. When they did get married, Tierney's father did everything in his power to have the marriage annulled.

Oleg challenged Margaret, saying he would not slink away quietly. Thinking that he may actually have had the kind of spunk her husband would appreciate, she decided to reserve judgment about him. Meanwhile, Grace didn't say a word. "I was furious with her," Oleg recalled.

Eventually, Jack did met Oleg during a weekend in Ocean City with the family. However, after a quick introduction to him, both Jack and Kell refused to even acknowledge Oleg's presence, not responding to questions from him, never even speaking to him at meals. It was one of the worst weekends, he has said, in his life. "I was dead meat to them," he now says. "They didn't want me in the family, even if I had been made of gold and diamonds."

Grace decided not to marry Cassini, bowing once more to her father's will. "I loved her dearly," Oleg recalled. "She said to me at the time, and I believe it to be true, that she loved me as much as she had ever loved anybody."

For the next year or so, Grace found herself on an emotional roller-coaster, juggling Oleg with French actor Jean-Pierre Aumont. Right after she met the Prince in Monaco, she spent time with Jean-Pierre in Paris, much to Oleg's consternation. The couple enjoyed as much time together as possible, lunching in romantic bistros and holding hands while engaged in what seemed to be deep, meaningful conversations, exchanging kisses whenever the mood struck. Many photos of Grace and Jean-Pierre kissing and looking romantic surfaced in the press, causing Grace to have plenty of explaining to do to her parents. She stopped seeing Jean-Pierre when she suspected that he was arranging with paparazzi to have his photo taken with her to publicize his career.

By late spring 1955, Grace felt emotionally drained by her romantic entanglements, none of which held for her the promise of future happiness. Also, she was exhausted by her treatment from a media so fascinated by the facts—or fictions—of her life.

Though Grace had managed to master the art of maintaining the façade of charm and beauty the world had come to expect from her, she was actually filled with a sense of sadness. It was an unhappiness that stemmed from feeling unloved by her domineering father, and one that manifested itself in many ways, not the least of which was her obvious search for validation and approbation from older consorts. It doesn't seem, based on what she told friends about her life—not to mention what she said in press interviews—as if Grace recognized the reasons behind some of her decisions. "We lived our lives as best we could, made the best choices we could make and moved on," said Rita Gam, Grace's good friend and roommate when she lived in Hollywood. "We didn't spend a lot of time deliberating over things, as we might today."

The constant meddling of her parents in her love life didn't make matters easier for her. After all, she was no longer a teenager. She was a twenty-six-year-old Oscar-winning actress, one of the most famous women in the world. Obviously, Grace Kelly's success in life thus far didn't matter much to her parents, especially to a father who would continue to treat her as if she were unable to make her own choices.

Anxiety seemed to envelop Grace Kelly by the time she returned from Monaco in May 1955, an urgency about the future brought on by the fact that all around her there seemed to be husbands in the offing, children on the way.

When Lizanne married Don LeVine, Grace was her maid of honor at the June ceremony. The excitement surrounding the occasion made her wish that, one day soon, such plans might be made for her own special day. She said that she loved her new two-bedroom accommodations at 880 Fifth Avenue, "but am I going to be living in it alone for the next twenty years, going back and forth from Los Angeles and movie locations like a yo-yo on a string?"

By this time, Grace's sister Peggy had been married for years. Grace enjoyed spending time with Peggy's small daughters, Mel and Mary Lee. Her friend Carolyn Scott Reybold was also raising daughters, both of whom Grace adored and upon whom she doted (and for one of them, Jyl, she was godmother). Sally Parrish Richardson was pregnant, while another friend, Bettina Campbell, was enjoying the daily chaos provided by a three-year-old at home. Rita Gam had divorced and was ready to try her hand at love again, cautiously optimistic about her future with a man who had just asked to marry her. Charlotte Winston, another friend, was also engaged to be married.

After she returned to America from France, Grace began confiding in her friends that she felt restless in her life, and that she now wanted to experience the joys of motherhood, of family. "She wanted what we had," said Rita Gam, "and the fact that she didn't have it had begun to stir something in her. It was funny because we thought that, as a star, she had it all. But, as it happened, she thought the same of us."

Father Figure

Like the Kelly family, the Grimaldis often found themselves invested in the melodrama of difficult familial relationships. However, unlike Grace's family members, who at least tried to work out certain difficulties and did so privately, the Grimaldis never made any secret of their intrafamily feuds. Like most royals, they were raised to accept with little sentiment the fact that there was seldom real warmth between them. The Grimaldis often fought bitterly and, generally speaking, seemed to dislike one another intensely, from one generation to the next. However, no Grimaldi ever seemed to be affected by disagreements, no matter how bitter. Instead, each went blissfully on with his or her life, never really caring what relatives thought about any of it. Antoinette's son (and Rainier's nephew) Baron Christian de Massy, born in 1949, put it best when he wrote in his memoirs, "I entered this bizarre family, inheriting a legacy of fathers hating sons, mothers hating daughters, children hating parents, sisters hating brothers, a tradition in the blood of our family of constant conflict."

Since Rainier's father, Prince Pierre, and his wife, Princess Char-lotte, had divorced when Rainier was a child, the young Prince, as noted earlier, was raised mostly by his grandfather, Louis (as well as various housekeepers and schoolteachers). There was always a sense of dissension in the air, as he has explained it. "When we were with Mother, we were always being told, 'When you see your father don't say anything to him about me or your grandfather,' he recalled. "Then, when we were with Father, we were always being told, 'Don't say anything to your mother or your grandfather about me.' That wasn't easy. Like any child who is the product of divorced parents, I felt hurt by it."

Because Pierre made an effort to keep in contact with both his children, he and Rainier tried to maintain a good relationship. However, any father-son bond between Pierre and Rainier was hard to come by, since the vengeful Charlotte made it difficult, often im-possible, for Pierre to see his children. At one point, when Rainier was ten, Prince Pierre tried to kidnap him just to spend time with him. He was stopped by the threat of serious jail time. Charlotte's father, Louis, later had Pierre banished from Monaco—not unusual in royal settings, where, if a powerful person was annoyed enough by a lesser person, he could just banish the problem-maker to a far-off land and be rid of him. After Louis died and Rainier came to the throne, he let his father return to Monaco and arranged for him to stay at the Hôtel de Paris in the heart of Monte Carlo. He also es-tablished the Prince Pierre Prize in Literature, an award to be given each year to an outstanding European author.

In years to come, Grace would find it difficult to adjust to the no-tion that the dysfunctional royal family members were so uncon-cerned with each other's feelings that they could often say terrible things to each other, mistreat one another, and then go on with their days as if nothing important had occurred. Though she and her parents had always had their problems, those issues were dealt with in one way or the other. Even though many matters remained unresolved over the years—and maybe not even discussed—they weren't simply ignored. However, as Rainier would tell Grace,

"This is Europe, not America. We think differently here, and you'll have to get used to it."

Not only could Rainier Grimaldi not always count on a true father figure in his life, he also never had many friends. Whereas Grace had many chums upon whom she could always depend, Rainier was generally treated by the Monegasques in his life as if he were out of the ordinary, as if he didn't need anyone in whom to confide because he couldn't possibly have problems, could he? After all, he was a Prince! Even if he did seem to need assistance from time to time, most people in his life felt it presumptuous to offer him suggestions. Basically, Rainier was surrounded by yes-men who generally agreed with all of His Serene Highness's opinions. However, Rainier was obviously as human as anyone else, and he did need in his life a person in whom to confide, someone upon whose advice he could depend. He found such a sounding board in one man, a person who would take on the role of a father figure to him: Father Francis Tucker, the trusted chaplain who would play an integral part in joining the lives of a lonely Prince and a restless movie star.

Father Francis Tucker was born to a poor Irish-American family in Wilmington, Delaware, in January 1889. By 1955, Tucker was sixty-six years of age, bald, and bespectacled. He had earned doctorates in philosophy and theology by the age of twenty-one. He was ordained in Rome in August 1911, a member of the Oblates of St. Francis de Sales, a French religious order that he was the first American to enter. In 1924, by direct Vatican appointment, he was named founding pastor of St. Anthony's, a new and primarily Italian-American parish in Wilmington, where he remained for twenty-five years.

Raised a Roman Catholic, Rainier has been devoutly religious throughout his life, adhering to the fundamental teachings of the church. Early in 1950, Rainier was granted an audience with Pope Pius XII. During their conversation, they discussed the local Monaco parish of St. Charles's—Rainier's preferred of five local churches because its congregation was mostly French and Italian with few aristocrats. It was also the church that attracted the most tourists, as it was located in Monte Carlo. In Rainier's view, the priests and congregation at St. Charles had become complacent; the church was in desperate need of a spiritual reawakening. He complained that the Italian clergy (known as Clerks Regular of the Mother of God) were only concerned with one's fate after death, providing prayers for congregants in hopes of assuring a divine hereafter for them. Rainier's concern was as much for quality of life in the here and now as it was for life after death. He also hoped to enhance the social life of the church's communicants, excite them about living in Monte Carlo, and, from there, cause a ripple effect that would, hopefully, inspire the rest of Monaco as well. "It begins with the church," he explained. "Everything begins with the church, the center of all activity."

As a result of Rainier's request, and after months of deliberation, in April 1950 the Vatican released the previous clergy and brought in Father Tucker of Delaware as new pastor of the parish, as well as five clergy from his own Oblates of St. Francis de Sales order. (The previous clergy were not happy to be ousted; in protest, they took all of the rectory's furniture with them, including the bathtub, which they actually pulled out with its moorings.) Father Tucker was chosen mostly because of his multilingual skills in French, Italian, classical Latin and Greek, and, of course, English.

In February 1951, after significant spiritual, liturgical, and social changes had taken place at St. Charles's, Father Tucker accepted Prince Rainier's invitation to serve as Grand Chaplain to the royal family. It was the first time in European history that such a position had ever been offered to an American priest—demonstrating, perhaps, how seriously Rainier looked upon his own personal religious convictions, and how much he admired and respected Tucker. "Can't you forget that I am a Prince and just treat me as one of your boys?" the twenty-eight-year-old Rainier wrote to Tucker shortly after the priest accepted his new position. In public, Tucker always referred to Rainier with the respectful "My Lord Prince," or at least "Your Highness." However, in private, he did call him "my boy."

Now, as well as his work at St. Charles, Father Tucker would supervise all religious services at the Palace and act as a personal chaplain, confessor, and adviser not only to Rainier, but to any member of his family in time of need as well as to more than seventy members of the Palace staff. However, Tucker's rapport with Rainier did not mean that the two friends were always in complete alignment. From time to time they engaged in battles over church policies, one in 1952 so heated that it caused Tucker to attempt to resign. So familiar was Rainier with Tucker that he would criticize him during such arguments, telling him that he was "acting like a girl."

In a 1952 letter to Rainier, Tucker—who always typed his correspondence—complained about getting "a Princely kick in the ass by a guy who has the memory of an elephant."

In an angry return missive, Rainier—who always wrote his letters by hand—noted, "May I remind you that *you are at my service*."

Tucker shot back with, "Your very hatred for me tells me that you love me."

When Rainier didn't immediately respond, Tucker, who seemed insecure at times, wrote to him, "Am I to interpret your silence as giving consent to my resignation?" Then, with a touch of Catholic guilt thrown in for good measure, he mentioned as an aside, "Your dear Mother has just sent me a word of thanks for my Xmas present, 'with much love.'"

A couple of years later, in February 1955, Rainier revealed his imperial side when Tucker announced to him that he was going to Rome on business. In a scolding letter to the chaplain, Rainier wrote, "You used to say, 'may I . . . do you mind . . . if Your Highness does not need me . . . would it be any trouble if I went to Rome.' Well, I supposed those were the days!!! . . . Times change, don't they? And so do all men, even those devoted to Holy Matters!!!"

Later that month, Rainier again became emotional in responding to a letter the priest had written having to do with Palace business that had not gone well. He charged that Tucker now viewed him as "some kind of failure and a growing fast MONSTER . . . the boy you despised—and have now learned to hate or detest!!!"

These outbursts characterized a relationship between the two men that was more than what one might ordinarily expect between a chaplain and His Serene Highness. Indeed, Father Tucker was a father figure to Rainier Grimaldi—for better or for worse—and remained so for thirteen years, from 1950 until 1963. Though some of the correspondence between the two during those years might suggest that they were a bit high-strung as personalities, their informal relationship was unique in Rainier's world, an environment in which people usually moved about him carefully and treated him not as an equal but a superior.

They had their disagreements, but one matter upon which they were in complete alignment was the vision Rainier had for Monaco: Only a Princess would make it complete. Many years later, Father Tucker's nephew, Joseph A. Tucker, Jr., put it best: "For Monaco to work, the royal family itself would have to reflect a Catholic Christian ethic. A single, life-loving Prince wouldn't do it. There would have to be a Princess. But what a woman it would have to be. The kind of woman the Vatican hoped the Prince would find was rare, indeed. Without her, scratch Monaco."

Principality at a Crossroads

In the early 1950s, Monaco found itself struggling to find its own identity. Prince Rainier had been charged with the responsibility of somehow molding this once sleepy seaside gem into the crown jewel of the Mediterranean. He felt the weight of royal responsibility deeply.

Long known as a spectacular resort town, Monaco also had its share of seamy neighborhoods. For the most part, these regions were avoided by Prince Rainier's chauffeur. However, one day each year the Prince would venture into such forbidden territories. It had become a ritual: On the first business morning of each year, Rainier would climb into the backseat of one of his staff members' cars and tour regions that were home to many of the day laborers of Monaco. He would make mental notes of which street signs had gone missing, which rooftops had begun to collapse, which families seemed to be in particular need. He would see to it that some of the less fortunate Monegasques would have their lives bettered by his visit.

Rainier knew that his generosity and kindness would not be enough to keep his subjects well fed, clothed, and housed. It would take vision and planning to bring old-world Monaco into what was fast becoming the Communication Age. The most stubborn Monegasques were more than just resistant to change; they were militant about their dreams of an untouched Monaco. For instance, when the first telephone poles were erected, a group of elderly women held a vigil, claiming that Satan was behind the effort to connect their fair village to the rest of the world.

The Prince faced a thorny challenge if he planned on building an economy for his principality that could not only support its people, but also allow them to flourish. Rainier spent many hours consulting with his counsel, clergy members, even world-renowned economists, to create a strategy for generating revenue. No matter what plan he and his roundtable came up with, he realized it would make enemies for him. He also knew that the best interest of his principality had to be his priority. Inaction would lead to decay. Decay was not an option. In his view, his subjects' devotion to an unchanged Monaco was unrealistic, and while many would call his plan to revive it a sacrilege, it was, as he put it, "a bitter pill that will have to be swallowed."

During one especially long and grueling summit, Rainier and his counsel took a break and headed onto one of the many Palace terraces overlooking the sparkling bay. It was during that recess that Rainier is said to have decided on his plan. As he looked down upon his paradisaical land, it hit him: tourism.

Of course, Monaco had always been a popular tourist destination, but there were limits to the amount of revenue that vacationers could generate for the principality, due to the simple fact of its crumbling infrastructure. At this time, Monaco was bursting at the seams with civic-planning issues. The sewage system was archaic, the plumbing system substandard at best, and the trash removal system one of the country's dirty secrets: Barges of refuse would head out to sea, crest the horizon, and dump their cargo into the water. While it was not an unheard-of garbage disposal practice in those days, Rainier was never fond of it, and he began to formulate a way to both curb the practice and create more of what was lacking in Monaco: land. In order to create more room for the tourists he planned to welcome, he would literally create more real estate.

The Prince envisioned adding possibly as many as fifty acres by layering rock and refuse in more than 150 feet of water, thereby enlarging the country by nearly 20 percent. Though it would take decades to see such a pioneering idea come to fruition, word of it spread quickly. It seemed impossible to most Monegasques, a waste of money. Besides, Monaco was large enough, or so it was argued by his critics. More land only meant more tourists—and Monaco, they complained, already had enough of *them*. When word spread that the Prince had plans to dump the city's junk into the sea at the shoreline—a reductive explanation of a broader plan—tempers flared.

Whenever there was the slightest blip in Prince Rainier's popularity, his sister, Princess Antoinette, would seize the opportunity to remind her brother that his role as public punching bag was one from which he could easily step away. Her son, Christian, was ready and willing, to hear her tell it, to assume the duties of leadership. Since he was too young to do so, Antoinette would gladly step in as regent until he was of age.

Poor Antoinette—twenty-seven months older than her brother—had been jealous of Rainier since they were just tots and she had to share her beloved English nanny with him. Before Rainier was born, Antoinette had gotten all of the nanny's attention. However, that soon changed when Rainier came along. The nanny, who was a cousin of Winston Churchill's, then preferred the boy because she knew he would be the one to inherit the throne.

Antoinette was not the favored child, which caused immediate resentment on her part. Then, when she was about five, she figured
out that Rainier would be Prince and would one day rule over the
principality. Though she wasn't sure what it meant to rule over
Monaco, she did understand that he, not she, would be the one
doing it. She had a distinct sense of having lost something to her
brother before she even knew what was at stake.

Now, decades later, Antoinette was still trying to get back what
she had lost: the throne. When she visited Rainier's office at the
Palace to make her proposal—just the first of a number of times she
would have such a self-serving idea over the years—she outlined
her reasons for wanting to replace her brother. She burst in while
the Prince was entertaining a guest, who then witnessed the heated
exchange between brother and sister. "She claimed that Rainier
wasn't protecting Monaco from the rest of the world," he recalled.
"It was as if she wanted it to remain separate, somehow. The Prince
thought that had been the problem in the first place. He wanted
the world to *discover* Monaco."

When Rainier went on to tell Antoinette that he had even contacted a mid-priced American hotel chain about possibly building
there, she became enraged. "You have the dreams of a common
man," she told him, according to the guest. "How you were born
into this family, I'll never know." With that remark, she stormed
out of the Palace.

Though Prince Rainier had always seemed irritated, even hurt, by
Antoinette's frequent attempts to force him from the throne, this
time he seemed somehow inspired by her insubordination. It was as
though he had finally realized that he had a responsibility to change
the course of his bloodline. The selfish, uncaring Grimaldis had
been in the game long enough. He knew that with his choice of a
wife, he could, and he would, create a new branch on this withered
family tree. His Princess would have to be carefully chosen, for her
reign would be one step toward undoing the generations of misery
his Palace had seen. He needed a Princess—now more than ever.

A Prayer for a Princess

Father Francis Tucker was not fond of Prince Rainier's girlfriend, Gisele Pascal, the actress he had referred to as Rainier's "little playmate" in a letter to his older brother, Joseph, in June 1951. The problem with Gisele, as Father Tucker saw it, was simple: She had been divorced. According to Catholic dogma, divorce is immoral, a law considered absolute in the 1950s even if it does have more flexibility these days.*

Gisele had applied for an annulment of her marriage, but that would entail a long legal process. In the meantime, it would seem that Father Tucker played a part in ending the romance of Rainier and Gisele during the time that Gisele ran off to be with Gary Cooper in Paris. "Family lore has this account," recalls Tucker's nephew Joseph A. Tucker, Jr. "When word reached Monaco of the Gary Cooper affair, it fell upon Father Tucker to tell the Prince about it since no one else would dare. The Prince said, 'I don't believe it.' Father Tucker said, 'Come with me to Paris to see for yourself.' The Prince agreed. In Paris, the two went to a fashionable Parisian restaurant, where they found Gisele and Gary together. The meeting was cordial but final. Rainier knew she was gone and that he would have to look for someone else to be Princess. That was vital, and he knew it."

Rainier's search for a wife and Princess was the most important quest in his life. He had considered the long list of available women he'd met over the years—the many exotic European beauties who had arrived at the Palace as if at the end of a long journey, as if they never

---

*According to current canon law, "If civil divorce remains the only possible way of ensuring certain legal rights, the care of the children, or the protection of inheritance, it can be tolerated and does not constitute a moral offense." However, even today a divorced person is not permitted to remarry in the Catholic Church, or accept the sacrament of Holy Eucharist. (The only exception would be in a case where the papacy was asked for special dispensation.)

wanted to leave—and, though each would have given anything for a place in his monarchy, none interested him. When Father Tucker put forth the idea of England's Princess Margaret as a potential spouse for Rainier, it was agreed that her sister, Queen Elizabeth, would probably not allow her to convert to Catholicism. Tucker also had British actress Deborah Kerr on his "wish list," as well as Americans Eva Marie Saint (who had won an Oscar for her supporting role in *On the Waterfront*) and Natalie Wood, just eighteen but making an impact on the movie industry as a result of *Rebel without a Cause*. For his part, Rainier couldn't help but go back in his mind to the one woman, also an actress, who seemed as if she was just passing through: Grace.

"I may have found her, Father," Prince Rainier said of Grace Kelly a few days after meeting the famous star, according to what Father Francis Tucker once remembered. "I think she may be the one. We didn't spend much time together, but I do have a feeling about her."

"Well, who is it?" Father Tucker wanted to know. This was big news; the chaplain could scarcely contain his excitement.

"The American actress, Miss Grace Kelly," said the Prince. He explained that she had been to the Palace for a publicity session, "And, though I never expected it, I was enchanted by her."

"Ah, yes, Grace Kelly," the priest said knowingly. "Now that's a fine girl." Could she be the one?

The Prince would have to marry not only someone he loved (if at all possible, though not absolutely necessary since arranged marriages were commonplace in royal circles), but also someone suitable for the throne. Grace was young enough to give Rainier an heir; she was beautiful; she had been brought up with wealth; and she was Catholic—all points in her favor. However, like Gisele Pascal, she was also a famous actress—which didn't necessarily bode well for her.

But how much joy did Grace derive from acting? Was it her passion, or just her job? Would she give it up for the throne? The answers to those questions would be crucial to Rainier's decision, because in order to sit at his royal side, Grace would have to abandon her acting career. No reigning Princess would be permitted an additional vocation of acting. Such a profession was deemed unworthy of the throne, which was one of the major reasons Gisele had never made it that far. Indeed, the woman Rainier eventually did marry would have to prove herself to be a woman willing to make certain sacrifices—if not acting, then the sacrifice of any profession or hobby or lifestyle she enjoyed that was not befitting a Princess—and rebuild her world accordingly. Was that Grace?

Days after meeting Grace, Rainier requested a private showing of Grace's film *The Country Girl*, for which she had won the Oscar. He may have been surprised at how dreary she looked in that movie, as dictated by the role. He also asked to see *To Catch a Thief*. Never had Grace been more beautiful than she was in that film, though her acting wasn't perhaps as convincing as in *The Country Girl*. It's doubtful, though, that Rainier cared much about her abilities as an actress.

After seeing the movies, Prince Rainier called upon Father Tucker and told him to gather his things for a journey. They were going to Lourdes, he said, where, according to Catholic history, the Blessed Mother had miraculously appeared to the fourteen-year-old Bernarde Soubirous. There they would pray to the Holy Mother for a woman with whom Rainier could enter freely into a sacred union. "Either prayer works, or it doesn't," the Prince said. "And I believe it works." The chaplain readily agreed to accompany his Prince.

During the long drive to Lourdes, the two discussed the kind of woman they hoped would be the answer to their prayers. "She shall be the center of all of Monaco's beauty," Father Tucker told Prince Rainier, according to what he later relayed. "She shall be the focal point, the manifestation of all that we hope for and dream about in Monaco," he said, in what was practically a prayer. "She shall be the perfect Princess, a good wife, a good mother. And we shall find her, God knows, with the help of the Blessed Mother, Mary."

Prince Rainier III of Monaco knew that he had a mission to fulfill, and if it took him to every landmark of biblical legend, then so be it. His selection of a Princess would not be the result of a hasty decision. His country, his people, his legend deserved more than that.*

---

*In 1979, the government of France chose Princess Grace and her son Prince Albert as its official representatives at Lourdes. The two were photographed while praying in the grotto, the same location where, twenty-four years earlier, Prince Rainier had prayed for a Princess.

The Swan

Upon her return from the Cannes Film Festival and her highly publicized side trip to Monte Carlo where she'd been charmed by the dashing Rainier Grimaldi, Grace spent a brief time in New York with friends. Then she went to California to film her next movie for MGM. With her suspension from MGM having been worked out by attorneys for both sides—and the promise of Grace's getting more latitude with the films she might make so as not to repeat the *Green Fire* debacle—it was time to get back to work.

After photos appeared of Grace with Rainier, there was widespread media speculation of a possible romance blooming between the two, even though no such relationship yet existed. Still, Dore Schary, then Metro's head of production, felt obliged to exploit this situation in the only way he knew how: by coming up with a movie for his beautiful star that might presage the events yet to unfold. A former journalist, Schary was a savvy, astute practitioner of the art of promotion. With Grace riding the crest of international acclaim and box-office popularity, he had to find a property worthy of the jewel in MGM's crown.

Schary found *The Swan*, a creaky old Ferenc Molnar comedy/drama of manners in the MGM vaults, which had been filmed twice previously—in 1925 with Frances Howard and in 1930 with Lillian Gish. He wanted to provide this new version with the famous MGM treatment, feeling that a lavish production in Technicolor and CinemaScope would help to mitigate the dated plotline:

A beautiful young woman of noble lineage, Alexandra (Kelly), is betrothed, by arrangement of her mother, Beatrix (Jessie Royce Landis), to Crown Prince Albert (Alec Guinness), ruler of fictional Ruritania. However, the Prince seems more interested in his dairy cattle than in Alexandra. After meeting Alexandra's tutor, Dr. Nicholas Dyl (Louis Jourdan), in a game of football, the Prince invites the handsome professor to that evening's Palace ball. He then watches as his betrothed and the professor dance, realizing that the two have fallen in love. In a situation of art imitating life, the "reel" Prince (much like the "real" Prince, Rainier) must find an appropriate mate in order to assure the future of the ruling family. The film even features a matchmaking monk, not unlike Father Francis Tucker.

Grace loved the story, having appeared in a production of it at the Bucks County Playhouse, as well as in a television production. Not only did this, her tenth film, provide a way for her to mend matters with MGM and reinstate her as a contract player there, but some have said its royal theme especially appealed to her after her visit to Monaco.

The Swan began filming in September 1955 under the direction of Charles Vidor. For this movie, Grace would finally have single top billing (the only time in her career that she would have such a distinction). As honored as she may have been by the billing, Grace still seemed distracted for much of the production. Alec Guinness recalls having observed her staring into space, seeming lost in a place that, at least from the distant look in her eyes, seemed far away. In fact, the entire time Grace worked on The Swan, she had good reason to be preoccupied. Indeed, what was going on in her private life was more fantastic than what was happening in the fictional story in which she was currently involved.

It had started with a mysterious letter from Father Francis Tucker. "I want to thank you for showing the Prince what an American Catholic girl can be," the priest wrote, "and for the very deep impression this has left on him."

After receiving Father Tucker's letter, Grace Kelly wrote back to the priest. She said she had enjoyed her visit with Rainier, and that she hoped to see him again in the near future. Her discreet enthusiasm, it would seem, was all that was needed to get the ball rolling. When Father Tucker reported back to Rainier that Grace seemed interested in him, as Tucker later reported, the Prince was "all aglow" as he uttered "little exuberances."

Still, Grace didn't seem immediately impressed by her original correspondence with the Prince. Her studio hairdresser for *The Swan*, Virginia Darcy, spoke to her every day during the filming of the movie. "One day, she said, 'You know, I met the Prince of Monaco while I was in France, and now the guy is writing letters to me. It's strange. So what do you think of that?' I said, 'Well, why is he writing to you?' And she said, 'I truly don't know. He likes me, I guess. He said he wants to see me again. But you know, I'm not really interested. He was nice,' she said, 'and we had a wonderful meeting, but what would we have in common?'"

"Not much," Virginia answered blithely.

Grace shook her head. "Not much at all," she repeated.

"It Must Be a Sign"

In May 1955, the same month Grace Kelly returned to New York from France, Father Tucker arrived in Wilmington, Delaware. While there, he began looking into Grace's background, questioning East Coast friends of the Kelly family, networking into their circle of acquaintances, trying to understand who Grace was—and projecting in his mind who she might become. His was a discreet investigation and, it would seem, based on some of his conclusions, maybe not such a good one, at least when it came to some aspects of Grace's private life.

Father Tucker's nephew Joseph A. Tucker, Jr., concludes, "Father Tucker found that there was currently no man in her life, nor scandal. She had caused no divorce, had taken no other woman's husband. Gossips will say that while that is true, she may have done some short-term borrowing." It turned out to be in Grace's best interest that Tucker spoke only to friends, who painted her in the best possible light. Luckily for Grace, it would seem, Tucker wasn't exposed to many reporters at the time, nor to any of the current press coverage about Grace. For instance, when asked if it were possible that Grace was not a virgin, Charles Fish, Jr., a real estate agent in Philadelphia who had known Grace since she was a teenager, exclaimed, "Absolutely not. And I don't think anyone could be closer to that situation than I was. Grace is a straight-arrow Catholic lady, and I'm a Protestant bastard. God knows I tried."

"She was not exploitive and couldn't stand people who were," Tucker's nephew observed years later. "She would permit no cheesecake exploitation by her studio. She did not like conflict and could cry easily. She was poised, gracious, tough, and tenacious. He [Father Tucker] also realized that, by her choice of careers and success in it, she would need a 'theater' for both motherhood and a wifely role. But it would have to be real. She had a passion to be real. I am sure that Father Tucker could conceive of no better choice to be the 'real' Princess that Monaco would need. A 'green light' for the Prince."

Although he usually appeared at ease in public, in private the Prince was a shy, sometimes moody man who was better able to communicate with his private-zoo animals than with people. He was at his best when he took pen in hand. Some have spoken of pages-long letters they received from Rainier—who was fluent in both English and French—in which he would expound on everything from world politics to affairs of the heart. He was an astonishingly literate and even poetic man whose letters were worth saving for posterity, not only because he was a Prince, but because what he had to say was so profound. It was by way of persistent mail communication that he had attracted Gisele Pascal. After first meeting him, Gisele hadn't even been interested. However, when she read his letters she began to appreciate his religious and often thoughtful outlook on life. It's not surprising, then, that Grace felt that she began to know Rainier through similar correspondence to her. And, as fate would have it, Rainier placed great value on her brief letters to him, later referring to them as his "secret treasure garden."*

Charlotte Winston, a friend of Grace's from Philadelphia who attended school with her there and who remained in touch with her throughout her lifetime, recalls a conversation between the two of them that, in retrospect, sounds like two high school girls giggling about the cute boy in English class.

"Grace called me from Los Angeles after she finished *The Swan*. She said that she had enjoyed a couple of telephone conversations with someone she wanted to tell me about. She said he was an interesting gentleman, someone she had met while in France, and then she went on and on about him, how she wasn't sure how she felt about him at first, but then how wonderful their conversations had been. She said they could talk on and on about many things, and she was surprised by it. Then she asked, 'Do you think it's possible to actually fall in love with someone over the telephone?' I thought, well, no. However, in Gracie's case, who could say for sure?

"There was always a sense of serendipity about Gracie's life. It was infused by a sense of destiny. She was still a deep believer in astrology, tarot cards, and other mysticisms. She had stacks of books about horoscopes. She loved giving us readings from *The Book of Destiny*. So, when something preposterous would happen in her life—something that seemed to make no sense at all—it always felt preordained, and you didn't question it. So I said, 'Of course, Gracie. You could fall in love that way. Why not?'"

After about thirty minutes of talking about him, Grace disclosed in an offhanded way, "Oh, and by the way, Charlotte, he's a Prince."

Charlotte recalls having been confused by the revelation. "Do you mean he's a prince of a guy?" she asked.

---

*Today it would seem that none of the letters shared between Rainier and Grace have survived. If they do remain, no one seems to know where they might be hidden. The Prince says that he did not save Grace's letters ("I'm not the kind of person to have done that"), and he isn't certain as to whether or not Grace kept his correspondence to her. The Kelly family has said that they have never seen these letters. It seems unlikely that Grace, who was a sentimental person, would have discarded correspondence that had so moved her. Perhaps she left some of them to her children. Maybe one day these historic communications will surface.

"No, darling," Grace said. "What I am saying, my dear, is that this man is *royalty*, a Prince."

Charlotte laughed and said that she was not a bit surprised by Grace's news. "Only you would end up involved with royalty," she observed, "and at the exact time that you are making *The Swan*, a movie about the same thing."

Grace agreed, further observing that it all "somehow makes sense." She wondered how she could ignore it all. "Surely, it must be a sign," she said.

After all the sadness and turmoil that Grace had experienced with various men, she now clearly hoped that romantic matters in her life would change for the better. At heart, she had always been idealistic. Or, as she told Charlotte, "I want to believe that something like this can happen, that something magical can occur." She then asked Charlotte her opinion as to whether or not she should return to Monaco and once again visit Prince Rainier.

"Have you lost your mind, Gracie?" Charlotte answered. "Why, he's a Prince with his own country. Have you any other choice?"

The two women laughed.

As it happened, Grace didn't have to return to the Palace to see her Prince. He had already decided to come to her.

"Just Like Cinderella"

Edie and Russell Austin were Philadelphia friends of the Kelly family, two people who were always on the guest list at Jack and Margaret's raucous Henry Avenue parties. Grace and her siblings actually considered Edie and Russell to be part of the family, referring to them as "Aunt" and "Uncle," even though they were not related. When the Austins visited Monte Carlo in 1955, they unwittingly became key players in the royal history of Monaco.

As it happened, Edie and Russell wanted to attend the Red Cross Ball gala, the biggest Riviera event of the season. However, much to their dismay, no tickets were available. While trying to figure out a way to take his wife to the ball, Russell remembered that, at a Kelly party, someone had mentioned that Grace had once met Prince Rainier of Monaco. Armed with nothing more than that tidbit of information, he decided to "give it a shot," and called the Palace. Dropping Grace Kelly's name, he requested tickets to the gala, further fibbing that Grace had told him that if he had any problem in Monte Carlo, he should contact Palace officials. Then he waited to see what would happen next.

Much to Russell Austin's utter amazement, his moxie paid off: He soon received a return telephone call from an exuberant Father Francis Tucker. What crazy luck!

"That call was clearly divinely inspired," Father Tucker later posited. Of course, he would honor the Austins' request. Not only would the priest arrange tickets to the gala for them, courtesy of Prince Rainier, but he would also invite them to the Palace to meet His Highness—if they had time in their busy schedules. They had time.

At this time, as always, Rainier Grimaldi was a busy man. Not only was he recovering from a recent appendectomy, he was in meetings regarding the serious instability of the Monaco Precious Metals Society, the principality's biggest bank. Also, Greek shipping magnate Aristotle Onassis had just taken over management of the casino and was moving much of his other business to Monte Carlo. While Rainier and Onassis were usually on friendly terms, they often disagreed on their vision of what Monaco might become in the future. Their arguments were emotional, and distracting to Rainier. Yet, the Prince still found time to sit down with Edie and Russell and ask questions about Grace Kelly. The tourists answered the Prince's questions as honestly as they could and, in the process, painted a positive portrait of Grace. She was a wonderful woman, they said, loyal and trustworthy and able to handle many responsibilities. As an actress, she had few peers, they enthused. As for gossip about her, there was little, they told him—and none of it was true. Rainier and Tucker were satisfied.

Russell Austin then suggested that the Prince "drop round for a visit sometime" at their home in Margate, New Jersey! The notion of His Serene Highness, the absolute monarch and Prince of Monaco, traveling all the way to the United States to visit two people he barely knew in Margate, New Jersey, may seem absurd in retrospect, but at the time it must have made perfect sense because Rainier said he would do it! He intended to visit the States soon, he said, and he promised to contact them. (Imagine the story Russell and Edie had to tell their friends when asked, "So, how was the vacation?")

As soon as she got back to the hotel, Edie placed a transatlantic telephone call to Grace, telling her all about her audience with the Prince and also saying that he would love to see her again. Grace acted unimpressed. Perhaps she didn't want Edie to think that she was going to end up playing matchmaker when, actually, Grace and Rainier were already exchanging correspondence. Grace even said that she found Rainier to be "short," and wasn't really that interested in him. Edie was a bit put off by Grace's attitude and told her to "be nice to the Prince," adding that she would be angry at her if Grace exhibited any of that "frosty cold-shoulder stuff you're so known for." Grace promised her "Aunt Edie" that she would be cordial to Rainier when she saw him again. No doubt, upon hanging up, Grace must have had a good chuckle about this unlikely turn of events. The truth, as she would later recall it, was that she had already begun to think that she might be falling in love with the Prince. "I almost knew I was in love with the Prince before we even met for the second time," she would say. "I don't know how I knew . . . and yet, something . . ."

When Edie Austin returned to the United States, she telephoned Grace's mother. "We saw the Prince of Monaco," she told her. "And did you know he is single? And looking for a wife?"

About a month later, Grace heard from the Prince that he would be coming to the United States during the winter, and that he would like to see her at that time.

Grace began calling her friends to tell them what was next in store for her where the mysterious Prince was concerned. Virginia Darcy recalled, "I got a phone call from Grace one day and she said, 'Well, Virginia, you will never guess what. Between my relatives and everyone else in my life, it seems that I am destined to meet that Prince I told you about. He's coming here, and I'm going out with him.' I was a little surprised. I thought it was about the strangest thing I had ever heard. 'You know, he's got this amazing zoo,' Grace said. 'I just hope he doesn't bring any of those monkeys with him.' We laughed. I told her to just have fun with it. Why not? It wasn't every day a Prince came a-courtin'."

Charlotte Winston recalled, "Grace called me and she said, 'That Prince I told you about, he's coming here to see me.' I thought, well, this is an interesting turn of events, isn't it? I asked if he was coming to look for a bride. Grace said she didn't know. We talked for a time about whether it was possible that she was on a list of women he was coming to meet, or if he was coming just to meet her. She said that she had the impression he was coming to see her, and her alone. Then she added with a laugh, 'If he is coming to meet other women too, well, how dare he waste my time.' Then, after much more enthusiastic discussion about it, she said, 'This is just like Cinderella, isn't it?'

"There was a sense of amazement about the whole thing," Charlotte Winston says. "Since that time, I have read many accounts of this time in Grace's life, and they have all painted it as being a series of events that Grace took in her stride. In fact, from my perspective, she was bowled over by the whole thing."

At about this same time, Prince Rainier gave an interview to David Schoenbrun for a story in *Collier's* entitled "Where Will the Prince Find His Princess?" If Grace read the story, one can only imagine her reaction to it. "A bachelor's life is lonely, empty and particularly so for a Prince," Rainier was quoted as having said. "I cannot behave like an ordinary bachelor. I have no private life. I cannot go out without being followed, watched and gossiped about. Every time I am seen with a girl, someone starts a rumor about a love affair. Why, only recently I met your lovely American actress, Miss Grace Kelly, a charming girl, and the next day I read in the press that I was going to marry her. That sort of thing embarrasses both me and the girl. It is difficult to be natural and at ease with a girl when both of you are secretly wondering whether something will come of it, and then the whole world is openly speculating about marriage.

"You see," he continued, "my greatest difficulty is in knowing a girl long enough and intimately enough to find out if we are really soul mates as well as lovers. I consider it a duty to my people to get married."

The interview with Schoenbrun had been arranged by Father Francis Tucker. Rainier was given quote approval prior to its publication, probably to make certain he hit all the right points. If ever an orchestrated campaign was in the works, this was it.

Before leaving for America, Prince Rainier felt compelled to quash rumors of his search for a bride, which had been running rampant in Monaco for weeks. If he returned without a spouse, the entire principality would be crushed, he felt. On October 11, 1955, Rainier went on Radio Monte Carlo to say that "the question on my marriage, which rightly preoccupies you, interests me just as much and more. Just give me another three years and then we shall see."

Barely a month later, in early November, he alerted the French government of his true intentions: to find a bride in the United States while he was there to attend the charity ball "A Night in Monte Carlo" in New York on January 6, 1956. According to the Franco-Monegasque treaty of 1918, the French government has to approve of any Monaco marriage that might affect the succession of the royal lineage. Rainier talked of his plans with the minister of state—though he pointedly did not mention Grace Kelly's name—who then took it up with the French consul general in Monaco. Grimaldi hoped, he said, that he would be proposing marriage—if all went well. However, it would seem that Grace Kelly wasn't the only woman being considered for the role as Princess. From all evidence, she was the only one in whom Rainier was actually interested, or had even met. However, the resourceful Father Tucker had actually composed a list of eligible American socialites on the Eastern seaboard who would also be considered if matters could not be worked out with Grace or her family.

Many years later, Rainier would continue to insist that he had no plans to ask anyone to marry him in America during his visit, to avoid making his trip seem, in the light of history, a calculated attempt to find a bride. However, on November 30, 1955, eight days before the Prince was scheduled to leave for America, the French Consul General sent a letter to the Minister of State confirming His Highness's intentions, "on the eve of Prince Rainier's departure for the United States where he intends to propose marriage to an American."

Meanwhile, Father Tucker also had reasons other than those relating to a Princess for Monaco for his presence in the United States at this time. He was scheduled to celebrate the fiftieth anniversary of his religious career in the Order of the Oblates of St. Francis de Sales on January 8, 1956—his sixty-seventh birthday—at St. Francis's Church in Wilmington, Delaware. Rainier intended to be at his chaplain's side for the celebration. Before sailing, Tucker visited the Prince's mother, Princess Charlotte, at the family's estate at Marchais to tell her of Rainier's intention to find a Princess in the United States. She asked the priest to tell her son that he had her blessing for his venture.*

Prince Rainier Grimaldi was filled with enthusiasm about the trip to America, his first. It was also worked into the schedule that he would have a physical checkup at Johns Hopkins University hospital to make certain that all was well after his recent appendectomy. However, he seemed healthy. This was a good time in his life: He was young, he was powerful, he was rich . . . and he was ready to meet the girl of his dreams. The plan was for the Prince to take an ocean liner to New York on December 8, 1955, and then fly to Los Angeles to meet Grace there. Afterward, they would fly back to Philadelphia together. Delaware would also be an itinerary stop for the Prince, and, if necessary, he would go to Baltimore, and

---

*Rainier's family estate, Château de Marchais (six times the size of Monaco), is at the foot of the Ardennes, near Paris. It includes two working farms, complete with Manchurian camels and roaming cows. Grace, Rainier, and their children would later spend many weekends here.

then Palm Beach, Florida, to meet the other eligible candidates found on Father Tucker's list of suitable bachelorettes.

Rainier would be accompanied not only by Father Francis Tucker, but also by a secretary and a doctor, Robert Donat, a young physician from Nice. Dr. Donat would accompany Prince Rainier to Johns Hopkins for his physical, but he would have another duty as well. He would supervise the examination of the woman finally chosen to be Rainier's Princess of Monaco, for it was imperative that she be a woman fully capable of having children.

"The Book"

Close friends still remember one of Grace Kelly's favorite pastimes, which involved what she called "the book." Grace often visited with her New York friends Carolyn and Malcolm Reybold and actress Rita Gam. After coffee and dessert one summer night in 1955, Grace sat down on the floor, her legs crossed Indian style. "Go and get the book, Malcolm," she said, clapping her hands. Malcolm vanished for a moment and then returned holding a blue leather-bound book with gold lettering embossed on its cover. It was Grace's favorite, *The Pursuit of Destiny*.

"What is that about?" Rita asked.

Malcolm explained to Rita that he, Carolyn, and Grace "swear by" this tome. Grace agreed, reminding Rita that she was a firm believer in astrology ("I *live* for it") and that "the book" revealed predictions about the future that would otherwise never be told. "Hurry up, Malcolm," she urged. "Go ahead. Read our charts."

Malcolm read the astrological analyses of the women, finally getting to Grace's. He held up the page upon which Grace's "sign" was illustrated—a pyramid with the sun blazing at its top, its rays emanating in every direction. The entry indicated that Grace, born a Scorpio, was living her life "in complete serenity." Others would always assist her in fighting her battles, according to the text, and would lead her to her "next great achievement." She would rarely have to exert much energy to get to the "next stage"; rather, she would simply be taken there by chance, by happenstance, by serendipity . . . at least, according to "the book."

"Well, that's certainly one way to live," Rita said. "So much for auditions."

Grace smiled, delighted.

Grace's chart also showed a strong affinity for Leos—and it was true that most of her best friends had been born under that sign of the zodiac. In fact, in August of that year she hosted a birthday party for all of the beloved Leos in her life—at least a half dozen—and presented to them a cake that featured frosting emblazoned with a confectionery, roaring lion.

Also, and most important, according to *The Pursuit of Destiny* a Scorpio such as Grace Kelly should "never, ever end up with a Gemini, the two signs are unsuitable for one another."

"Well, I won't be choosing a Gemini for a husband, that's for sure," Grace said.

"What man do you know who's a Gemini?" Rita asked.

"I wouldn't even *know* a man who was a Gemini," Grace answered. She added that if she ever discovered a suitor to be a Gemini she would "go running in the other direction." She didn't seem to be joking, either.

Actually, Grace didn't realize it yet, but she did know a man who was born under the sign of the Twins. He was Prince Rainier III of Monaco.

Prince Rainier Meets the Kellys

At first, the plan had been that Prince Rainier would visit Grace Kelly on the set of *The Swan* in Los Angeles, trailed by two photographers from *Look* magazine who had been assigned to cover the meeting. It seemed that little could occur between Grace and Rainier without the participation of the media, and, to be accurate, it wasn't as if the press could simply barge into a private date. It was clear that the two actually welcomed and authorized such photo opportunities—this one was set up with the couple's individual permissions through Rupert Allan and Bill Atwood, an editor at *Look*.

However, because the movie's production was behind schedule and it would not be completed until a few days before Christmas, plans were made for the Prince and Grace to see each other on Christmas Day. Rainier was contacted to let him know he should go straight to Philadelphia, not Los Angeles. Then the Christmas visit was switched from the Austins' home to the Kellys'.

The Kellys attempted to act nonchalant about the Prince's arrival, Jack Kelly saying that they really didn't know much about Rainier, "so why get all worked up about it?" However, in truth, an electric current of excitement ran through the entire family—the entire neighborhood, for that matter, since word of the visit swept from home to home like a brushfire. After all, while sports figures were always on the Kelly invite list, it wasn't every day that a true Prince showed up at 3901 Henry Avenue in East Falls for Christmas dinner.

One of Grace's relatives recalls a conversation with her during which Grace confessed that she "feared" the Prince was planning to propose marriage during this time. The relative—close to Grace and accustomed to the sharing of confidences with her—was dumbfounded. "Grace said that she and the Prince had been enjoying a letter communication, and that he had implied in one of his letters that he might ask for her hand," said the relative. "Grace said she was nervous. She didn't know how she would respond. 'I don't want to give up acting,' she said, 'but I know that if I marry, him or anyone else, I'll probably have a battle on my hands where my career is concerned.' I told her I thought she could do both, marry and have a career. 'Maybe,' she said. Then she said, 'Imagine how my father would react if I married a Prince.' I hoped she was joking . . ."

Prince Rainier was scheduled to show up at Henry Avenue late on Christmas Day. Charlotte Winston recalls, "This was a pressured time for Grace. I spoke to her on the telephone on Christmas Eve to wish her happy holidays, and she sounded rattled."

"Whatever is going on with you, Grace?" Charlotte asked, concerned.

"He's coming," Grace said. "Here. To Henry Avenue. For Christmas."

Charlotte says she was astonished. Charlotte recalled, "Gracie no longer sounded giddy about the prospects. Rather, she sounded concerned. She said she was worried about how her father would act toward Rainier. She feared that he would embarrass her. 'One wrong word from Rainier and it could be over before it begins,' she said of the evening. She said she had telephoned her sister [Peggy] and begged her to be there, at her side."

At 7 P.M., Prince Rainer, Father Tucker, and Dr. Donat arrived at the Kellys' home. "Sit on down, Father Tucker," Jack Kelly said, slapping him on the back. He seemed to have an immediate affinity for the Irish-American priest. "How'd you like a cigar?"

Jack hadn't been sure how to address the Prince and—out of earshot of Rainier, while he was talking to others—suggested that he might refer to him as "Your Majesty." However, Father Tucker quickly corrected him, telling him that the proper way to refer to Rainier would be as "Your Highness." Though it seemed incomprehensible to Jack that he should have to address any guest in his home in such a fashion, he played along anyway—though he did hasten to add, "Royalty doesn't mean much to us."

Father Tucker introduced Jack to Rainier, saying, "Sir, may I present His Serene Highness, Prince Rainier of Monaco."

"Hey, nice to meet you, Rainier," Jack responded, shaking his hand. "So how's about a drink? Cigarette?"

The big surprise to all observers was that Prince Rainier seemed so at home on Henry Avenue, as if he'd been born in the suburbs, lived the better part of his life in that house, and had just come home from a vacation. He moved about the guests with ease, so effortlessly that it seemed as if he already knew the people in his presence, all Kelly family members and a few of their friends.

Much to her relief, Margaret Kelly found the Prince to be a pleasant, sometimes wry conversationalist. She'd been concerned at first as to what he would be like, and wasn't even clear from which country he'd come. She thought he was the Prince of Morocco, until someone set her straight.

Often Grace was seen glancing in Jack's direction, trying to discern what he was thinking. Was he impressed? She would later say that she "truly could not tell." His expression was inscrutable. "It was as if Rainier was just anyone," Grace would tell her sister, "and Daddy treated him that way."

From time to time, Grace and Rainier managed to steal away for a few private moments. As they spoke in low voices, everyone present strained to hear what they were saying.

When the hour got late, Father Tucker agreed to let Jack drive him to a nearby rectory to spend the night. On the way, according to what Tucker later recalled, he confided to Jack that the Prince was considering asking for Grace's hand in marriage. Jack said that he had felt as if "something like that was going on," and said that he would reserve judgment until the unfolding of such events. If surprised—or excited—by the news, he did not let on. He did say that he would give his permission for the marriage, provided that it was what Grace wanted as well.

Meanwhile, Grace, Rainier, and Dr. Donat went to the home of Grace's sister Peggy, where they played cards until late in the evening. At one point, Peggy and the doctor went into the kitchen, leaving Grace and Rainier in the living room alone. When they returned about an hour later, Peggy noticed that Rainier's suit was flecked with hair that had shed from the family's pet dog. "Oh my God, look at you," she said. "I'm so embarrassed." She ran into the kitchen and came back with Scotch tape. "Here, use this," she said, handing His Serene Highness the roll with which to clean his suit. As Peggy and Grace went off to a bedroom for a private talk, Rainier looked at the roll of tape as if it were the first one he'd ever seen in his life.

"Well, I think he's fascinating," Grace told her older sister, according to a later recollection. "What do you think?" Peggy agreed; he was "nice." The two then chatted about Grace's feelings, and what might be in store for her and Rainier. The Prince's arrival was thrilling, the kind of fantastic occurrence shared best by sisters who are close and want to see each other happy in life. After their brief conversation, the Kelly sisters, with Rainier and Dr. Donat, returned to Margaret and Jack's home. Ma then made her guests comfortable in two of her guest rooms. Grace joined her mother in the master bedroom while Margaret prepared for bed.

"So what do you think?" Margaret asked her daughter. According to Margaret's later recollection, she was seated at her vanity while talking to Grace, studying herself in the mirror and brushing her hair. Grace stood behind her. "Well," she answered, slowly. "I think he's most attractive." Then, putting her hands on her mother's shoulders, she added, "I think he's rather nice, don't you?" While looking at each other's reflections in the mirror, mother and daughter smiled knowingly. Grace held her mother close from behind and then grasped both her hands as the two women continued to talk about their fascinating guest. They seemed closer than ever, as Margaret would later tell it.

No doubt Margaret would ordinarily have had serious reservations about Grace becoming romantically involved so quickly with someone she barely knew, unless that person were a rare fellow. She would have done everything in her power to prevent Grace from romancing a director, for instance, that she had just met. However, Rainier was a Prince, *royalty*, and in terms of how things "looked," well, this looked pretty good. Because it had been Jack and Margaret's hope that Grace—that all of their children, actually—marry into Philadelphia society, this latest turn of events involving Rainier was an intriguing way to go in terms of enhancing the family's social status. On the night that they met Prince Rainier of Monaco, the Kelly parents must have recognized the value of their Gracie moving forward with Rainier, and even marrying him. Or, as Margaret might have put it, "That would sure show those Main Liners a thing or two about *real* class, wouldn't it?"

PART TWO

Engagement

Love at First Sight?

There has been much speculation over the years about how Grace and Rainier could possibly have fallen in love after having known each other for such a short time. Their first meeting had been brief and under intense scrutiny by studio representatives and magazine photographers. However, afterward, they spent months corresponding via letter and telephone. Writing letters was Rainier's strong suit. Though he was often shy in person, his written words could be eloquent. Perhaps by wooing Grace through the mail, he made a better impression than he would have made in person. Even though they had only met once, as Grace read and reread his letters she began to feel attracted to the man she imagined him to be. It was during Rainier's first night in Philadelphia, apparently, when the couple began to feel genuine affection for each other. Was it true love? Who, except the two of them, could say? And in a sense, Rainier cleared it up in 1997, when asked by Diane Sawyer if it was "love at first sight" for him with Grace. "No," he said, simply. "No," he repeated. Then, ever the pragmatist, he concluded, "I don't believe in love at first sight anyway." He added that such a sentiment was "a wishy-washy expression, which I don't use."

The day after he arrived in Philadelphia, Grace and Rainier had lunch privately in the country, a simple picnic of sandwiches and wine, eaten under a clear blue winter sky filled with white puffball clouds and brilliant sunshine—with the Prince's bodyguards at a discreet distance, serenely eating a similar meal next to an old elm tree. (Grace would recall years later that she had no idea how Rainier's guards got their own food when she and the Prince went on picnics, "since I certainly didn't prepare it for them. I was vaguely aware that they were even there. However, when Rainier approaches them, they bow deeply, which is so fascinating to see.")

Later that day, Grace telephoned Charlotte Winston to tell her that she believed she was in love with Rainier.

"But Grace, is that possible?" Charlotte asked. "You don't even know him yet."

Grace said that she didn't know what was and was not possible when it came to love. "However, one thing I do know is that my father would approve of this kind of relationship," she concluded, "and that's nice."

Only those close to Grace knew of the concealed flip side to her seemingly impermeable public exterior: the deep sadness she felt in knowing that her success would never be enough to win her dad's approval. It was a disappointment with which she had lived for a long time, brought on by years of his indifference toward her accomplishments. However, to her credit, she never let feelings of inadequacy undermine the intensity of her ambitions. Rather, they urged her onward, perhaps in the hope that one day she would star in that extraordinary film or win that extraordinary award that would finally make her look less ordinary in her father's eyes. But she had already starred in a number of memorable films, and had already won an Academy Award—yet Jack Kelly remained unimpressed.

Years later, Charlotte Winston recalled, "Frankly, my fear was that she was going to get involved with this stranger just to get her father's approval. After all, how much better could she do than a Prince? So I asked her, 'Grace, what is this really about? Is it about your feelings for Rainier? Or is it about your feelings for your father?' She didn't answer. Instead, she promised to call again soon."

Later that evening, Grace and Rainier went to Lizanne's house for dinner. Lizanne hadn't been present for the Christmas Eve gathering, since she was in Pittsburgh with her husband, Don's, family. So this gathering at her home was her first opportunity to meet the Prince. She recalls having been astonished when Monaco's head of state rose from his chair and went into the kitchen to help her with the dishes. "He was quite the charmer," she recalls, "nothing like what one might expect, I mean, in terms of being . . . imperious, I guess."

Later, Grace sat next to her sister on the sofa, stealing a few private moments with her. "How do you like him?" she asked Lizanne.

"Seems nice," Lizanne said with a shrug, indicating that she really didn't know him well enough to have a strong opinion about him one way or the other. Lizanne was never the kind of person to be easily bowled over by anyone. Too practical to take any situation at face value, she always looked deeper at the true meaning of life's unfolding circumstances than did her siblings.

Grace paused. Then, fixing her sister with an earnest look, she said, "I'm going to get married, Lizzie. We're getting engaged."

Lizanne was stunned. "Oh my God, Grace!" she exclaimed. "But you don't even know this guy."

Grace smiled and said that she knew all she needed to know about Rainier. At that point she was summoned by someone across the room—saved by the bell, so to speak. She rose. "See you later, alligator," she said to Lizanne.

"In a while, crocodile," her sister answered halfheartedly.

"Like everyone else, I couldn't believe it," said Lizanne years later. "I was astonished."

During the next few December days, Grace and Rainier spent more time with each other, taking personal histories, sharing confidences . . . and also laughing together. Though she certainly didn't appear to be ambivalent about him, more time alone with Rainier would serve to clarify her true feelings. She soon learned that he had a wicked sense of humor, that he was a practical jokester. Good humor was important to Grace. In her view, there was nothing worse in a man than a lack of humor—she enjoyed a man who could laugh loudly and raucously, not just give out a chuckle every now and again.

Thomas D'Orazio was one of the bodyguards who'd been hired from a private security firm in Philadelphia to guard the Prince during his visit to the United States. He recalls that conversations between Grace and the Prince were "the kind you'd hear during a blind date. She was asking him questions like, 'So, what's it like to do what you do?' 'Do you enjoy your life?' 'What were your parents like?' He asked similar questions. Sometimes they held hands.

When he wasn't watching, she would check him out. And when *she* wasn't watching, he was doing the same. At one point, she got on a pay phone to place a call. I believe she was talking to someone about her next movie [*High Society*]. She was pretty annoyed and said, 'Look, I don't like that particular dress for that scene. We'll have to find something else. So do it, and don't bother me about it until it's done.' Rainier looked at her curiously, took out a notepad from his vest pocket, and jotted something down."

Grace discovered that she and Rainier had certain life experiences in common. For instance, they'd both been lonely as children. In her family, she had felt like an outsider. Similarly, Rainier felt weighed down by his responsibilities to the throne. He had never been able to act like, or mingle with, boys his own age. He too felt like an outcast. Both he and Grace were often shy. Their public personas were all a matter of charade, they agreed, and if they could wish for any personality trait it would be the ability to truly *be* outgoing while at social functions, not just *act* outgoing. (However, to be accurate, Rainier may have felt as if he were bashful, yet few would have that perception of him, especially based on his interactions with the Kelly family.) They both enjoyed having intelligent, witty people in their lives. They could not tolerate those who did not share their zest for life, their sense of excitement about the unfolding events of each day. This is not to say that Grace and Rainier didn't have bad days—but, as they agreed—they tried to make the best of each situation.

There was also discussion between Grace and Rainier about their personal religious convictions—both Roman Catholic—and about Grace's interest in having children. According to what she later recalled, she told him that she had recently been experiencing maternal urgings. The sooner she could have a child, she said, the happier she would be for it.[*] "I hope it's not presumptuous of me to say, but I expect you to be the most glowing of expectant mothers," he told her. "I shall look forward to that occasion."

---

*Grace and Rainier, as if to accommodate Princess Grace's "maternal urgings," became parents about nine months after their marriage.

A day or so after the picnic with Rainier, a panicked Grace called Charlotte Winston, saying that she had learned "the most awful thing," and now didn't know what to think.

"What is it, Gracie?" Charlotte asked.

"Rainier. He's a Gemini."

It took Charlotte a moment to recall what *The Book of Destiny* had to say about Geminis—that people born under that astrological sign should "never, ever" end up with those born under Grace's sign, that of Scorpio. The two zodiac signs were incompatible; a pairing of them would result in disaster. "Well, you have to forget it," said Grace's chum. "I mean, c'mon Gracie. It's just for fun."

"Not for me it isn't," Grace said. "I'll have to really think about this."

Grace said she couldn't believe that "after all of this time," she hadn't thought to ask Rainier about his date of birth. Her friend suggested that perhaps the reason for such an oversight was because, in truth, it wasn't really important to her. "Well, I don't know how to explain it," Grace said, bewildered. "Usually, that's the first thing I find out about. How did this slip by me?"

Gemini or not, Grace couldn't seem to resist the Prince.

"He was charming," observed Virginia Darcy. "He could charm the birds off the trees. You should have seen him in those days: He was impressive. Cute—not handsome, but cute. And he had such personality. Compared to what was out there in Hollywood, all those actors with so little to offer but scandal, I mean, how could he not win any competition for a girl's heart? He was a Prince! It didn't hurt that she knew she was going to be a Princess. Who didn't want to be a Princess, after all?"

Not surprisingly, on the days Rainier and Grace strolled the sidewalks of Philadelphia, hand in hand, stopping to window-shop or have a bite in an intimate bistro, they were under the careful scrutiny of paparazzi. "I have lived my life in recent years under their watchful eye," Grace told the Prince during the couple's visit to a friend of the Kellys in Philadelphia. The two were seated on a sofa in the living room of the home of the family friend, enjoying a cup of tea. A small group of people whom Grace had known for years chattered away, trying not to stare at the couple but attempting to eavesdrop on them anyway.

"I have had to deal with them as well," Rainier observed of the pesky photographers. "How do you tolerate it, my dear?"

"Generally, I find it easy to overlook their rudeness," Grace said. She added that their existence in her life had never stopped her from living it to the fullest, "though it probably should have from time to time," she joked. Moreover, she had never been one to complain about the price of her success. She said that she had a marvelous life and "I thank God for it every day. How lucky I am," she exclaimed. She always seemed so full of life, grateful for every day.

When Grace put down her cup of tea, the Prince put down his cigarette. He clasped both her hands and looked at her warmly. "You, my dear, are an exceptional woman," he observed, giving her a flirtatious look. "Do you know that?"

Grace blushed. "Why darling! There are people here, listening," she said, motioning to her friends, all of whom were eavesdropping and grinning.

"But I am not saying anything they don't already know," he continued, now loudly so that all could hear. "I'm quite taken with you, Miss Grace Kelly."

Grace smiled and put her head on his shoulder. "What a dear man you are," she remarked. Then, turning to their audience, she repeated, "What a dear, dear man."

The Proposal

On December 27, Grace was scheduled to begin vocal lessons in Manhattan in preparation for her role in *High Society*, a musical reimagining of MGM's 1940 movie version of Philip Barry's *The*

Philadelphia Story (which had starred Cary Grant, James Stewart, and Katharine Hepburn).

In *High Society*, Grace would play Tracy Samantha Lord, a spirited but spoiled, rich Philadelphia Brahmin. MGM's name change was probably meant to deflect comparisons between the two films. Alas, comparisons are inevitable—with the musical version coming up short. As Tracy, Kelly proves she's no Hepburn. She is gorgeous to behold and properly upper-crust, but she lacks the tart-tongued delivery and icy edginess that made Hepburn's performance so memorable.*

Still, *High Society* would go on to become the year's number one box-office movie and a fitting valedictory to the film career of Grace Kelly, whose position in the firmament only four years earlier was established in the much-lauded *High Noon.*

Prince Rainier and Dr. Donat both accompanied Grace to New York. They were driven by Thomas D'Orazio. "I sat in the front with the doc," he recalls, "and the Prince and Grace were in the backseat. I checked the rearview mirror at one point and realized that we were being tailed by a car with four guys in it, and behind them was another car. Both cars had their lights on, in daylight. I mentioned it to the doc, thinking they were press and we needed to ditch them. But the doc said, 'Never mind them. They're with us. Just drive.'

"Maybe a half hour later, I looked again in my rearview mirror, and Grace was back there with her head on the Prince's shoulder, looking about as relaxed as you can get. At one point, she rolled down the window, turned around, and said, 'Do you know we're being followed?' The Prince said, 'Yes,' and she said, 'I was going to

---

*Prior to filming, Grace was nervous because she realized she wasn't really a singer and would be paired with one of the world's most popular vocalists. That most of the production people involved in the film felt that she should use a voice double, de rigueur for nonsingers such as Rita Hayworth and Ava Gardner, didn't help matters. However, Grace was a consummate professional and wouldn't hear of such fakery. She was determined to work as hard as she could to get her contralto voice in shape to handle the simple melodic range of "True Love" with Crosby. It worked so well that when "True Love" was released as a single, it sold almost a million copies, earning Grace a gold record and royalties for years to come.

ask that we pull into a rest stop, but now I'm too embarrassed to have all of these people wait for me. So forget it.'"

While in New York City, Grace became further acquainted with the Prince; the two stayed in adjoining rooms at the Waldorf-Astoria. Their first evening together as part of Manhattan's exciting nightlife would become the subject of copious column items and photographs in the next day's newspapers. Of course, the importance of this time with the Prince in Grace's life was unknown to the media and the public—and it would most certainly have generated a surprise headline or two had it been revealed.

The official story that has been passed on year after year in Grace Kelly biographies is that the Prince proposed marriage on New Year's Eve. Actually, he proposed on December 28. Leanne Scott, who was a nurse hired to assist Dr. Donat while he was in America, says that she was told by the doctor that the proposal took place on a chilly evening after Grace and the Prince had enjoyed a romantic dinner at the Waldorf-Astoria, alone. Rainier later told Dr. Donat that, while eating their dessert of pears poached in wine, he presented Grace with a gift. "If you are to be at my side," he reportedly told her, "then you may need this."

When Grace unwrapped the box, she found a lavish, pictorial history of the Grimaldis in Monaco. As she turned the pages of the book, Rainier told her that he didn't expect her to actually read it. However, he suggested, she might find the need to at least refer to it in the future.

Rainier later said that as she studied the book, Grace observed, "I think I would love to live in this place . . . and to live there with you would be wonderful."

Rainier then gave Grace a brief oral history of Monaco, including some of the myths about it, such as the so-called curse of the Grimaldis. According to the legend, at the end of the thirteenth century, Rainier I—known as the Admiral General of France—abducted a Flemish woman after a battle. The maiden turned herself into a witch after he raped her, and then cursed Grimaldi and all of his descendants, stating, "Never will a Grimaldi find true happiness in marriage."

Rainier laughed when he told Grace the story—even though, if he had ever thought about it, he must have realized that Charles III wasn't happy in his marriage, and neither were Albert I and Louis II and many other Grimaldis along the way.

Grace did not find the legend the least bit amusing. Unbeknownst to Rainier at the time, she was fascinated by the occult and held fast to her own superstitions. Though Rainier told her the curse was "utter nonsense," Grace said she would prefer that he never again bring up the subject.

While it seems that Rainier had planned to propose to Grace during dinner that evening, it never happened. Perhaps discussion of the curse of the Grimaldis had given him an uneasy feeling, after all, or maybe it just dampened the mood, because he decided on a secondary plan. He asked Grace to join him for an evening stroll in Central Park. That locale would be the perfect spot, he may have thought, since Grace had always been fond of it. The Prince knocked on the hallway door to Grace's hotel room, choosing not to use the door that connected their adjoining suites. Not surprisingly, when she appeared at the door, she was a vision of beauty, her upswept hair revealing diamond earrings. As evidenced by photographs taken that night, she looked elegant in a dark ranch mink coat and long leather gloves.

The two descended in the Waldorf elevator. Unfortunately for Rainier, when the elevator reached a lower floor, in walked Dr. Donat and his nurse, Leanne Scott. While making small talk, Grace invited them to join her and Rainier on their stroll through Central Park. Once again, the Prince's plans were foiled.

Outside of the hotel, Rainier must have known that he couldn't propose in a caravan of four, because he took drastic measures. As the group waited to cross Park Avenue at 50th Street, the Prince decided to put a bit of distance between the two tagalongs and his would-be fiancée. Just before a long stream of traffic, Rainier grabbed Grace's wrist and yanked her out into the street. Horns blew, but the two made it safely to a grass-covered median that lay between Park Avenue's north-and southbound lanes. Through the rush of traffic, Donat and Scott saw Rainier reach into his pocket and present Grace with something. "She let out a small squeal," says Leanne Scott. "And she said, 'Yes, yes, yes, I will marry you' so loudly that the others, who hadn't crossed, could hear her. At that point, the doctor and his friends crossed over and caught up to them.

" 'What's all the fuss about?' " Dr. Donat asked.

" 'Why, the Prince asked me to marry him,' Grace told him, her face flushed pink with excitement. On her finger, she flashed what would be a temporary ring: a band set with diamonds and rubies. Rainier told her he was having a ring created especially for her with emerald-cut diamonds. [Later, the Prince would give her a Van Cleef & Arpels pearl-and-diamond necklace and earring set as an engagement gift.] 'And I said yes,' Grace continued, 'I would love to marry him.' "

"He told me that Grace seemed happy, and that the Prince was grinning from ear to ear. They then locked in an embrace and kissed, right there on the sidewalk in front of everyone. He and everyone who observed the kiss did the only thing they could think of to do: They applauded."

Once back at the Waldorf, Prince Rainier telephoned Father Francis Tucker, who was in Wilmington, Delaware, at the time. According to what the priest later told his nephew J. Clifton Tucker, Rainier said, "Father, I owe all of this to you. It's all because of you that this wonderful thing has happened to me. Look at how blessed I am, to have found this wonderful woman."

"Oh, no, my boy, you don't owe me a thing," Father Tucker said. "Do you remember our pilgrimage to Lourdes? Well, this is the 'Grace' the Blessed Mother gave to you and to you alone."

Many months later, when Father Tucker shared with Grace Kelly the story about his and Rainier's trek to Lourdes to pray for a Princess, she was surprised. "Why, Father," she said, excited. "You will never believe this, but my confirmation name is Bernadette."

"Somehow, I believe it," Father Tucker told her. "In fact, it doesn't surprise me a bit."

"I Have Made My Destiny"

The next morning, on December 29, 1955, Grace Kelly telephoned her parents with the news that she had already told her sister Lizanne: She was going to marry Prince Rainier Grimaldi of Monaco. She told her mother, according to a later recollection from Margaret, that she was "very much in love." Jack said he already knew about it, and explained that Father Tucker had told him about Rainier's plans to ask Grace for her hand. Margaret was also not surprised because, apparently, Jack had already told her the news. They both seemed happy and accepting; this was one relationship in which they were not going to meddle. "When a daughter comes to her mother and says she is marrying a Prince, well maybe that's when you stop disagreeing with her on her choice of men," Margaret said at the time. To a reporter, she clarified: "Imagine, here I am, a bricklayer's wife, and my daughter's marrying a Prince."

Rainier never actually asked Jack's permission to marry Grace. As Margaret once explained, "Father Tucker formally notified my husband that the Prince wished to marry Grace. My husband said, 'You know, Father Tucker, a title does not impress us. The only thing my wife and I are interested in is the happiness of our daughter.' The Father spent a good deal of time telling Jack about the Prince's family background and character. He assured us that the Prince was of nobility not only in birth but in deed and character. It was settled."

Margaret had made it clear that she wanted Grace to be married in Philadelphia. When told by the Prince that such a plan would be fine, she believed him and began thinking of a Philadelphia ceremony. By this time, Margaret was already fond of Rainier and, it would seem, fairly swept away by the idea of being his mother-in-law. She had already taken to calling him "Ray," an abbreviated version of Rainier (and also because, as she later explained it, "he did bring a ray of light into our home"). Rainier had confided in her, as well, that he sometimes called himself "Shorty." In a newspaper article Margaret wrote at this time, there was no mistaking her feelings. She wrote that she had always hoped her daughter would marry somebody of distinction. "But a Prince! And such a charming Prince! And such a handsome Prince! Even as I write these lines, I still feel a sense of unreality. Just think—my daughter is marrying a Prince!"

Grace's sister Lizanne says, "I don't think Grace was in love. She didn't have time to *really* be in love. She had been more in love with other people than she was with Rainier when she first met him. But there was a great attraction between them. Other than that, I don't know why she decided to marry him so quickly."

Melvin Shiffle, whose father, Theodore, was a cement contractor in Philadelphia and a good friend of Jack Kelly's, recalls, "My old man told me that he got a phone call from Jack one day, and Jack said, 'Finally, my Gracie is doing something right. She's marrying royalty.' My dad was used to Jack's B.S. He said, 'Jack, what the hell are you talking about? Is Gracie marrying some kinda king, or what?' Jack said, 'Just you wait and see. This is gonna be the biggest news of all time, and Gracie is right in the middle of the whole thing. You think it was big when she won that acting award [presumably the Oscar]? Forget that. That was small potatoes compared to what we got in store.'"

Later that day, Grace wrote a letter to Jean-Pierre Aumont to tell him about the engagement, rather than have him read about it in the press. Then she began telephoning select friends and relatives.

Recalls her lifelong friend Rita Gam, "She called me after New Year's Eve and invited me to a cocktail party to meet her intended; she also asked me to be a bridesmaid at her wedding. 'Rita darling, won't you come and meet my Prince?' I accepted with great joy, assuming 'my Prince' was just her romantic way of referring to Oleg. To my surprise however, her Prince was a real one."*

Grace's friend Marianne Dressler, who had known her since high school, recalls a telephone call she received from Grace at this time. "I was sitting at home, reading about the two of them in a newspaper column when my phone rang. It was Grace. 'My gosh, I was just thinking of you,' I told her. She said, 'Sit down. I have good news.' Then she told me about Rainier.

"'But Grace, you cannot marry this man, I don't care if he is a Prince. Why, you don't even know him,'" Marianne said, according to her recollection.

"Well, don't try to talk me out of it," Grace countered. She added that her mind was made up, that she had never been more certain of anything, nor had she ever been happier. Even if he was a Gemini, she said, she was going to marry him. "Plus," she observed, "I'm not willing to let go of this magical thing that is happening to me now." Then she concluded that even her father seemed excited about the prospect.

"But, Grace, listen to reason—"

Grace hung up. Ten minutes later, she called Marianne again. She apologized for the previous disconnection and explained that "a lot of people will be against me on this, and I need your support. So, are you with me?"

"Of course I'm with you," said Marianne. "But what about love, Gracie? Do you love him?"

"Oh, that," Grace said dismissively. "I've had plenty of that. Now," she concluded, "I want peace." She then hung up.

Marianne recalls, "I decided not to fight her. However, I think most of us who loved Grace felt the same way: that she deserved more than this kind of whirlwind courtship. As young women, we all wanted to be romanced; we wanted to be dizzy in love. I felt she

*Rita Gam had her own successful career as a contract player in the 1950s and '60s, cast in films such as the thriller Night People with Gregory Peck, the biblical epic King of Kings, and, most notably, 1952's The Thief, whose gimmick was that it had no dialogue. Her appearance in that movie generated a Life cover story for her. Her costar in The Thief was future Grace Kelly costar (in Dial M for Murder) and lover Ray Milland.

was being cheated, and I also felt she was doing this to make an impression on her father. Though I knew even then that true love rarely played a part in royal marriages, still, I hoped for more for Grace."

Grace had told her friend that she wanted "peace" in her life. Indeed, that reason for her sudden decision to marry Rainier seems clear when one considers her tumultuous history of romantic entanglements with William Holden, Clark Gable, Ray Milland, Oleg Cassini, and the rest. Many of Grace's friends have theorized that by the time she met Rainier, she was drained by all of the strategizing involved in hiding previous romances from not only her scrutinizing public but also her domineering family. Moreover, she may have wrestled with the moral conflict between her traditional Catholic upbringing as a youth and her erotic private life as an adult. Also, so many men had let her down. Rita Gam adds, "In the fifties, anyone you took to bed, you took to heart. You had to fall in love with the man you were making love with. Grace was used by some of these men. For them, it was not serious. For her, it was. They could not have suffered as desperately, or as silently, as she did."

There had been so much drama in Grace's romantic life for so many years that by the time she met Rainier she was ready to settle into an easier life. After all, he was stable, reliable, loyal—comfortable. He would also provide a safe haven for Grace at a time when she was feeling uneasy about her domestic future. Her romance with Rainier Grimaldi was a legitimate one that, obviously, could be carried on proudly, in full view of the world. She was definitely her mother's daughter in the sense that she did care what people thought, she did care how things "looked"—and what could look better than marrying a Prince?

Also, Grace had said that she never wanted to be in a relationship with a man who would feel belittled by her success. "I couldn't bear walking into a restaurant and hearing the maitre d' refer to my husband as Mr. Kelly," she had said.

Moreover, Grace obviously believed that Jack Kelly would be pleased if she married the Prince. That in itself seemed to be almost reason enough for her to do it. Lastly, as a result of her relationship with Rainier, she had never been closer to Margaret. Grace was smart enough to know that her parents had their own rationale for their joy over the presence of Rainier in their lives, which had as much to do with social climbing as it did with their daughter's happiness. However, the end result was the same: All three—mother, father, and daughter—were in alignment, a rare occurrence in young Grace's life.

In the end, at least in Grace's view, it made perfect sense that she should marry Prince Rainier Grimaldi of Monaco. True to the manner in which she had always lived her life, she said, "Sometimes you just have to make a decision, make a choice, and then do it."

In the days to come, Grace would also confide in Oleg Cassini about the marriage, and wished to do so in person rather than by telephone or correspondence. It was interesting that she first arranged a meeting with him in public, accompanied by Virginia Darcy. "I went with her so that she could tell him in person that she was marrying the Prince," recalled Virginia. "She said, 'I have to see Oleg and tell him good-bye. But it's better to be done in public. Then, if His Highness asks any questions, it can't be said I had a secret meeting. No one could make anything out of it.' So, we met at the bar of the St. Regis Hotel in New York. She talked to him, I didn't pay attention. I stood on the side and just minded my own business."

If Virginia had been eavesdropping, she might have realized that Grace actually did not end it with Oleg that afternoon at the St. Regis. Apparently, she had merely staged the meeting as an alibi, in case she ever needed one. Actually, she later met the designer in private, on the Staten Island ferry.

Because it had rained earlier that day, a sticky dampness lingered in the air when the two met on the commuter boat. "Oleg, I have made my destiny," Grace told her former lover. (Notice that she did not say she had "met" her destiny. No, she had "*made*" it. True to form, she felt she had created her destiny, rather than just stumbled upon it.) Grace then told Oleg of her plans to wed Rainier. This is how Oleg remembered it:

"Grace, one of the reasons I believe that you're marrying this man is because this is the best script you ever received in your life," Oleg told her. He had always been a straight shooter. "You're going to have a life that is glorious for a month or two. Why, the publicity will be enormous. But then what? You're an actress, and you want to be in that milieu. You would be more comfortable with me as your husband and you know it."

Grace said that marrying Oleg was "out of the question," adding, "we're beyond that now, Oleg."

"Another reason you are doing it is to please your father, isn't it, Grace?"

Grace smiled. She could always be honest with Oleg. "Well, Daddy does like Rainier," she said, "and I must say that it's nice to not be fighting with him."

While they spoke, the two former lovers were enveloped by a thick fog, as if on the set of a movie. According to his memory, Grace put her head on Oleg's shoulder. "You do have your own way of looking at things, don't you?" she said to him.

"It's not good, marrying a man to please your father," Oleg offered.

Grace smiled. "There are worse things in life," she opined.

"But do you love him?" Oleg persisted.

"I will learn to love him," she answered, according to Oleg's memory.

That was the last time Grace Kelly and Oleg Cassini ever spoke to one another.

The "Fertility Test"

It's been continuously reported over the years that the reason Prince Rainier did not marry Gisele Pascal—who had for many years lived in the Beaulieu villa where he spent most of his time—

was that it had been determined by a "fertility test" that she was unable to bear children.

Actually, there existed at that time no such test that a woman could simply either pass or fail. Because it was imperative that Rainier's wife be able to bear an heir to the Monegasque throne, any woman who intended to marry him would have to be examined to make certain that she could conceive—not so much a specific test as a mere physical examination. When informed that she would have to be so examined, Gisele had produced a letter from her French physician stating it would not be necessary, that she was certainly able to conceive. However, it was still decided that the Prince's physician should be the one to examine Gisele.

It has been reported that three examinations of Gisele came to the same conclusion: She would not be able to conceive. Rainier was supposedly told that if he married Gisele Pascal, he was taking a chance on not having an heir to the throne. Upon receipt of that bleak news, as the story goes, he left her. "If you ever hear that my subjects think I do not love them, tell them what I have done today," Rainier supposedly told his confidant, Father Tucker.

Of course, the truth about the breakup of Rainier and Gisele was that she left him because she was tired of waiting for him to make up his mind about her. Moreover, the story of Gisele's not being able to have children, still so accepted as a part of Monaco history, is actually a rumor that was spread by Rainier's sister, Antoinette, who so disliked Gisele that she told many stories about her— though none as enduring as this one. Anyway, according to the by-laws of the 1918 treaty, Rainier and Gisele could have adopted a child, so the matter of Gisele's ability to have a child of her own would not have been a sole reason for that relationship to end. Ironically, Gisele Pascal did go on to marry Raymond Pellegrin and have a daughter.

Now Grace Kelly would have to undergo an examination to determine if she were fertile. Even if they could adopt, Monaco officials still wanted to know what to expect and, no doubt, at least try to convince the Prince not to marry a woman who couldn't bear children. Actually, such circumstances are not unusual in royal circles. Just as the ability to produce an heir has been the raison d'etre for entering into a marriage, the inability to have a child, especially a male child, was the official reason for at least one major high-profile divorce in the modern era: Mohammad Reza Pahlavi, the Shah of Iran, divorced his second wife, the beautiful Soraya, when she failed to produce an heir. His first wife, equally infertile, was the sister of King Farouk of Egypt. After the divorce from Soraya, the Shah immediately married the former Farah Diba, who provided him with two sons and two daughters in quick succession. (Soraya never remarried and died in October 2001.) It was also asked of Diana, Princess of Wales, that she undergo an examination before she could marry Prince Charles, also to determine if she could bear children.

Grace Kelly hadn't fully understood the specific reason for Dr. Donat's presence at Rainier's side when he showed up in Philadelphia, and simply assumed, she later said, that he was there to attend to the Prince in the event of a medical situation, and also to be at his side for an examination at Johns Hopkins. However, it became clear while she was in New York with him that Donat's purpose was to supervise her examination—not to be present for it but, rather, to serve as a conduit between the examining physician and Palace officials.

Because she understood the reasoning behind it, Grace wasn't upset about the examination, which she was told would focus on her process of ovulation and menstruation. She would also be x-rayed to ensure that her fallopian tubes were free of blockages, and that the uterine environment would be suitable for implantation of a fertilized egg. It was also explained to her that if the exam concluded that she had problems, she would be treated and given advice on what to do when trying to conceive. "In other words, she wasn't going to be abandoned," said Donat's nurse, Leanne Scott. Grace was also told that she would be asked certain questions about her family's medical history to be certain that hereditary diseases such as hemophilia did not exist in her lineage, though it has been presumed that these kinds of inquiries had already been made in one way or another by someone (perhaps Father Tucker) long before the Prince even showed up in Philadelphia.

Always a woman who did whatever was necessary to achieve her goals, whether in her personal life or in her career, Grace Kelly decided that the examination, as explained to her, would be harmless enough and that the information imparted to her during it could even be useful in the future. She was no more annoyed by the proposition than she would have been by a last-minute glitch in a contract negotiation with MGM. "Nothing ever goes easily, does it?" she asked one relative. True, it had always been one thing after another for Grace, and this was, in her view, another "thing." However, she also decided not to tell her family about this "thing" because, as she told Charlotte Winston, "I don't think they would understand it at all, and I'm not going to try to explain it to them."

However, Grace did have some apprehension about a matter that was sure to be revealed as a result of a physical examination: that she was not a virgin. Though Grace hadn't been a virgin for some time, the Prince was apparently under the impression that she was still "chaste." Despite all of the media coverage of her personal life at the time, many people would still have been surprised by an absolute admission that she was sexually active. Today, in a more cynical age, the public would never believe that a twenty-five-year-old woman as alluring as Grace Kelly and living the kind of fast-paced, show business life that she was, in the company of so many famous, sexually charged men, had not been intimate with someone along the way. However, in the 1950s it was assumed that a woman was a virgin until proven otherwise—not the other way around.

"Yes, she was concerned about what would happen if he found out she was not a virgin," says one friend of hers. "She and I were having lunch at the Barclay Hotel in Philadelphia's Rittenhouse Square when she told me about it. I was appalled that she was expected to go through with the exam. She, however, was practical about it. 'Look, you do what you have to do in this life,' she told me. 'It was time for me to get a checkup anyway. And, besides', she laughed, 'this way he's paying for it, not me.'

"However, the fact that it might be learned that she wasn't a virgin did bother her. 'Maybe I will say I was in some kind of sporting accident in school,' she said. Her voice held a note of panic. Trying to calm her, I said, 'Grace, you weren't very good in sports, remember?' And, with typical humor, she smiled and said, 'All the more reason I would have an accident, then, isn't it?'"

As much as she was concerned that the Prince would learn that she wasn't a virgin—and the notion of a Princess in 1956 not being pure was practically unthinkable—Grace was also a practical woman who knew that it would not serve her image or career if word got out that she had taken a physical exam and was declared impure as a result of it. Her imagination ran wild as to what the ramifications of such a revelation would be. Would the studio use the morals clause of her contract to cause further problems for her? How would her fans react? Would her box-office appeal be damaged? Worse, what would her parents think? "It was a lot of pressure," says her friend Don Richardson, "and coming at a time when she certainly didn't need it."

The physical examination would eventually be conducted by a female gynecologist Grace knew and trusted at a women's clinic in Bucks County, Pennsylvania. In the end, it showed that Grace could have children.

Later, Grace said that the physician never even asked if she was a virgin, and, as she put it, "if she was any good at all, she would know that I wasn't one. But she didn't ask, and I didn't offer. It wouldn't have been polite, anyway, for her to ask."

It's not known if Grace Kelly and Rainier Grimaldi had any discussions about her virtue. Considering the kind of whirlwind romance he was spearheading with her, would the Prince really have taken the time to quiz her about the specifics of her sexual encounters with men like Jean-Pierre Aumont and Oleg Cassini? He didn't need to know *everything* about her. It could also be argued that she was not obliged to tell him everything either.

The Dowry

In weeks to come, the world would think of Grace Kelly's decision to marry Prince Rainier of Monaco as an extraordinary and sweeping fairy tale, one in which a beautiful American actress falls in love with a handsome Prince and, by the wonder of his love, is magically transformed into a reigning Princess. It would be fair to observe that Grace believed it as well. Perhaps she also believed she was in love.

However, behind the scenes—unknown to the public, but well-known to some members of Grace's and Rainier's inner circle—were occurring the kinds of negotiations that would have astonished even the most jaded of celebrity watchers. Surely even the most romantic of people would have had to view the proceedings that followed Rainier's proposal through rose-colored glasses in order to continue seeing it as a complete fairy-tale story.

First, there had been the so-called fertility test. Grace had managed to get through that matter, her dignity intact. The next challenge would be the matter of a dowry, the European tradition whereby a woman brings an amount of money, or other goods, to her husband in marriage. It was Father Tucker who first explained the dowry to Jack Kelly: $2 million was the sum—it is unknown as to how it was arrived at—that was to be paid to the Prince in order for Grace to marry him.

It seemed strange to the Kellys that Grace Kelly, a mere actress, would be asked to give money to Rainier, ruler of a principality. Was he marrying her for her money? To Jack Kelly, that scenario seemed a possibility. "Forget it," he told Tucker. "It's not gonna happen. We're not giving him money."

Later, Jack informed his wife that he "told off" the priest. "Oh, he really did carry on about it," recalled Grace's Aunt Marie McGee of Jack's reaction to Tucker's news.

In fact, a dowry was more a common practice when a marriage was arranged, explained Jeffrey Trent, a Philadelphia accountant at the time who was a friend and business associate of Frank Cresci, Rainier's consul general of Monaco from 1954 to 1993. (Trent was also tangentially involved in the Kelly family's finances.) "The problem, of course, was that this wasn't exactly an arranged marriage. However, in the sense that it was a royal marriage, a dowry of some kind was still expected. The dowry was supposed to be money, goods, or estate that the wife would bring to her husband, which was technically provided by the bride's family. In return, the groom promised to provide for and support her. It was completely archaic, even back in the fifties, and I recall Frank and many of Rainier's American associates being puzzled as to why it was even necessary. However, some European traditions die hard, and this was one of them. There was also a sense, as I recall it, of not wanting to push too hard for fear of alienating or even offending the Prince. One really had to walk softly on this terrain."

In a series of tense meetings over the next few days, Father Tucker explained that if Jack wanted Grace to marry a Prince, there would be no way around a dowry. Tucker explained that the marriage of the Prince of Monaco was an affair of state, and there could be no exceptions to common law: A woman who marries into such a situation must present a dowry. This tradition would not change for Grace Kelly, nor for any other woman the Prince chose to marry.

It wasn't as if the Prince needed the money, the priest explained. After all, Rainier was still a wealthy ruler, even though slow tourist trade in Monaco had squeezed the casino's revenue into an economic crunch, especially in recent years. He did have significant real estate holdings, including his Palace and his share in the huge family estate, Château de Marchais.

No matter what Father Tucker had to say, however, it did not sit well with Jack Kelly. To this protective father, it sounded more than ever as if Rainier were a "broken-down Prince" (as he put it) in need of $2 million. He wasn't about to pay anyone to marry his daughter. After all, if news of such a deal ever started churning through the gossip mills of Philadelphia society, how would it look?

In truth, Rainier's Palace was in need of some repair. Since the end of the war, the crown jewel of Monaco had been on the decline. At the very least, it needed a new coat of flamingo pink paint—not to mention updated electricity systems and plumbing fixtures, heating and air-conditioning units, carpeting, and more. If a wedding was to take place there that would garner worldwide attention, the old girl could stand a facelift.

"Two million dollars might have helped, but let's be reasonable, it wasn't as if Rainier was marrying Grace for her money," Jeffrey Trent explained. "I've heard such things in the past, and the notion is preposterous, even if it did seem to be the case to Jack Kelly and some other observers—which was also understandable, given the circumstances as they perceived them. My understanding of it was that tradition must be adhered to, and that was just the way it was going to be.

"It could be said that two million dollars was not a lot of money," he added. "But at the time, yes, that seemed like a lot. The Kellys were having trouble adjusting to the fact that *any* money had to be paid. Grace got used to the idea, as I recall it, quicker than anyone else. To her, it was just money. 'I can always make more money,' she said."

It would seem that Grace wasn't as annoyed by the notion of a dowry as she was about the way it seemed to have been sprung upon her and her family. After the surprise of the physical examination, the revelation of a dowry hit her hard. Rainier had never mentioned it to her. Instead, he had gone directly to Jack Kelly—and, even more egregiously, via an intermediary, Father Tucker. Still, that was proper protocol in this particular situation. "Oh, for crying out loud," Grace said, according to Jeffrey Trent. "If it's not one thing it's another."

After a few days, Grace began working as conscientiously as Father Tucker and the Prince's own attorneys to resolve the matter of the dowry, if only so that she could proceed with the wedding plans. Rather than continue to debate the notion of a dowry, she simply offered to pay it out of her own pocket by liquidating certain stocks. Jack refused Grace's offer, maybe out of pride.

Grace was frustrated. To think that the entire wedding could be scuttled because of a money matter was inconceivable. In the days that followed, she told Don Richardson that her father was being "impossible" about the dowry, and that she didn't know how to handle him. "It was a surprise to her, all of this business about finances, and she really found it unpleasant," said Richardson. "The money meant nothing to Grace, other than another snag in the process. It meant a lot to Jack, however, in terms of the principle behind it."

"I'm sick about it," Grace told Don, according to his memory. The two were on the telephone; Grace seemed to be in tears. She also said she was concerned about how such a revelation would be perceived if it were made public. "If the press finds out about this thing," she observed, "well, forget it. We're cooked."

"Then tell him to back off," Don told her. "He doesn't need the money, for God's sake."

Grace seemed baffled, and admitted that she too wondered about Rainier's finances, especially after what her attorneys had told her about the state of the Palace. "They say the Palace needs paint," she said. "It did look a little beat-up when I was there." When Don asked the facetious question of how much it costs to paint a palace, Grace laughed and said, "Two million dollars, I guess."

When Don suggested that Grace ask Rainier about his finances, she said she couldn't possibly do such a thing, that it would be inappropriate. He then suggested that she still had time to reconsider her decision to marry the Prince. "He's a good man, I'm sure," Don said, "and any woman would be lucky to have him. But you, Gracie, are not just any woman. Why, you're Grace Kelly. You have a life. You have a career. You don't need this. You've already created your life."

"I've created a life, all right," Grace said. "A life alone. I may not need it," she added, "but I *do* want it." Her tone was absolute, her attitude as determined as one might expect from a woman who had managed to make it to the top of Hollywood's list of elite actresses of the 1950s. She assured Don that the marriage would go forth as planned. Twenty-six years later (in 1982, just seven weeks before her death), in an ABC-TV interview, Grace would make a statement that seemed to clarify what she viewed as the mixed blessing of being a strong and independent woman in Hollywood. "Very often," she said. "I think the price for independence and freedom is often solitude and loneliness."

In the end, the Kellys agreed to pay the dowry. It has been said within the Kellys' inner circle that half—$1 million—came from Jack, and the other half from Grace. It should also be noted that with the passing of the years, any dowry presented to the Prince has been redefined by spokesmen for Rainier as "a financial arrangement, but certainly not a dowry." Whatever one chooses to call it, all available evidence points to the Kellys having paid a sum, as requested.

Explained one family member, "The family was determined that he [Jack] not put the kibosh on things, even Ma Kelly, who eventually said, 'Oh, just pay him the money. I want Grace to be a Princess, and it's what she wants as well.' Not only was Jack pressured by his family to pay the money necessary for the wedding to go forward, but he, like Margaret, was enticed to do so because he recognized the social and promotional value of having Grace marry Prince Rainier. 'As long as no one finds out about it,' he concluded, 'I guess the dowry doesn't make any difference. It's a business transaction, in the end, isn't it?'"

The Marriage Agreement

After the unpleasantness of the physical examination and then the matter of the dowry, Grace Kelly might have thought that nothing else would interfere with her plans to marry Prince Rainier.

If so, she would have been wrong.

In weeks to come, a marriage agreement would have to be negotiated between the Kelly family's attorneys and accountants in New York and Prince Rainier's in Monaco, and the give-and-take, back-and-forth on this written agreement would prove to be a further complication for Grace—but one that, in the end, she would handle with aplomb. A marriage agreement, or contract, was commonplace in Europe, especially among wealthy families. Though such an agreement between the two marrying parties may now seem unusual, it really isn't—today it's simply called a prenuptial agreement. In America in 1956, such a document was unusual, thought of by most people as the instrument of a business merger rather than a romantic union.

In France, couples customarily marry under community property laws. However, Grace's attorneys were informed that she and the Prince would have to be married under a total separation-of-property agreement—*séparation des biens*—meaning that, despite what the term seems to imply, everything each party brought to the marriage would belong to both of them equally, as well as everything acquired during the marriage.

Predictably, Jack Kelly wasn't happy about the Palace's proposed arrangement, saying he would prefer that his daughter enter the union with a specific division of property—meaning that all that she and the Prince brought into the marriage would remain their own, and what they accumulated after the union would be jointly owned. Jack had intended to gift Grace with a large stockholding in his business, Kelly for Brickwork, as a wedding present, as he had done with his other daughters. However, he wasn't eager to make such a gesture if he felt it was going to end up tied to the principality's assets.

A smart businessman, Jack did his own research and learned that the flip side of the proposed arrangement meant that Grace would have certain responsibilities toward certain outstanding bills related to her home, which would be the Palace. It was unclear as to what the total of these expenses would amount to, but whatever it was going to be was too much, as far as Jack was concerned.

It was during discussions about the marriage agreement that Grace may have realized that her Prince was not as amiable as he had appeared to be up until this point in time. During their brief courtship, Rainier was on his best behavior—as people tend to be at the beginning of an incipient relationship. No doubt Grace was putting her best foot forward as well. However, when she first attempted to discuss the troublesome marriage agreement with him, she found that Rainier was not eager to discuss it. His controlling behavior, some thought at the time, might be a precursor to future problems Grace would have once they were married.

Laurence Lanier was one of the Kelly family's New York attorneys who, along with Grace's lawyer, Henry Jaffe, had negotiated the matter on Grace's behalf. "I was right out of law school," he recalls. "We had a meeting in my office—Jack, Grace, me, the Prince, and an attorney for the Palace. It was a big day for me, having a Prince in my office. I had my secretary take a photo of all of us."

In the black-and-white snapshot displayed by Lanier so many decades later, Grace is wearing a simple two-piece dress with a small hat. Somehow, despite her simple outfit, she still looks intensely glamorous. Rainier is in a conservative dark pinstriped suit. Jack Kelly, Laurence Lanier, and two other attorneys are also in dark business suits. Whereas everyone in the photo is smiling, Jack Kelly is the exception. His expression is stern, unhappy, perhaps indicating his feelings for the subject of this meeting. Everyone is puffing away on cigarettes; there is so much smoke about them that they appear to be standing in a fog.

"Rainier, you know I'm a little unhappy about all of this business with the marriage agreement," Jack Kelly began, according to Lanier's memory. "It doesn't seem right to me."

"Well, this is something that cannot be helped," Rainier said with conviction. "It is what it is, and that's the way it must be. It is also fair." He added that everyone present must realize that he would not take advantage of Grace.

"But, Rainier, please, can't we—" Grace began.

Rainier put his hand up, cutting her off. He told her that the matter should not be discussed by the two of them. As he motioned to her father and the attorneys present, he suggested that she leave this situation to be worked out by the men.

"Well, I disagree," Grace said. She was a woman who was used to dealing with real sharks in Hollywood, accustomed to at least being heard in a disagreement even if not always having her way. "What I think is—"

Again Rainier cut her off. Smiling, he put his arm around her. "Now, you listen to me, dear," he said tenderly, as a father would in speaking to his child. "What I am proposing is fine and fair." He asked if he had her trust.

"I don't see that as being the point," Grace answered with a frozen smile.

"Fine, then," Rainier concluded, ignoring her iciness. "Let's move on, now, shall we?"

Grace glared at Rainier. She then opened her black velvet purse, took out her lipstick, and applied a deep slash of red in a way harsh enough to convey exasperation.

"Oh, yes, she was disgruntled," recalled Laurence Lanier many years later. "When they left, Grace was not holding the Prince's hand—as she had been when they arrived. She didn't once look at him after their small exchange. I didn't have a good feeling about it.

"Later, Jack said to me of the Prince, 'How dare he be so dismissive of all of us? Does he think I just fell off a turnip truck?' It was all Jack could do to not tell him a thing or two about the way the Kellys operate.

"I told him, 'Look, Jack, if it was me, I would put an end to all of this, now. The Prince is unresponsive to her concerns,' I told him, 'and it troubles me.' Jack said, 'I agree that this deal has not gone well, from the beginning until now.' But he said that Grace would never speak to him again if he tried to stop the wedding, and neither would her mother. 'I have to let her do what she wants to do, but it's killing me that I can't protect her,' he told me. He then asked me to find out if there could be some movement on the matter, and then get back to him. He wanted me to at least determine the exact amount of money she might end paying in Palace expenses.

"I never did learn what kinds of expenses we were talking about. The agreement was vague. The clock was ticking. Communication with the attorneys in Monaco was unsatisfactory. Everyone wanted to get past this matter and move on."

About two days later, the attorney received a telephone call from Grace.

"I want you to know what Rainier and I have decided," Grace said, according to the lawyer's memory. She then said that she and the Prince had discussed the matter privately, and that they had agreed that she would retain a large amount of stock on her own, as well as certain other assets. Putting it simply, according to what Grace told the attorney, she and Rainier had made a compromise and agreed that, while certain of their monies would be commingled, she would also have her own assets, which would be supervised by the Kelly family accountants and maintained in banks in America.

"Basically, she won, if indeed you want to call it a battle," said Lanier. "It felt to me at the time like she was a smart woman hedging her bets. If things didn't work out in Monaco, she was wise enough to maintain her own money, and he [Rainier] was, I suppose, smart enough not to make it a major issue between them. Still, there were some ambiguities having to do with the Palace and certain responsibilities she might have for the upkeep of it."

Lanier tried to protest. "I think I need to discuss this with your father," he told her.

Grace said that she had already discussed the matter with Rainier, that they were in agreement, and that there would be no further discussion about it with anyone.

"This is worse than dealing with MGM, all of the back-and-forth for weeks and weeks now," Grace said. "Let's end this now, shall we?"

Jack Kelly and some of his attorneys and accountants and business associates, including Jeffrey Trent, had lunch the next day at the Oak Room in the Plaza Hotel to discuss the negotiations. Though Grace was supposed to make an appearance, she didn't show up. "Oh, she's just being Grace," Jack said by way of explanation. "Busy, I guess. Shopping, probably."

"So what do you think about this whole thing?" Trent asked Jack, speaking of the marital agreement.

"Well, I want Grace to be happy, and if this makes her happy, then fine," Jack said, according to the accountant's memory. "I've wanted all my kids to go after what they want in this life." Jack further stated that he was "damn proud of my Gracie" for reaching an equitable agreement with Rainier where her finances were concerned. "So I say, good for her," Jack decided. "She, a woman, managed to do what a whole team of you bastards couldn't do. She sure as hell surprised me," he said. Then he added with a wink, "Don't you dare tell her that either. If she gets a big head, she'll be worse than her mother."

People who knew her well were not surprised that Grace had found a way to reach a compromise with Rainier. "Even at such a young age, she was able to negotiate with people in a way that they wouldn't feel bad about giving her what she wanted," said Virginia Darcy, her MGM hairdresser. "She never had to hurt anybody's feelings to get her way. She knew exactly how to sway them to her way of thinking. She was fair, diplomatic, and, face it, beautiful—and that helped. I think, at least during the early stages of their relationship, it was hard for Rainier to resist her if she was adamant about something."

"Men would go gaga over Grace," said her sister Lizanne. "I don't know what quality it was that made people want to do things for her, but she had it. I even found myself doing things for her. Though she was a powerful woman, she did sometimes have a help-less quality about her. She was far from helpless, though. She was talented and efficient and could do anything she chose to do, but all the men she knew wanted to do things for her and, boy, they would—it was unbelievable."

However, there was at least one condition upon which Prince Rainier would not capitulate, no matter how charming Grace might have been in her discussions with him about it. It was a par-ticularly startling clause in the agreement, specific in its intention: If the marriage should fail and either party should choose to end it, Grace would have to surrender to Prince Rainier any children she might bear during their marriage.

The Announcement

On Friday, December 30, Grace organized a dinner party at her Fifth Avenue apartment so that her friends could meet Rainier. It was a pleasant evening; Grace's friends were impressed with this Prince who quickly charmed them by insisting they dispense with formalities and simply call him "Rainier." It wasn't his looks that at-tracted people. Although short, he was handsome enough, if not as good-looking as many of Grace's suitors over the years. Rather, it was a blend of self-assurance, sense of humor, and the ability to put others at ease that made him so attractive. He was immensely com-pelling. When he spoke to a person, it was as if he were speaking only to that person—and as if no one else in the room mattered. There was also a sense of intrigue about him. After all, he was roy-alty. Prince Rainier III was, in a word, *powerful*, and, as Henry Kissinger once put it, power is its own aphrodisiac. Before long, he had impressed most of the people at the party, many of whom had been skeptics out of concern for Grace.

"He's everything I've ever loved," Grace told one of the guests. She ticked off the Prince's qualities, as she saw them: "He's enormously sweet and kind. He's strong. He wants a close and loving family, just as I do. He's bright, has a wonderful sense of humor, and makes me giggle. I love his eyes. I could look into them for hours. He has a beautiful voice. He's a good person."

The major topic of discussion that evening had to do with the announcement of the upcoming nuptials: How would it be made, and when? At one point in the evening, Grace—tired of being asked repeatedly—rounded everyone up and said that Father Tucker would explain to them how the formal announcement would be made to the world. "Listen," she told her guests good-naturedly, "and listen well, because this will only be explained once."

Father Francis Tucker then stood in the middle of the living room and clarified that His Highness and Grace Kelly would return to the Kelly home in Philadelphia, where the announcement would then be formally made. There would be one photographer present, he said, whose job it would be to document the moment by taking two pictures: one of the happy couple, and another of the happy couple posed with Grace's happy family. Those two pictures would then be distributed to the press.

There was a moment of silence as the chaplain's words sunk in. Somebody let out a long, low whistle, as if to say, "Uh-oh. This is trouble."

Only two photos? To be *distributed* to the press?

Everyone present excitedly voiced astonishment and disapproval. Clearly, Grace's friends wanted to protect her from an embarrassing announcement that would make it appear that she was hiding something. She sank in her chair and closed her eyes, perhaps hoping to bring some order to whatever chaos was going on in her mind. After all, she had been in show business for years and knew that this sudden turn in her life would be a headline-making event and would have to be announced in a way that suited its newsworthiness.

Rainier didn't say a word. From his expression, he was clearly disgruntled. Later, he was overheard having a heated discussion with Father Tucker in a corner of the room. "Who do these people think they are?" he hissed angrily, trying not to bring more attention to himself, yet making his position clear to his confidant. "They are mere actors, show business people. I am a reigning Prince! And you, my priest. How dare they disagree with us?"

"Now you stop it right there," said Father Tucker, wagging his finger at Rainier. "Don't you dare become a royal pain in the ass now, do you hear? These are Grace's friends, and you'd better respect them. Or you will lose her, I can guarantee you that much."

Rainier walked away, angrily muttering to himself, smoking a cigarette.

Father Tucker then told the group that he would take all of their suggestions "under advisement." However, by this time the atmosphere had cooled considerably. Rainier soon began treating the guests as if they were his royal subjects, rather than friends. "Get me a vodka," he said to one partygoer, giving him an order as if he were a Palace servant, "straight with ice and lime." In turn, the guests began referring to him as "Prince" rather than "Rainier."

Grace was distressed that the evening that had begun so well turned out so badly. "I suppose he could be a bit more flexible," she said to one guest, referring to Rainier. "I can see now that there'll be a good way to appeal to him, and a not-so-good way . . . and in front of strangers may not be the good way. He is a Gemini, after all," she added, though she didn't elaborate.

If there were any tension between them because of the past, it had dissipated by Tuesday night, January 3, 1956, when Grace accompanied Rainier to the Stork Club in New York. Jack O'Brien, a columnist for the *Journal-American*, came to their table and slipped Grace a note that said he had it from a reliable source that she and Rainier were about to announce their engagement. Would she simply write on the bottom of the paper, he asked in the note, which day she planned to make the announcement and then give it back to him? When Grace showed the note to Rainier, he chuckled. She rose, walked over to the writer, and said, "I can't answer this question right now. But I can on Friday." She smiled. He got the message.

After he heard about the way the Prince planned to announce the engagement of his daughter, Jack Kelly sprang into action. Jack, who had an experienced understanding of the media and how it worked, had a meeting with Rainier and explained that such an important announcement could not be made without calling a press conference. "So, that's the way it has to be," he told Rainier, according to attorney Laurence Lanier. "You do things your way in your kingdom, or whatever it is," he said, "and here we have our way. So you'll have to swallow this one, pal." Though Rainier wasn't used to being spoken to in such a way, he did find Jack's blunt manner amusing. He smiled, shook his hand, and agreed that there would be a press conference. "See, you just gotta talk straight to the guy," Jack told Lanier. "He's okay. People kiss his ass too much, that's all." Then, with a big Jack Kelly grin, he added, "If people kissed my ass that much, I'd love it too. Nothing wrong with that."

In order to announce his daughter's engagement privately to friends, family, and certain dignitaries (including Governor and Mrs. George M. Leader as well as Mayor and Mrs. Richardson Dilworth), Jack Kelly hosted a luncheon at the Philadelphia Country Club on Thursday, January 5. Plans were made that the engagement would be simultaneously announced in Monaco by the Minister of State. Grace, who wore a simple gold-brocaded dress with a pink chiffon scarf around her neck, seemed to glow that afternoon. On her finger was the engagement ring, which consisted of a large twelve-carat diamond with smaller rubies—representing the red and white national colors of Monaco.

As he raised a glass of champagne, Jack beamed and said, "We are happy to announce the engagement of our daughter, Grace, to His Serene Highness Prince Rainier of Monaco. We drink a toast to them." Later, Grace said that Jack had never seemed happier.

After the luncheon, Jack invited the press to his red-brick manse for photographs and questions. About one hundred reporters descended upon Henry Avenue, all eventually assembling in the Kellys' living room with their cameras and lights placed atop the family's grand piano, their equipment plopped on all of Margaret's "good" antique chairs. The air was full of excitement. Anything—and everything—seemed possible if such a thing like this could occur in the suburbs of Philadelphia: a celebrated local girl announcing her wedding to a mysterious royal, perhaps giving up her skyrocketing movie career, most certainly moving to a strange country few had even heard of. Grace later said that she had to repeatedly pinch herself that afternoon to ensure that she wasn't dreaming: That's how surreal the press conference seemed to her. Months earlier, she didn't even know Prince Rainier Grimaldi of Monaco. Now this . . .

Grace and Rainier posed for the cameras, doing what they knew they had to in order to placate the enthusiastic reporters and photographers. All the while, the media jostled for the best angle, shoving and pushing so much that the pregnant Lizanne scurried upstairs to escape the possibility of an accidental elbow in the stomach. Grace smiled, self-assured, confident, and looking radiant—in her element. After all, this was her world, giving quotes to reporters, having her picture taken, being a star.

"So what's the deal here, Prince?" one reporter shouted out. "Is this an arranged marriage, or what?"

"How does it feel, Grace?" another asked. "Are ya happy?"

"So where exactly is this so-called kingdom you got there, Joe?" asked another, addressing Rainier as if he were the guy who sold pretzels on the corner in front of the Philadelphia Museum of Art.

"Gonna be giving up your career, Gracie?" another demanded to know.

As the questions came at the couple fast and furiously, Jack watched the scene and smiled proudly. "Now, this is really something," he said to Paul Renquist, a freelance photographer working that day for the *Philadelphia Bulletin*. "We're talkin' headline news here. I mean, look at this frenzy, will ya? My Gracie has gone and done it now, hasn't she?"

"Well, sir, obviously Grace Kelly has been a star for some time . . ."

"Well, not like this she hasn't," Jack said.

"But the Oscar," Paul said as he shot a picture of Jack holding up a glass of champagne in toast style.

"Aw, that was nothin'," Jack said with a grin. "But this," he said, motioning to the fracas, "now, *this* is *somethin'*."

With that comment, Jack walked over to Grace and put his hand on her shoulder as she answered a question from an inquiring reporter. Father and daughter exchanged smiles; she reached up to touch his cheek, and then cupped her hand on top of his. "She glowed like a little girl who had come home from school with an A-plus," recalled Paul Renquist. "And I remember thinking to myself, 'Ah-ha, now I get it. Now it all makes sense.' If I had been a writer instead of a photographer, I would have been able to crack the mystery of why Grace Kelly was marrying a man she hardly knew, based on observing that one single moment between her and her ol' man."

Though Grace held up well during the press conference, Rainier's smile vanished after about five minutes. He did his best to get through the ordeal of having to answer the same questions and pose for the same kind of photos repeatedly, until, finally, he seemed to buckle under the pressure. Weary from the bombast that surrounded him—and no doubt annoyed by the ill-mannered press people—he dragged his sleeve across his eyes. "Look, I'm not tied to MGM," he told Father Tucker. "I want this to be over, now." However, when Tucker shot Rainier a warning look, the Prince backed down.

The next day's newspapers were filled with stories about Grace and her "Prince Charming." Observed the Associated Press report, "Hollywood, used to surprises, seldom has been more flabbergasted . . ."

The next night, Grace and Rainier endured more of the same kind of publicity at a charity ball they attended at the Waldorf-Astoria in New York, appropriately dubbed "A Night in Monte Carlo." This was the event Rainier had been scheduled to appear at, which he mentioned the first time he met Grace. The ball's organizers had hastily constructed a "Royal Box," complete with

The official wedding portrait: Princess Grace and Prince Rainier of Monaco.
(PHOTOFEST)

Grace Kelly, precocious in 1931, at age two. (Retro-Photo)

Rainier Grimaldi, a little prince in 1926, at age three. (Paragon Photo Vaults)

Prince Rainier III of Monaco in 1955, still unmarried at age thirty-two. According to the terms of a treaty between Monaco and France, Monaco would revert to French control should its prince die without an heir. It had become a dynastic imperative, therefore, that Rainier find a Princess to bear him a child. (The Academy of Motion Picture Arts and Sciences)

Prince Rainier became official heir to the throne on June 2, 1944, shortly after his twenty-first birthday. This photo was taken at his Installation. From left to right: Rainier's sister, Princess Antoinette; his mother, Princess Charlotte; Rainier; and his father, Prince Pierre. (PARAGON PHOTO VAULTS)

April 6, 1955. When Grace Kelly and Prince Rainier III of Monaco shook hands in the Palace of Monaco for the press, little did they know that their entire lives would be changed by the publicity gimmick. (PICTORIAL PARADE)

By the spring of 1955, twenty-five-year-old Grace Kelly was at the top of her profession as an Academy Award-winning actress. However, she had found only unhappiness in romance and was ready to make a change in her life. Never would she have imagined what was in store for her. (PARAGON PHOTO VAULTS)

After meeting Grace, Prince Rainier took his Palace chaplain, Father Francis Tucker, on a pilgrimage to the holy site of Lourdes. There they would pray for a Princess. "Either prayer works, or it doesn't," Rainier said. "And I believe it does." (RETRO-PHOTO)

Rainier and Grace are pictured with Grace's proud parents, Margaret (far left) and Jack Kelly, as all admire Grace's engagement ring. (PHOTOFEST)

The Kelly family was swept off its feet when royalty showed up at its front door. Prince Rainier (bottom left) holds Grace's arm as the couple poses with the Kelly family. Top row, left to right: Kell's wife, Mary; Lizanne's husband, Donald LeVine; Grace's brother, Kell; Peggy's husband, George Davis; and Grace's younger sister, Lizanne. Sitting in the middle is Grace's mother, Margaret, with Grace's father, Jack, and Grace's sister Peggy. (PHOTOFEST)

Grace and Prince Rainier pose in New York in January 1956 during the "Night in Monte Carlo" benefit at the Waldorf-Astoria. Though Rainier had made it clear that Grace would have to abandon her film career to become his princess, she thought there might be a way to change his mind . . . later. (PHOTOFEST)

Was it love at first sight? Rainier answered the question years later. "No," he said. "I don't believe in love at first sight, a wishy-washy expression, which I don't use." He and Grace finally got to know each other while in New York in 1956—*after* she accepted his marriage proposal. (PHOTOFEST)

Grace Kelly, on her way to Monaco to marry Prince Rainier, gazes out to sea as the liner *Constitution* passes the Azores on April 12, 1956. As she later recalled it, while strolling aboard the ship, it suddenly hit her that she was a woman without a home—without a country, even. Not yet a Monegasque, and no longer an American at heart, she really did feel as if she were lost at sea. (BETTMAN/CORBIS)

Grace and Rainier in the salon of the Prince's yacht, *Deo Juvante II*, on April 12, 1956, the day Grace arrived in Monaco for the royal wedding. (PHOTOFEST)

Prince Rainier and Grace Kelly sit in the Throne Room of the Royal Palace on April 18, 1956, just before their civil marriage ceremony. From the expression on Grace's face, she had a lot on her mind . . . perhaps second thoughts about all she would have to sacrifice in order to be royalty? (PHOTOFEST)

As Palace guards keep the throng at a distance, Grace is escorted by her father, Jack, into the Cathedral of St. Nicholas on her wedding day. (PHOTOFEST)

Grace's big day, April 19, 1956. Has any bride ever looked more stunning? (PHOTOFEST)

Princess Grace and Prince Rainier, as husband and wife, immediately following the ceremony. "Thank you, darling," Grace told him, "for such a sweet, intimate wedding"—a tongue-in-cheek reference to the media chaos that had nearly ruined their special day. (PHOTOFEST)

Grace's parents, Margaret and Jack, with their new son-in-law, Prince Rainier, and his wife, Princess Grace, at the wedding reception. (PHOTOFEST)

Home sweet home? Illuminated by floodlights, the Monaco Palace gleams like a fairy castle in the dark of a Riviera night. Imagine living here! This photo of the Grimaldi home was taken in the spring of 1956. (BETTMAN/CORBIS)

streamers, which looked so preposterous that the Prince was reluctant to even occupy it. However, in keeping with the benevolent spirit of the evening, he allowed photographs of himself and his bride-to-be to be taken in the contraption.

His Serene Highness appeared dignified in black tie and tails with royal decorations. The superbly cut suit hung with precision. On this night, he seemed larger than life, taller than his actual height, alive, vital.

For her part, Grace also looked smashing in a strapless white satin Dior gown, a corsage of orchids pinned to her bosom, wearing low heeled shoes so as not to appear much taller than her fiancé. She appeared cool, self-possessed, and more striking than ever.

Before Rainier was to speak to the throng of guests, Father Tucker was asked to say a few words. Standing in front of the microphone, the chaplain appeared to be so emotional that he would, at any moment, dissolve into tears. "This is a time my Prince and I have prayed for," he said, "a time of joy, a time of love, for we are about to welcome the most wonderful of women into our world, the lovely Miss Grace Kelly." At that, there was a huge round of applause. Grace, with tears in her eyes, stood up and acknowledged the applause. The priest continued: "They say that God works in mysterious ways, but I disagree with that. It is no mystery to me whenever God puts the best of people together to spend their lives in joy, harmony, and love, and such is the case here. May God bless my Prince, and may He bestow equal blessings upon the Prince's fiancée, Miss Grace Kelly."

Following the priest's comments, Prince Rainier rose to speak to the assembly. He graciously singled out Edie and Russell Austin, the couple who had visited him in Monaco and acted as intermediaries upon his arrival in Philadelphia. Smiling at them from the podium, he said, "You have done more for me by this than anyone else has done in my life." It was a courteous gesture, one that must have made two people feel proud, even though, in truth, Rainier had had the power to meet Grace again if he chose to do so, and certainly didn't need Edie and Russell to assist him. As he spoke, Grace clung to the Prince's arm, as if never to let go.

After the Waldorf event, Grace and Rainier went dancing at the Harwyn Club. Later, in the company of bodyguard Tom D'Orazio, Grace acknowledged Rainier's efforts at being so cooperative. "I know you're not used to this kind of thing," she said, holding both his hands and gazing into his eyes. "It's been awful for you, hasn't it?"

"At times," he said, nodding his head in confirmation. "But, for you, my dear, I would do anything." When he lifted her white-gloved hand to his lips and kissed it, Grace's blue eyes lit with pleasure. Rainier then took her by the arm and escorted her onto the dance floor. Once there, the couple gently swayed to the music of what would become "their" song: "Your Eyes Are the Eyes of a Woman in Love," from *Guys and Dolls*.*

As they danced, the Prince slid his hands down Grace's back and then over her buttocks. The movement, which seemed curiously provocative in public, was caught by a photographer for the Associated Press. In that one instant, perhaps these were not two well-known celebrities but, rather, two people doing their best to seize a private moment together. As the couple floated across the floor, seemingly lost in their own world, hundreds of adoring friends, family members, and fans encircled them, captivated by their sensual dance, struck by their obvious rapport, enchanted by their sudden romance. Who, after all, doesn't enjoy a good fairy tale?

His Highness Lays Down the Law

In the weeks to come, Grace Kelly would find Rainier Grimaldi often blunt about his opinions, sometimes unnervingly so, espe-

*The song, written by Frank Loesser for the movie to provide a solo for Marlon Brando, was not in the original Broadway production of the durable musical.

cially when it came to her career. Though at times he seemed to waver and imply at press conferences that Grace might continue making movies after taking the throne, privately his position had never changed: When Grace became his wife, she would have no choice but to abandon her career.

The Prince had never been fond of show business and the people it attracted. Also, Rainier may not have had many things in common with Jack and Margaret Kelly, but they did share a concern about appearances. He felt strongly that it didn't "look right" to have his wife, the Princess, making love with another man on-screen, and he knew that such a scene was inevitable if she were to continue her career. It was simply "beneath" a Princess to appear as an actress in a movie.

Rainier and Grace discussed the matter of her career several times after he came to America, so it was not news to her that he wanted her to retire after taking the throne. If she had told him in unequivocal terms that she would never, under any circumstances, abandon her career, there's little doubt that he would have continued his search for a Princess. Father Tucker had a list of women he had intended for the Prince to meet, and the only reason that list was discarded was because Grace had accepted his proposal. However, Grace wasn't firm about her position, feeling that she could negotiate the terms of her future in movies later—after she was Princess.

Bodyguard Thomas D'Orazio recalls, "Once, we were in a car being driven somewhere and Grace said, 'You know, I do hope there will be a way to continue my career after I'm the Princess.' The Prince said, 'I'm sorry, my dear, but as I have said, that is an impossibility.' She said, 'Well, Your Highness, you know that anything is possible.' And he said, 'I can tell you right now that this is one thing that is not possible. So you must forget about it.' He sounded like a domineering autocrat.

"I glanced over to her and she was staring straight ahead, seeming pissed off," recalls D'Orazio. "After a few moments, she said, 'I'll have you know, Your Highness, that my contract with the studio has four more years left on it. I just can't stop because you want me to. So don't be so sure of anything."

"I glanced over again, and now *he* was the one staring straight ahead. I thought, 'Hmmm, this is going to be one interesting little marriage.'"

Still, Grace felt compelled to warn her agent, Jay Kanter, that her days in films might be numbered. "She came to my office on Madison Avenue and said she had something important to tell me," recalled Kanter. "In view of her upcoming marriage, she said, it might become difficult for her to continue with her career. She was pretty matter-of-fact about it. I was happy for her, and I felt sad as well because she really was at the peak of her career. I didn't express any unhappiness, nor did I engage in much conversation about it with her. I just told her that I was happy for her and wished her well."

Grace under Pressure

On Saturday night, January 7, 1956, Grace Kelly and Rainier Grimaldi attended a formal dinner in honor of Father Francis Tucker, who the next day would celebrate fifty years with the Oblates order. Dolores Donato of Philadelphia was present because her parents were friends of the hosts, Mr. and Mrs. W. F. Raskob. Twenty years old at the time, she attended the gathering with her parents and sister. Years later, she recalled, "It was the most wonderful experience, just to have Grace Kelly, this famous and glamorous woman, in our midst, not to mention her handsome Prince. Grace was close to Father Tucker, always at his side, more so, I thought, than even at the Prince's. I remember at one point, Grace was asked to say a few words. She really did not want to do it. The people there—maybe twenty-five of us—kept chanting, 'Speech, speech!' Grace looked terrified. She turned to the priest. He stood up and said, 'Please, let's not force Miss Kelly to do something she really does not want to do. As difficult as it may be for us to believe it, especially in that we have all seen *Mogambo*, she is actually a shy young lady.' That got a real round of laughter."

Instead of Grace, according to Dolores Donato, Jack Kelly stood up and delivered his own speech. While everyone expected him to talk about Father Tucker, Jack went on to speak about Grace. Some observers speculated that he may have had too much to drink.

"He went on and on about how much he loved Grace and how proud he was of her, and how he always knew she would eventually amount to something. She looked a little mortified. He then said that he also always knew she would marry well, 'but not this well,' which got him another laugh. Actually, he was charming. Then he walked over to Grace and kissed her on the cheek. It looked as if she had made him happy. My own father turned to me and said, 'I hope you one day make me as proud as Grace has made her own father today, though I don't expect you to marry royalty to do it.'"

On Sunday morning, January 8, Grace and Rainier attended a solemn High Mass at St. Anthony's in Wilmington, Delaware, to honor Father Tucker's anniversary with the church, and also his sixty-seventh birthday. Grace's parents attended, as did Mr. Marcel Palmero, Consul General of Monaco, and his wife; August F. Walz, Mayor of Wilmington; and hundreds of close friends and family. That afternoon, Grace left for Los Angeles to begin work on *High Society*, with Bing Crosby and Frank Sinatra. Rainier was set to join her there later in the month after a trip to Florida. He and Father Tucker had intended to go to that state in case the situation with Grace did not work to their advantage. Since all had gone so well, they decided to go south anyway, for a vacation, since Rainier had never been to Florida.

All was peaceful in the Kelly household . . . at least for another week.

On January 10, the *Wilmington Morning News* ran the headline "Prince Leaves for Florida with Nuptial Plans Cloudy." Paul

Noches, chief of the Prince's private cabinet, announced to the press that the marriage ceremony was to take place in Monaco. According to Monaco law, Noches explained, if and when the Prince married, it would be in Monaco. This disclosure contradicted what Rainier had promised Margaret Kelly, which was that the wedding ceremony would take place in Philadelphia. Upset, Margaret telephoned Grace in Los Angeles to discuss with her the inappropriateness of the groom's camp making a final decision about the wedding's location. Grace defended Rainier, telling Margaret that she had discussed the matter with him and that he was unaware that Noches had intended to make any such statement to the media. She also explained that the law was clear: The wedding would have to take place in Monaco. While Rainier hoped to somehow get around that rule, there was no guarantee that he would be able to do it. Grace and her mother discussed the matter heatedly for about thirty minutes. Finally, Grace needed to get to the studio. She hung up, not willing to give the matter any more of her time.

Margaret was angry. It would be a disappointment to her if Grace's wedding could not take place at St. Bridget's, the Kelly family's 102-year-old parish church in Philadelphia. From the moment her daughter became famous, Margaret had longed for the day Grace would return to their local church and walk down the aisle to be wed. Of course, she was a mother who wanted to see her child happily married, but she also had other motives. With Grace the focus of such attention, Margaret wanted to share the spotlight. Such a high-profile event in Philadelphia could afford her the opportunity to show the world that her famous daughter had not accidentally come by such refinement and elegance. In Margaret's view, the idyllic wedding for Grace, one that would be talked about for years to come, could serve to acknowledge her influence on her daughter. A well-orchestrated, classic wedding planned and organized by Margaret Kelly would prove to the world that her sense of style and sophistication was the seed from which had sprung her daughter's stardom. However, because it didn't look as if she would get her chance at such glory, Margaret decided that the message would have to be conveyed in another way.

Mrs. Kelly had always obeyed Grace's pleas to avoid giving long-form interviews with celebrity journalists. Yet now Margaret had her own tale to tell. She had been the quiet, supportive mother long enough—and on January 15, 1956, the world would hear her story.

That January morning, Grace woke up in her leased, oceanview home in Pacific Palisades, California, to breakfast in bed (prepared by her cook and served by her maid) with her morning *Herald-Examiner* newspaper and the headline "My Daughter Grace Kelly: Her Life and Romances," by Mrs. John B. Kelly as told to Richard Gehman. (Gehman was a prolific freelance writer and husband of future Oscar-winning actress Estelle Parsons.) Much to Grace's surprise, she soon realized that what she held in her hands was only part one of a ten-part *series* about her life, dictated by her mother to Gehman and circulated to Hearst newspapers worldwide by the King Features Syndicate. An editorial at the beginning of part one explained that Margaret's "royalties for this series of articles are being sent in entirety to the Women's Medical College of Philadelphia," her favorite charity.

Grace could barely believe her eyes. According to the first day's article, when the Kellys first heard about the Prince's existence in Grace's life, they thought of him as "only one of a vast horde of men." Moreover, some of her "affairs of the heart" in the past had been "trifling." However, Margaret noted, "I hasten to add, I never interfered even when I did not approve." Margaret mentioned Gary Cooper, then Clark Gable, and, "after that, in rapid succession, she [Grace] was going about with Ray Milland, Jean-Pierre Aumont, Bing Crosby and several others. The list is really too long for me to remember."

Over the next few days, Margaret would go on to reveal her impressions about relationships she had previously hoped to conceal from Grace's public. "Next in line was Oleg Cassini," read one passage, "and I don't mind telling you that this situation had us all concerned. The mere thought of Grace's considering a divorced man was distasteful to us. For a time, I felt that she might well go against our wishes and marry him." In part three, Margaret wrote, "If she added a charm to a bracelet for each [marriage] proposal, she would scarcely be able to lift that bracelet today." In part four, of Don Richardson (whom she didn't name) Margaret explained how she had "advised" Gracie not to marry him, even though he could help her in her career, "and she was so intrigued by the idea of becoming a big star." She added, "Mother did some logical talking . . . and today," she concluded, "that young man is still an unknown." In part ten, she spilled the beans about Rainier's need for "an heir to his throne: If he and Grace should remain childless the country will revert to France. That would be too bad for Monaco, but it would be just as sorrowful for the Kelly family."

Not surprisingly, Grace was displeased. She later said she could not remember ever being as angry with her mother as she was that morning. Still, she decided not to say a word about it to her until the entire series ran. Then, on day ten, she telephoned Margaret in a rage, making her feelings clear about what she considered an invasion of her privacy. Never had she spoken to her mother in such an incensed manner. Margaret seemed to be stunned by her daughter's attitude, and acted as if she had no idea why Grace was upset. She explained that the writer had twisted her words and that she didn't really mean what was written, "not exactly." Plus, "it's all for charity."

"Why couldn't she just bake some cookies, if she wanted to do something for the college?" Grace later complained to her friend Maree Frisby. "I cannot believe she would to this to me. She's ruining everything."

Some of Margaret's friends felt that her true intention for the series was to rehabilitate Grace's image. Margaret was well aware of the gossip about Grace's romantic life in her social circle, and had even recently confided to Dorothea Sitley, director of publicity for the Gimbel's department stores, her concern that if the whispers became any louder they might somehow impact adversely on Grace's marriage plans. Still, it was odd that she would air so much dirty laundry in public. After all, she was a woman to whom appearances had always mattered. It seemed out of character for her to have cooperated with a series that was, at least in some respects—and especially for the times—a "tell-all."

Grace had her own theory about the motivation behind Margaret's journalistic venture. She felt that the reason her mother had authorized the sensational "biography" was to enhance her own public image. In Grace's view, Margaret wanted to ensure that the public recognized the magnitude of what she had been through as a mother with her foolish daughter's imprudent romances. Grace's love life had taken its toll on Margaret, at least according to the subtext of the series. However, ever true to the indomitable Kelly spirit, Margaret had persevered. She had managed to advise her daughter every step of the way, so much so that eventually Grace was able to attract a decent man like the Prince into her world. "She's trying to take credit for my good fortune," Grace decided in a discussion about it to one friend. "It's so transparent."

Most of Grace's friends had never heard her speak of either of her parents in any way other than in glowing terms. Regardless of how she may have felt about them from time to time, she had always been a model of discretion. She cared what others thought and never wanted anyone to view Jack or Margaret as uncaring or thoughtless people. This incident with the series, however, caused her to finally lose her cool, at least where Margaret was concerned.

Charlotte Winston recalls an afternoon with Grace during which she brought up the subject of the series while the two were having a "little lunchie," as Grace called it, of tuna sandwiches, potato chips, and ice-cold tomato juice at the Griffith Park Zoo. Charlotte, a graphic artist at the time, had come to Los Angeles from New York on business.

"I really don't think it's that bad, Gracie," Charlotte said, according to her recollection. "At least she makes you sound like a virgin."

"Are you crazy?" Grace said. She pointed out that even when her mother wrote something of a complimentary nature, she countered with "something awful, like mentioning my 'old nasal whine.'" Grace turned to the article and read aloud: "Her enjoyment of food gave her a little extra weight. She was nobody's Princess Charming in those [teenage] days. I wonder if Prince Rainier would have thought of her if he had seen her *then?*"

"My, she was certainly in an expansive mood when she wrote that, wasn't she?" Charlotte said, trying to lighten the moment.

However, Grace wasn't ready to make light of anything in the series. She said that she had never read anything about herself as damaging as this material, "and I've read a lot of rubbish about me. So what if she makes me sound like a virgin?" she asked bitterly. "Everyone thinks I'm a virgin. That's not news."

Grace handed Charlotte part four with the headline "Never Finished Any Project She Started." Charlotte recalled looking at it and saying, "Oh, no. That can't be good. I don't even want to read it, Gracie." (In this part, Margaret wrote that Grace "is not the neatest individual in the world." She said she had heard that Rainier's Palace has 250 rooms and asked, "I wonder if there will be enough people in his retinue to pick up after Gracie in 250 rooms?")

When Charlotte asked what Grace planned to do about her mother, Grace said that she was at a loss. She didn't know what to do, short of telling her how she felt—and she'd already done that. "The last few months have been like a dream, and I'm afraid I will wake up and find that it isn't true, that the Prince doesn't really exist in my life," Grace said, adding that she didn't want anyone to ruin it for her, "especially not my mother."

Eventually Grace came to the same conclusion that many children of erratically behaving parents have reached at one time or another. "She's my mother," Grace Kelly said. "What can I do?"

Suddenly, out of the corner of her eye, Grace apparently saw a movement in the bushes. She composed herself and sat straight in her chair. "Smile," she ordered her friend, her voice dropping to a whisper. She had detected a photographer taking pictures of the two of them from behind a bush, "and the last thing I need right now is a picture of me in the papers looking unhappy. So smile, darling," Grace concluded, "and it'll all be just fine."

"Look What I'm Giving Up"

In January 1956, popular Hollywood reporter Maurice Zolotow asked Grace Kelly if she intended to retire after marrying Prince Rainier, as had been suggested. He wrote that Grace "laughed and shook her head." She responded, "Why, there isn't anything to do in Monaco, you know? It's such a little country. Of course I'm going to continue with my work. Right now, I'm reading a dozen different scripts, trying to choose among them. I'm never going to stop acting."

Just days after that article appeared, Grace woke up to find another in the *Los Angeles Times* in which Rainier was quoted as saying, "I don't want my wife to work. She and I have agreed that she will end her career after this next film, and we're happy with our decision." In truth, they had come to no such "decision." Rainier had now gone to the press with his edict that Grace must give up her career. Whether or not it was his intention, it now seemed as if he were applying pressure on Grace to see things his way by using one of the most powerful tools at his disposal—the media.

Grace wanted nothing more than to marry and have children; the Prince came into her life at a time when, confused and lacking direction, she was beginning to feel hopeless about the prospects for her future. But give up her career? That was not what she intended to do. Perhaps she would take some time off, she had said to friends. The notion of never again making another movie was unthinkable.

Panicked, she telephoned her friend Don Richardson to ask him his opinion of what course of action she should now take.

"You tell me, Gracie," he said, according to a later recollection. Grace had earlier told him that marrying Rainier was "the solution to my life." Don had always been one of those who thought she was making a mistake. Now he asked her if she truly wished to abandon all that she had worked so hard to achieve, in terms of her fame and celebrity, not to mention the actual art of acting.

"You know as well as I do that I hate the business of it all," she told him. However, she said that she had always enjoyed acting, and that she didn't know what she would do without it in her life. "It's what I do best," she concluded.

"He has your heart, Gracie, he doesn't need your career too," Don told her. "Don't do it," he warned. "You know you are only doing this to impress your father."

Grace disagreed with Don's conclusion, saying that she didn't understand how he could possibly come to it. Don then reminded her of the time, years earlier, when he visited her at the family's Ocean City home. He had noticed on display various plaques and awards given to her father, mother, and Kell, and other mementos celebrating the lives and achievements of Peggy and Lizanne. There was nothing on display to memorialize anything Grace had ever done.

"That's because I never *did* anything, Don," Grace told him, sounding defeated.

"What bullshit," he said, before reminding her of all the magazine covers she'd been on by that time in her life, as well as the many television programs and commercials. "Grace," he demanded, "wake up, damn it!"

She slammed the phone down.

"It would be weeks before we would again speak," he recalled many years later. "It's been reported in the past that she was eager to give up her career. Not true. She had serious reservations about it. I think she hoped to take a couple of years off, but then have the door left open to return. Closing the door entirely? No. That was not her intention. However, she also did not want to contradict Rainier. She was afraid of the bad press that would result from publicly disagreeing with him. She felt backed into a corner."

Her friend Rita Gam put it this way: "I don't think Grace really believed she was going to give up acting. I think the reality of that probably struck her somewhere in the middle of the Mediterranean after the honeymoon began."

Her friends' concerns were mirrored by MGM's. The studio was not pleased about the possibility that one of their Academy Award–winning actresses would abandon her career when it was at its apogee. At this time, Grace still had four years left on her contract; her next film was to be *Designing Woman*, in which MGM hoped to reunite her with Jimmy Stewart.

"There was little they could do," recalled Grace's agent, Jay Kanter, succinctly. "They couldn't very well force her to make movies, could they?" (Eventually, *Designing Woman* was re-cast with Lauren Bacall and Gregory Peck. It was released in 1957.)

Moreover, there was such media chaos in the country about Grace's fairytale-like engagement to a Prince, and her inevitable ascension to a throne, that MGM executives realized that if they pressured her to adhere to her agreement by litigating against her, it would only generate bad publicity for the studio.

Grace had hoped, as she told some of her friends, that the studio would actually cause more of a problem for her. There were executives at MGM who had never been shy about making her life difficult from time to time. At least whenever Grace and Rainier had a discussion about it, she had always been able to point to MGM as the culprit as to why she couldn't end her career. Much to her dismay, MGM did not form an alliance with her against the Prince—not that she asked for one, but she certainly would have appreciated it. Instead, the studio graciously agreed to release her from her contract, as long as she never made another movie for anyone else during the term of the deal, and promised to return home to MGM should she change her mind and decide to act again after her MGM deal expired. (Eventually, a "quasi-extension" was added to the deal, to which Grace eventually agreed. It would—needlessly, as it happened—tie her to the studio until 1966.) Then, to make matters even more "heartwarming," the studio offered Morgan Hudgins, one of its top publicists, to handle the media surrounding the upcoming wedding. (Monaco had no official press office. In fact, Father Tucker was the first real "publicist" Rainier had ever had in service!) The studio also paid nearly $8,000 for Grace's wedding dress, designed by the studio's costume designer, Helen Rose. Moreover, Grace's MGM hairstylist, Virginia Darcy, as well as Helen Rose, would accompany her to Monaco—as if she were starring in a movie, and not in a wedding. As even more of a bonus to Grace, for her trousseau, the studio would give her all the outfits she wore in *High Society* as a wedding present—and another $65,000 as a bonus above what she would be paid for the movie. "A fine time for them to suddenly become so nice," Grace told Don Richardson ruefully. "We've battled for years over movie roles, and now that I need them to play hardball, they become a bunch of Santa Clauses over there."

In return for all it was giving to Grace Kelly, Grace and Rainier agreed that the studio would have the rights to a documentary to be made about the wedding in Monaco, to be called *The Wedding of the Century*. This was a deal that had been suggested by Rainier and brokered, for the most part, by his attorneys; it would be filmed by a Monegasque crew. After a 30 percent distribution cut, Rainier and Grace would split the balance with the studio. (The Grimaldis would then donate their share to the Monaco Red Cross.) Tied to the matter was MGM's agreeing to let Grace out of *Designing Woman*.

The entire venture made Grace uncomfortable. "He doesn't want me to make movies, yet he's making one in which I'm the star?" Grace said to Charlotte Winston during another Los Angeles luncheon. (Now it looked as if she really would need her studio hairdresser and costumer!) Grace said that she was "becoming unhappy." Charlotte suggested that she talk to Rainier about it. However, Grace said that whenever she and the Prince discussed her career, "it always turns into a big argument. And you know how much I hate confrontation." When her friend offered that it would be a shame for her to give up her successful career simply because she wasn't able to stand up to the man she was about to marry, Grace said, "I can't believe it myself. I have had to stand up to so many people over the years, and it's never been easy. For some reason, I can't stand my ground with Rainier."

"How much of yourself are you willing to give up for this man, Grace?" Charlotte recalled asking her.

Grace didn't answer. Instead, she reached into her purse and pulled out a magazine. It was *Time*. On its cover was a lush painting of a beautiful woman under the headline "Grace Kelly—Gentlemen Prefer Ladies." The issue had just hit the newsstands that morning. Grace put the magazine on the table between her and her friend. She didn't say a word. Instead, she just allowed the astonishing validation of her success sit for a moment between them. Charlotte stared at it.

Finally, Grace spoke. "So, darling, there I am," she said. She waved at the magazine with her hand, holding a cigarette. "Can you fathom it? Me on the cover of *Time?*"

Her friend was speechless. "Gracie, look at you!" she exclaimed.

"I know," Grace said glumly. For a woman on the cover of one of the most prestigious newsmagazines in the world, she didn't seem particularly happy. She said that she had been staring at the magazine all morning, "and," she concluded, "all I keep saying to myself over and over is 'My God! Look what I'm giving up.' Well, I am not going to do it," she decided, finally. Then, after a moment, as Charlotte recalled it, Grace added with somewhat less certainty, "At least, I don't think so."

Father Tucker to the Rescue

By mid-February 1956, a final decision had still not been made as to where the wedding ceremony of Grace Kelly and Prince Rainier would take place: in Philadelphia as the Kellys wished, or in Monaco as the Council of Monaco required by law. There was not much Rainier could do about the matter, if he wanted to do anything at all. He acted as if he wanted to please the Kellys by insisting that the ceremony be in Philadelphia at St. Bridget's, the Kelly family's parish church, but he wasn't convincing in his efforts. Interestingly, when Jack Kelly learned from Father Francis Tucker that

Grace wouldn't have the same kind of pomp and circumstance in a Philadelphia ceremony that she would have in Monaco, he began to waffle on his position, as did Margaret Kelly. "If we're going to do this thing, we should have it all," Jack said, "the whole shebang."

It was by the brilliant diplomatic intervention of Father Tucker that the matter would be worked out to everyone's satisfaction. After he returned to Delaware, he wrote a long letter to Rainier. In it, he tried to set the matter straight.

In an important letter to Rainier, Francis Tucker wrote that he considered himself "liaison" between the Prince and the Kellys, and that he was now concerned by the way matters had begun spiraling out of control. He noted that he was inspired by the way the Prince had handled delicate matters pertaining to Grace and her family and, indeed, the entire country's perception of himself and Monaco. "To the great delight of the American people," he wrote, "you have sold Yourself to them as a Man rather than as a Prince, without detracting from but adding to the dignity and worth of Your Sovereignty." He understood that Paul Noches's announcement that the wedding would take place in Monaco put Rainier in a delicate position; Rainier should not look as if he had no control whatsoever over his own government (yet in fact he really didn't, at least where this kind of protocol was concerned). It also appeared that Rainier was being discourteous to the Kellys by ignoring the wishes of the bride's family.

In his missive, Tucker further noted that Jack Kelly was "terribly obligated" to the citizens of Philadelphia because so many had voted for him when he made his unsuccessful bid for mayor. (He was also careful to add that Kelly was certainly not as obligated to Philadelphians as Rainier was to Monegasques in that Rainier's title was "far superior" to anything Kelly had ever achieved.) Moreover, the Father added that Jack Kelly would never be able to change the long-standing American tradition that a marriage ceremony should occur in a locale determined by the bride and her family, not the groom and his—even if the groom is the reigning Prince of a principality.

Though it was clear to Tucker that Monegasque law must be obeyed, he wrote, it couldn't appear as if the law was being imposed upon Grace Kelly, her family, Philadelphia, and the rest of the nation. He wrote, "You are right in not wanting to be 'Mr. Grace Kelly,' but then Grace wants to be Your Wife and Your Princess and not 'Mrs. Monaco,' subject not to You, nor to Noches . . . and Co. Please understand that the Kellys LOVE You very, very much and they respect You. Mrs. Kelly always refers to You as His Highness and so does John in public life. They will give You their all, but in their own way. They are giving You the BEST they have, and all America thinks that they too are giving You their BEST. And they give her willingly to You, thanking God that it is You."

Father Tucker then begged Rainier not to let "these simpletons step in [meaning the Monaco government], with their fifteenth century ideas which I know You loathe."

He concluded that the Kellys had now agreed to have the wedding in Monaco, but that Jack Kelly did not want it to appear to the public that he had no choice in the matter, that it had been a decision imposed upon him against his will. It was Jack's idea, then, according to the Father, to have him (Tucker) make a statement indicating that the Prince had also been eager to have the ceremony in Philadelphia. However, if that were to occur, Grace couldn't be accorded the prestige and royal honors that she would receive if the wedding took place, instead, in Monaco. It would be a slight to Grace, then, if the wedding were to occur in Philadelphia. Tucker's implication was that all of Philadelphia—indeed, America—loved Grace Kelly at this time, and no one would want her to be deprived of the full ceremony she deserved as incoming Princess.

Tucker wrote that John Kelly had asked him to make a statement that would take him "off the hook" and placate his family, Philadelphians, "the people of America," and also the Monegasques: that the Kellys had decided the wedding should take place in Monaco so that Grace could have what she deserved to have.

In that same letter, Father Tucker expressed his opinion that Rainier should change his plans and not meet Grace in Los Angeles while she was working on her new movie. Rainier's intention was to rent a home in Bel Air and remain on the West Coast for a month, to see as much of L.A. as possible, as well as to be with Grace. Tucker noted, "Don't forget that you are in LOVE and so mentally imbalanced." He was of the opinion that Rainier would have nothing to do in Los Angeles since Grace would be so busy with *High Society*, and that anything he did in terms of recreation would be viewed suspiciously by the media since Grace would probably not be able to be constantly at his side. He felt that Rainier's time would be better served by taking Margaret Kelly to Europe to visit Princess Charlotte, the Prince's mother, so that the two women could meet, and hopefully bond. Also, from a public relations standpoint, he wrote, such a gesture would be a success. Then, he strategized, they should have Jack fly over to Europe to bring his wife home.

Prince Rainier agreed with Father Tucker that his tactics were the best way to placate everyone involved in the controversy regarding the location of the wedding. An announcement would be made, then, that the wedding of Rainier and Grace would take place in Monaco, in April. However, he vetoed Tucker's idea about taking Margaret Kelly to meet Princess Charlotte, saying that he really did want to spend more time with his fiancée. Instead, he suggested that Father Tucker join him on the West Coast so that any gossip could be tempered by the notion that at least the engaged Prince had a priest at his side whenever he went out and about in Los Angeles. Tucker agreed. Ironically, after he and Rainier got to the West Coast (by car, via Louisiana, Texas, New Mexico, and Arizona!) Rainier's father, Prince Pierre—who had not at first been enthusiastic about the idea of Grace Kelly joining the family—decided to fly to Los Angeles to get to know her better. Grace was concerned that her *High Society* filming schedule would keep her too preoccupied to be at her best with her future, and apparently displeased, father-in-law, but she would do her best to win him over. (Eventually, she did just that. In fact, because Pierre liked Grace so much, Princess Charlotte, who always took the opposite tack from her former husband, disliked Grace before even meeting her.)

With Pierre's arrival, there was no room in the Bel Air house for Father Tucker, so he had to pack his suitcase and take a room at the convent of the Marymount School. (In a letter to his brother, Tucker grumbled about this turn of events, calling it "quite a change" from socializing with Mrs. Gary Cooper, Jack Warner, Rosalind Russell, Jane Wyman, Bing Crosby* and Zsa Zsa Gabor to living with a bunch of nuns.)

Grace Kelly stayed in Los Angeles after the completion of *High Society*, since as the previous year's Best Actress winner, she was expected to present the Best Actor award that year at the Academy Awards (to Ernest Borgnine, as it happened, for *Marty*). It would be her last public appearance before her wedding. Meanwhile, Prince Rainier, Prince Pierre, and Father Tucker were scheduled to return to Monaco on March 16 to begin planning what promised to be one of the greatest weddings of the century.

---

*Father Tucker had made such a name for himself in America via his connection with Grace and Rainier that Leo McCarey, producer and director of *Going My Way* and its sequel, *The Bells of St. Mary's* (both starring Bing Crosby as a priest), approached him with the idea of making a movie based on his life. Tucker was enthused, as long as all proceeds benefited the Oblates of St. Francis de Sales. (As an Oblate he had taken a vow of poverty and could not accept remuneration from a Hollywood studio.) The film, however, was never made because Rainier felt it was inappropriate for his personal chaplain to receive this kind of attention from Hollywood.

PART THREE

Marriage

Taking to the High Seas

It was April 4, 1956, when the SS *Constitution* sailed from Pier 84 in New York into a thick fog en route to Monaco for a 4,000-mile, high-seas adventure that would take eight days to complete. There were so many reporters and well-wishers to see the seventy-odd members of the Kelly entourage off that the departure had been delayed forty-five minutes. Besides most of the Kelly family and friends (including three of the six bridesmaids), more than a hundred reporters were also aboard—not to mention all of the other passengers who happened to have made vacation plans at the same time. (These travelers may have thought they were lucky at first, but the Kelly contingent took over many of the public rooms and, along with the media, crowded other passengers out of their own vacation. By the time the trip was over, many probably wished they had taken American Export Line's offer of upgraded accommodations on other ships. Sixty-six passengers actually did just that.)

The presence of so many media persons aboard the ship was contrary to Grace's express wishes to the American Export Line. Somehow, she had fantasized that she and the Prince would be able to marry without much media scrutiny. She couldn't understand why there needed to be press on board the ship. However, they were present, and she would have to deal with them, with the assistance of MGM's trusty press agent, Morgan Hudgins. As the newspeople set up their equipment all about, Grace Kelly—wearing a champagne-colored toque (an Easter present from Rainier), a tan dress and blouse, a white silk scarf crossed at her neck, matching white gloves, and brown leather pumps—walked alone to the edge of the ship. She later recalled gazing out into the fog, wondering, "What is going to happen to me now? What sort of world is waiting for me on the other side of that fog?"

"The trip was bedlam," she would recall years later. "There was such confusion, mounting hysteria everywhere. Leaving New York was frantic. I hardly saw my mother the day we departed."

The press was relegated to cabin class and was not allowed to mingle with the wedding guests, all of whom had first-class accommodations paid for by Jack Kelly. There had been one press conference before the ship sailed, and it had been such a melee, with writers and photographers pressing in so close to Grace, that she admitted to being frightened by the deafening scene. From the expression on her face, it was clear that she was again asking herself the question she had earlier posed to Oleg Cassini: "What have I gotten myself into?" After that unruly affair, the reporters were kept at bay, so efficiently that some of them began to vent their frustrations in critical stories cabled to their home papers. When friends of Jack Kelly in the States read these reports and informed him of the bad press the group was getting, he was incensed.

Jack Kelly could not tolerate bad press. In his view, the whole purpose of Grace's wedding to Rainier was to enhance his and his family's image, not tarnish it. He had always had a good working relationship with the media in Philadelphia—one of the reasons he insisted that the wedding announcement be handled with two press conferences, one in his own home. Anyway, in his view, that was as much *his* party as it was Grace's; any rancor he might have felt about the nuptials not being held in Philadelphia appeared to have been forgotten. In order to placate the newsmen and -women, he insisted to Grace that she hold scheduled press conferences where the media could question and photograph her. Though Grace was unhappy about the prospect of cooperating with "those people," as she called them, cooperate she did. (Later she said she should have gotten a "battle ribbon" for her efforts.) Jack also encouraged the other guests to be friendlier to reporters. As a result, the ensuing articles were much more favorable.

Even Grace's former roommate Prudy Wise had asked if she could author an article about the wedding for a New York publication. Because of their shared history, Grace felt that she couldn't turn Prudy down—though it seemed strange to some that Prudy wasn't a bridesmaid. Before she boarded the *Constitution*, Grace wrote Prudy a letter saying that it was "okay" for her to cover the wedding, as long as it was not "on the spot." (Not even an invitation for poor Prudy? She wasn't even aboard the ship! *Something* must have happened between them.) Moreover, she suggested that "it would be a good idea" if Prudy did not let anyone know that she was writing the story until after she had published it. "Also," she wrote, ominously, "I would rather you not mention in the by-line that you were ever my roommate or secretary." (Though it sounded like a death knell to their relationship, the letter apparently was no such thing, since Grace and Prudy continued their correspondence for many more years.)

One of the more important press duties to which Grace readily agreed was to broadcast a greeting to the Monegasques over Radio Monte Carlo:

"I am deeply moved as I prepare to leave the United States, where I was born and spent my early years. But I also have the great joy today of bringing to the Monegasques the sincere affection of their American friends. All those who know the principality want to go back there; many would like to remain. I was there one year ago and I am going back again—to stay. I would like to tell my future compatriots that the Prince, my fiancé, has taught me to love them. I feel I already know them well, thanks to what the Prince has told me, and my dearest wish today is to find a small place in their hearts, to share their joys and sorrows as well as their hopes and aspirations."

Grace's stateroom, completely redecorated for the voyage, was comfortable, though inundated with baskets of fruit, flowers, and other presents, not to mention luggage. The chairs, couch, bedspread, and drapery were all meticulously color-coordinated in champagne-toned raw-silk fabrics. The stateroom opened onto a sundeck, which was enclosed by glass and provided a stunning view of the ocean.

It turned out to be a sociable crossing for everyone. At the captain's reception, held in the observation lounge, Grace sat with a few friends, including bridesmaid Maree Frisby and writer/publicist Gant Gaither. Gaither recalled, "She spoke of the Prince. 'I loved someone once and fluffed it,' she said. 'This time, I had the oddest feeling I was being given a second chance for happiness.' She added that she had hoped everyone present would like Rainier. Florence Merkel, who had been Grace's baby-sitter when she was a child [indeed, it seemed *everyone* she ever knew was aboard—except for poor Prudy], said, 'I'm sure we will if you do.' A little frown crossed Grace's brow and she said, 'I haven't always gone with boys you could say that about, Flossie.' 'No,' Florence agreed, 'and you didn't marry any of them, either.'"

After dinner, as Grace pulled her stole up over her shoulders, a monogrammed Prince's crown with two inverted G's underneath became visible. Maree Frisby looked surprised; it did seem strange that Grace had already monogrammed some of her clothing. "Do the two G's stand for Grace Grimaldi?" Maree asked. According to Gant Gaither, Grace shook her head and explained that the initials were the royal way of monogramming "Grace." Then, as if it were the most normal thing to talk about, she nonchalantly explained, "Darling, I shall be called Grace-Patricia de Monaco. Not Grace Grimaldi. They will also use my middle name, Patricia. I'm eliminating the crown from the monograms on my wardrobe, but I'll use it on my stationery and all official correspondence." There certainly wasn't much Maree could say in response to that but "My, my, my."

Later, on the way to the Boat 'n' Bottle Bar, Grace told Maree, Florence, Gant, and the rest of the group, "The Prince has said that he might bestow an order on me before our marriage. That is, if I behave myself. He's not sure. It all depends on whether or not I'm a good girl." Gant Gaither recalled that the entire time she spoke of Rainier, she "unconsciously fingered the twenty-franc gold piece with his profile on one side and the crest of Monaco on the other, which dangled from her charm bracelet—the only charm she wore on that special bracelet."

One of the *Constitution*'s public rooms, set aside for "Gracie's group," became off-limits for anyone not a member of the party. Usually her close friends would end their evenings there, singing old show tunes, playing charades, doing impressions of celebrities (Grace's of Zsa Zsa Gabor was a crowd-pleaser), and sipping champagne. Grace's spirits were buoyed by the fact that she was surrounded by so many loved ones and so many of her good friends from New York, and she would remember many details of the trip fondly. Because she sensed that her Atlantic crossing was meant to be an exciting time for her, she wanted to focus on the adventure, if at all possible. "I'll never live this time again," she had said, "and I want to really live it."

However, at times Grace was seen walking the deck alone, seemingly lost in thought. While she did have fun aboard the ship with her friends, her solitary moments during the journey to Monaco were emotionally difficult for her. Grace's belief in astrology, fate, and the occult kept her preoccupied during much of the voyage. As she drifted from her country of origin, from her family, her friends, and the career that she had put so much of her heart into, she soon became overcome by the enormity of the decision she had made.

What had she done? What did it all mean? The opportunity to live a fairy-tale existence had certainly led Grace down a more difficult path than she had anticipated: the physical exam to prove her ability to have children, the discord over the dowry, the acrimony over the wedding agreement, the ambivalence about her ending her career. As she later recalled it, while strolling on the ship it suddenly hit her that she was a woman without a home—without a country, even. Not yet a Monegasque, and no longer an American, she really did feel as if she was lost at sea.

While her head was spinning from scenarios of what could and might have been, as Grace recalled it, her mother approached her. Seeing that her daughter was troubled, Margaret took the opportunity to clear the air. While she stopped short of apologizing for her tell-all newspaper accounts from the weeks prior, she did speak with regret of her participation in the stories.

As the two walked the deck, at times hand in hand, Grace spoke of her uncertainty regarding the wedding. Margaret suggested they retreat to the privacy of her stateroom to finish the conversation. "If you are going to do it," Margaret then told her, "you must be certain that it's something you want to do. God forbid you should grow to hate your husband because you blame him for that kind of decision."

Grace said that she could never "hate" Rainier, that if she made the choice to never make another movie she would hope that it would be *her* choice, or a choice she and her husband would make jointly. Margaret, a smart woman, was not convinced that the decision would be made in such a cooperative manner. After having been around Rainier for a few months, she realized that he was used to having his way. She was concerned that Grace would have no choice in the matter at all, "and then how will you feel about Rainier?" Grace said that she couldn't imagine feeling anything but love for Rainier, ever. As she recalled it, she then decided to change the subject. "You're a grown woman now," her mother reportedly told her, wrapping up the matter. "I trust you to make the right choice." Grace said that she began to cry, and that her mother held her "for a long time." Having her mother's trust meant a lot to Grace Kelly, there could be no denying that much. It's not known exactly how she felt about this conversation—certainly there was plenty of so-called food for thought there—but it would seem fair to say that she must have been moved by Margaret's attempt to finally treat her like an adult.

As sophisticated as she was, there was still something of the little girl about Grace Kelly. One evening, she and her father were in the Boat 'n' Bottle Bar when it was announced that bingo was being played on the ship. Grace turned to Jack. "Bet you can't guess what I want, Daddy," she said with a girlish toss of her head. "Money," Jack answered. He dug into his pocket and extracted a few dollars.

"See you later, alligator," Grace said.

"In a while, crocodile."

"All the money she makes," Jack told the bartender, "but when it comes to shelling out some, who does she come to? 'Papa.'"

Because of the nightly festivities on board and the rounds of pre-wedding events in Monaco, the guests, especially the women, had to take an enormous amount of luggage to accommodate formal wear such as tuxedos and floor-length gowns. Grace herself had two vanloads of suitcases and several large steamer trunks full of clothing. Fashion consultant Eleanor Lambert assisted her in the buying of more than $25,000 worth of new wardrobe (in addition to what MGM had provided from *High Society*!), including a $7,000 sable coat and $4,000 mink, twenty hats, and twenty-nine pairs of shoes. (As well as two specially made pairs of wedding slippers that her shoemaker equipped with built-in pennies for good luck. In a *Life* cover story [April 1956], Grace is pictured holding a shoe, index finger to forehead in deep deliberation as to whether or not she should buy it. The magazine dutifully noted, "She didn't." Indeed, everything Grace did, or didn't do, seemed to be major news.)

Grace's wedding dress was stored in a steel box resembling a coffin, an idea that sprang from the imagination of MGM publicist Morgan Hudgins, who wanted to ensure that no reporter was able to sneak a peek at the gown. "My goodness, it looks like a casket," a horrified Grace said upon seeing it. (In fact, when it was delivered to her Fifth Avenue apartment, the doorman directed the deliverymen to a funeral home around the corner.) At one point during the journey, Jack Kelly, who was always trying to stay busy and useful, went into the hold of the ship to make sure that all of the luggage and other boxes were secure. Much to his dismay, the "coffin" holding Grace's wedding gown was somehow turned upside down. Jack raised hell with the chief baggage steward until he finally agreed to find crew members to set the box straight. When Jack told Grace about the mishap, she said, "Well, if I don't get some sleep soon, they're going to have to carry me off this boat in that box!"

Such heavy baggage would pose a challenge when the passengers reached Monaco, which was not a regular ocean-liner port of call. Because there were no berthing facilities for a ship that large, the *Constitution* would have to dock outside the harbor, and the wedding guests and their belongings would be taken ashore in launches.

For Grace, her friends, and her family, the time aboard the *Constitution* seemed to fly by. Every night, before retiring, Grace wrote a lengthy letter to Rainier about the day's events. She didn't bother to mail them, however, realizing that she would get to him long before the letters. Later, she told Gant Gaither, "I'll hand them to

His Highness when I board the yacht. At least he'll know my intentions were good."

Some of Grace's friends found it odd that she so easily and readily referred to the man she was about to marry as "His Highness," or at least "the Prince." When one friend made a blue joke about how Grace would refer to Rainier on their honeymoon night ("Oh, Your Highness, now that was *wonderful!*"), another friend said, "If Grace hears you joke about the Prince, she will have you thrown right off this ship."

The night before they arrived in Monaco, Grace's good friend Bettina Campbell (not the same Bettina Campbell who would later work for Grace at the Palace) came over to Grace to say good-bye to her. "But I'll be seeing you in the morning," Grace replied, confused.

"Yes, but from tomorrow on, it will be different for all of us," Bettina said, a sadness in her voice. "It'll be a new world for you, Gracie. I just wanted to say good-bye to you in this world, the one we've shared."

"But, darling," Grace began, with tears in her eyes, "we shall *share* the new world."

Somehow, as Bettina would remember it, she knew better. Maybe Grace knew better as well.

With tears still in her eyes, Grace embraced Bettina. "I will never forget you, my friend," she said, emotion rising within her. "And I will never forget my wonderful life with all of you. Let's just say goodnight," she concluded. "Not good-bye."

The Arrival of a Princess

It was an azure morning, April 12, 1956. Though the Mediterranean was choppy, no restless sea could stop boats of all sizes and shapes from sailing out to greet the new Princess-to-be as she arrived in Monaco. Some carried musical bands, while others had trios, duos, or soloists aboard. Since no two groups seemed to be playing or singing the same tune, the result was sheer cacophony. Meanwhile, to heighten the drama, helicopters with photographers hovered overhead, some of them dodging small planes from which banners streamed (with welcome messages as well as with corporate advertisements). With the sun shining brightly upon the festive scene, it was as if the entire country were in celebration.

Promptly at 10:30 A.M. Prince Rainier's 340-ton, freshly painted white yacht, *Deo Juvante II*, appeared from the inner harbor.*As it approached the Bay of Hercules to greet the *Constitution*, Grace materialized on deck in a light rain, as if a vision. There she stood, wearing a navy blue coatdress with a small white scarf tucked into its V-neck. A bit of white cuff peeked beneath her three-quarter-length sleeves. She wore wrist-length white gloves and the white organdy and Swiss-lace, wide-brimmed hat that would be cursed by every photographer present because of the way it covered her face. She also wore large sunglasses. Indeed, the next day, many newspaper reports chastised Grace for her choice of headwear. Still, she looked modest, demure, and virginal. Her only other accessory was Oliver, her black French poodle, wearing a white satin bow.

"I see him! Look, there he is!" Grace said to her parents when she finally spotted her Prince, wearing a dark suit, white pocket handkerchief, and a tie, standing on the bow of the approaching yacht. She waved wildly to him; it had been almost a month since she'd seen him. In response, he stood straight—perhaps looking more handsome than ever in her eyes—shot her his best lordly look . . . and gave her a crisp salute. Grace's face broke into a broad grin.

When *Deo Juvante II* was finally alongside the *Constitution*, a contingent of the yacht's crew saluted Rainier onto the deck. Protocol

---

Deo Juvante roughly translates to "God Willing" or "With God's Help." In New York, during a press conference, Rainier mistakenly translated it as "God Help Us," much to the delight of the assembled reporters.

dictated that Grace come to the Prince. After a gangplank was rigged between the two vessels, Grace—who had one hand on the rail and the other holding Oliver—cautiously made her way down it. She was followed by her beaming parents. While holding Oliver, Grace extended her free hand in greeting Rainier. "Darling," she said. He took her hand and kissed it lightly. Then Rainier reached to take Oliver, almost knocking Grace's hat off in the process. Once everyone was aboard, the Prince himself took the helm and circled the *Constitution*. The royal couple waved; the cheers from 20,000 Monegasques, journalists, and tourists, observing the arrival from casino terraces and streets along the shore, grew even louder.

As the yacht steamed toward the inner harbor of Monaco, Rainier wrapped his arms around his fiancée. Holding her large hat on with one hand, Grace snuggled up and put an arm around his shoulders. As they got closer, the beautiful view of Monte Carlo unfolded before her.

At first, the mountains of Monaco seem to rise up out of the bluest of blue seas. As one approaches the shore, a stunning landscape of white buildings—a mad patchwork of plaster—erupts from rolling, pine tree–covered hills. Light seems to spill out from everywhere—seldom is the fresco-like sky ever cloudy.

The coastal water is uncommonly serene in Monaco as waves cozy up to a crescent-shaped white beach. Fat boats and sleek yachts of every size hug the shore. Open-air restaurants and bars are scattered everywhere, each teeming with suntanned, smiling people in bathing suits and bikinis. Some are on vacation, but many are Monegasques living the good life.

Why would anyone live anywhere else? By the early 1900s, the casino here was generating more than 50 million francs a year, thereby practically financing the entire government. So wealthy is this place, its subjects don't even pay taxes, and haven't since the 1880s. (Because Rainier's great-great-grandfather did not want his subjects to incur gambling debts, no Monegasque is permitted to gamble at its tables.) There is also no property or inheritance tax, no military service, no unemployment, just fun and sun. Monaco boasts more millionaires per square foot than any other place in the world. *This* is living—and all a bit less than one square mile.*

In response to Grace's arrival, sirens blared and a twenty-one-gun salute shattered the air. Crowds lined the quay waving the red-and-white flag of Monaco and the red, white, and blue colors of the United States. At one point, a seaplane circled mysteriously before finally dropping thousands of red and white carnations upon the proceedings, a colorful and surprising gift from Aristotle Onassis. (Onassis, watching the spectacle from the deck of his opulent yacht, the *Christina*, turned to a friend and said, "A Prince and a movie star. It's pure fantasy.")

After the yacht finally docked, Prince Pierre and officials from the Monaco government boarded it to welcome Grace, privately, with a champagne toast. After an hour, the Prince and his fiancée emerged from the yacht to the cheers of reporters who had congregated in anticipation of a photo session with the couple. Unfortunately, Grace's large hat proved a source of frustration—one simply could not view her entire face. Despite continuous pleas that she remove it, of course she could do no such thing. There was no telling what her hair looked like beneath it, and that would certainly not have been the time for her to have to deal with any such surprise.

Following more speeches, photos, and applause from onlookers, Grace and Rainier entered the Prince's green Chrysler and began their drive up winding streets toward the Palace. The view was, and is, overwhelming, with military ramparts, imposing towers, sturdy walls, sentry boxes, and the glorious red-and-white, high-flying flag (always at full staff when the Prince is in residence). As the car meandered along, crowds of people lined the way, cheering them on and tossing flowers to them every step of the way. Upon entering the Palace gates, the Prince's honor guard, dressed in red and wearing white gloves, sprang to attention and saluted the couple. A flourish of trumpets then rang out, as the Prince escorted his future

---

*The *New York Times 2001 Almanac* lists the population of the principality as 31,693: 47% French, 16% Monegasque, 16% Italian, and 21% others. At just less than one square mile, it is the most densely populated nation in the world.

Princess into the entrance of her new, 220-room home. Once there, Grace met the Palace staff. Then she and Rainier and Margaret and Jack Kelly went into the Palantine Chapel with Father Tucker to say prayers in gratitude for having had a safe journey.

Afterward, Margaret and Jack were led through a mazelike series of corridors and staircases to the second floor, where the private residential apartments—some of which were huge—were located (they were built over a ruined wing torn down after the French Revolution). Jack immediately began to complain about the stairs, saying that they were going to "kill" him, and he noted his embarrassment about the fact that he would never be able to locate his apartment without an aide's assistance. "And why all the noisy birds?" he wanted to know. "It's like a zoo in here." Indeed, there seemed to be cages with exotic birds in them everywhere.

Gant Gaither recalled the Kelly parents' accommodations: "[The apartment] overlooked the village square . . . the handsome, all-white foyer had *boiserie* of gold leaf decorating the panels, and on the Louis XV console table there was a vase of long-stemmed Monegasque red roses. Mrs. Kelly led the way into the salon, which was bordered with gold *boiserie* and had gold brocaded draperies. On both sides of the marble fireplace were shelves holding exquisite antique porcelain figurines and plates . . . a delicate hand-painted desk stood in a bay-window."

Across the Hercules Gallery from Margaret and Jack was Grace's apartment. Again, Gaither, who was in both suites: "Instead of paneled walls, Grace's were covered with leaf-green brocaded silk. Her suite was furnished with antiques of the Empire period of France and upholstered in matching tones of green. Oliver [the poodle] quickly found Napoleon's bed to his liking. Off the bedroom was a vast bathroom of pink marble, with matching appointments. Opposite the bathroom was an office with a wrought-iron gate and a single step-down into her sitting room . . . [The entire apartment] was wreathed in calla lilies, orchids, carnations, tulips, tuberoses, ordinary roses, extraordinary roses, and roses, roses, roses, from floor to ceiling."

"The unpacking of her trunks, now *that* was funny," Virginia Darcy recalled. "Gracie was a frugal person, still wearing some of the same clothes she'd had in high school and college! For instance, she had packed so many old shoes, I couldn't believe my eyes. I asked, 'What are you doing with these? These are awful, Grace.' And she said, 'Well, I'm going to have walk through the Palace gardens, now, aren't I? I do need sensible shoes, don't I?' I said, 'My God, Grace, buy some new shoes, *please*. Don't take these ten-year-old shoes to the Palace.' She had also decided that she would pack sheets and towels. Sheets and towels! As if they wouldn't have sheets and towels at the Palace.

"Later, she told me, 'Oh my God, Virginia, I am so embarrassed. I went to unpack my stuff and, suddenly, all of these maids materialized from nowhere to do it for me. I wanted to die. I had to stand there and watch as they unpacked my old shoes and sheets and towels. So I told them, "Oh, those are for the Red Cross. I brought them for the Red Cross." One of them gave me such a look, as if to say, "You brought this old stuff all the way from America, across the ocean on the *Constitution*, just to give to the Red Cross?" I was going to come up with something else,' Grace said, 'when it hit me that they wouldn't dare question me. And, of course, they didn't. One of them just told another to start taking the stuff down to the boat to give to the Red Cross. However,' Grace added, 'as she was leaving, I thought to myself, boy, I sure hate to see those good old shoes go to the Red Cross.'

"We had such a good laugh over that. That was so Gracie."

Grace's New Family

In the hope that the Grimaldi and Kelly families could become better acquainted, on the day of the Kellys' arrival, Prince Rainier planned a luncheon for the families at the home of his sister,

Princess Antoinette, at Eze, a French village midway between Monaco and Nice.

As she prepared for the gathering, Grace asked Madge Tivey-Faucon (an Australian woman about Grace's age who was on staff as the Palace's expert on etiquette; she would soon become Grace's lady-in-waiting) if she thought the enormous hat Grace had worn upon her arrival in Monaco might be appropriate for the luncheon. Madge took one look at that oversized hat and blanched. "Oh, I think not," she said in a condescending tone. It was clear from her expression that Madge had strong reservations about the Prince's choice for a Princess. For her part, Grace later said that intuition told her Madge would present future problems for her. Then, when she checked her out, she learned that Madge was a Virgo. That was bad: "Scorpios and Virgos don't get along," Grace said, "so there's bound to be trouble." As usual, Grace's instincts would not fail her, nor would astrology: There *would* be trouble with Madge, and plenty of it.

Despite Prince Rainier's good intentions, the luncheon event he planned came off like a French farce. If it had been a stage play, it would have been comical.

Of course, Rainier's long-divorced and ever-warring parents, Prince Pierre de Polignac and Princess Charlotte, were both present.

Pierre had spoken out against the notion of Grace as Rainier's bride, but after having bonded with her in Los Angeles, he was now enthusiastic about the marriage.

Charlotte—also known by family members as "Mamou"—arrived at the Palace with her chauffeur, René Gigier, who wore a skintight white uniform. As it happened, Gigier was a renowned jewel thief who was part of Charlotte's household; she had taken to using paroled jailbirds as servants. "Well, I thought the air and sun would do him good," Charlotte said in explaining René's presence. "His health is delicate after his years in prison." (A few days later it was discovered that two of the wedding guests had had $58,000 worth of jewelry stolen, including Grace's loyal friend Maree Frisby, who lost $8,000 in jewels. Indeed, it seemed as if Grace Kelly's film with Cary Grant, *To Catch a Thief*, was being replayed for real.)

Charlotte's odd relationship with the chauffeur wasn't too surprising to those in the family. After she divorced Pierre, she'd had a number of intense romances. One with a doctor almost ended in disaster when he told her he was leaving her. Charlotte took out the gun she kept at her bedside and shot at him; he narrowly escaped death by throwing himself to the floor in the nick of time.

When Charlotte heard that her ex-husband, Pierre, now thought highly of Grace, she decided that Grace wasn't a worthy candidate to marry her son. From this luncheon onward, she would not like Grace, and would not hide those feelings. "When Grace shook her hand," recalled Rainier's nephew Christian de Massy (Antoinette's son, present at this luncheon also, and the ring bearer for the ceremony), "Mamou made no secret, through her expression, of her contempt for the new arrival." In years to come, Grace would fight a losing battle in trying to win over her mother-in-law.

Rainier's sister, Princess Antoinette (known within the family as "Tiny," due to her diminutive size), was also present. At the time of her brother's wedding, Antoinette was separated from her first husband and having an open affair with Jean-Charles Ray (a Monaco government official whom she would later marry). From the start, she disapproved of Grace. It didn't help that Grace committed a dreadful, though certainly unintended, breach when she asked Antoinette to be a bridesmaid. She had even brought her future sister-in-law a yellow dress from America, matching the ones to be worn by the rest of the bridesmaids. As Rainier's sister, though, Antoinette could never be a mere bridesmaid; she was insulted by the suggestion that she was only as important as Grace's New York girl-friends. "But I brought the dress all the way from America," Grace cried when told the news that Tiny was offended. "I was only trying to be nice." For poor Grace, it was all downhill from there where Antoinette was concerned. Of her brother's marriage, Antoinette said, "It won't last two years. Grimaldi marriages seldom do."

Actually, Antoinette and Grace might have had common ground for discussion, if they ever could have opened up to one another. Antoinette had never gotten along with her extremely critical, belittling mother. Estranged for years, they made a point of avoiding each other. At a small gathering such as this one, their feelings toward each other were obvious; neither took pains to hide them. Throughout her youth, Charlotte had constantly put Antoinette down, causing the young Princess to become an unhappy woman, filled with insecurities. Unlike Grace, Antoinette had no outlet for her frustrations, no way to distinguish herself as Grace had done with acting. She had no choices to make in her life, other than to just stay put in her royal, and unhappy, world.

Though their relationships with their mothers may have had certain similarities, Antoinette and Grace never bonded; in fact, Antoinette was barely cordial to Grace. Besides the inevitability of Grace providing an heir, Antoinette had another reason to be wary of her. As long as Rainier did not have a wife, Antoinette could take on the hostessing duties that Grace would later assume—just as she did when he was dating Gisele Pascal. Antoinette would now have to play second fiddle to the new Princess.

One of the only royals in Grace's corner was Princess Ghislaine, Rainier's step-grandmother (his late grandfather Louis's third wife), who was also a former actress (known then as Ghislaine Brullé). Long ago, she and Rainier had become adversaries when he contested Louis's will, which had left half his fortune (millions of francs) to Ghislaine, and the remaining half to him, Antoinette, and Charlotte. First Rainier had used his powers as Prince to block the will, and then he had filed a legal action to have it be considered null and void (claiming that his grandfather had no right to bequeath his money to his actress wife since it was a royal fortune, not a personal one). Poor Ghislaine ended up with only a modest income, and none of the money willed her. She was able to keep her jewels and any gifts Louis had given her during their union. She was also permitted to live in the Palace apartments, which she did for a while (though she and Rainier never spoke to one another). However, despite the bad blood between them, Rainier decided not to prevent Grace from becoming close to Ghislaine in years to come, probably reasoning that the two might have some common ground since both had been actresses.

Although Grace had heard stories about bad feelings and infighting among the Grimaldis, she had certainly not expected the coldness from them that she and her family received. Of course, it didn't help that Grace's mother slapped Rainier's mother on the shoulder and cried, "Hi, I'm Ma Kelly." If the truth be known, her boisterous greeting probably didn't make a bit of difference. Stress was the immediate fallout whenever these people socialized, no matter the presence of outsiders.

Fortunately—or maybe unfortunately—Grace Kelly was too overwhelmed by her surroundings to fully recognize that the clash of personalities that day would, in many ways, foreshadow her life as Princess. Had she known, she might have rowed out to the *Constitution* and headed right back to Hollywood.

Meanwhile, her family—dressed formally, like everyone else—seemed to be having a wonderful time, oblivious to any tension. With a butler positioned behind the chair of every guest, Jack Kelly could not have been more impressed. "The servants had so much braid," he enthused, "you couldn't tell them from the generals."

The placement of the butlers was the ingenuous Father Francis Tucker's idea, explained his nephew, Joseph A. Tucker, Jr.: "Each place setting would have a multitude of glasses, china, and silverware to be used in proper order during the feast. A reputation could be ruined by selection of the wrong spoon, knife, or fork. His solution was elegant. Each guest would have a regally dressed attendant standing behind him or her to provide service. Uncle Francis would arrange with the attendant a set of discreet grunts to signal which utensil to use. It was an Irish solution."

Desperate for news, members of the media set about trying to find anyone connected with the wedding to interview. They also resorted to extreme measures. For instance, a photographer threw himself in the road as the Prince's car approached on his way back to the Palace after the luncheon at his sister's. Rainier managed to stop in time, but just barely. Grace, in the front seat, was not amused. Jack, sitting in the back, was outraged. "Lemme at 'im," he cried. Meanwhile, Margaret linked her arm around Jack's to keep him in the car while Rainier tried to settle matters outside the vehicle with the offending newsman. By the time he got back into the automobile, Rainier was as angry as Jack.

Afterward, the Prince issued a statement saying, "There are certain limits of good behavior that should not be passed, and they have been passed." Rainier then decided that only three photographers would be allowed to document the civil ceremony, and none would be permitted to cover the party afterward. This decision caused an avalanche of discontentment. Everyone from Jack (who told the press, "I'll have to talk to that young man. He needs to learn to roll with the punches") to Father Tucker (who called the Prince "a spoiled boy") reacted negatively to Rainier's dictate. It was with Tucker, rather than with Kelly, that the Prince had the bigger problem.

Bodyguard Thomas D'Orazio accompanied the Prince's entourage to Monaco at Rainier's request. "He liked me. He turned out to be a real regular guy," says D'Orazio. "He had a sense of humor about things, until he got back to Monaco. Then he became pretty surly, but it was understandable. It was a mess there."

After the near-accident with the reporter, D'Orazio overheard Father Tucker telling the Prince, "Listen, my boy, you have to have daily briefings of the press, or this thing will be the biggest circus in history."

"I'm not going to do it, Father," Rainier said, adding that the week had already turned into "the biggest circus in history. Grace is upset."

"Well, listen to me, Grace is going to have to put up with it," Tucker said, further observing that she was "a star, she's been through this before." It seemed that even Father Tucker was losing track of how difficult the matter had become for Grace.

"Can't you see how upset she is?" Rainier argued, according to his bodyguard's memory. "This promises to be the worst day of her life, not the best."

"Oh, stop acting like a little baby," Tucker said, chastising the Prince and telling him that it would "all be over soon enough."

"I remember thinking how odd it was that a priest would speak to a Prince like that," says D'Orazio. "But I figured, well, that must've been their relationship. Rainier stood there and took it while biting his fingernails.

"Later, I remember Grace going to Father Tucker and saying, 'Will you talk some sense into Rainier? He's letting too much press coverage occur. What is wrong with him?' And the Father said, 'Yes, dear, I will talk to him. It is out of hand, isn't it?'"

Finally, Rainier agreed to allow himself and Grace to be photographed several times a day, though he naively wanted approval of all of the pictures that were published—which could never have occurred, and didn't.

The few days after the luncheon were more than a whirlwind of activity. A hurricane would be a more apt description of the days' events—and Grace and Rainier were right in its path. Princess Charlotte and Princess Antoinette stayed in the Palace with Grace and her parents during the days before the wedding, so everyone could get "close." Meanwhile, Rainier wisely stayed out of the way by retreating to his Villa Iberia at St.-Jean-Cap-Ferrat.

With close to 1,500 media representatives from around the world crammed into about one square mile, and all of them clamoring for the same story, there was bound to be bedlam. Even Gloria Swanson—not much of a reporter but a great coup as a correspondent— was present, on "special assignment" for UPI (apparently the result of her personal experience, having once been wed to a titled aristocrat, the Marquis Henri de la Falaise de la Coudrage). The wedding was scheduled to be televised live to more than 30 million people in nine countries. Grace's biographer Steven Englund put it best when he wrote that the press "outnumbered the Monegasque army eight to one, the guests more than three to one; they outnumbered the police, including the reserves sent in by France; and at many events, they even outnumbered the crowds of spectators."

Before Rainier and Grace announced their engagement in Philadelphia, Rainier had planned to let one paid photographer record the event. It had taken Grace's lawyer. Henry Jaffe, and agents John Foreman and Jay Kanter, to convince Rainier that the engagement was news and that the media were going to get the story one way or the other, so he might as well cooperate with the press. Rainier gave in, grudgingly. He may have thought that the engagement was one matter and the wedding would be another, since the ceremony would be on *his* turf and he would be able to control the show. He could not have been more wrong. It didn't help that Monaco's press office—brand-new in recent weeks—consisted of one inexperienced publicist, who spoke only French.

Despite Rainier's best efforts to control what was being said and seen, and by whom, a number of unflattering stories appeared from inside the Palace, such as that of Jack Kelly summoning servants while dressed only in his underwear and holding his glass of rye. Or, worse yet, of poor Jack getting lost in the Palace, not able to find the bathroom or even ask for directions because he couldn't speak French, and then ending up taking a limousine to a friend's hotel room to use the facilities. There were other stories about Peggy and her children wearing shorts while in the royal quarters. Other reports were about Grace's hairdresser, the flamboyant and fun-loving, red-haired Virginia Darcy, on loan from MGM, arriving first thing in the morning and remaining at Grace's constant beck and call throughout the day.

During the first few days of Grace's arrival, there were a number of official portraits to be taken. Grace, as a movie star and soon-to-be Her Serene Highness, knew quite well the importance of image. She owed it to her public to look spectacular.

As the wedding day approached, the rounds of parties and the demands of the press seemed to take their toll on Rainier, who grew more and more irritable. It had been reported that he was suffering from a toothache, but actually he was annoyed by the media and exhausted by all of the work necessary to plan for the nuptials. Three miles of red carpet were laid throughout the principality (Grace's dowry money at work?).

There were luncheons and dinners and galas and parties—and Prince Rainier was the one who had to make most of the final decisions. A bachelor party at an inn in southern France was supposed to be a relaxation for him. However, even that turned out to be the subject of media scrutiny when Father Tucker wasn't invited to it. It was reported that Rainier was angry at Tucker for "hogging" so much of the limelight, with all of the interviews the prelate had given to the media. The truth, of course, was that inviting a priest to a bachelor party would have caused an even bigger media sensation, which is why Rainier decided against it.

The night of the party, Rainier was particularly stung by a telegram he received from Queen Elizabeth II of Great Britain, who sent her regrets and, later, a gold serving tray as a wedding gift. It was a snub of the first order; the Prince was hurt. Because he was ruler of a sovereign state, it would have been courteous for Elizabeth to have attended his wedding, or at least to have sent her sister, Princess Margaret. That the Queen made the decision not to attend speaks to the way the world, especially other royals, viewed Monaco. When Grace learned that the Prince had never even met Elizabeth, she became confused as to why he was so angry. "Protocol," he told her, according to a source in the Palace, "is everything. The fact that we have never met is irrelevant. This is still a slap in the face." The probable truth was that Rainier's ego was bruised.*

The Queen's snub was followed by regrets from President Dwight Eisenhower, who had also decided not to attend the wedding. The truth was that, at the time, Monaco was looked upon as a small and expensive resort with a big gambling casino, and its rulers were thought of as quarrelsome, spiteful people who made news with their sometimes outlandish behavior. If the Grimaldis had been rulers of a large and powerful country, they probably could have indulged in their scandals and the world would have winked. However, Monaco was so inconsequential that some of her Princes hadn't even bothered to live in the country they ruled. And when European royalty wanted to marry, the Grimaldis were not usually considered contenders. Monaco was simply considered a lightweight in the world of royals.

President Eisenhower asked hotel entrepreneur Conrad Hilton to be his representative in Monaco. Hilton said he didn't know why

---

*Princess Grace's ego may have taken a bit of a beating as well a couple years later when she finally met Princess Margaret. Margaret sized her up from head to toe and said, "My dear, you don't *look* like a movie star, now do you?" Never one to let anyone get away with a putdown, Grace countered with, "Well, I wasn't *born* a movie star, now was I?" Those present didn't quite grasp the meaning of her retort; perhaps it was the first thing that came to her mind. However, of Margaret, Grace did later remark, "How dare she? Certainly, *she* doesn't look like a Princess, not that I ever would have brought it to her attention."

the President had chosen him to act as his emissary, that he had never even met the Prince but had once seem him "somewhere or other." However, he would be happy to attend the services, though he would be bringing no gift from the White House, nor would he have one himself.

Jack and Margaret Kelly were both gloomy about the President's decision not to attend the ceremony; it certainly didn't "look good." "Why, the nerve!" Margaret said, in front of a press person. "His not showing up is bad enough. But no gift either? At least he could spring for a coffee pot, for goodness' sake!" Grace gave her mother a stern look and, indicating an eavesdropping reporter, whispered, "Mother, not in front of *him*."

The next day, Margaret Kelly's comment appeared in an Associated Press report.

Locusts!

For Grace Kelly, regrets from the Queen of England and President of the United States were matters about which she could do nothing. The show would still have to go on, and she was up to the task of it. Still, the stress she felt had become apparent at the wedding rehearsal; she had such pronounced dark circles under her eyes that she wore sunglasses to avoid photographers taking pictures of her looking so haggard. As Rainier gnawed nervously on a fingernail, Father Tucker explained how the complex ceremony would unfold. With a serious expression on her face, Grace took frantic notes as if in preparation for a complicated scene in one of Hitchcock's thriller movies. "Darling," she told Tucker, "this is so *much* to remember! Surely, there must be a simpler way!" At one odd point in the rehearsal, Grace was about to make her way down the aisle when her mother pulled her aside. "Gracie, it's bad luck for the bride to walk down the aisle during a rehearsal," Margaret said. "Allow me." Grace then stood aside as Margaret took the bridal march, slowly and deliberately all the way from the back of the grand cathedral to its stunning altar, while photographers snapped her picture. Afterward, Father Tucker told the media that the wedding rehearsal had gone well and that Grace "has done the Prince more good these past few days than I would have been able to do for him in six months. I have never seen my boy so happy. Clearly, my work here is done." Also, he explained that the rehearsal was organized "so that Grace doesn't fumble the ball on the day of the big match."

That same day, Fred Sparks of the Scripps-Howard news service filed a particularly troubling report. "I hate to be offering Grace any advice but she is public property like the *Mona Lisa* and I urge her to stop, look and listen before she lets her head be turned by dreams of marbled halls. The marbled halls of Monaco lack central heating and the plumbing would worry a camel and the furniture belongs in a museum and collects pyramids of dust."

"After I read that story, I telephoned Grace, concerned," recalled Charlotte Winston, who was not present at the wedding because she was eight months pregnant at the time. "Reaching her by telephone was practically impossible. I left several messages. Finally she called me back. She seemed on edge. 'Have you read what they are writing? Those damn reporters,' she said. 'They're ruining everything. They've descended upon us like locusts. Thank God you're not here,' she told me. 'You would hate it.'"

"Gracie," Charlotte said, according to her memory, "you sound like a wreck."

Grace said that she *was* "a wreck." She then recounted a litany of events that had transpired since her arrival in Monaco, dubbing the proceedings "The Carnival of the Century," instead of "The Wedding of the Century," as it was being promoted by MGM. She further stated her disbelief that she was going to be "stuck" in such a small country for the rest of her life. "Do you know how claustrophobic this place is?" she asked. She then compared Monaco to "taking all of the city of New York and squeezing it onto the head of a knitting needle."

"What are you going to do, Gracie?" Charlotte asked.

"What do you think I'm going to do?" Grace responded, her tone uncharacteristically edgy. "The whole goddamn world is waiting for me to get married. I can't very well not do it, now can I?" She said that she now believed Philadelphia would have been a more ideal location for what she called "such a melee. My mother had the right idea," she observed, adding that her father could have at least controlled the media in Pennsylvania. Grace concluded, "Much to my surprise, Rainier can't even control his own people, let alone reporters from all over the world."

It wasn't long before everyone around Grace got a taste of what life would be like for her at the Palace, and those at the Palace realized what it might be like for them with Grace in residence. There was so much inflexible protocol going on around the Kellys that they finally decided to ignore it and get through the days as best, and as normally, as possible. One morning, as she waited for Grace's hair to dry, Virginia Darcy went through some of Grace's mail. She recalled, "Grace said that Rainier wanted to have any mail that asked for photographs separated from the bunch because he viewed that as fan mail. 'No fan mail,' he had said. 'That part of her life is over.' So she asked me to put the official mail in one basket, the fan mail in another."

As Virginia was doing her task, Madge Tivey-Faucon happened by, saw what was going on, and objected to it. "Why, this is entirely inappropriate," she said, her tone that of a schoolmarm. "Only the Princess is permitted to read her mail, or even *touch* her mail. She is royal. One must always remember one's position, mustn't one?"

Madge then turned and walked from the room with a flourish, her exit as dramatic as any Grace had ever made in her most dazzling cinematic moment. "Oh my, now aren't we hoighty-toighty?" Virginia said. At that, Grace burst into uncontrollable laughter.

The Civil Ceremony

On the morning of April 18, 1956, Prince Rainier Grimaldi and Grace Kelly were married in a civil ceremony in the Throne Room of the Palace, the room reserved for the most formal state occasions. The last wedding to have taken place in the room was that of Rainier's parents on March 19, 1920—obviously not a successful marriage.

The room held about one hundred people. Because they had to invite local dignitaries as well as representatives from twenty-five countries, just the closest family members and friends were invited to attend. Of course, Grace's six bridesmaids were there, all girlfriends from New York, but only as observers at the civil wedding. Her sister Peggy would be her witness.

Lizanne, Grace's younger sister, due to have a baby at any moment, was the only close family member not at the wedding. In a 1983 interview with Stephen Birmingham in *TV Guide*, Lizanne jokingly recalled, "They didn't want me there. They were afraid I'd have the baby in the church." Prior to sailing, Lizanne and Don LeVine did have a few tearful moments with Grace; Lizanne slipped into Grace's hand the same lace handkerchief Grace had given her, the "something borrowed" for her own wedding. (Lizzie named her baby, born in May 1956, after Grace.)

A television crew, the only media allowed at the wedding, transmitted the half-hour ceremony to 30 million viewers watching on Europe's major television outlets. Everyone was seated when Grace and Rainier entered the gold and red velvet Salle du Trône (Throne Room). The Prince wore a cutaway coat, pearl gray vest, and gray striped trousers. Grace was dressed in a rose-beige, lace-over-taffeta suit with a small collar, full midcalf skirt, and three-quarter-length sleeves. She wore matching silk pumps and kid gloves, and carried a small nosegay of roses. Her brimless, off-the-face organza hat, also the same color as the dress, was trimmed with a fabric flower over her right ear. It was restrained and elegant, but the constant demands of the past week were etched on her face.

It was an odd yet necessarily formal moment when Grace sat in a large high-backed gilt-and-damask chair, facing the Prince in a similar chair. (The actual throne had been removed and replaced by huge floral displays of Easter lilies and white lilacs.) As the two looked at one another, the TV cameras trained on their every movement, it seemed to some observers as if they didn't even know one another. In fact, both Grace and Rainier looked tense and barely glanced at each other during the proceedings.

Prince Rainier in particular showed an economy of emotion. He had warned Grace that, in his position, he was not to show personal feelings during such ceremonies, so she shouldn't be upset if he seemed cold and aloof. A public display of emotion for royalty was bad form—it had been that way for centuries and would never change. There would be no tears, no kissing, and she should always refrain from such displays.

As the ceremony concluded, Grace glanced at Rainier, who, as expected, stared straight ahead. She studied him carefully as he ran his finger under his collar, bit his fingernail, and then pulled his mustache. Grace caught Peggy's eye. The two sisters smiled conspiratorially, a silent mischievous thought passing between them. For a moment, it looked as if they would be rendered speechless by laughter. Luckily, they stifled the impulse.

Although an elaborate religious ceremony would follow the next day, the civil ceremony was the one required by Monegasque law. The mayor or other official usually performed such a ceremony; on this day the person who read the long list of duties ("the wife is obligated to cohabit with her husband and follow him wherever he goes") was Judge Marcel Portanier, Minister of State of Monaco. Portanier also read a list of Rainier's 142 titles. Grace now had 134 titles of her own. She was the most titled woman in the world: twice a duchess, once a viscountess, eight times countess, four times marchioness, and nine times baroness. (To these were added 110 other titles, which translate into "Lady.") Grace's and Rainier's answers (mostly "*oui*") were barely audible, and Grace's hand shook when she signed the document.

The air in the Throne Room was humid, thick and heavy with the presence of so many people. Grace could probably hear people stirring and shuffling, it was such an uncomfortable experience for so many witnesses, some of whose signatures had to be recorded: the parents of the bride and groom, Margaret and Jack and Prince Pierre and Princess Charlotte; Grace's brother, Kell, and sister Peggy; Rainier's sister; his cousin Count Charles de Polignac; and his friend French army Lieutenant Colonel Jean-Marie Ardent. Later Father Tucker and Conrad Hilton, representing the United States, would also sign.

Afterward, the press descended upon everyone involved. "So, what do you think of your new son-in-law?" an Associated Press writer asked Jack Kelly.

"Who, Ray? Well, he seems to be a nice boy," Jack said. "If he is half as nice as the other two we have, he'll be all right. We call him Ray, you know."

"Does this marriage give you any titles?" the reporter asked.

"I don't think so," Jack said. "I want only to be the padrone of the Falls of Schuylkill. That's where I did all my rowing. My son too. You know, the Kellys are as distinguished a family as the Grimaldis. In Ireland, every Kelly is a king. There were over six hundred Kellys killed in the American Revolution. They came over to fight the British wherever they could find them. Two of my ancestor Kellys came to America to fight in the Revolution, and then returned to Ireland."

The civil ceremony and the filming marked the beginning of what was to be a long day: a luncheon for the wedding guests at a sidewalk café on the wharf in La Condamine, followed by a 4 P.M. reception for the 3,000 Monegasque citizens, who ate a specially baked wedding cake and toasted the newlyweds in the Palace's Court of Honor, with its resplendent stairway of seventeenth-century frescoes showing the twelve labors of Hercules, and also his death. One by one, the Monegasques shook Grace's hand and curtsied in front of her. It must have been the oddest experience for Grace, who may have looked like a Princess and acted like one, but really was still a Hollywood actress playing a role—and playing it well. Still, to the Monegasques invited to meet her on this day, she was their new Princess, not a film star, and the sooner she adjusted to her new position, no doubt the better she would be for it. It was a complete and utter mob scene in the Court that day, the kind of mad chaos to which Princess Grace would have to become accustomed whenever she would venture forth among her loyal subjects.

Jack and Margaret were visibly moved by the Monegasques' response to Grace, clinging to her as if she—not Peggy or Kell—had always been the favored child. For once, Jack was speechless when asked by a reporter how he felt about the fact that Grace was so loved by the Monegasques. "Ask me later when I can speak," he said, choked up.

Wednesday, April 19, ended with an evening gala, a ballet performance entitled "The Stars Dance for the Princess," held in the magnificently appointed Opera House. All the opulently clothed and bejeweled guests were to be present before Their Serene Highnesses arrived; no one would be permitted to leave until Their Serene Highnesses exited their Royal Box, walked down the marble staircase, along the red carpet (lined with uniformed guards in black jackets, red-striped trousers, white belts, and matching gloves), and into their black stretch limousine.

Wearing a white organdy embroidered ball gown, opera-length white gloves, and a white mink stole, Grace was replete with diamonds—gifts from the Prince—that sparkled when they caught the light. She also wore a diamond tiara, a suitable accessory considering her new status, in hair that was pulled into a chignon. Though crowns are featured on all of the Palace's crystal, china, silverware, and linens, there actually is no crown of Monaco. As history has it, someone absconded with the original crown during the French Revolution. Because of superstitious belief, it was never replaced. Therefore, as the country's Princess, Grace Kelly would not have an official crown. On occasion, she would wear a tiara—such as the one placed on her head this evening by Virginia Darcy—but only for appearance' sake, not because it actually had official significance.

As Virginia placed the tiara on Grace's head, the hairdresser began to choke up. She had, just months earlier, done the exact same thing for a scene on the set of *The Swan*.

"But this time it's not a prop, Grace," Virginia said. "And we don't get another take. You really are a Princess now."

"But, darling, how can this be?" Grace asked, suddenly seeming overwhelmed by the enormity of what was occurring in her life.

"You're asking *me*?" Virginia answered, now laughing. "But good for you, Gracie," she added. "It's not like you could do any better, is it? He's a real Prince, for heaven's sake! Now, don't cry, whatever you do." Years later, Virginia explained that Grace's skin was so fair, it would immediately redden and appear puffy whenever she cried, "and that wasn't the look we wanted that evening, now was it? She was only twenty-six. People tend to forget how young she was. She had to be in complete control. Image was everything. She handled it all so beautifully."

Most impressive-looking on Grace this night was the red-and-white sash that went from her right shoulder to the left side of her waist. It was the Order of St. Charles, Monaco's highest honor, which Rainier bestowed upon his bride as a public acknowledgment of his high esteem and love. He presented it to Grace in a private ceremony. (She must have proven herself "a good girl," as she had said [on the *Constitution*] she would have to be in order for Rainier to bestow her with such an honor.)

As Grace and Rainier stood in their Royal Box, the national anthem of the United States was played by the immense orchestra, immediately followed by the Monegasque anthem. Then, as applause broke out, Rainier presented his Princess with a sweeping, royal gesture. Grace stood erect, a slight smile on her face, as she looked out at hundreds of faces, some familiar (if she could even make them out, sans her tortoiseshell-framed eyeglasses). Her parents, Jack and Margaret, her brother, Kell, and sister Peggy were all in the Royal Box with her and Rainier. Standing below and gazing up at them were some of Grace's beloved and loyal New York girlfriends who would be her bridesmaids, such as Maree, Rita, and Carolyn. Even her dentist from Philadelphia was present, not to mention her former baby-sitter; journalist Rupert Allan; her Hollywood agent, Jay; her MGM publicist; her MGM hairdresser Virginia, who could not stop weeping; and dozens and dozens of others who had known and loved Grace Kelly for years, all present for her now and acknowledging her not as an Academy Award–winning actress but as a Princess, Her Serene Highness of Monaco. There could not have been a dry eye in the house.

The Wedding

A gloriously sunny morning and cool ocean breeze promised a prototypical "bride's day" on Thursday, April 19, 1956, the day six hundred guests would fill the Romanesque Cathedral of St. Nicholas for the most highly publicized and promoted wedding in modern history. Early in the morning, cannons had begun booming from harbor battleships just opposite the cathedral, heralding the exciting morning that had at long last come to pass.

In preparation for the ceremony, St. Nicholas's had been thoroughly cleaned for the first time in years, ridding it of decades of accumulated grime. Now magnificently decorated with ornate floral designs of white lilies, lilacs, and hydrangeas, it seemed the ideal showplace for the most important event ever to occur in Monaco's history.* Celebrities present included so-called special assignment reporter Gloria Swanson; the David Nivens; and Aristotle and

---

*The wedding was said to have cost the principality the equivalent of $500,000. However, it was also reported that the Prince made $450,000 just on commemorative postage stamps featuring the royal couple, still a collector's item on the Internet site eBay today!

Christina Onassis. Ava Gardner flew in from Madrid and was escorted by Rupert Allan, the journalist who had initiated Grace's life-changing adventure by insisting that she attend the 1955 Cannes Film Festival. (Many years later, in 1989, Rainier would name Allan a *Chevalier de l'Ordre de Grimaldi* [Knight of the Order of Grimaldi], one of the country's highest honors.)

During the previous evening, Grace had expected to sleep in the arms of her Prince. Spending the night with Rainier would have been the panacea she needed to restore her spirits. However, much to her consternation, she and her new husband were to retire in separate suites. In the eyes of his constituents, as Rainier explained it to her, he would not be officially wed until the church ceremony. "That is absolutely Victorian," Grace complained. Still, she slept alone in a luxurious oversized bed in a luxurious oversized room. In the end, she was probably too exhausted to care. On the morning of her wedding, she still did not look rested. Though luminescent from afar, upon close inspection she looked exhausted, dark circles under her eyes betraying her.

At about 10 A.M., as 30 million television viewers watched, Grace Kelly made her entrance into the cathedral on the arm of her pleased father. As she stood waiting at the back of the church for her cue to proceed, Grace appeared precisely as one might expect a Princess bride to appear: radiant. She was draped in a dramatic gown, the loving creation of MGM's head costume designer, Helen Rose. Four hundred and fifty yards of Brussels rose-point lace—made only in Belgium—and silk taffeta were sewn into a fitted bodice, high neck, long sleeves, and full skirt (whose V-shaped slash in the back was filled with lace that cascaded into a train three yards long). Her lace-trimmed veil, embroidered with seed pearls and orange blossoms, attached to the beaded Juliet cap. It fell to her waist in the front and became part of the train in the back. She carried a small white Bible covered in the same material and rose-point lace as the gown, with the cross embroidered in small pearls, as well as a small bouquet of lilies-of-the-valley. The entire picture was magical; Grace seemed somehow to just float down the aisle.

In direct reverse of the American tradition, Grace and her father proceeded down the aisle first, followed by the six bridesmaids and the maid of honor in their yellow organdy dresses and matching stiff-brimmed hats, the four young flower girls in their white dresses, and the two young ring bearers dressed in white ruffled shirts and satin knee breeches. Perfume wafted through the air as the women made their way to the front of the church, the scent mingling with the fragrance of white snapdragons in large gold baskets that had been hung between each column on both sides of the aisle up to the altar.

Margaret Kelly sat in the first row, watching the proceedings with a breathless excitement obvious to any observer. No doubt she must have marveled at the strange twists of fate that had brought her, a Philadelphia bricklayer's wife, to this great cathedral, as mother of a Princess bride. All in a bit more than a year!

Custom dictated that commoners must wait for royalty. At the wedding rehearsal, Grace was told by the bishop, "A Prince waits for no one. Not even his bride." So, there stood the nouveau Princess in her ivory tower of silk and diamonds, waiting for her Prince. Monaco's Bishop, Monsignor Gilles Barthe; Father Cartin, the Kelly family's priest from Philadelphia; and Father Francis Tucker all stood before Grace at the altar. White candles in antique gold candelabra bathed the area in a warm glow.

No official circumstance would be complete without a bit of the theatrical from Jack Kelly. When Father Tucker instructed him to take a seat while his daughter waited for her groom, Jack said that he would prefer to stand at her side until the Prince made his appearance. Tucker nodded and smiled knowingly. Actually, it was an emotional moment for anyone aware of the strained history of father and daughter. Jack obviously felt that Grace shouldn't be left standing alone at the altar, if even for a few moments. (At the rehearsal, Rainier had joked to Grace, "Whatever you do, don't wait for me for more than half an hour.")

After a hush came the sound of blaring trumpets and the appearance of the Prince's aide-de-camp, Count d'Aillières, followed by the Prince himself. Rainier looked striking in his self-designed Napoleonic wedding uniform: a black tunic with gold-embroidered cuffs and epaulets, a multitude of medals, including the red-and-white sash of

the Order of St. Charles, and sky-blue trousers with gold bands down
the sides. In his white-gloved hands he held a light blue bicorn hat
trimmed in ostrich plumes. His sheathed sword hung at his left side.

Throughout the prayers, the hymns, the promises of love and devotion, Grace remained wrapped in her own ethereal beauty, shim-
mering and soft in silk and lace. Her mood was impossible to
discern. She never once smiled, nor looked at anyone other than
the priests and Rainier. She didn't even realize that her cousin, Jean
Goit, had fainted and had to be carried out of the church. Also, of
course, she had been told by Rainier to refrain from displaying any
emotion—and she did just that.*

Meanwhile, Father Francis Tucker was constantly at the elbow of
Grace and the Prince, telling them with whispered asides and quick
gestures where to stand and where to kneel.

"Rainier Louis Henri Maxence Bertrand, will you take Grace Patricia, here present, for your lawful wife, according to the rite of our
Holy Mother, the church?" The question (in French) from Bishop
Gilles Barthe seemed, if just for a moment, to take Rainier by surprise. He replied, "*Oui, je veux,*" though no one present, except
perhaps the bishop, could hear his response. The Prince's chin was
so set that it looked as if it might crack with the merest of smiles.

"Grace Patricia, will you take Rainier Louis Henri Maxence
Bertrand, here present, for your lawful husband, according to the
rite of our Holy Mother, the church?"

She responded in a whisper: "*Oui, je veux.*"

With the words "I declare you united in marriage in the name of
the Father, the Son, and the Holy Ghost," the newlyweds exchanged
rings and faced each other as man and wife. They didn't kiss. After
looking at each other with unmistakable love, they genuflected and
turned to face the congregation. Rainier offered his arm to his wife,
and they walked up the aisle and out of the cathedral. They were not
smiling, but rather, as tradition dictated, serious in their demeanor,
not about to break what appeared to be a magical spell.

*Unlike at the civil ceremony, the press was allowed in the church; the clicking of cameras almost
drowned out the words of the ceremony.

When the royal couple emerged into the sunshine, they smiled at each other for the first time that day. They worked their way through the mob scene outside the cathedral, and stood before a waiting Rolls-Royce, which would take them back to the Palace for a grand reception. Afterward, a seven-week, high-seas honeymoon was in store for Rainier and Grace. No doubt the notion of making love to the romantic sounds of the sea caressing the *Deo Juvante II* must have seemed appealing, especially after all they had been through together.

Finally, the dust had settled; the fray was over. Once outside, Jack and Margaret Kelly hugged their daughter; Jack seemed unable to let go of her. Husband and wife both looked relieved. Kell and Peggy appeared a bit stunned, almost as if they simply could not believe that their sister, little Gracie, who, as the family roles had always had it, never seemed to be able to do much, had done *this*.

Before entering the cream-and-black, open Rolls-Royce, Rainier clasped his hands in joyful exultation, as if to say, "By God, we did it!" Grace leaned over, crinkled her eyes, and whispered something into his ear. Rainier tugged at his collar and grinned broadly. He looked at his wife with affection. What a shame no lip-reader was present. However, one of Grace's girlfriends later asked what she had said to Rainier. Grace recalled having whispered, "Thank you, darling, for such a sweet, intimate wedding."

PART FOUR

Life at the Palace

Transition: Grace's

Once Grace Kelly decided to marry Prince Rainier of Monaco, everything changed for two families on two continents, for Hollywood, and for a "kingdom." Like a modern-day Cinderella, Grace had, in seemingly a heartbeat, chosen to abandon life as she knew it for a man she had only recently met. In the process, she would have to live in a foreign country she had previously visited only one time. Had she carefully considered the reality of what she was doing, or had she recklessly thrown caution to the wind for the promise of living a fairy tale?

On January 23, 1957 (nine months and four days after the wedding), Grace gave birth to her and Rainier's first child, the blue-eyed Caroline Louise Marguerite, thereby guaranteeing the continuation of the Grimaldi lineage, and the freedom of Monaco from France as per the terms of the 1918 treaty. Still, after the excitement and anticipation about the wedding wore off, Rainier's subjects did not fully embrace his wife, as one might have expected they would have, judging from the bombastic reception they had accorded her when she first appeared in Monaco on the *Constitution* that spring day in 1956. Even the fact that she had given birth to a girl was a disappointment to some Monegasques, who had wanted an immediate male heir.* Perhaps because she felt some pressure to do so, Grace became pregnant again just five months after giving birth to Caroline.

On March 14, 1958, the Princess gave birth to Albert Alexandre

*Apparently, Jack Kelly agreed with those Monegasques. "Aw, shucks. I wanted a boy," was his response when told that Monaco's sovereignty was assured with the birth of a baby girl.

Louis Pierre, a son and heir. Rainier, who had been "wishing very hard," as he put it, for a son, was overjoyed. Even the hopeful Father Francis Tucker had cigars wrapped with cellophane that said "It's A Boy!" six months before the baby was born—just in case. According to Monaco's constitutional law at the time, the first child succeeds the Prince until a male child is born, who then takes precedence. "Let us thank God for this new happiness," Rainier announced in a radio broadcast, "this proof of His special blessing." The Monegasques shared his joy. In celebration, the people danced in the streets, singing and laughing. The harbor and streets were filled with revelers, friends and strangers hugging and kissing one another, throwing flowers into the air.

Later, Grace and Rainier emerged on the royal balcony of the Palace, where they would always make special appearances, standing just above the Grimaldi crest carved in stone, now with their newborn son, Albert. The cheering of the crowd was overpowering. Prince Rainier waved to his subjects as his beautiful Princess cradled their son, smiling broadly. It was a joyous moment.

However, though she tried to focus on her new life and responsibilities as Monaco's Princess, Grace began to regret her decision to turn her back on the past, specifically on her acting career—if in fact it could be said that it was her decision, and not her husband's, to do so. This wasn't surprising, since she had earlier expressed such ambivalence about the matter. Between 1956 and 1960 there were many anxious transatlantic telephone calls from Grace to close girlfriends in America, all of whom she had kept in her life—no doubt her way of staying connected to her original identity, "Grace Kelly." She complained of feeling a sense of disorientation, as though she was in the middle of a dream. Did she really now live in a palace? With the passing of time, it somehow made less—not more—sense.

Bettina Campbell worked at the Palace at that time as secretary to Marie Claire-Tenniere, Grace's personal secretary. (Many of the secretaries at the Palace had secretaries of their own!) "In those first years away from America, there had been times that she didn't want to speak on the telephone to anyone who wasn't a trusted friend from the past," said Campbell. "She would become sad when the telephone rang and we had to tell her it was anyone other than an American chum. Finally, there were days when she would say, 'I don't even want to know who is calling unless it's Maree or Rita or Charlotte . . .' She had a list of first names that I soon memorized."

Of course, there were many moments when Grace would forget her sadness and go on with her life. After all, as Princess, she maintained a demanding schedule, attending official functions, most of which she dreaded. She enjoyed her work in improving the Monaco Hospital, renamed after her in 1958, and also in bettering Monaco's home for the aged. She was president of the Monaco Red Cross, a position she took over from her husband and to which she was resolutely committed. She had two children, a husband. She couldn't spend all of her time bemoaning the fact that she couldn't make movies. When in public, Princess Grace always exuded strength and confidence.

Many days were spent in boredom. Deep in thought, Grace would walk alone through the Palace's lush gardens, beautifully planted with red and white cyclamen, sometimes in the rain—*especially* in the rain because she preferred it—trailed by one of her poodles. Sometimes she would spend the entire day reading; when she got to the Palace she bought a complete library of five hundred books about Ireland from a retired Irish diplomat, determined to read every one of them.

On the worst of days, she would feel so exhausted by despair that she would simply take to her bed. "At first when she went to bed in the middle of the day, I thought she was ill," recalled Madge Tivey-Faucon, her lady-in-waiting. "I had to get used to it. And so did the Prince. The telephone can ring, the visitors can wait, the Princess sleeps, and orders are given not to wake her."

In the summer of 1960, John Brendan Kelly, the man who had provided Grace with the catalyst to marry well in order to win his approbation, became ill. Though his doctor had told Grace that he would be fine, the tone in her mother's voice during another telephone conversation had convinced her otherwise. She left Monaco as soon as she possibly could, en route to the States. When she got to Philadelphia and was able to see Jack, she was told the truth: stomach cancer. Though it went unspoken between them, as had so much over the years, it was clear that her father, now seventy, was dying.

Grace's times with Jack during their last two weeks together were good ones—certainly it was not the time for him to be judgmental of her, nor was it the time for her to dredge up the painful past. Grace had her own children now and, though they were young, she was beginning to understand that a parent's relationship with a child is complex.

Not only had Grace felt emotionally alienated from the Monegasques when she moved to Monaco, in some ways she had felt equally forsaken by her father. After the excitement of the courtship and wedding was over, Jack wasn't as impressed by Grace's new station in life. Yes, it had elevated his social status in Philadelphia, as expected. However, that done, his daughter's union with a Prince meant little to him. In his view, she was still just "Gracie," and as exasperating as ever. "Oh, he was just Daddy," Lizanne explains. "Of course he wasn't going to change. We accepted him as he was, you know? We loved him so much but, yes, he could be frustrating."

When Jack did visit the Palace, he was annoyed by the many servants whose jobs involved catering to his every need. Many a morning he would take out a clean shirt, decide not to wear it, put it on the bed, and then go back for it ten minutes later only to find it gone—already picked up by a functionary and sent to the Palace laundry. Two hours later, the shirt would be returned, now with the sleeves pleated! "Jesus Christ!" he would bellow. "Now I look like a fruit."

Jack also couldn't help but compare himself to his daughter's new husband. A proud man, he was accustomed to being the center of attention, not to mention the focus of his daughter's world. At the Palace, he was a guest, merely the Prince's uncouth father-in-law, a man some of the servants even thought of as a "commoner." He could sense it, and it wasn't a good feeling for him. He decided to avoid it as much as possible. He only visited Grace at the Palace twice. If Grace wanted to see her parents, she would have to fly to the States, which she did often. The Kellys loved their grandchildren dearly; Grace wanted to ensure that her parents had a strong relationship with Caroline and Albert.

Grace did not confide in her parents her unhappiness about giving up acting—at least not that anyone has ever recalled. Margaret had said, while on the *Constitution* with Grace, that she trusted her to make the right decision. That had been a big moment for Grace, a giant step forward in her relationship with her mother. It wouldn't have surprised anyone who knew her that Grace would never want Margaret to feel that her trust in her had been misplaced. As for Jack, she had ample reason to believe he would be judgmental of her.

However, once Jack Kelly died on June 20, 1960, Grace didn't know what to make of her life. She had had many reasons for marrying the Prince, chief among them the desire to win her father's approval—and, as it would happen, she never did win it. Now, he was gone and she was stuck in Monaco.[*]

For her part, as Margaret aged, she softened toward Grace, even showing admiration for the way her daughter handled herself as a Princess and blended into her royal surroundings. Margaret couldn't very well be critical of the people in Grace's life now in that they were all the cream of the crop, in terms of social status. "Things were much better between Grace and Mother after Grace got to Monaco and had a family of her own," said her sister Lizanne. "When she had her kids, Grace started to see our mother through different eyes. You're a little more patient with your mom when you see firsthand what it's like to be one, at least that was the case with Grace, with me, and with Peggy. And also, I think Mother saw Grace differently as well. She was so proud of her, and supportive of her, unlike our father, who, to tell you the honest-to-God truth, sometimes just would not give Gracie a break."

---

[*]Three years later, in June 1963, a six-foot-high statue of John Brendan Kelly was erected in his honor on the east bank of the Schuylkill River.

After Jack was gone, Grace was filled with mixed emotions. How much had she given up in order to impress this man? Had his approbation not meant the world to her, would she still have married Prince Rainier? "On the way home from the funeral, she told me that she wanted so much to be loved by that man," her secretary and good friend Phyllis Blum Earl once recalled. "She said that she would have done anything for his love and approval, and she'd done a lot to get it. However, she said, 'I don't think I ever had it. Not really.' She was in tears, upset."

"She was oversensitive to the Kellys," Prince Rainier would later say. "They mattered terribly much to her—more, it certainly seemed, than she mattered to them. Though there were strong family ties with the Kellys, there wasn't a lot of heart."

A talk with Father Francis Tucker helped Grace. Tucker, who felt close to the entire Kelly family, attended Jack's funeral in Philadelphia. Afterward at the funeral home, he told a distraught Grace something she did not know: that Jack had asked him to watch out for her in the Palace, to stay by her side and be there for her should she ever need him. "John B. Kelly specifically asked him to do so," noted his nephew Joseph Tucker. "Kelly knew the first few years would be difficult for Grace." It lifted Grace's spirits to know that her dad did care enough about what happened to her once she left America to ask the chaplain to keep a protective eye on her.

Now that she was officially Her Serene Highness of Monaco, Grace Kelly—thirty-one in 1960—would face her longest, most difficult, and final role. Her Prince would do what he could to please her. However, the question remained: Would she ever be happy as a Princess . . . or had she truly made the biggest mistake of her life?

Transition: Rainier's

By June of 1960, His Serene Highness, Rainier Louis Henri Maxence Bertrand de Grimaldi was thirty-seven years old. He was the absolute ruler of his own principality and enjoyed a life of wealth, deference, and power. His wasn't necessarily in the "real world," as most people tend to think of it, but then again, neither was the one from which his wife, Grace Kelly, had come—a world wherein a wealthy sophisticate emerges from the Philadelphia suburbs to become a world-acclaimed, Academy Award–winning Hollywood actress. He was as unfamiliar with her world as she was with his. However, unlike Grace—a woman who had had the experience of several life-altering romances with passionate, worldly men— Rainier was naive when it came to dealing with matters of the heart. Trained to be a ruler from an early age, he was a practical person, not an emotional one. His decision to marry Grace had been one based as much on necessity as on any romantic ideal.

Rainier loved his wife, inasmuch as he knew what love was and how to express it. His pragmatic view of such matters was worlds away from the romantic notion Grace had had in mind when she confessed to her New York girlfriends that something was "missing" in her life, that she yearned for a husband and children in order to feel more whole and complete. Of course, Grace didn't marry just anyone in order to paint that portrait of domestic bliss. She, like the Prince, had reasons for her choice that had little to do with head-over-heels romance.

Insofar as each chose the other as a way of solving specific personal problems, they were well suited not just for a marriage, but for a mutual agenda. He needed a Princess to bear him an heir in order to avoid the fate of French domination, as per that irritating yet mandatory 1918 treaty with France. She needed to marry well in order to gain freedom from a father's constant disapproval, as well as to fill the emptiness that overshadowed her otherwise scintillating success. However, how much thought had they given to what their future together would look like once those troubling issues were behind them?

To the Prince, Grace was a fascinating creature. She was perceptive and thoughtful, unlike most members of his family. She took her life into her own hands, rarely allowing others—besides her parents, anyway—to dictate her circumstances. He knew that she had been at the top of her field, a difficult profession at which most people are never successful. She was ambitious, yet also sensitive. She was beautiful, more so than any other woman he'd ever met. She had a quiet dignity. She was articulate. She was charismatic. He'd never known anyone quite like her. As far as Princesses go, obviously she was the perfect choice.

However, with Grace as his wife, Rainier faced an uncertain future. After all, he was married to a woman who, from the start of her reign as his Princess, had made it clear—at first just by her behavior, but later with actual discussions with him about it—that she feared she had made a mistake by coming to Monaco . . . and she didn't know what to do about it. Because she was his wife and the mother of his two children, his greatest wish for Grace was that she be happy and fulfilled. Yet it was his decision that she not be permitted to do the one thing she wanted most: act.

It was inevitable. By June 1960, when a depressed and heartbroken Grace Kelly returned to Monaco from her father's funeral in Philadelphia, Prince Rainier Grimaldi realized the truth: He really did not know, nor did he completely understand this woman—and she felt the same about him.

Strengthening a Marriage

Because he had official business to attend in Monaco and could not leave on short notice, Prince Rainier III did not accompany his wife to her father's funeral in Philadelphia. Instead, he asked Father Francis Tucker to go in his place and watch over Grace.

Most of those who knew her well felt that Grace needed her husband's support during such a difficult time, especially considering the tumultuous relationship she had with Jack Kelly and what were sure to be emotional repercussions of his death. However, all of those people lived in America, not in Monaco, and none felt close enough to Rainier to offer him unsolicited advice about his marriage. True to his emotional composition at the time, the Prince was not able to intuit his wife's emotional needs. When she said she understood he could not be with her, that he needed to stay in Monaco, he believed her. He was certainly not raised to look for the subtext of what a person said, but rather to simply take that person at his word.

It seems that, understandably, Grace wanted him to insist on going with her to Philadelphia, or so she told friends on the East Coast once she got there. Perhaps because she was upset with him, Grace didn't say good-bye to Rainier when she left the Palace. Instead, she and her secretary, Phyllis Blum, slipped out while he was in a meeting. Rainier was mystified by the suddenness of Grace's departure, not understanding why she was upset.

Problems between the couple had actually begun a few weeks earlier when Grace, who had just heard that her father was ill, decided to fly to Philadelphia to be with him. It happened to be Rainier's thirty-seventh birthday, May 31, 1960, when she left.

That night, with Grace gone, Rainier celebrated his birthday with a party, dancing until the early-morning hours with a striking

Latin woman, Zenaide Quinones de Leon, whom he had recently hired as a new assistant for his wife.

Bettina Campbell, who worked at the Palace at that time as secretary to Marie Claire-Tenniere (Grace's first personal secretary at the Palace), recalled, "While the Princess was in Philadelphia, a so-called friend of hers called her to tell her that Rainier and Zenaide had carried on behind her back. Much to everyone's amazement, the Princess seemed to believe that something indecent may have occurred between them. She returned from the trip in a depressed state. Her father was not well and she knew she would have to return soon. She was distraught. I overheard an angry confrontation between Their Serene Highnesses over the matter of Zenaide."

According to Bettina Campbell, when the Prince and Princess discussed the matter over breakfast in the Palace dining room, Rainier insisted that he was innocent of any wrongdoing. Just as Campbell walked in to present him with the morning mail, she heard Rainier say, "Look, I danced with all of the women there."

"And that's supposed to make me feel better?" Grace responded.

The Prince added that Madge Tivey-Faucon had been present at the party, had witnessed everything that occurred, and could attest to his innocence. Tivey-Faucon was, at least in Grace's view, probably not the best witness in Rainier's defense. Grace felt that Madge—an Australian friend of Gisele Pascal's who had been assigned her position at the Palace by Rainier—had never approved of her, and she was probably right. Madge was one of the cynics in Monaco who felt that the former actress really wasn't "Princess material."

It had been Tivey-Faucon, a stickler for protocol as required by her original position at the Palace, who had chastised Grace's studio hairdresser, Virginia Darcy, for opening the Princess's mail the first week Grace was in the Palace. In describing Madge, Virginia recalled, "She was big on the typical English secretary's outfit—tweed skirt, sweater, and hat. Most of the time, I thought, she was dressed like that so she wouldn't be noticed lurking about the Palace. She had an attitude. I remember that after the wedding, we friends of Grace's were hanging out of one of the Palace's windows as His Highness and Grace walked below on their way to the honeymoon. We were all yelling good-bye, waving and screaming as we Americans will do at weddings. Suddenly, Madge walked in and said, 'This isn't appropriate at all. It is most inappropriate, in fact.' We said, 'But this is what we do in America.' She said, 'Well, you are not in America now, are you?'

"Unfortunately, after the wedding, Madge Tivey-Faucon was someone upon whom Grace had to rely because she was the only one around the Palace truly fluent in English. But you always had a feeling that maybe she couldn't be completely trusted."

When Grace asked Madge about the matter, she corroborated Rainier's version of what had happened at his birthday gathering: nothing.

Over the course of a few days, this disagreement between Prince and Princess became one about which most people who worked at the Palace were well aware; Rainier and Grace were uncharacteristically indiscreet. Rainier told one relative that he was surprised by the way Grace had handled the matter and, as he put it, "I guess you never really know a person until you marry her."

Actually, Grace didn't know Rainier any better than he knew her, which was the real problem. For them, it would be a matter of trial and error if their marriage were to work.

Inevitably, it was to be precisely the kind of marital difficulty presented by the appearance of Zenaide Quinones de Leon in their lives that that would test the very union of Grace and Rainier. If they were to be successful as a couple, they would once and for all now learn about each other's temperaments. More importantly, they would have to learn that abandonment was not an option—this marriage would have to be permanent.

It was clear to Rainier that Grace's despair over his alleged unfaithfulness and her father's illness was almost more than she could bear. Madge Tivey-Faucon recalled, "I can still see her, seated beside her husband on the little balcony that overlooks the Cour d' Honneur. There was a concert that night and they were playing Chopin. Suddenly, she was overcome with some emotion. She had to get up and go into the *salle des gardes*. Everyone thought, for a moment, that she was seeing herself once more on her wedding day, coming down the great marble stairs on her father's arm."

In Rainier's view, it would have been best for Grace to ignore idle gossip. Instead, Grace decided to fire Zenaide Quinones de Leon. She felt that she had no choice, but to some her decision only served to make Rainier appear guilty of some wrongdoing.

It wouldn't be until a week after Jack Kelly's funeral that the couple would finally be able to put the matter behind them. Grace was the one to apologize.

Years later, Princess Grace recalled the entire incident to Charlotte Winston as the two ate lunch in the Throne Room during one of Winston's visits. While picking at her *fiori di zucchine fritti* (deep-fried zucchini flowers), Grace said that she finally realized she hadn't been "thinking straight." She had been so distraught over her father's illness that she had become "irrational."

"The rumors pushed a lot of old buttons for me," Grace said, according to Winston's memory. "Suddenly, there I was, back in Hollywood again with people whispering about my life behind my back." She said that she couldn't imagine that such a thing was happening to her again, and thousands of miles away from Hollywood, in Monaco. "And I just wouldn't have it," she concluded. "Poor Rainier, though. I really put him through the wringer. I felt like such a dummy afterward."

When Charlotte noted that Grace was fortunate that Rainier had been so patient with her, Grace agreed. "I think the situation with Zenaide strengthened our marriage," Grace concluded. "Afterward, Rainier said to me, 'If we got through that, we'll be fine.'"

Rainier Stages a "Coup"

Throughout the fifties, and into the sixties, Prince Rainier III had to deal with financial and political problems that constantly threatened not only his royal sovereignty but also Monaco's independence as a principality. During much of this time, Rainier was regarded as ineffectual by critics who believed his organizational and leadership skills to be weak. They pointed to the disorderly drama that threatened his magnificent wedding to Grace Kelly as a principal illustration of his incompetence. The events surrounding the 1956 royal nuptials had spiraled out of control. Rainier had not appeared to know how to handle most of the volatile situations that arose, particularly those concerning the press. A stronger ruler, at least as argued by his critics, would have prevented much of what had occurred that chaotic week. However, in his defense, there were more than just the Prince's "own people" involved in the wedding fracas; media and guests from around the globe had converged upon his small, ill-equipped principality. It was a mad scene, unlike any that had ever occurred before, really. Even today, so many decades later, Rainier Grimaldi still wishes he had handled it differently. However, in light of all Rainier has since done for Monaco, the wedding's circus atmosphere now really means very little.

When Rainier came to the throne in 1950, Monaco was in dire financial straits. There was probably not just one reason, but a combination of many, that caused casino attendance to fall by 75 percent. The principality's income had depended on tourists coming to gamble, and World War II impoverished the once wealthy European nobility who had flocked to Monte Carlo in the past. Now newer casinos were springing into existence at other places along the French Riviera. And Las Vegas, with its star headliners and glitzy shows, provided more exciting entertainment than the traditional ballet, theater, and opera offered by Monte Carlo. Furthermore, Monaco suffered from the taint of having been pro-German in World War II; Louis, Rainier's grandfather and ruler at the time, had aligned his country with the French Vichy government, supported by Germany, and had refused to fire his openly pro-fascist Minister of State. Because the Italian border was so close, many Italian officers spent recreational time in Monte Carlo, joined by their Nazi counterparts.

In May 1951, at a time when Monaco was in desperate financial need, one of the richest men in the world, forty-three-year-old Aristotle Onassis, sailed his yacht, *Olympic Winner*, into the harbor and leased the extravagant Château de la Croe, in which the Duke and Duchess of Windsor had once resided. The small-statured and squat Onassis was a new and intriguing presence in Monaco, a cigar-puffing character in dark-tinted glasses with an abundance of well-coiffed, ink-black hair. He was immensely charming, particularly to any of the principality's beautiful women who might cross his path. He was also married to young Christina Livanos, heiress to the Stavros Livanos shipping fortune. They had two small children who played on the estate's expansive grounds with gazelles given them by the King of Saudi Arabia. Tended to by a legion of servants, housekeepers, maids, cooks, chauffeurs, and the rest of what became known among the townsfolk as "Ari's army," Onassis and his family seemed to love publicity, posing for photographs whenever such an opportunity presented itself. The fact that the only other man around who had this kind of ego, and who held such allure for the townsfolk, was the Prince himself, made Onassis even more a fascination for Monaco's residents. "The word at first was, 'Who is this person and what does he want in Monaco?'" recalled Prince Rainier in one interview.

When Onassis finally established office space in a neglected old building on the Avenue d'Ostende overlooking the harbor, word spread through the city that he was a shipping tycoon, wealthy beyond all measure, whose business, Olympic Maritime, was about to be headquartered in Monaco. At first, Rainier welcomed Onassis's presence in the tiny nation. After all, his was the kind of successful enterprise the Prince had hoped to attract to the principality.* Rainier was also entertained by Onassis's flamboyant manner, amused whenever the charismatic Greek tycoon was in his presence. The two became uneasy friends.

Rainier, fond of all things maritime, was particularly impressed with Onassis's mammoth new luxury yacht, the famously opulent *Christina*. When that "baby" (as Rainier called the vessel) docked in Monaco's harbor it became the biggest and most mesmerizing attraction there. Rainier didn't even mind the fact that the 125-yard-long yacht dwarfed his own *Deo Juvante II*, though the symbolic discrepancy in the sizes of the two ships certainly did not escape the notice of some of the more wary Monegasques. Even Christina Onassis, Aristotle's wife, cattily remarked, "Rainier doesn't have to worry about the fact that the ceilings on his yacht aren't very high. Neither is he. But Princess Grace is a rather tall girl, now isn't she?"

Within two years of his arrival, after Aristotle Onassis had acclimated himself to the environment and decided that he liked it enough to want to invest in it, he attempted to purchase the dilapidated Winter Sporting Club building as a tax-exempt site for his shipping company. Rainier had gotten to know Onassis by this time and was suspicious that the aggressive Greek mogul was considering a campaign to infiltrate Monaco and control as much of it as possible. When the Prince refused to approve the purchase, the S.B.M. (Société des Bains de Mer, or Sea Bathing Society) informed Onassis that the club was not for sale. Rather than take no for an answer, the savvy tycoon found a way to get around the S.B.M.—by purchasing it! His secret takeover of the casino corporation was implemented by acquiring directly, and also via certain companies of which he was a covert owner, a majority of the S.B.M.'s shares. In about a year, Onassis staggered the S.B.M., and

*Onassis also founded Olympic Airlines, the Greek national air carrier.

Rainier, by announcing that he now had a controlling interest in the corporation.

"My first reaction was that here was a man whom I could get really excited about the S.B.M.'s future," Rainier told writer Peter Hawkins. "There is no doubt he was interested. He was then in a family situation which drew him much more into the social life of Monte Carlo, too." However, after some consideration, Rainier became unhappy with the way Onassis had, in his view, "tricked everyone" by taking over the S.B.M., the most politically powerful organization in the land, and had done so in such a surreptitious manner. However, the Prince decided to focus on the possibility that the wealthy and influential magnate would be an asset in his cause to reinvigorate the principality, especially after Onassis indicated approval of the Prince's vision of a new Monaco. Onassis assisted Rainier in the plan to remodel the Belle Epoque architecture of the already impressive Hôtel de Paris (built in 1864 and situated on the Golden Square of the Place du Casino), personally selecting many of the improvements, right down to the marble utilized in the staircase leading to its entrance. With its sweeping views of the Palace, the casino, and rows of gleaming white yachts in the harbor, Hôtel de Paris is today one of the most stunning hotels in the world and certainly a tourist fascination. Onassis did have ostentatious taste, but Rainier rightly felt it served Monaco.

Aristotle had also maintained that a famous American woman would gloss the luster of Monaco and increase its worldwide appeal as a vacation spot. Because he had recommended that the Prince choose a celebrated woman as his wife, the National Council hoped that his marriage to Grace Kelly would smooth matters between the two powerful men. In many ways, it did just that. Onassis was excited by the addition of Grace Kelly to the royal fold, so much so that he donated a million francs to the Red Cross in honor of the marriage.

Grace and Rainier would join Ari and his wife, Tina (and, later, his mistress, opera star Maria Callas), aboard the *Christina*. Grace,

Tina, and Maria all got along well.* Still, the fact that Onassis had a controlling interest in the S.B.M. couldn't help but gall Rainier.

A bit of background about the S.B.M. is necessary in order to understand the impact of Onassis's takeover of it. Its name—the Société des Bains de Mer—does not nearly describe its vital role in Monaco. Besides the famed casino, the S.B.M. owns three of the principality's best hotels, the country club and golf course, the beach resort, and most of its more profitable tourist attractions.

The S.B.M. got its start almost a century before Rainier came to the throne. Reigning Prince Charles III felt that life in Paris was much more exciting than in Monaco, then not much more than a hard-to-reach backwater. After going through his wife's dowry, Charles still needed more to maintain his lifestyle. His mother came up with the idea of turning Monaco into a spa, similar to those in Germany that combined "taking the waters" with gambling casinos. Monaco had perfect climate, breathtaking scenery, and a harbor untainted by sewage. Thus, even though the principality did not have the mineral water that German spas had, it still had clean (although somewhat rocky) white beaches, and in the late 1850s the Société des Bains de Mer was established, with plans to turn the principality into a tourist attraction. Nearby Cannes and Nice had already begun to attract many rich English visitors during the winter, and Monaco wanted to do the same.

Planners were hired to put out glossy brochures to attract investors. Work began slowly. What was built bore little resemblance to the brochures, and it was difficult for the few visitors who ventured forth to reach their destination. Boats seldom stopped at the harbor, and the once-a-day, four-hour horse-drawn carriage ride over the uninhabited mountainside ran the risk of encountering stray boulders careening into the path.

Things lumbered on in this fashion until 1863, when another group of investors, which included the famous Rothschild bank-

---

*The first time Grace Kelly had met Aristotle Onassis was when she was on the Riviera making To Catch a Thief with Cary Grant. During a yachting excursion with Onassis, Grace was so quiet and withdrawn that he thought, or so he claimed, that she worked for Cary. As they were leaving, Onassis told Grant, "Do come again, and bring your lovely secretary, too."

ing family, took over. Within two years, the shoddy hotels and casino were rebuilt into elegant establishments. Magnificent gardens were planted. The area was named Monte Carlo (Italian for Mount Charles, named after the Prince). Beach cabanas flourished in the Condamine section of Monaco. Houses were built and the permanent population increased, many coming from nearby Italy and France. (As already noted, Monegasques are barred from gambling there.) A flotilla of boats brought passengers daily, and carriage service improved as a safer road replaced the old one. The final boost to success came in 1868, when the railroad line between Nice, France, and Genoa, Italy, began stopping in Monaco.

Since its inception, the Grimaldis have received a portion of the S.B.M.'s earnings. Most of the rulers before Rainier had little interest in Monaco and were more than willing to use their money to live in comfort elsewhere, usually France. However, when Rainier came to the throne, he had visions of diversifying Monaco. He wanted to attract businesses to enjoy the principality's tax-free status, and he wanted to have tours bring in middle-class visitors, rather than rely on the wealthy gamblers who had visited before but were coming no longer.

In 1955, Rainier faced the most serious challenge of his sovereignty. After foolishly investing in a radio and television conglomerate, the country's biggest bank, the Société Monégasque de Banques et de Métaux Précieux (Precious Metals Society [P.M.S.]) declared bankruptcy. Rainier's closest staff, as well as certain members of the Grimaldi family, sat on the board of directors that had made the ill-fated investments. Moreover, influential members of the National Council of Monaco were also investors in P.M.S., and now had lost investments in its bankruptcy, which did nothing to ingratiate Rainier to the Council.

From the time Rainier Grimaldi became Prince at the age of twenty-six, his relationship with the conservative National Council of Monaco (which had been formed decades earlier to oversee the financial business of the principality) had been a contentious one. Revolutionary improvements, such as the Prince's ambitious undertaking of building a railroad tunnel through Monaco, were discouraged by the traditionalists who sat on the Council, most of whom were intent on spending as little money as possible. Also of continued interest to Rainier was the landfill project he felt promised to add acreage to the principality, upon which could be built offices and apartment buildings. In Monaco, where the coast was— still is—literally crammed with buildings, there was so little room for growth that the only way for expansion was to do it in an upward direction with modern high-rise structures. However, the Council was concerned that Prince Rainier's improvements would only serve to destroy the quaint charm of the seaside principality, transforming it from an old-world resort into just another stark European metropolis.

Though Rainier was raised to believe that his was the final word in all matters of family and state, that wasn't entirely the case. In governmental matters, he was bound by a constitution that stipulated that the principality's Council—not its Prince—had final authority on economic solvency. However, the Council's power was limited in that it couldn't outright veto any of Rainier's plans, but could only delay them by making finances unavailable in the budget, or by issuing forth mountains of tedious and interfering red tape, not unlike the U.S. Congress.

After months of acrimony over the matter of the P.M.S. bankruptcy, the National Council finally insisted upon the resignation of three of Rainier's trusted advisers. Though Rainier was vehemently opposed, he was eventually forced to accept the resignations. The failure of the bank would be used as ammunition against Rainier for years, with foes on the Council expressing skepticism that the young Prince would be able to handle the expensive undertaking of his proposed modernization projects when he couldn't even keep an important Monaco bank in the black.

By utilizing his wide-reaching influence with several wealthy investors, Aristotle Onassis was able to swoop in and rescue the Monaco Precious Metals Society from any final declaration of bankruptcy. "All's well that ends well," said Onassis triumphantly.

It was while Rainier was distracted by the P.M.S.'s complex

bankruptcy that his sister, Princess Antoinette, made another of her bold moves toward the throne. Sensing that public opinion would be against her brother in the P.M.S. matter, Antoinette and her lover (later her husband), Jean-Charles Rey (president of the Finance and Fact-Finding Commission of Monaco's Council), conspired to have Rainier deposed (again!) and have her son, Christian de Massy, named as his replacement. Of course, as had been her plan in the past, since Christian was too young to rule, Antoinette would come to the throne as regent. As Christian later recalled, "The bank scandal had provided the breach into which my mother now proposed to rush." Rainier learned of his sister's scheme and managed to thwart it. He had always known that his sister had traitorous intentions, but this time she had gone too far. He was actually amazed at her gall, and mystified as to how she ever thought she would have gotten away with her plan. He knew that he could make Antoinette face trial as a traitor, and that was a strong possibility. She clearly had no love for him, so why should he show mercy toward her? Or he could just do what princes in his position often did when unhappy with a family member: banish her forever from Monaco. The problem for Rainier, however, was that Antoinette was a popular fixture in Monaco since she had always been at her brother's side at so many royal functions. Either decision could cause serious consequences.

At this point, Aristotle Onassis stepped forward with the observation that Monaco would never really achieve financial stability if it did not first have the kind of political stability a friendly royal family would ensure. Rainier listened, though he wasn't thrilled with the notion that Onassis even had an opinion, let alone a platform to express it. Though extremely upset at feeling backed into a corner, Rainier issued a statement claiming that the whole idea of a coup by his own sister was nothing more than rumor. The city's major newspaper then published photographs of Rainier smiling at Antoinette with his arm around Christian. It worked. Still, Rainier knew now more than ever that he couldn't trust his sister, and that he should have as little to do with her as possible.

Rainier also viewed Onassis's involvement in Monaco's business with suspicion. He knew that the Greek mogul had little respect for him, viewing him as nothing more than a puppet of the National Council of Monaco—a figurehead, rather than a Prince with any true authority. Because it was the S.B.M. that had to approve all building and improvements in Monaco, Rainier's greatest passion, the Prince and the entrepreneur would spend years battling over control of it. Rainier only owned 2 percent of the S.B.M., but, luckily for him, as Prince he had the power to veto any decision. So he began vetoing them as fast as Ari could make them, causing conflict between the two. Both were powerful, stubborn men who liked to have their own way. They fought with each other constantly, voicing their feelings to the world media. As often as they quarreled, they made up, only to start the cycle once again.

Obviously, Onassis's interest in Monaco was anything but altruistic: He was a businessman who wanted to make a profit. Ranier, however, had other goals besides making money, goals having to do with tradition, history, and a future for his subjects long after Onassis had made his "killing" and was gone. Both agreed that the no-tax law for residents would continue to bring business into the principality, so that law could never be jeopardized. Onassis had already made Monaco the hub of his shipping empire, which brought in more business. However, the two clashed violently about the way Monaco should look to the world and to the people who would visit. Onassis wished to keep Monaco an exclusive playground for the rich: "Monaco will always be prosperous so long as there are three thousand rich men in the world." However, Rainier wanted more than that for his principality; he wanted to attract middle-class Americans. He continued to hold talks with American hotel corporations about future building in Monaco—and he wanted his subjects to trust him, *not* Onassis.

It was in August of 1956, when Rainier announced that Grace was expecting their first child, that he took the opportunity to relate the future of the Grimaldi line to the future of the principality. "The significance of this awaited event is clear to all of you," he said. "Now, I find it indispensable to link this guarantee of the principality's surviving in its independence and privileges to the absolute necessity of establishing an era of total trust and confidence. The projects for economical and technological development which have received my approval are neither unreasonable, imprudent, nor opposed to the true interests of our country. They answer new needs which stem from a normal and desirable evolution of our great economy. In light of this news [of Grace's pregnancy], it seems impossible that we should not strengthen our trust in the future. One chooses one's future and then starts building it. I ask you to trust in the choice I have made for Monaco's future, and also to remember that the principality has endured, and will only endure, as long as its Sovereign Prince has full and complete exercise of power."

While the situation with Aristotle Onassis was one with which he had to live, Rainier's ongoing troubles with the National Council had become, by 1958, unbearable. It was as if he always had one problem or another to deal with, which left him tense and irritable most of the time—certainly not the same man Grace had married. Whereas he had been humorous and romantic in New York when courting her, he was now surly and dismissive, and Grace would just have to live with it. As far as he was concerned, his wife was there to support him, not criticize him. Therefore, she should keep her mouth shut. Despite her annoyance at his temper, Grace was still unwavering in her support of her husband, and would do anything she could do to make his life easier, if only in acting as a sounding board to his grievances.

By 1958, Rainier had managed to see work on his railroad make progress, even though he had fought the National Council every step of the way. The project was more costly than he had expected and the Council never let him forget he was over budget. In his view, the eventual result would be well worth the money spent, whatever the cost, and he was annoyed that the Council couldn't see past the budgetary concerns. "Why can't the vision be expanded past the finances involved?" he asked in one published interview. "In fifty years the money will have been long spent, and the tunnel will still serve Monaco." There was only so much the Council could do to thwart Rainier's modernizations; making the money unavailable or griping about the cost was about the extent of its power. Because there was a strong faction of Monegasques, however, who agreed with the Council that Rainier was out of control, soon the principality was split in its assessment of its Prince.

While trying to see his railroad tunnel project through, the Prince proposed additional financing for the Oceanographic Institute and Museum. His timing couldn't have been more wrong. This additional request for funding was all the Council needed to cause bigger problems for him. To teach him a lesson, the Council voted not to approve the 1959 annual state budget, an extreme and rare move on its part and one that, basically, imparted the message that Rainier's critics were correct: He really *was* inept. Grace put it best in layman's terms when she said, "What a slap in the face!"

Actually, as it happened, it was Grace who influenced Rainier's next major decision, a drastic step. According to what Madge Tivey-Faucon once recalled, Grace and Rainier engaged in a discussion about the Council's decision while the two were in the library, where Grace was painting a seascape. She sometimes enjoyed dabbling in pencil and paint work, her favorite subjects all being things of nature. Though she never exhibited her works, she would sometimes gift a friend with one if she thought it special enough.

Uncomfortable sharing his indecision, his problems, Rainier didn't like opening up to Grace. It wasn't easy for him; it was simply not the way he was raised. However, Grace was a good influence on him in that, in her own gentle way, she was able to encourage him to share his concerns with her. When he did, it was usually to his advantage. Grace's perspective was often different from his, and it was worthwhile for him to hear it.

"I don't understand why you are letting them bully you like this," she observed of the National Council, according to Madge Tivey-Faucon's memory. "You're supposed to be the boss around here, aren't you? I don't get it."

Rainier explained that there was only so much he could do, that he was bound by the constitution. "I have to play by the rules. You know that as well as I do," he told her. "It's just like in show business."

"Are you kidding me?" Grace asked. "Why, in show business, the big shots make up the rules as they go along. You think Mayer ever cared about rules? Darling, he changed the rules to suit himself," she groused, referring to her old MGM boss, Louis B. Mayer.

A couple of days later, Rainier met with Father Tucker for private counsel and prayer. He then "changed the rules."

Reflecting upon Monaco history, Rainier recalled that Albert I and Louis II both had had problems similar to his with the Council, and both had done what many in present-day Monaco thought to be the unthinkable: They had abolished the National Council, promising that there would be an election to replace its members. After much deliberation, Rainier took the same action. Putting the constitution on suspension and announcing that there would soon be "a new constitution," he explained to his subjects that, in his view, he had no choice. Either he had power or he didn't. The principality was astonished at the Prince's audacity. Then, to make the point that his was indeed the final word on the matter, he outlawed the public's right to demonstrate for political purposes, causing his foes to then label him a "dictator." In fact, Rainier's decision *was* unconstitutional, but there was no one to stop him. Grace would later say that she couldn't have been more proud of her husband, or, as she told one reporter, "He took matters into his own hands and did what he had to do. He made a choice to upset the apple cart and, to me, any decision is a good one as long as it's one in which you firmly believe."

Grace Banishes Antoinette from the Palace

It had been a revelation to Prince Rainier that his Princess could be of assistance to him in moments of crisis, that she could be much more than just a figurehead at his side. She did have strong opinions, a way of looking at things that could be helpful. She brought to the principality a different viewpoint, an American one that, in some ways, related to the entertainment business—and if Monaco wasn't about entertainment, then what was it about?

"What I admired from the beginning in the Princess was her way of analyzing people," Rainier would say years later, in 1974. "A woman's intuition is much more acute than a man's. I found she was asking questions about people I'd worked with and taken for granted for years, people whose motives I'd never thought to question."

As it happened, it was Grace who influenced Rainier's next major decision, one that was dramatic and historical.

One of those whose motives Princess Grace carefully scrutinized was Rainier's sister, Princess Antoinette. The two had been only begrudgingly cordial since their first meeting, and as the years passed, their jaws only clenched tighter when they were in each other's company. Of course, in her view, Antoinette had good reason to continue to dislike Grace, if not for who she was, then certainly for what she represented in Monaco. The principality had always needed a female representative, and Antoinette had once viewed herself as the chosen one. When Grace swept into town, however, all eyes fell away from Antoinette. It had to be tough on her.

Though Grace tried, at first, to win Antoinette's approval, she quickly learned that her sister-in-law's blood connection to the

Palace would never allow her to fully accept Grace's presence there. Grace was rarely at ease in the presence of Antoinette, and her being at the Palace was always a possibility since she had convinced her brother to allow her to maintain royal quarters there. Grace had only bristled at that arrangement upon her arrival in Monaco, but as the years passed she noted the liberties her sister took with it, and would often share them with Rainier. "Does she have to just come and go when we least expect it?" Grace wanted to know. "It's very unnerving." For the most part, the Prince brushed aside any ill-will between the two women as being mere cattiness. However, there came a time when a serious miscalculation made by Princess Antoinette allowed Princess Grace the opportunity to illustrate just how much power she had in the Palace.

As Rainier was fighting what he saw as a necessary battle to retain his power, Antoinette was one of those who felt his views were archaic and that he was acting as a dictator. His sister's opposition was no surprise to Rainier; it had always been such, and he could count on her for a dissenting viewpoint. It was Grace, however, who made Rainier see just how egregious Antoinette's statements against him had become. "Before retiring one night, Grace told Rainier, 'She wants to topple you,'" shared an American friend of Grace's. "'She wants to see you fall. I'm sure of it.'" Before the couple fell asleep that night the decision was made: Antoinette would be asked to clear out her rooms (she then had a number of chambers at the Palace due to her growing family) and leave the Palace, never to return. This dramatic banishment for which Grace campaigned would disallow Antoinette from attending any official family functions, be seen in the presence of the royal family, or even so much as speak to any of them, from the oldest, Rainier, to the youngest, Albert. Not only that but her fiancé, Jean-Charles Rey, formerly of the National Council, and her children, Christian de Massy (who had been ring bearer at Rainier and Grace's wedding), Elisabeth, and Christine, would also be ostracized, not permitted to set foot in the Palace or have any contact whatsoever with the royal family.

There was one snag, however: Rainier didn't seem firm in his decision. Grace may have feared that the light of a new day would bring forgiveness to her husband, and he would be unable to follow through with such a serious act. "So the Princess told him she would do it," said her friend. "She told him, 'Putting your foot down halfway is just a can-can dance. I'll speak to Antoinette myself.'"

Wasting no time, the next morning Princess Grace had one of the servants deliver an invitation to Princess Antoinette, asking her to a consultation. Within the hour, Antoinette appeared, looking a bit unkempt, wanting to satisfy her curiosity quickly, even before benefit of a morning spruce-up. Grace, however, was stunning. She hadn't been able to sleep much the night before, so she had decided to start preparing for the meeting with her sister-in-law as soon as the sun rose.

The details of the meeting are unknown, but Grace did tell a number of American friends that, according to one, "Antoinette's jaw was in her lap. She told Grace she was going to go pack, but Grace told her it would be unnecessary, that all her things were being boxed as they spoke." Antoinette didn't take the news of her banishment lightly, according to what Grace later recalled.

"You've had this planned from the start," Antoinette said. "I'm sure you're pleased to see the back of me."

As her sister-in-law stormed from the room, it was Princess Grace who had the last word. "It's the best part of you, darling," she said. "Believe you me."

The Lonely Princess

Prince Rainier III once remembered a conversation he had with Princess Grace in the fall of 1960 that, in retrospect, best encapsulates his wife's mixed experiences in the Palace those first few years. A gloriously sunny day found Grace in a Palace courtyard surrounded by government officials. She had just presided over an official luncheon. Still looking like a stunning movie star, she appeared naturally elegant in a knee-length pale pink silk dress, her honey-blonde hair cascading loosely to her shoulders. Gaily, she tossed her head back as she laughed at comments made by Monegasque dignitaries. She shook hands and wandered through the crowd with patrician grace. Women curtsied in her presence. Watching her, one would have thought that she was one of the most contented women in the principality, maybe the entire world.

Afterward, over dinner, according to Rainier's later recollection, he and Grace engaged in a conversation about the day's events. "Lovely afternoon, wasn't it?" he said. "You were marvelous, my dear." (At the time, Rainier kept a pad of paper next to his plate upon which he often took notes about the meal. "The leg of mutton is not cooked enough," read one.)

"I'm an actress, darling," Grace told him while picking at her food. She seemed miserable. "I act. Better, apparently, than some of my critics even know."

The Princess then placed her fork on the table, rose, and walked away, leaving Rainier alone with his thoughts. "I knew she was unhappy," he would later recall, "but I thought, in time, she would grow into the position." Though he wouldn't later speak much about it to his official biographer, Peter Hawkins, he did allow that Grace's adjustment to Monaco was "really very difficult, though she tried to hide it." Or, as he more pointedly later told writer Douglas Keay, "She has this ability to put on a mask when necessary. It's all to do with her studies in dramatic art."

"Grace didn't know how she was going to get through those first years at the Palace," says her sister Lizanne. "Rainier tried to help, but it wasn't really his problem. She was the one who had to make the difficult adjustment. She felt alone and isolated, even after she had the two children. She missed us, her family, even after Dad died. We were five thousand miles away. She would sometimes call me and sound so sad, I didn't know what to do. I felt powerless.

However, I knew how hard she had worked at everything in her life up until that point, so I prayed to God that she would begin to work as hard at this [her life in Monaco] as she had at her acting career. I knew she had the courage, if she could find it. We all had it; we got that from our mother and father. The problem, I think, was that it was truly another world over there. You have no idea how different it was."

When Princess Grace first took residence in the Palace, her uncle, Dr. Charles V. Kelly, Jr.—chairman of the English department at La Salle University in Philadelphia—visited her in Monaco. He witnessed many odd moments. He once recalled an evening when he, Grace, and Rainier were seated for dinner in the Palace dining room. As they enjoyed their *boeuf bourguignon* with noodles, one of the housekeepers entered holding a large bowl of dog food. She handed it to the Prince. He inspected it and nodded his approval. He handed it to the Princess. She inspected it and nodded her approval. The Princess then gave the bowl back to the housekeeper, who gently placed it in a corner. The servant then went to a door and opened it with a grand flourish. Suddenly, two large Dobermans galloped into the plush dining room and scrambled into the corner, where they began to dig into their meal as if it was the first they'd had in weeks. Charles Kelly was astonished. "Either they go, or I go," he told his niece, pointing at the animals. "I have no intention of eating my meal with a pair of slobbering beasts." When Grace clapped her hands, the housekeeper once again appeared in the room. In French, Grace instructed the functionary to escort the animals from the room, which she did—but not until after they had completed the task at hand. (No one in her right mind would have tried to prevent two starving Dobermans from finishing their royal dinner.)

Aside from tending to spoiled animals, there was so much protocol for Grace to remember, she once said that "it almost drove me mad." (Rainier didn't understand her problem with stringent protocol, thinking of it all as simply a question of good manners and public order.)

For instance, Grace had to wear a hat during all public functions, even those at the Palace. She didn't like wearing hats—odd, considering the enormous one she sported when she first arrived in Monaco. In 1960, when General Charles de Gaulle and his wife visited the Palace, the Princess met them wearing a glamorous mink coat—and no hat. They were scandalized, and made note of it later to the French press. "Oh my," Grace said when she read the report in a gossip column, "I do hope they get over it. A whole country to run and the poor dears are worried about hats." (Later, de Gaulle grew to admire Princess Grace, calling her *l'Aphrodite américaine*.)

More protocol:

No one was allowed to be seated if the sovereign, Rainier, was in the room and he was standing. Nothing was more annoying to Grace when, at dinner parties, Rainier continued to stand and speak to guests as servants waited to serve food that was growing cold. "If you don't sit, dear, we shall never eat, now shall we?" Grace would often be heard to observe to him. When Jack Kelly visited the Palace, he would always seat himself before Rainier, on purpose. As Grace would stare at him with wide eyes, trying to signal him to stand up, he would look at Rainier and, patting the chair next to him, say, "Take a load off, Ray." (In the privacy of the Grimaldis' apartment, this rule was, of course, not observed. However, when in public, Princess Grace was expected not to sit unless her husband was seated first.)

She always had to sign her name as "Grace de Monaco," this coming after having spent years signing autographs as "Grace Kelly."

She wasn't permitted to leave the Palace grounds unless in the company of her husband or Madge Tivey-Faucon. (Some of Grace's comments made it seem that this rule was not official protocol but, rather, something Rainier dreamed up to keep her under surveillance. "He has me cornered," she told Micheline Swift, wife of her friend filmmaker David Swift, when the two visited the Palace in the sixties. "I can't move. I can't go anywhere. I have no freedom.")

When she referred to Rainier, it was as "His Highness." When she mentioned him in correspondence, it was "He," or "Him," with a capital H.

She had to speak French in public, a huge obstacle because she sometimes did not speak or understand French, the language of the principality, as well as she would have liked. Madge Tivey-Faucon was responsible for fine-tuning Grace's French, but she wasn't much of a teacher in that she had little patience with her pupil. "The Prince enjoyed working with her on her language skills, and it did bring them together," Father Tucker once recalled in an interview. "I remember after one particularly draining session, the Princess addressed one of the servants and requested something be brought to her, in French. The Prince said to me, 'Look at how perfect her French is, Father. It's amazing, isn't it?' And I said, 'My dear boy, I knew love was blind, but I had no idea it was deaf as well.' We all had a good laugh."

Because she had such difficulty with the language and feared embarrassing her husband, Grace usually chose silence when in public places, forcing a faint smile and creating an image that many Monegasques simply mistook as cold detachment, or even petulance. (One citizen was quoted by the *Sunday Express,* in June 1956, as saying, "Our Princess acts more like a Queen than any Queen does.") Also, she refused to wear her tortoiseshell glasses in public. Because she was so nearsighted, she would suffer from headaches if forced to endure long stretches without them, which made matters more miserable for her.

"There was nothing more painful than accompanying her to the opera," Madge Tivey-Faucon recalled, "especially on a gala night. She would enter the box at her husband's side as though she were going to an execution. If they played the national anthem and if the house applauded, she might give a faint smile. People would shake their heads and say, 'She just does not know how to do it. It would be so easy to love such a beautiful Princess.'"

In all her years at the Palace, Grace made few—if any—true friendships. In her "old" life, she had been surrounded by trusted friends, colleagues in the acting world, people upon whom she depended for moral support and who relied on her as well. A gregarious, social woman, Grace took pleasure in interacting with people. She had always been warm, full of life, ready to take on the world and bring her friends along for the ride. However, in her "new" life, she was forced to be a loner.

Grace was accustomed to meaningful, deep relationships with her friends. However, the few times she invited Monegasques to the Palace in hopes of befriending them turned out badly. Most of these were women who had never left Monaco's city limits, and if they had they'd ventured only as far as Nice. They had nothing in common with Grace in terms of worldly experience. Moreover, they were Grace's subjects; they felt awkward in social situations with her. After all, how could these people who were supposed to curtsy to her (and to her husband) confide in her about their lives? And how could she confide in them about hers?

"The Princess's idea of opening up the Palace by inviting local people to dinner parties was not a success," Rainier would later observe. "The Monegasques have this notion that they are a part of the Prince's family, but they are also very shy and respectful, and when we invited them here for meals they became formal and difficult to entertain.

"But it was the same for both of us," he continued, when speaking of trying to make friends.

"I think that with everybody, in whatever walk of life, as you reach maturity, you realize that you can count your true friends all on the fingers of one hand. These are the real friends, maybe including relations, that you count on at any moment, and they are scarce. We discovered that this was still more so for us, because of our position, and we had to learn to accept it, to live with it. And I don't think there is any way of getting it corrected."

The Prince was accustomed to this situation; it was all he'd ever known. He wasn't the kind of person to look for intensely personal relationships anyway. It was rigid in Monaco where royal protocol and the Monegasques were concerned (and it's still that way today). Monegasques referred to Rainier as "Mon Seigneur" ("My Lord"). Princess Grace was referred to as "Your Serene Highness" or, at the very least, "Ma'am" (which she hated), Caroline (and

later, Stephanie) was referred to as "Madame." Albert is, like his father, *"Mon Seigneur."* No wonder Grace longed for honest, stimulating communication with someone—*anyone* of the hundreds of
servants milling about would probably have done fine. However,
she could no sooner traverse the boundaries of protocol that existed
between her and most others than she could sprout wings and soar
out of the stifling Palace to sweet freedom. Besides, Grace was still
her mother's daughter: She cared what people thought. So she tried
to act dignified and self-assured when in the presence of others in
Monaco.

It didn't help that Rainier also limited Grace's contact with certain of her friends, particularly those, it seemed, with jobs in show
business. Virginia Darcy, her MGM hairdresser, was a good example of a woman who got along famously with Grace, but who also,
perhaps, gave her too much information about Hollywood for the
Prince's comfort. "I don't think it was that he wanted to cut show
business out of her life as much as he didn't see the reason for her
to have it always in her face," said Virginia. "When Grace and I got
together, of course what we talked about was show business, the
gossip about who was doing what . . . and maybe to whom. Rainier
wasn't happy about such conversations. There was a moment I remember when she and I were talking about the business while
doing her hair for a stamp or a coin, or something, and Rainier
walked in and said that he had someone he wanted her to meet—
immediately. Grace said, 'But Virginia and I are talking.' And he
was put off by the fact that she didn't just jump. 'These people are
more important,' he said. The next thing I knew, I wasn't doing her
hair any longer. Grace and I never discussed it. I just couldn't get
through to her anymore. He, or whoever, wouldn't give her my
messages, I assumed. I realized what was happening, and I wasn't
heartbroken. I knew it wasn't Grace, but rather the circumstances
in which she found herself."

Meanwhile, the world's press profiled Grace in one way or another on practically a daily basis; she constantly appeared on the
covers of magazines published on virtually every continent. Particularly in America, her story of actress-to-princess was viewed as a

true fairy tale. She was featured on a regular basis in women's magazines, posing alone or with Rainier, or with her children, for indepth features that went on endlessly about her fabulous life. Only her husband, her true friends in America, and a few intimates at the Palace privy to her world—such as her secretary and certain other Palace staffers—were aware of Grace's true melancholy . . . and they weren't talking.

The Stubborn Prince

A few years after her marriage, Princess Grace observed to a reporter, "The biggest change in my life wasn't the Palace. It was the adjustment to marriage itself. I lived alone in New York and in California, and the entire schedule of my life centered around my work. I had to get to the studio on time. I had to arrange my meals to fit my schedule. My career was the central focus of everything I did. Now my life centers around my husband."

Indeed, Grace's only sounding board at the Palace was Rainier, and she knew that she couldn't discuss most of her interests with him. Theater held no fascination for him, and neither did movies. He would usually fall asleep at the opera, to be awakened only when she kicked him gently in the shin lest the royal couple be embarrassed in public. Much to Rainier's disappointment, Grace did not share his interest in motorcar racing, skin diving, archeology, or zoology. Besides their children and Catholicism—which Grace turned to more than ever while at the Palace—the royal couple really had little else in common.

Grace learned early on that Rainier wasn't the easiest person to live with. She came from a world in which she usually got her way; she had been a pampered Hollywood star, after all. However, at the Palace, she found herself playing the most subservient role of her life, spouse to a man who was not only ruler of a principality, but also of a palace, his home—much like her father had been in his house. In his view, he was never wrong, again like Jack Kelly. If a dinner party went on too long, he would sometimes fall asleep at the table. Once, the Prince and Princess were entertaining the elderly Queen Victoria Eugenie of Spain, often referred to as Queen Ena, who was also Prince Albert's godmother. As the Queen—who was the mother of the Spanish pretender Don Juan—told a long story about how she was almost assassinated on her wedding day in Madrid in 1906, Princess Grace tried to act captivated. She hoped to keep the Queen's eyes on her because, seated right next to the Queen was Rainier, sound asleep. Later, when Grace challenged Rainier about it, he defended himself by saying that he and Grace had heard Ena's "big story" a dozen times, and "I can sleep anywhere I wish, anytime I wish, because it's my Palace."

"He would blow up. Oh boy, would he ever!" said Grace's sister Lizanne good-naturedly. "Now, *that* was something to see."

For instance, in 1961, Grace decided she wanted to cut her wheat-blonde hair even though she realized that, at this time, Rainier preferred it to be just above shoulder length—and not just because he liked it that way but because he believed in continuity of image in annual photographs, coins, and stamps. A whimsical hairstyle change was not supposed to occur in royal circles, at least not a dramatic one. Explained Virginia Darcy, who styled Grace's hair for the photo session from which the stamps were made, "His Highness wanted her not to look like a Hollywood actress on the stamps and coins. That was most important to him. He said she was to look royal, not Hollywood."

Princess Grace and Countess D'Aillères, wife of the Grand Chamberlain, went to the Hôtel de Paris to confer with the stylist there, Alexandre from Paris. (Because Grace was not permitted to leave the Palace without her, Madge Tivey-Faucon also tagged along.) Finally, after much discussion, Grace decided upon the new, trendy "artichoke" style. Recently created by Alexandre, the haircut was described by a *Look* magazine reporter as "locks cut in the shape of leaves, nesting one over the other." (Basically, the cut was short at the neck and bouffant on the top.) After her hair was so styled, Grace was pleased. "However," she said, "I fear Rainier will blow a gasket over this." For the next two hours, the Princess and Countess drank martinis in the hotel's American Bar, perhaps fortifying themselves for the Prince's reaction to Grace's insurrection. On the way out of the lobby, Grace noticed the statue of Louis XIV sitting upon a horse. "Legend has it that a person will have good luck if he touches the knee of this animal," Grace said, "and I think we may need it." She placed her hand on the statue and seemed to make a silent wish.

The Princess returned to the Palace a short time later with her new "artichoke" look. She happened to be standing in the library with Gaia Magrelli (an Italian designer who knew Grace during this time and who had visited her several times at the Palace in consultation regarding renovations there) when Rainier walked into the room. Upon seeing him, Grace struck a flamboyant "Hollywood" pose, her hand on her hip. "So, darling," she asked, "what do you think?" Rainier took one look at Grace, turned beet red and threw his drink to the floor, showering their feet with glass. As he stormed away, Grace must have suddenly realized that she didn't care quite as much as she thought she did—or maybe those martinis had finally kicked in. Without missing a beat, she rolled her eyes and turned back to Gaia. "Anyway," she said, "as I was saying . . ."

Lizanne first visited her sister at the Palace in 1960, actually her first time there, since she had been unable to attend the wedding due to her pregnancy. "Grace was spoiled, true," recalled Lizanne, with a chuckle. "But, I must say, Rainier was even more spoiled. While Grace could accept not having her way, he couldn't accept the idea at all, not without a fight. I don't know how she lived with him, really, at least not at first. She would say, 'Ooooooh, that man!'"

Rainier Grimaldi was raised as the scion of a powerful family—a youngster destined to one day become the Serene Highness of a principality. It's safe to say, at least based on all available evidence as well as the recollections of those who knew him well, that he rarely found himself in the position of having to reconsider any view where his personal life was concerned. Although it seems difficult to imagine a person rarely having to concede the fallibility of his decisions, the truth is that members of royal families often do not. That they would have final say in any matters regarding right or wrong is for them a privilege intrinsic to their position. Rainier was no different.

A person born into such a paradigm of absolute authority and power, such as the Prince, would certainly become skewed in his perceptions of both himself and his fellow man. It is the reason why such men often grow up myopic in their views, hopelessly ignorant of what things are like in the "real world" and for those who occupy it. Of course, it would be untrue to state that Rainier *always* had his way, that he was able to *force* others to do his bidding. In Monaco, the Prince was at the mercy of a governmental council with which he was often at odds. He was also at cross-purposes with opponents such as Aristotle Onassis, who was buying up shares in Monaco faster than Rainier could keep track of them. In matters of state, he didn't always get his way and didn't expect to have it. At home, it was a different story.

Grace was also less likely to humor Rainier when she didn't feel inclined to do so. For instance, she was once having an urgent discussion with a functionary in the library when the Prince burst in and interrupted her to tell her that one of his chimpanzees was pregnant. Grace ignored him, as he had often ignored her in front of the staff, and went on with her discussion. She couldn't have cared less about the animals in the Palace zoo, and rarely went there. "You don't understand, Princess," Rainier said urgently. "Tanagra is pregnant!" Grace didn't say a word. "It's rare for a chimpanzee to breed in captivity!" he pressed on, waiting for a reaction. Finally, Grace whirled around to face him. "All *rightie*, then," she said impatiently. "I'll knit her something." She then went back to her business.

Another incident Palace workers often spoke about happened

while Grace was preparing one of the guest apartments for a visit of the Brussels minister and his wife. She ordered the placement of a few pieces of furniture to be changed, thinking it would make the couple more comfortable. Though she wasn't supposed to move furniture without prior approval from the Prince, she usually ignored that rule, judging it, as she once said, "too ridiculous to take seriously." As often happened at the Palace, someone "told" on her, reported her to the Prince. That night the Prince and the Princess apparently discussed the matter as they walked in the Cour d'Honneur (Court of Honor) on the way back from the Palace's theater to their private quarters. It's not known what Rainier said to his wife since he kept his voice low. However, many people overheard Grace's response. "How dare you speak to me that way!" she challenged him, her voice raised. "I am the Princess here, in case you haven't noticed. I am not your maid."

Though he and Grace would argue noisily and reconcile feverishly, Rainier would not change. Marriage can be challenging under the best of circumstances, but for the Prince it was especially the case. He wasn't accustomed to compromise. He also wasn't used to considering another person's feelings; sensitivity wasn't his strongest suit.

"My, dear, you look fat in that dress," he once told Grace before the two left for an important function about which she was apprehensive. She was wearing a white silk sheath, designed by Flora Villarreal of Madrid.

Crushed, the Princess burst into tears and ran back into the bedroom.

"What did I say?" the Prince asked Madge Tivey-Faucon. "I'm trying to protect her. If she is unhappy with the photos in tomorrow morning's newspaper, her whole day will be ruined."

"Yes, Your Highness," Madge recalled having said. "That's certainly true."

Perhaps Grace did look "fat" in Villarreal's creation and Rainier was being protective as well as honest. However, few women would countenance such a degree of honesty from their spouses.

Another time, Grace put on a simple, large and inelegant rain-coat for a walk in the Palace gardens. Rainier sized her up and quipped, "Who would have guessed that I would one day marry an immigrant?" (Grace laughed that one off, taking the jibe with good humor.)

Though unlikely to change his own opinions, the Prince wasn't always successful in getting others to accommodate them. Early on in their marriage the arguments started between him and the Princess, mostly stemming from his trying to tell her how she should feel. Much to his dismay, his attempts to control and shape the viewpoints of his loved ones were often frustrated by the stead-fastness of their own beliefs and their intransigence at changing them. He would have to learn to accept the fact of free will, the re-ality that it was one domain over which his authority was not ab-solute. For instance, he approved of few of the choices his sister, Princess Antoinette, had made over the years—going all the way back to her rumor-mongering campaign against Gisele Pascal—but he was never able to stop her. Still, he rarely missed an opportunity to at least try to control someone he loved, a pathology to which Grace would be immediately exposed.

For instance, Grace was unhappy—and that was just the way it was going to be for her until she decided that she was happy. There was no point in trying to tell her that she shouldn't feel as she felt. Bettina Campbell recalls, "I know they had disagreements about Grace's seeming stubbornness to adjust to her new life in Monaco. It was exasperating for him to see her moping about all the time. He would say, 'My dear, you simply have to make the best of it. Why not just be happy? You are a Princess now. Truly you can't be as unhappy as you have convinced yourself that you are.' And she would say, 'Please don't tell me how I feel. I can accept that I am unhappy—and you will have to as well. I'll get through it,' she would tell him, 'but let me feel the way I feel.'"

Grace Kelly was a woman who usually honored her true feelings, even when they involved sadness. After all, she had been an actress who had worked for years digging to the core of how she really felt. One of the reasons she had trouble early in her career (when she was displeased with many of her early performances) was because she couldn't access certain emotions, she had become so used to stuffing them for the sake of her family. She got past that—and she won an Academy Award for it. Now that she was in the Palace, suddenly she found herself being told to stuff her feelings once again. She had no precedent for being who he wanted her to be. She could only be herself.

" 'Please, let me be miserable,' she would say to the Prince," recalled Gaia Magrelli. "But he was always trying to make her not feel that way. It was bad enough that she wasn't happy . . . but unbearable that she had to *act* as if she were, just to keep the peace with him."

"How many times I saw the Princess coming out of her room, sniffling, red-eyed," recalled Madge Tivey-Faucon. " 'I have a cold,' she would tell me to hide her embarrassment. She seemed to have an everlasting cold."

Still, to characterize Rainier as unfeeling or uncaring where Grace was concerned is not entirely true—just as it would have been to paint Jack Kelly with that wide a brushstroke where his own wife was concerned. A demonstration of the Prince's fervor to please his Princess is found in an idea he had that, at the time, struck some observers as a bit unusual: He arranged for Grace to speak on the telephone to Godfrey "Fordie" Ford, the beloved servant/chauffeur who was practically a member of the Kelly family. One of two black "housemen," he kept the cars polished, supervised the bartenders at parties, and worked in the garden.

One afternoon, the Princess, Gaia Magrelli, and Madge Tivey-Faucon returned to the Palace, exhausted at the end of a long day. After tending to the children, Grace walked into the family's old-fashioned drawing room (where they often enjoyed coffee with friends in front of a crackling fire). She slumped into a chair and kicked off her heels. Rainier walked over to her and handed her the telephone. "Someone wants to speak to you," he said, according to Gaia Magrelli.

"Oh, please, I just walked in," Grace said, irritated. "Can't I even have five seconds to myself?" Still, she took the phone. After a beat, she jumped to her feet and squealed with delight: "Fordie! Oh my God! Fordie!"

Rainier, Gaia, and Madge, all beaming, left Grace in the drawing room, where she then spoke privately to the Kelly houseman for thirty minutes. When she emerged, she had tears in her eyes. She rushed to Rainier. "Darling, that was the most wonderful thing in the world," she said, embracing him. "Fordie means the world to me. My God, how did you ever think of it?"

"My dear, of course I remember Fordie," Rainier said, brushing away her tears. "And I remembered how much he meant to you."

"You truly are the most wonderful man in the world," Grace told Rainier. The two then walked off, hand in hand.

"See you later, alligator," Grace said to Gaia as she walked away. It had been so long since Gaia heard Grace use that expression— the Princess had been so sad lately—that she almost forgot the response. "In a while, crocodile," she finally said.

"More Palace Drama"

To keep her busy at home, Prince Rainier encouraged Princess Grace to make the Palace's nine-room private apartment more to her liking, since she had felt from the beginning that it was too impersonal and solemn an environment. Their apartment, located on the ground floor of the west wing of the Palace, comprised a kitchen, dining room, drawing room, library, bar, bedroom, bathroom, and two dressing rooms. Large nursery facilities adjoined it, consisting of two bedrooms, a day room, a kitchen, a bathroom, and a laundry. Before Grace moved in, Father Tucker described it as being "like a mausoleum . . . the deadest place imaginable."

When Grace asked Rainier if she could bring her furniture from

New York to Monaco, he agreed to allow it, believing that her eighteenth-century French pieces would not be out of place in the princely ancestral dwelling. However, when Grace then hired her decorator, George Stacey, to work on the apartment, the Prince was unhappy. A mere "decorator" involved in Palace decor? Never! Such choices were only made by Palace officials. However, Rainier acquiesced to Grace in her remodeling decisions and, for a while, the work kept her occupied and contented.

Grace and Rainier shared a bedroom that looked out onto the Palace gardens, lush with blooming mimosa, bougainvillea, and orange trees and, farther in the distance, the sports stadium and the harbor. They slept in the same bed—in the middle of the flower-filled room—for their entire marriage. Bedside tables on both his side and hers were always littered with medicine bottles, magazines, books, papers, water glasses, and coffee cups. The Palace maids were asked not to disturb the items on these tables because, as Rainier put it, "I like to know where my private things are."

She also spent time redecorating their vacation retreat, Roc Agel, the two-story provincial, Moorish-inspired villa with a roof of red tiles in the middle of sixty acres, about two hours from the Palace. There, Grace had a vegetable garden she enjoyed tending as Rainier rode his horses in peace. They had a more casual lifestyle; Grace prepared Mexican or Italian meals in a kitchen she designed (with American plumbing). Rainier enjoyed donning his asbestos gloves and cook's apron and cooking steaks on the barbecue grill he had brought back to France from America. Though still watched over by guards who bowed low whenever they walked into a room, and coddled by busy assistants who fussed over them constantly, the family was far more self-sufficient at Roc Agel than they could be at the royal Palace, which suited Grace. At sunset, Grace and Rainier could often be found holding hands on one of the terraces at Roc Agel, facing the peaceful Mediterranean and the far-off coast of Italy, feeling, perhaps, alone in the world.

Back at the Palace, even some of the servants—such as Madge

Tivey-Faucon, as well as those in positions of far less importance—had ambivalent feelings about Grace, thought of her as an interloper, and did not often hide their disapproval of the former American actress in their midst. In front of Rainier, of course, they would act respectful toward her. Out of his presence, however, it was clear how they really felt about her. Or, as Grace told one New York friend, demonstrating that her sense of humor was still intact, "Why, I'm an unwelcome guest in my own Palace!" It didn't help matters that she would sometimes do the strangest things, such as when she gave many of the servants a single bar of scented soap for Christmas. Perhaps she thought it was an appropriate gift—perhaps it was even an "expensive" soap product—but the people who received it felt she was trying to tell them to bathe more often. (And, who knows, maybe she was!) Once, Grace bought Madge Tivey-Faucon a mauve feather duster. Since the cleaning of the Palace was certainly not part of Madge's job, she was insulted. Was Grace trying to tell her something as well? No, Grace explained. "I simply know how much you like the color mauve."

So, there was no love lost between Grace and most of the Palace "help," some of whom even attempted to sabotage their Princess from time to time. For instance, Bettina Campbell remembers the time Rainier walked into a guest suite that had been decorated with white chrysanthemums by Grace and Madge, in preparation for a visiting official.

"What is this?" Rainier shouted at Grace. "Chrysanthemums are used for funerals, not guest rooms in the Palace. What is wrong with you?"

"But how was I to know?" Grace asked in her own defense.

"Why, even a peasant would know such a thing," Rainier said before charging off.

"As well as any 'peasant,' Madge Tivey-Faucon should have known such a thing," observed Bettina Campbell, "and she was the one who suggested those particular flowers for that occasion, not Princess Grace. Later, the Princess just chalked it up to what she called 'more Palace drama.'"

Unlike his appointed Palace staff members, Prince Rainier's own flesh and blood—his mother, Princess Charlotte, and sister, Antoinette—didn't feel the need to mask their harsh judgments about Grace. They continued to openly resent her and did whatever they could do to complicate her life.

Princess Charlotte posed the greatest challenge to Grace's peace of mind, with letters and telephone calls constantly reminding her of protocol. Luckily, Charlotte didn't visit Monaco much, preferring to stay either in Paris or at her country home in Marchais, which Grace described in a letter to Don Richardson as surroundings "colder than a witch's teet." (She had originally written "tit," but must have thought it inappropriate because she crossed out the word and replaced it with "teet.") By this time, Charlotte, always a real character, had taken to collecting small terrier dogs. Wherever she went, she had seven to ten small dogs following her, barking up a storm and biting anyone who came near her. "How charming," a sarcastic Grace would say whenever Charlotte and her team of ankle-nippers walked into the room.

Grace could always rely on both Grimaldi women—intensely jealous because Grace had the full power of the Palace at her disposal, and they did not—not only to criticize her, but also to align themselves with her many detractors in the principality. Because she was accustomed to disapproval from her own parents, Grace was able to deal with that of the Grimaldis. However, it was still painful for her to know that there were those in her life who did not like her. After all, she was not a woman who, prior to this time, had ever had people in her world who didn't appreciate her for the good and decent person she had always been.

"What they think of you doesn't matter," Father Francis Tucker told her, according to his later recollection. "What you think of yourself, now that's what matters."

Doing her best to overlook the Grimaldi women's petty natures, Princess Grace kept busy with the daily scheduling of a life to which she felt no authentic connection. Truly, she was just acting the role of Her Serene Highness as she went about her charity work, shaking hands, being gracious, posing for photographs with a bright smile, or as the self-aware Grace would have to admit, acting like "a big phony." She wanted to like the Monegasques, and perhaps they wanted to like her—but, at first, it was an uneasy alliance between Princess and constituency.

"Let's face it, a similar thing happened more strongly for the Queen of Spain," Prince Rainier once explained, drawing a historical parallel, "when she married Alphonse XIII. By this I mean that she wasn't a Spaniard, she was blonde, and the people put a moral embargo against her. Here—there was this astonishment, you know, not knowing how to approach a Princess who came from another country and spoke another language. What would be her reactions? What would she think of them and how much would she want to change their ways? It was certainly difficult . . . and painful for her."

Many years later, Rainier would be even more clear when assessing Grace's early relationship with her subjects. "The simple image people here have of a Hollywood actress is Mae West, and it doesn't go much further," he explained. "They didn't know what kind of mentality the Princess had, and so they retracted. I realized this would be the case and probably it would have been better if she'd spent some time here with her parents before we married. Looking back, I was also probably too impatient that she should fit in and feel at ease. Often, I didn't understand her outlook on things; I have to be honest and admit that much."

Rainier Encourages Grace's Comeback

By early 1962, Prince Rainier III had become concerned enough about his wife's depression to take on a more proactive role in trying to resolve it. He knew that the source of her feelings had to be the many sacrifices she had made on his behalf: abandoning her career, her life in America, her family, and her close friends. After Albert was born, Grace would suffer two miscarriages, which would only add to her unhappiness. ("It was a terrible experience and has left me shaken both mentally and physically," she wrote to Prudy Wise after the first miscarriage. Then, because Prudy was pregnant and Grace was concerned about the tone of her letter, she added as a postscript, "Sorry to send such a downbeat letter.") Rainier recognized that what she really needed was a renewed sense of satisfaction and fulfillment in her life, something that for Grace would always arise from the same thing: making another movie.

Four years earlier, Grace had appeared, playing herself, in an hour-long film entitled *Invitation to Monaco*, a fictional story about a young girl who visits Monaco to give a kitten to young Caroline. Though Frank Sinatra and Prince Rainier also appeared in the film, it was really just a promotional movie to encourage tourism in the principality. "It's not a real movie, no matter how you slice it," Grace had said. It did little more than whet her appetite for something more substantial.

Grace's potential return to Hollywood had always been a thorny issue for Rainier. The idea went against the standards of royal and familial propriety, in whose strict adherence he had always believed without question. He couldn't imagine Grace, as he put it to one aide, "parading about on a movie screen with an actor, doing who knows what." The thought of it made him shudder. The only place where photos from Grace's movies were on display was in a guest bathroom at Roc Agel—not exactly an honored site. Occasionally, Grace enjoyed showing her films in the luxurious Palace screening room, formerly the stables. When she did, the Prince sometimes banned Palace employees from seeing the movie, depending on which one was being shown. While the staff was permitted to see *The Country Girl,* they were not allowed to watch *To Catch a Thief.* He had his reasons, and he never explained them.

Rainier also was unimpressed by Grace's show business friends, believing that their presence in her life could only lead to distraction for her. Former MGM colleague Esther Williams recalled there being a "wistfulness" about her when she saw her in Monaco. "We were seated next to each other at a fundraiser, and she wanted to talk about the studio, who was there and who wasn't. You don't do that if you're through with something." Former Paramount production chief Robert Evans says he was snubbed by Grace at the Red Cross Ball in 1967, which he attended with David and Hjordis Niven, and with Princess Soraya on his arm (she had just been divorced from the Shah of Iran because she could not bear him a child). Evans had known Grace since her modeling days and felt that her dismissal of him was probably a reaction to Rainier's not wanting her to socialize with old friends from her time in show business.

However, Grace would often have her showbiz chums—people like Rita Gam, her former roommate, who had also been one of her bridesmaids, and her agent, Jay Kanter—visit Monaco and would invite them to the Palace for important formal functions. Grace, who had always been a fun-loving person, occasionally couldn't resist kicking off her shoes and having fun when her friends visited, even if she was supposed to be "Princess" that day and not "Gracie." From across the room, one might hear, "Hey, Gracie, c'mon over here. Let's play charades!" Rainier would cringe, as would Madge Faucon-Tivey. Though it was stultifying for Grace to have to constantly keep up her royal pretense, Rainier and Madge—her new "parents"—never approved of her really letting loose. "This familiarity destroys at one blow the careful staging built up by protocol around the Prince and Princess," Madge once said.

In 1961, when Grace's *To Catch a Thief* costar, Cary Grant, visited Monaco with his wife, Betsy Drake, for Easter weekend, Grace was so excited about their arrival that she went to the Nice airport to personally meet their plane. Rainier warned her that such an honor from a Princess was sure to be misinterpreted by the press, even if she had never actually had any kind of romantic relationship with Cary Grant.

According to Barbara Tuck Cresci, widow of Frank Cresci, who was Rainier's Consul General in New York, "Every time an article came out about her former boyfriends, Rainier would fly into a rage. That just about ruined their marriage. However, I didn't blame him, you know? It was a horrible thing to always have to be reminded of her life before she was his wife. My husband, Frank, told the Prince, 'Look, you married her from that day forward. Forget it! Just forget it.' But the press never would let him or her forget."

Predictably, there were photographers waiting at the airport for the Grants' arrival, and their excitement at the surprising appearance of the Princess was practically palpable. The next morning, photographs of Cary and Grace (none of Betsy) were published all over Europe, with accompanying innuendo about the two movie stars who had once appeared to be so passionate about one another on film. Rainier was annoyed enough by the coverage to smack his newspaper onto the breakfast table and say, "So there you have it, Princess. How nice for us."

Rainier was then distant toward the Grants during their visit. One day, the foursome went to a tennis tournament in the afternoon, and then the opera at night. Rainier never said a word to Cary or to Grace the entire day. He spoke only to Betsy—and didn't say much to her either. Grace ignored Rainier as much as he ignored the Grants, determined not to allow him to ruin her good time. At the end of the evening, when Cary slipped on the polished marble floor and fell on his backside on the way to his Palace apartment, he and Grace laughed so hard their sides hurt. However, Rainier remained stoic. "I don't know how such a fun-loving girl stays married to that fuddy-duddy," Cary later said. (What a shame. The Prince actually had a marvelous sense of humor—though one couldn't have convinced Grant of that.)

When the Grants left Monaco, there was friction between Rainier and Grace, and rather than blame himself for the arguments they had about what had occurred, he blamed the presence of movie star Grant at the Palace. "Being married is having the same argument over and over again," Grace said at the time. She told one friend that she wished she "could have more fun, the way I did when I was acting."

"By this time, she was really regretting her decision, I think," said her ex-paramour Oleg Cassini, perhaps stating the obvious. Though he and Grace were not speaking, Oleg was still in touch with many of her friends. "The life that she really liked, she could not conduct," he said. "Her husband disliked many of her friends from Hollywood, and they all knew it. It was two cultures clashing. Culturally, she and Rainier were different people. It wasn't a marriage of convenience as much as it has been a marriage of reason. But, suddenly, it seemed unreasonable." (As recently as 2002, Oleg maintained that he and Grace would have been the better couple. "She would have been happy as my wife, continuing doing pictures and being the great star that she was. Instead, she gave it all up for the glamour of the . . . the *moment*, really.")

It speaks volumes about Rainier's concern for Grace, then, that he would try to overcome such deeply held opinions against her show business friends and Hollywood career by encouraging her to reenter that milieu. He felt that he owed her a debt of gratitude. Though he had certain regrets about the way he had managed the madness surrounding their wedding, he could take heart in the fact that, by the end of the 1950s, it was clear that his having married her was precisely what had been needed to extract Monaco from its recession. She had certainly infused some much-needed glamour into a depressed postwar Monaco. Thanks to the worldwide publicity generated by "The Wedding of the Century," much of a world that had previously never heard of Monaco now wanted to vacation there. With gambling revenues at an all-time high, the principality's annual income had grown to the tens of millions of dollars by the end of the fifties. Grace gave as much as she could in her position as Princess. She was a good mother, a loyal wife. Now it was time to pay up . . . to let her do this one thing she wanted to do most: make a movie.

Prince Rainier later explained to his biographer Peter Hawkins, "There have been times, you know, when the Princess has been a little melancholic—which I understand—about having performed a form of art successfully, only to be cut away from it completely. Let's imagine that we had gone on living in New York, or London, or Paris, she would still have been able to keep up with acting activities. She found herself cut off from this, and she loved her profession." Rainier was stretching the truth in implying that the reason Grace had to abandon her career was because she was now residing in Monaco instead of in a metropolis like Paris, but perhaps his was a royal right to "misspeak," especially to his own biographer.

Over the years, it's been reported that Hitchcock had the idea of a film project for Grace and that he approached her, and Rainier, with his concept. (Rainier even repeated that story in his biography.) It now seems that Rainier actually telephoned Hitchcock to tell him that Grace was despondent, and that he would like for her to make another movie in the hope that it would lift her spirits. Besides, she had been so supportive of him during recent difficult political times. It was only fair, said the Prince, that he do something for her now. It was ironic, and much like the way Grace's charmed life had worked before she got to Monaco, that Alfred Hitchcock was at the same time wondering how he might go about hiring Grace for a film he was planning to film in the summer of 1962.

The film Hitchcock had in mind was *Marnie*, from a novel by Winston Graham. It is the provocative story of an attractive woman plagued by sexual problems and such a fear of intimacy that she becomes violently ill whenever she realizes that a man is interested in her. Her distrust of men manifests itself in compulsive kleptomania. In the novel and screenplay, Marnie—also a liar and a forger—eventually comes to terms with her fear of men with the help of a love interest (to be played by Sean Connery), who helps her to realize that the source of her problem is rooted in a dysfunctional childhood at the hands of abusive parents. In a climactic moment, Marnie recalls that, as a child, she slept in bed with her prostitute mother while the woman engaged in sexual activity with clients. Later in the story, she is violently raped.

Not surprisingly, when Prince Rainier read a draft of the script, he wasn't particularly pleased with it. Was there any way to produce *this* movie in a dignified, tasteful way? Of course, if it was to be an Alfred Hitchcock movie, what could he expect, especially in the explicit early 1960s?

Of course, there was some show business precedent in the Grimaldi family: Princess Ghislaine, the widow of Rainier's grandfather Prince Louis II and step-grandmother of Prince Rainier III, had once been a famous actress and still longed to return to the theater. Because she no longer lived at the Palace, it was a bit easier for her to give show business another try. In 1958, she appeared in a Nice presentation of *Mrs. April's Diamonds*. Afterward, she told the press that Rainier was "very understanding." However, because Rainier and Ghislaine were not friendly, it's doubtful that he was so "understanding" and more likely that he just didn't care. After all, Ghislaine was almost as little-known inside the principality, of which she was First Lady for nearly three years, as she was outside it.

Princess Ghislaine frequently visited the principality at Princess Grace's invitation. "Grace asked Ghislaine to come to the Palace to talk about *Marnie*," says Bettina Campbell. "For years after, Ghislaine would speak about what she had suggested to Grace. 'You must do that movie and you mustn't let anyone stop you,' she told her. 'If you have Rainier's permission, who cares what anyone else thinks? He's the Prince. You are a brilliant actress, and you should not allow that talent to be wasted. As long as Rainier approves, what is to stop you, my dear? Nothing but yourself.'"

"Don't Tell Father"

Father Francis Tucker—seventy-one years old as of January 8, 1961—was still a formidable force in the Palace because of his strong influence over Prince Rainier's decisions, both personal and governmental. Few held as important a role in the Prince's life as his chaplain, who served Mass for Rainier and Grace every single morning, with both receiving daily communion.

When the priest's brother Ed died in February 1961, Rainier was deeply upset. He wrote a letter to Tucker that revealed much about his growing insightfulness, some of which may be attributed to a marriage that had forced him to dig deep within himself for understanding and compassion. In his letter, he recognized that attributing Ed's death to God's will was really of little consolation. Yet he added that God "knows so much better than we poor mortals . . . the value of life . . . and when 'time is up' for each of us." He reminded Tucker that he could always find "a family" for himself in Monaco at the Palace and concluded that the Lord is "good and generous" and "fond of you." He then signed the letter simply, "Rainier."

"Both seem to cuddle up to me more than ever, which pleases me a lot," Tucker proudly wrote to his older brother Joe about Rainier and Grace.

On August 10, 1961, Father Tucker celebrated his "Golden Jubilee" with the church, fifty years as a priest, the first American of the Order of the Oblates of St. Francis de Sales to reach such a milestone. Though he would be feted with a big celebration in a couple of months at St. Charles's in Wilmington, Delaware,* he spent August with Rainier, Grace, Prince Pierre, Caroline, and Al-

---

*Grace's mother attended the celebratory Mass for Father Tucker at St. Charles's, and also sat next to the guest of honor at the gala banquet. A telegram from the Grimaldis was read at the banquet: "Don't forget to come home," signed simply, "Rainier and Grace."

bert at the country home at Roc Agel. There, Father Tucker performed a Mass for the family in the Grimaldis' private chapel. "It was a special service," Rainier later reported. "How wonderful it was for us to have the good Father here on such an auspicious occasion. He also says mass for us in the chapel for the children's birthday every year. God is always here."

While in Delaware, Father Tucker told a family friend, "The Prince is alarmed by the Princess's constant state of unhappiness at the Palace. He and I discussed it. He asked me to talk to her. She tries to stay busy with her many duties and with the children, but we all knew she had lost something important to her, her career. However, in my view, there wasn't much that could be done about it."

Tucker had previously told a reporter that if she were to ask his advice about a future career in the cinema, "I would most certainly advise against it." He told another writer—as always, Tucker still enjoyed granting interviews—"They couldn't offer her a role in Hollywood as good as the one she is playing now."

It was Rainier's difficult decision to keep from Father Tucker any news about Grace's return to movies. He realized, say those close to him, that the Catholic Church would never approve of Grace's returning to movies, let alone in a movie such as the one proposed. Though he discussed all personal and state problems with his personal chaplain, he decided not to consult with Tucker about this one for fear of putting him in a difficult position with the church.

Thomas Sartre recalled, "There was a Palace meeting about *Marnie*, and Princess Grace was present, though not talkative. She looked around and suddenly said, 'But, darling, where's Father?' Rainier said, 'Don't tell Father about this, Princess. It'll just be hard on him, as much as we need his counsel now. I think he could lose his post over this.' Grace nodded her head in agreement. 'This is hard enough on everyone,' she said. 'I guess we should spare Father Tucker.'"

"God Help Us,
When This News Gets Out"

Though it had been years since Grace Kelly made movies for MGM, the studio never stopped receiving requests for interviews with her. Thomas Sartre was at the time a young publicist who worked as a press liaison between the Palace (under Emile Cornet) and MGM. He also worked with Rupert Allan to field press requests. "Emile Cornet and I had many conversations with the Prince about *Marnie*," recalled Sartre, "and he told me that everyone he knew in Monaco was against the idea. When I asked him how he felt about such opposition, he was philosophical about it. 'I have never had anything other than opposition in whatever I have proposed for Monaco,' he told me, 'so why should this be any different?' Emile asked him how the press should be handled regarding the matter, and Rainier made it clear that it should be left to the Princess. 'She understands the way these things should be handled,' he told me. 'I will defer to her on all matters having to do with the media and *Marnie*. However, where I am concerned,' he added, 'I want it made clear that I am in full support of this movie. Even though my entire family will be in an uproar about this matter, I will stand by the Princess one hundred percent as she has always stood by me.'"

On the morning of March 16, 1962, Prince Rainier received a letter from Grace Kelly's mother. Along with it was a copy of an article Margaret had saved, written in 1956. The note from Mrs. Kelly asked Rainier to consider the article when making any decisions about Grace's return to movies. It's not known if, or when, Margaret knew that such a decision was being made. The article, written by veteran journalist Maurice Zolotow, was published in the magazine the *American Weekly*. In part, it read, "I do not believe that she [Grace] can be happy unless she continues to do the work that has come to represent for her the special and private fulfillment of all her creative desires. Acting symbolizes the solid ground on which she stands with her own two feet. It represents her triumph as a human being, her victory over all the doubts and insecurities that have haunted her life since childhood. To turn her back on all this, I believe, would be a terrible defeat for her. It would be like cutting the heart out of herself."

Thomas Sartre recalled the morning Rainier came into his office with the letter from Margaret:

"I jumped up, as you are supposed to do when he comes into the room. He asked me to read the letter. Mrs. Kelly started it with 'Dear Ray,' that, I remember. In it, she observed that her daughter never should have stopped making films, that she hadn't been truly happy since *High Society*. She was concerned, and thought Rainier should do something about it.

"Then he showed me the article from the magazine. After I read it, he asked me what I thought. I told him that, for me, the letter and the article were a persuasive argument as to why Princess Grace should make a movie. 'I think you're right,' he told me. Then he asked me what I thought about the fact that Mrs. Kelly had kept the magazine article all of those years. I said that, in my view, she was a woman who truly loved her daughter. He said, 'I think you're right about that, too.' "

Many years later, Sartre recalled, "The Prince went to the Princess with the letter from her mom, and the feature. I don't know what their discussion about it was; I never asked. Later that same day, I saw the Prince. 'Well, she's doing a movie,' he said. Then, with a laugh, he added, 'God help us all, that's all I can say, when this news gets out. Run for cover, my boy. Run for cover!' "

Early on March 18, 1962, Princess Grace summoned four Monaco court officials to inform them of her intention to appear in *Marnie*: Emile Cornet, Palace press officer; George Lukomski, Palace photographer; Monsieur Delavenne, Minister of the Interior; and Monsieur Jean-Claude Farjas, chief of the Centre de Presse de Monaco. While Rainier attended to business elsewhere in the principality, Grace would greet the officials in her green-and-gold-appointed office, located in one of the Palace's twin towers overlooking the harbor and the square of the old quarter, dotted with souvenir shops.

Just as everything was done at the Palace, the visit was conducted with an eye toward protocol. All four—even the two Palace employees—arrived at a side entrance of the Palace, where they were greeted by a fully decorated and uniformed concierge. After telephoning Grace's secretary, Phyllis Blum, to be certain that the Princess was expecting guests, he asked the men to follow him to the tower. Once they arrived at a gate leading to the tower, the group was stopped by a white-gloved *carabinier*, or Palace guard, whose job it was to carefully write the name of each guest—even the Palace employees—in a large guest book. The concierge then took his leave while the guard escorted the four men to Princess Grace's office—where they sat and waited for an hour. They couldn't help but notice that the biggest and most obvious picture in the room was an oil painting of Manhattan's Fifth Avenue, blanketed in snow.

"Gentlemen, I have marvelous news for you," Grace said upon finally arriving. The men jumped to their feet. Wearing a smart beige-and-brown tweed business suit and her tortoiseshell glasses, she looked like an actress playing the role of an executive. Seeming barely able to contain herself, she smiled broadly.

"I am going to make a film," Grace exclaimed. "Try not to look too astonished," she added with a laugh. At that moment, Cocoa, a parrot known around the Palace for being able to whistle "The Colonel Bogey March," better known as the theme to *The Bridge on the River Kwai*, flew into the Princess's office and alighted on her Louis XV desk. It had obviously escaped from its captivity; there were birds in cages everywhere, or so it seemed. "You know what we need around here?" Grace said, exasperated. "More birds!" As she reached for the small creature, it flew away, and then out of the room. Grace then turned back to her visitors and went on to explain that she was making a movie with Alfred Hitchcock. As she gave the details, Phyllis Blum typed up the official press release in an adjoining office. It was to be sent out via a telegram in French and English. It read:

"A spokesman for the Prince of Monaco announced today that Princess Grace has accepted an offer to appear during her summer vacation in a motion picture for Mister Alfred Hitchcock, to be made in the United States. The Princess has previously starred in three films for Mr. Hitchcock. The film to start in late summer is based on a suspense novel by English writer Winston Graham. It is understood that Prince Rainier will most likely be present during part of the filmmaking depending on his schedule and that Princess Grace will return to Monaco with her family in November."

One of those to almost immediately congratulate Prince Rainier on his decision to allow Grace to make the movie was Father Francis Tucker. At first, the priest was concerned as to why the Prince hadn't discussed the matter with him in advance. It made him feel less necessary in the Prince's life that such an important matter had not crossed his desk. Even if only for a moment, it was never good in the sometimes insecure relationship the two shared for either of them to feel unnecessary in the other's life. However, after Rainier explained his reasoning, his chaplain agreed that he had made the right decision to keep him out of it. The priest would surely have been obligated to at least try to change his mind about the movie, as would have been his duty as a representative of the church.

In a letter to "My Dear Lord Prince," dated March 20, 1962, Tucker wrote, "I am the more grateful to Your Highness for sparing me any and all direct intervention in the decision that might have provoked upon me an increase of scorn and contempt from the unmerciful."

As it happened, Father Tucker did have his hands full with the Vatican. The church came down hard on him regarding *Marnie*, making his life a misery of arguments about Grace's return to films. There wasn't much he could do about it, Tucker told the church representatives, explaining that the Prince and Princess didn't solicit his advice, and that if they had, he would certainly have relayed the church's point of view—but they didn't. In a letter to one of his superiors, Archbishop O'Connor, Tucker explained that the decision to make the Hitchcock movie was made during his stay in America for his fiftieth anniversary, "extending from October 1, 1961, to January 21, 1962." (Actually, the decision was made after January 21.) He also explained that the choice wasn't shared with him until after the press release was disseminated, and that he then learned from Rainier that "it was a joint decision taken in family counsel, and considered by them a strictly family affair." Boldly, Tucker further stated that he was actually "happy" that Rainier hadn't consulted him.

With the news ricocheting around the world, Grace's friends in the States were elated for her. Rita Gam was one of the first to call. She recalled that Grace's voice sounded like a schoolgirl's.

"How will it be for you, going back to work?" Rita asked.

Grace thought about the question for a moment. "Probably a little strange, at first," she said. "But, oh Rita, I honestly can't wait another second!" The Princess then laughed gaily, unable to hide her excitement.

The reaction from Rainier's friends and family was less enthusiastic. Thomas Sartre recalled, "Even Prince Pierre, who was terminally ill at the time, was unhappy about it, and he liked Grace.*

"I also remember that the Prince's mother called, upset," continued Sartre. "I spoke to her myself. 'How could you allow this to happen?' she asked, as if I had had some input in the Princess's final decision. 'Princess Grace, an actress? How revolting,' she said, as if the Princess had never acted a day in her life. 'I always knew she would not amount to much,' she said. On and on she went. She kept saying, '*C'est une Américaine*,' meaning, 'Well, she's an American, what can you expect?'

"Finally, the Prince got on the phone to speak to her. I remember him standing there holding the telephone about six inches from his ear as he spoke loudly. Rainier actually was a funny person. I can

---

*A letter from Father Tucker to his brother Joe confirms Pierre's dissatisfaction: "I have never seen Grace and Rainier more loving and devoted to one another than they are now. Of course the SNOBS such as Pierre de Polignac and Co. are shocked. And all the while, what Antoinette is performing in 'REAL' not 'reel' life is perfectly acceptable." Tucker was probably referring to Rainier's sister's ongoing antics of stirring up trouble.

still see him rolling his eyes and, with his free hand, making wild snapping gestures, as if to say that his mother was yakking on and on and on. I remember on his private office door, he had a sign that said, 'I would like to help you out. Which way did you come in?' That was the kind of person he was."

"How Dare They Do This to Me?"

Because it was obvious that Princess Grace's reemergence as an actress would be controversial, one would have thought that the press release and public relations that surrounded the announcement would have been handled with the utmost caution. However, this was not the case. The press release issued from the Palace was actually disconcerting, because it did not address obvious vital questions, such as how much the Princess would be paid for her services, and what she intended to do with the money. One would have thought that Rainier would have approved the release before it was distributed to the press. However, as he indicated to Thomas Sartre, he left the matter in Grace's hands. As soon as the release was issued, there was an immediate uprising from the subjects of Monaco, as well as the press, against the notion of Princess Grace appearing in any movie.

For some reason, Grace felt—and Rainier agreed—that making it clear in the press release that production would take place during the Grimaldis' so-called vacation would somehow placate the Monegasques. "Hitchcock gave his assurance that he could easily fit all the location and studio shots in which the Princess would have to appear into the two months in which we had already said we were going to be in the States, so I didn't see how anybody could be upset," Rainier later explained. "And I honestly didn't think so.

I even said that we could take a couple of servants with us. [I told her,] 'We can find a nice house, and not have to live in hotels, and so long as it's just for our holiday, I don't think it can go over badly. You'll be working with somebody who is very nice, he has a good name, and he makes interesting films. Let's do it.' If it had been a super-duper big production, I wouldn't have said the same thing, but this was merely a sort of fun enterprise."

That they thought it would make any difference to their subjects that the movie was being made during Grace's vacation demonstrates how much the Grimaldis had misjudged the situation. Also, contrary to what the Prince may have told himself about the project to reason it out in his mind, Alfred Hitchcock would most certainly not have produced anything other than a "super-duper big production" at this time in his career.

To the Monegasques, it seemed demeaning for their Princess to be making a movie—whether while on vacation or not—and it also appeared to some observers that Grace's decision was based on a "seven-year-itch" of unhappiness in Monaco. Would she be leaving the principality after the movie was made, in order to make other films? Would she divorce Rainier? The response from the Monegasques was loud and clear: Her Serene Highness should most certainly not appear in any upcoming movie.

What many didn't realize at that time was that Grace had been hiding from the public the state of her own emotional health. It had taken far more courage to make the decision to do *Marnie*, because she had been struggling to resurface from what she would later call her "darkest days." After finally making the decision, she was completely blindsided by the furor over her impending return to the big screen. It hit her hard. "The Princess is shocked beyond all measure," George Lukomski, not only the Palace photographer, but also a close aide to Rainier, said at the time. "She has been in grave danger of breaking down."

It appeared that what little energy she did have, Grace had been devoting to the coordination of her comeback. As a result, her physical health had suffered. "She was just pushing food around her plate during meals, she wasn't eating," said a Palace employee. "You could tell from looking at her that she was withering away. She also complained of sleeping problems."

The anxiety brought on by indecision about *Marnie* had been almost more than Grace could bear. Therefore, when she got word of the civil unrest that followed her announcement, the Princess collapsed. Had she been in better emotional and physical condition, she certainly would have handled the situation with more aplomb. A carefully worded press release would have been prepared addressing the concerns of her people, and, if well received, her trip to Hollywood would have gone on as planned. Yet her reaction to such an outcry from the Monegasques, as overreactive as it may have been, left her immobile. Distraught, she entered her chamber, turned the heavy gold key in the door, and refused to see anyone. Throughout that day, and into the evening, attempts were made to get her to answer the questions that were now swirling about Monaco. One senior employee of the Palace's press office (Centre de Presse) spoke to her from the other side of her door: "Please, ma'am, tell us what to say. Our phones are ringing off the hook. We can't just remain silent."

After a moment, the heavy bolt in the door echoed through the cavernous hallway, and a disheveled Grace peered out. "You can and you will remain silent. Tell everyone in the press office to go home early." Then, almost as an afterthought, she added, "And they can take tomorrow off as well."

As the Princess had instructed, the door to the press office stayed locked the following day, and all calls regarding her comeback plans went unanswered. Because no clarification was forthcoming regarding *Marnie,* the media invented its own "spin" on the story of Grace's sudden return to films. Reporters took to the streets of Monaco to ask the Monegasques what they thought of her decision, and the public's confused opinions then became the fabric for negative stories about the movie project. By the next morning, Grace was still in self-imposed exile when Rupert Allan, who was in Monaco to assist her with the *Marnie* press, folded the front page of a local newspaper and slid it under the door of Grace's room.

"Your people have spoken," he said to Grace through the massive door. After a moment, she allowed him entrance. According to his memory, she wore a mint green silk nightgown, her hair tied in a matching turban. "She walked directly to the window as I entered," he recalled, "keeping her back to me."

Allan picked up the tear page he had slid under the door. The headline and story implied that Grace's intentions were to leave Monaco permanently. "May I ask why you're so upset? Is there any truth to this?" he asked her.

Grace remained silent as she gazed out to the sea.

"I'm asking as a friend," he pushed. "Are you planning something? Off the record."

"Silly Rupert," Grace said, sounding bitter. "When will you understand? Nothing is off the record."

Allan began to protest, miffed by the implication that those around her, including himself, were less than trustworthy. "If I were less loyal, Princess, I might say 'How dare you?'"

"How dare *I*?" She spun and faced him. "How dare *they*? How dare they do this to me?" she said, pointing to the paper in Allan's hand. She asked him to leave. As he started out, Grace added in a sarcastic tone, "In the future I'll require no questions from you as a *friend*. My private intentions are of no concern to you."

"I just thought we had become close. You would be missed, Princess, if you were to take your leave."

"Sadly, that is a luxury unavailable to me."

Years later, Rupert Allan recalled, "I didn't quite understand what she meant at that time. She said to me, 'Do you suppose I'll ever be allowed to take one step without someone asking me where my tenth step will be?' I told her that the public asks questions, that it was a simple fact. She responded, 'And they expect those of note to have answers. But sometimes we have none. Sometimes there are only more questions in the place answers should be.'"

Princess Grace appeared to Rupert Allan to be on the verge of tears. After he attempted to console her, she apologized for having been so short with him and then asked to be left alone.

"The Sound of Hope, Dying"

Without any help from the Princess herself, the Centre de Presse augmented her original press release, clarifying that the $800,000 fee she would receive for appearing in *Marnie* would be donated to a charity for deprived Monegasque children and athletes. George Lukomski was charged with the responsibility of reporting to the Princess just how the people of Monaco were reacting to the releases. The news, he told Grace, "is not at all good, ma'am." When he outlined for her all the drama that had resulted from her announcement, Grace was all the more discouraged.

The despair that the Princess had fallen into was deep. While the *Marnie* project itself seemed to be unraveling, those close to Grace tried to rally her to action.

Princess Ghislaine, who considered herself a master of problem-solving when it came to the press, insisted on seeing Grace. Bettina Campbell says, "As I understand it, Ghislaine told Grace, 'Oh, screw the Monegasques. How dare they? Why, you are Princess Grace! Live your life as you choose.' Of course, Ghislaine had always lived her life the way *she* chose, which is how she was able to marry Prince Louis when she was forty-six and he was seventy-six! She told Grace, 'Public relations, my dear. This is all a matter of public relations. You can set this straight.'"

Grace, however, had given up the fight. The decision was made: Rather than participate in any "damage control," the Princess would let it go. Grace summoned a trusted reporter from *Nice Matin* and arranged for an interview to tell him—and her subjects—that she had decided against the movie. "I have been very influenced by the reaction which the announcement provoked in Monaco," she said, understating the impact of the Monegasques on her future. For both Grace and Rainier, it was now clear that there was no going back—Grace's glory days as an actress were over. Bettina Campbell says that after the reporter left, Grace apparently gave in to an emotional moment and broke a canvas over the corner of her desk in the library. Bettina later retrieved the broken artwork, a painting of a bird soaring high above a seashore. In the bottom corner were painted the initials "G.M." (Grace de Monaco).

That Grace had always hoped to return to Hollywood one day and make the occasional film may have been what motivated her to play the role of Princess with even greater stamina and enthusiasm. She believed that the more she gave of herself to the principality, the more it would give back to her in return. Many of her critics believed that her preoccupation with possibly returning to filmmaking—as unrealistic as it may have been—kept her from fully committing to Monaco.

Now the principality had effectively disabused Grace Kelly of her hopes. Any potential return to Hollywood was frowned upon and discouraged, and with an intransigence that seemed to leave little room for a compromise. The decision she had made of her own free will had now seemingly led her into a circumstance without choices. The realization was a major blow for Grace, a person used to choosing, to making her own decisions—a woman who had told former boyfriend Oleg Cassini that she had "made" her destiny. Distraught, she confined herself to a guest room.

Not surprisingly, Prince Rainier turned to Father Tucker for advice as to how he might help Grace handle the crushing disappointment. Tucker told him that he would have to be patient and focus on giving her more support and encouragement than ever before. He also promised to pray with Grace and to commiserate with her as much as possible. Tucker had been a source of strength for her ever since she moved into the Palace, living up to the promise he had made her father when she first moved to Monaco. However, at this time, Grace wasn't open to his comfort. She didn't want to share her disappointment with him, or with anyone else. "We can only pray for her," Tucker finally told Rainier, according to a later recollection. "This is a personal issue for her . . . it had to happen."

Father Tucker viewed Grace's turmoil as an inevitable turn of events in her life. During a long-distance telephone call with Father James McGinnis, a clergy friend of his in Delaware, he expressed his belief that *Marnie* presented Grace with a necessary, life-changing spiritual conflict between her past and her present; between who she had been and who she had become. Tucker had always believed that her nostalgia for the past would lead her one day to stoke a confrontation with the principality by attempting a return to Hollywood. If she was refused, as he knew she would be, the question for her would be whether or not she trusted that the "Highest Good," as he called it, had delivered the new terms of her life, and that she should capitulate to them as "God's will," whatever the outcome; or whether she should persevere, in the Kelly family tradition, and find some way to make her return to acting, despite the protestations of her subjects.

If indeed Grace was enduring the inner struggle described by Father Tucker, it didn't take her long to surrender once the reaction to *Marnie* was clearly a negative one. "It's what I would have advised, had she asked me," Tucker told his colleague. In Tucker's view, such a personal conflict could only result in good anyway, not only for Princess Grace but also for the often troubled principality she served. Father James McGinnis, who is now retired, recalled, "Father Tucker believed that once the Princess won the battle, she would finally be able to devote herself entirely to her work in Monaco. 'Never again would she ever have to wonder if she should, or could, make another movie,' he said. 'Never again would her career have such pull at her.'"

Though it may sound as if Father Tucker's loyalty was with Monaco and not with its Princess, he actually *was* considering her best interest. After all, he knew she was never to leave Monaco— not with her children, anyway. She was probably going to live in the principality for the rest of her life. Should she spend those years in misery, wondering what might have been? In Tucker's view—and it was shared by Father James McGinnis, who also knew Grace and Rainier—the sooner she relented and completely devoted herself to her family and her work as Princess, the better off she would be.

Tucker's "boy" Rainier needed Grace's support now more than ever, in light of the ongoing political crises faced by Monaco. To abandon her career aspirations, once and for all, would be a supreme sacrifice for Grace, both priests agreed. "However, it was her choice to make. She made it. Now she would have to find a way to live with it. That was Father Tucker's opinion," said Tucker's friend. "It's the only thing she could have done at that point."

"Honestly, we have never seen her like this," Rainier told a friend of Grace's, Antoinette Brucatto, widow of an Italian shipping magnate. Antoinette recalled, "I first met the Princess shortly after she arrived in the principality. She was so alive, so excited about the future. She and I often had lunch at the Palace to discuss our work with various charities in Monaco. It would be stretching it to say that we were friends, though we later did become closer. Never once had I said more than two words to Rainier; he was distant to me, cold. However, when I telephoned the Palace to talk to Grace about a Red Cross dinner, he came on the line."

"Do you know about the movie?" Rainier asked Antoinette. Antoinette said she had heard from a televised news report that Grace had changed her mind about making the film. "Well, you are one of Grace's dearest friends," he said, his voice strained. "What do you suggest we do? She is so upset, she won't talk to me. She won't see the children."

"Give her time," Antoinette advised Rainier. She said that she believed Grace would be fine. "After all, Princess Grace is so strong."

Rainier and Antoinette then had a brief conversation about Grace's depression, and how difficult the previous couple of months had been for her. He suggested that she call again in a few days. Perhaps she could speak to Grace at that time.

"When I hung up, I was drained," she said. "After just ten minutes on the phone with the Prince, I realized how desperate things were there for her. For days afterward, I kept hearing his voice in my head saying, 'She won't see the children.'

"My image of Princess Grace was that she was controlled and powerful, so to hear of this desperate situation from His Highness was more than I could take. I kept asking myself, how did this happen to her? She had it all, she had the world. How did this happen?"

Most of Grace's closer friends shared Antoinette Brucatto's sense of apprehension about her future. A confidante, who was a member of her wedding party so many years earlier, recalled telephoning Grace after the announcement, and actually speaking to her about it. She said that Grace sounded brave, as if she realized that she had made the only choice possible. "In the back of my mind, maybe hers as well, there was the thought that circumstances would present Grace with another opportunity to act again at a later date. But underneath I heard something in Gracie's voice I had never heard before." The confidante said there was only one way to describe what she heard in Grace's voice: "It was the sound of hope, dying."

A Crisis in Monaco

At the time of the announcement of Grace Kelly's impending return to feature films, Prince Rainier III found himself immersed in a tangle of serious governmental matters. If he had been able to focus his energy entirely on the public relations problems of Grace's announcement, no doubt certain troubles would have been avoided in the process. However, the timing for Grace's reemergence as an actress couldn't have been more unfortunate, not only for her husband but for every Monegasque in the principality—or at least that's how it seemed at the time.

It had always been the Prince's intention to modernize Monaco, to see it grow and prosper, no matter the expense. After he abolished the Council that had presented so much opposition to his plans (thereby creating space for a new and, hopefully, friendlier, one), Rainier's vision for Monaco finally began to take full form. He still had strong opposition on a daily basis—he had grown accustomed to never having, as he put it, "a peaceful moment"—but as Monaco began to grow and thrive, so did public confidence and trust in its Prince. Soon, hundreds of businesses began relocating to the principality, taking residence in the high-rise structures Rainier had built ("growing upward, not outward"). Rainier was satisfied, though his critics felt that Monaco looked increasingly like Manhattan. Even Grace said she could barely stand to leave the Palace. Years earlier, she had complained that Monaco was "like taking all of the city of New York and squeezing it onto the head of a knitting needle." By 1962, it was certainly more crowded than it was in 1956 when she had offered such a critical assessment.

The fact that there was no taxation in Monaco made it an attractive locale for foreign enterprise, with American, British, Italian, German, and Spanish businesses booming in the hills behind Monaco's picturesque coastline. Employment in the principality was at an all-time high; life was good. It was during this time of prosperity that Prince Rainier felt he could relax for a moment and focus some attention on his wife's unhappiness. However, by the time the solution to her problems began to surface—the Alfred Hitchcock film *Marnie*—so did the first major challenge to Monaco's sovereignty and independence in more than a century.

France had joined the rest of the world in relocating more than fifty businesses to Monaco, much to the dismay of Charles de Gaulle, who was deeply concerned about the loss of revenue in his own country. According to the 1918 treaty, Monaco was not to pose unfair fiscal competition to France. De Gaulle decided not to force the matter with Rainier, until the Prince took a stand against France's huge stock investment in Radio Monte Carlo. Concerned that he could lose control of Monaco's media enterprise to France, Rainier suddenly banned trading of Radio Monte Carlo on the Paris stock exchange. De Gaulle was incensed by Rainier's surprising move. Why, he asked, was it appropriate for Monaco to compete with France for corporate business dollars, yet unfair for France to compete with Monaco for control of a powerful communication enterprise?

At de Gaulle's insistence, Monaco's French Minister of State, Emile Pelletier, demanded that Rainier rescind the trade suspension. Not only did Rainier refuse, he fired Pelletier. "He was highly salaried by the Monegasque government and supposed to have the welfare of the principality at heart," Rainier explained years later. "I thought that he ought to resign, and I told him so. The result was that he went to Paris and said that I was anti-French and that I had spoken anti-French words, which I certainly had not done. This added fuel to a situation that was already smoldering because the French demands were quite disagreeable and menacing, particularly for the French people established in Monaco."

De Gaulle took swift action, retaliating in a way he knew would most impact Monaco: He declared that the principality had only six months (until October 11, 1962) to restructure its government to include resident and corporate taxation, the proceeds of which would be paid to France. Word was passed down that if Rainier refused, France would probably cut off its supply of water, power, and gas to Monaco. "The French," wrote Sam White in France's the *Evening Standard,* "can asphyxiate the Principality in a matter of minutes."

Not only did de Gaulle's action take Prince Rainier by surprise, it put him in a precarious position. After all, the major reason for Monaco's unique hold on new business enterprise was the absence of taxation in the principality. Without that perk, the principality was just another sunny European gambling resort. Moreover, if Rainier gave in to de Gaulle's demands, his subjects were sure to face serious hardships. No doubt, a carefree existence for Monegasques would be a thing of the past. Again, Rainier was faced with the question of who, as his wife put it, was "boss." This time, it wasn't the Prince against his own Council, but rather against an even more formidable foe: Charles de Gaulle. "I have great faith in my husband's ability to solve this situation," Princess Grace said in a statement. "I have met General de Gaulle, and I cannot believe that he will be unreasonable in the days ahead."

After praying about the matter with Father Tucker for more than an hour, the Prince finally decided he had no choice but to change his mind about the ban on trading, much as he loathed doing it.[*] He then wrote to de Gaulle to reaffirm his allegiance to France. However, de Gaulle did not back down from his intention to force taxation in Monaco. It was time, Rainier decided, for all Monegasques to unite against the threat now posed by France. As often happens in difficult times, factions that once opposed each other found it easy to work together against a common enemy. Rainier reestablished the National Council with a new election, deciding that if he had to work with his opponents, he would do so. Internal strife, after all, was preferable to the loss of freedom proposed by de Gaulle. Rainier also promised a new constitution that would limit certain of his powers.

The most bitter pill for Rainier to swallow, however, was that, along with all of the other concessions, he had to once again embrace his traitorous sister, Princess Antoinette, in order to present a united front to the world. Also, her husband, Jean-Charles Rey, would have to return to his powerful position on the new National Council. This was difficult; Rainier had ambivalent feelings about his sister and Rey, for obvious reasons. Grace, who three years earlier had been the one to give the news to Antoinette that she and her family were being ostracized, was also not eager to see her again. However, Grace, as a Kelly family member and also a showbiz veteran, fully understood the importance of public relations. Though she agreed with the Prince that their lives had been easier without Antoinette present, she encouraged him that he must now at least act as if he was reconciling with her and Jean-Charles. "Think of how it looks, this sister of yours and her husband not even being allowed to visit the Palace," she said, according to one source close to the family. "I don't like it any more than you do, Rainier, but we must do what we must do."

---

[*]"That Father Tucker was involved as a senior adviser on matters diplomatic and political is certain," noted his nephew Joseph A. Tucker, Jr. "He may have reached the peak of his influence during those years."

Begrudgingly, Rainier agreed, and Tiny's banishment was suspended, as was her husband's. The awkward reconciliation took place when Antoinette and Jean-Charles invited Rainier and Grace to dinner at their estate in Merez. According to Christian de Massy, who was present, "Rainier succeeded in disguising his true feelings; even his Oscar-winning wife couldn't have matched the performance he gave that night. He shook hands with Rey, embraced my mother, and hugged us with all of the affection we had remembered from his visits to our garden long ago. [Grace] took my mother's hand, and Rey's, without any definable expression crossing her face. Mummy went mechanically through her movements of reception and welcome. Rey did not cease bragging and striding about, excessively jovial and false. It was absurd."

The meal went as well as could be expected; Tiny and her husband were back in the royal picture. However, neither would actually live at the Palace, nor maintain quarters there, as had once been the case. Rather, they were permitted to just visit, if they called in advance—no dropping in, as in the past. Also, they were allowed to once again attend important state functions.

Even though Jean-Charles Rey and the other members of Rainier's new National Council attempted to negotiate with France, the impasse still existed—and worsened. French customs officials were stationed along Monaco's borders to pester tourists with red tape and technicalities, thereby discouraging visitors to the principality. Panic spread throughout the land, with rumors that French battleships might pull up to the emerald harbor and start shooting away, or that de Gaulle might even drop a bomb on the principality. There was talk that someone sighted a troop of battle parachutists descending into the casino square—untrue, of course. "Our problems with the French government are not being solved easily," Grace wrote to Prudy Wise, "so they may enclose Monaco with barbed wire tomorrow."

Thanks to the ascension of Grace Kelly to its throne, Monaco was no longer a place about which few people knew or cared. Because the world's press covered with great interest Rainier's conflicts with de Gaulle, nations became divided in opinions about the controversy, with most—including America—siding with Monaco. De Gaulle realized that he wasn't courting much favor with the world's superpowers by letting the threat linger that he might drop a bomb on Princess Grace Kelly. There were even rumors that one of the reasons Grace was making *Marnie* was to snub de Gaulle and make a demonstration of Monaco's independence. Perhaps she was also hoping to raise money for Monaco as well, reported the media.

De Gaulle eventually relented and offered Rainier a compromise: Only those businesses that had relocated from France to Monaco in recent years would be levied, thereby freeing all resident Monegasques and longtime businessmen from sudden taxation. Because Monaco would maintain its autonomy, the agreement was viewed as a clear-cut victory for Prince Rainier III, and his performance during this time is still viewed as one of his best moments.

At this same time in 1962, a new Monaco constitution was approved, establishing a separation of powers between the executive, legislature, and judiciary under the aegis of a constitutional monarchy. The Grimaldi family's sovereignty was confirmed, but the new Council would have even more governing power than it previously held.

Grace's Tortured Inner Life

In June 1962, a few months after she made her difficult decision about *Marnie*, Grace Kelly wrote to Alfred Hitchcock telling him that "it was heartbreaking for me to have to leave the picture." She said that she had been "excited" about working with him again, and she hoped to explain all of the reasons for her decision when next they met. She closed by saying it was "unfortunate" that matters worked out as they had, and she was "very sorry." In turn, Hitchcock wrote to her and told her that, in his view, she had no choice but to "put the project aside," that she had made "the best decision. After all," he concluded, "it was only a movie."

Perhaps fate was on Grace's side when it came to her return to movies. From the beginning, things went badly for Tippi Hedren, the actress who replaced Grace in *Marnie*. Before she even began work on it, Hitchcock sent her then five-year-old daughter, Melanie Griffith (now a famous actress in her own right), an expensive miniature doll of Tippi dressed as she had been in her recent Hitchcock film, *The Birds*. Most disconcerting was that the doll was in a small pine casket, a ghoulish gesture that was a harbinger of things to come for Tippi Hedren.

During production of *Marnie*, Alfred had a dressing trailer designed for Tippi with a ramp that led to his private office, so he could have private access to his star. He then began a persistent campaign of romantic overtures toward her, even though she was engaged to be married at the time. She asked that he back off. Hitchcock, married himself, was at first dismayed, then hurt, and finally, angry. He told studio executives that he couldn't understand how Tippi could reject him—except if she was incapable of physical intimacy with a man, like the character she was playing in his movie. He even sent Hedren's handwriting to a graphologist to look for evidence of such frigidity. It was downhill from there for Tippi as the emotional abuse from Alfred continued unchecked, culminating with a sexual proposition to her in her dressing room, which she rejected.

Of course, it can't be assumed that Grace Kelly would have suffered the same fate on *Marnie* as Tippi Hedren. Grace was a much bigger star than Tippi and probably wouldn't have put up with as much from him, nor would he likely have dished out as much.

It's also interesting that Hitchcock didn't seem particularly disappointed about losing Grace as the star of *Marnie*. In fact, many a film historian has wondered why he wasn't absolutely infuriated. After all, it would have been in his volatile character to have been outraged by the chain of events that had led to Grace's pulling out of the film. In truth, just as Grace had sensed that something was amiss with Alfred's personality when he visited the Palace to discuss the movie, he found something to be not quite right about her as well.

When Hitchcock returned to the States, he told trusted friends that Grace seemed bored. Hedren recalled, "He thought that she did not have much mental stimulation there, the activity that she was used to, and that it was hurting her emotionally."

Alfred also said that, in his view, Grace had lost her "warmth." One of the reasons he had always been so intrigued by her as a woman and an actress was because of the sexual heat so evident beneath her cool exterior. It was that paradox of personality that had always made Grace Kelly so compelling a screen star. However, when Alfred saw the "new" Grace in Monaco—*Princess* Grace—all he sensed of her was the chill, with none of the warmth. Grace had changed. By 1962, she was much more inaccessible, even to friends, than ever in the past. Most of her intimates and family members reasoned that her unusually frosty demeanor was a guise she had adopted as a result of her royal position. They laughed about her aristocratic air, figuring that if she was a true Princess she should act like one—and she was certainly doing that.

"She actually studied for it," Rita Gam told one of Grace's biographers, Robert Lacey. "She went to the library and got out the books on Queen Victoria. She studied English royalty. She studied the hairdos of power—big hairdos, with hairpieces and so on. If you are the tallest, you are the biggest. It was a calculated observation on her part. She studied the pictures and she did it." When writer Joyce Winslow interviewed Grace, she noted of her encounter with her, "She is seated in a way that allows her face to fit perfectly into the space left among the family portraits on the wall behind her. Such attention to detail characterizes her reign."

Still, it bothered many people that Grace wasn't the same person she had once been. Yes, she had always been a society girl, a little snobbish at times. However, when one knew her well, she was anything but chilly. Rather, she had been easy to know, eager to share. She was funny, happy . . . optimistic. However, that was the "old" Gracie. The "new" one—Princess Grace—was nothing like that. Those friends who thought about it—mostly her New York confidantes—realized that Grace Kelly had built a wall around herself out of fear. She was trying desperately to steel herself against the intimidating circumstances of a position for which she felt unqualified.

Moreover, day after day of feeling unhappy and unfulfilled can change a person, and it did change Grace Kelly. She had become distant, not the same woman. Her friends and family members noticed it. She was still Gracie . . . but not really. "There was a sadness about her during this time, a distance in her eyes, a wariness," said her sister Lizanne. "It was as if she didn't want anyone to get too close, or she would break down."

Grace had spent years accommodating everyone and everything else in her life, all at the expense of her own needs. She had suspended her deepest desires, placing her husband, her children, her subjects first. Now she seemed depleted and, yes, even angry. However, she was still her mother's daughter—so, appearances mattered. "When I hugged her good-bye, she pulled away quickly, as if she knew that to remain too long in my arms would mean she would break down into a hopeless heap," said one friend of hers from New York. "She could be relentlessly cheery at times, to the point that you knew it wasn't real. Then she could become quite sullen. My God, I thought, what is happening to her?"

"I ran into her while getting my hair done by a beautician at the Hôtel de Paris, where Grace also got her hair styled," said Antoinette Brucatto. "She was a different person, distracted. She seemed drained, robbed of her life force. When I started talking about a benefit I was planning, she snapped at me. 'Oh, for goodness' sake, Antoinette, don't bore me with the details. I'll be there, all right? Isn't that enough?' Then she reached into her purse, pulled out a French-language textbook and began studying it, completely ignoring me."

No one had expected this Monaco fairy tale to turn out the way it did, least of all its principal characters, Rainier and Grace. By the end of 1962, Rainier couldn't help but notice the significant changes in his wife. While she would sometimes complain that he was no longer the man she married, he could have offered a similar appraisal of her as not being the same person she was the morning she walked down the aisle to meet him at the altar in 1956. He didn't dare, at least not in the presence of any witnesses. After all, he knew that he was at least partly responsible for any change in Grace's personality. It pained him to see what had happened to the woman who had entrusted him with her happiness, her peace of mind, her life. The way Grace now acted around the Palace suggested that she had something she had never had before—a tortured inner life.

One day, as Father Tucker once remembered it, he and Rainier were in the private residence library, discussing the matter in the charming room filled with photos of generations of Grimaldis, as well as of the current Serene Highnesses and their two children. In the center of the library was a large round table upon which were stacks of magazines, piles of books, opened and unopened boxes, small toys, stuffed animals, "and a big mess, much like the library always was," Tucker said. "On either side of the library was a desk, one for Him and one for Her, upon which they conducted much of their daily personal business, such as answering mail."

"I wonder if we did the right thing bringing her over here," Rainier said, while rummaging through the boxes on the table. "I can't say the Princess has been happy a single day, except when being a mother to the children."

Rainier found what he was looking for, a small box. "This is a gift for Grace," he said while opening it. He pulled from it a diamond bracelet. "Perhaps this will make her happy. I don't know . . ."

Father Tucker told the Prince that it had been Grace's choice to come to Monaco, and that it had been the right choice. "We didn't force her," he said according to his recollection. "God brought her to us. God makes no mistakes."

While the well-meaning priest's words may have temporarily calmed Prince Rainier's apprehension about his beloved wife's state of mind, His Highness must have known the truth: While God does not make mistakes, people often do.

Grace couldn't very well change her mind about her marriage now, could she? Divorce would mean losing her children. Such was the law of the land, as it had been for centuries. It wasn't going to change, not then or ever, and she knew as much when she signed the marriage agreement with Rainier in 1956.

Moreover, if Grace were to actually be bold enough to leave the principality, and heartless enough to leave her children behind just so she could make movies in Hollywood, how would the world react to such a decision? It would take a genius of a publicist to turn that particular scenario around to her PR advantage.

No, for Grace Kelly, actress, it was over. Now, as Grace de Monaco, she was just as imprisoned as any of the many birds in the Palace. Yet her entrapment had a more torturous element to it. She was her own warden. She had the ability to stray at will—and she could venture just far enough from her gilded cage to see what she was missing.

Father Tucker Leaves the Palace

Few people were as important to Prince Rainier III and Princess Grace as Father Francis Tucker, the trusted chaplain who had been present for them whenever spiritual counsel was necessary—which had been on many occasions, especially recently. For twelve years, Father Tucker had celebrated Mass every morning, offering the Prince and, after she came to Monaco, the Princess, Holy Communion at the Palace and even at their Roc Agel country home. He was a wonderful man, a valued friend to Rainier, and especially after the death of her father, a confidant of Grace's as well. It was inconceivable to them that Tucker might one day leave the principality, but the reality was that by July of 1962 he was seventy-three years old, and ready to move on. In his view, the way the Prince had supported his wife during the difficult *Marnie* incident was proof that the couple could make it without him. As Grace recovered from her depression, Father Tucker wanted any comfort she might seek to be found in the arms of her husband. He realized that as long as he was there to console and counsel them, the Prince and Princess might not be as likely to cling to each other during times of trouble, as he felt they should. He also believed that Rainier and Grace now deserved a younger chaplain, one who could travel with them with greater ease. Tucker had suffered from a number of health challenges in recent years, which made traveling difficult for him.

Moreover, a breach in protocol also prodded Father Tucker along in his decision to leave Monaco. Charles de Gaulle of France had often complained about the influence of so many Americans over Prince Rainier, a grievance Rainier thought to be preposterous and that had never mattered much to anyone at the Palace—except to Father Tucker, who, despite his bravado, was sensitive to such disapproval (especially as he got older). Father Tucker told his brother Joe that when de Gaulle did not invite him to an important political function to which he felt sure he should have been invited, he took it as a sign of disrespect. Though de Gaulle's slight was viewed as a minor incident by most observers, it was apparently the catalyst for Father Tucker's decision. On May 1, 1962, Prince Rainier received written word from the priest that he planned to resign. Though he tried to convince Tucker to change his mind, he was not successful. Grace also did her best, but to no avail.

Father James McGinnis recalled, "Francis called me to tell me that he had decided to leave Monaco. Though there was a lot of red tape involved with the church and the Palace in relieving him of his pastorate, eventually he was cleared to go. However, he said that the Prince and Princess were not happy with his decision. 'I have never disappointed them before, but now I'm afraid I must,' he said. I believed then that he was having some health issues that he wasn't sharing with anyone. Leaving the Palace was something I thought he'd never do. I thought he'd die there, actually."

On June 1, while the Prince and Princess were on vacation with their children, Father Tucker slipped out of Monaco and headed to

Rome. He later said that he couldn't bear to say good-bye to them. A month later, Rainier received a letter from the priest, which concluded with, "my departure cannot sever the ties that bind me to Monaco's Cathedral—and, may I add, much less those that bind me to Monaco's Prince!"

Prince Rainier took Father Tucker's departure badly, becoming severely depressed over it for a number of weeks, not even wanting to play squash in the morning, which he had done every day for years. After all, the priest had been a father figure to him in many ways, and had certainly been more present in his life in terms of emotional support than his own father, Prince Pierre. He had been chiefly responsible for instigating the marriage to Grace, and had acted as his confessor during countless personal and political crises. "I know that all things must change," Rainier told publicist Thomas Sartre, "but this is a change that I never expected. I'm sick about it, I must say. It has brought forth in me a torrent of emotion I'm not used to dealing with."

A series of successors would replace Father Francis Tucker over the years, but none would ever come close to approximating the relationship the prelate shared with his "boy," Prince Rainier III, and his wife, Princess Grace. Sadly, it seems that after he was gone, jealous critics of the powerful American priest spread pernicious lies about him—untruths about why he left the Palace, published without substantiation in a 1994 Grace Kelly biography. In fact, after leaving the Palace, Father Tucker went on to serve as an adviser to the Second Vatican Council in Rome during a time when the church was undergoing great and important changes in its liturgy. He did return to Monaco twice—in January 1963 for the Feast of Sainte Devote (the patron saint of the principality), and then, finally, in November of that year to visit the Prince and Princess. "Leaving them that time almost killed him," said Father McGinnis. "It truly did. He was almost debilitated by grief; he loved them both so much. He called me from Rome and said that he nearly collapsed from emotion on the way out of the Palace."

In November of 1963, Father Francis Tucker finally returned to the United States to take on an assignment at the Villa Maria

Oblate Retreat House in Wernersville, Pennsylvania. The Retreat House had recently been purchased by the Wilmington Province of the Oblates; Father Tucker was assigned the role of director. He often served Mass at St. Anthony of Padua in Wilmington. "But his life was nothing as it had been when ministering to Rainier and Grace at the Palace," said Father McGinnis. "He told me often, 'I miss my boy.' Seven months later, Francis suffered a stroke and, though it was a small one, it hit him hard. He did manage to go to Rome and then Paris in the spring of 1966, but decided not to visit the Prince and Princess that time, saying he couldn't bear to see them again."

Father McGinnis further recalled, "After Francis left, Rainier called me to find out if he was coming to Monaco. When I told him that I seriously doubted it, the Prince was deeply disappointed. He said that the Princess had planned a dinner party in his honor and then, the next day, high tea in the Grande Salle à Manger. Rainier had told her it was not reasonable to expect a man of Francis's age to attend such functions at the Palace.

"The Princess then came on the line, seeming emotional, almost in tears. 'Why, if he's in Paris, so close to us, how can he not come to visit?' she asked me. 'Age has never stopped him from doing anything. I simply don't believe it. We must have done something to offend him!' The truth, I told her, was that it was just too emotionally hard on Father to see them again and then have to say good-bye. 'I understand that,' she finally told me, 'because it would be just as hard on me, and twice as hard on his boy [Rainier], who is already devastated.' Before hanging up, she said, 'Please tell Father to keep us in his prayers, just as we keep him in ours. The Palace is not the same without him,' she concluded, sadly, 'and neither are we.'"

Father Tucker would mark the sixtieth anniversary of his ordination in May 1971 with a Mass of Thanksgiving at St. Anthony's followed by a testimonial dinner attended by hundreds of guests, including the Bishop of Wilmington, the governor, the mayor, and Margaret Kelly, representing her daughter and Prince Rainier III. Margaret was startled by Father Tucker's frailty. She telephoned

Grace at the Palace to tell her that she felt the priest didn't have long to live. A week later, Rainier telephoned Father Tucker at the Salesianum School in Wilmington, a religious nursing home in which he now lived. "They spoke for an hour," recalled Father McGinnis, "going over old times, as would any father and son. Joseph telephoned me later. 'My boy is a man now, isn't he?' he observed. 'My God, how the years have flown.'"

Father John Francis Tucker died on November 2, 1971, at the age of eighty-three—sixty-one of those years spent as a priest.

Coming to Terms

In the winter of 1962, Princess Grace wrote a letter to her friend Prudy Wise while in Schonried, Switzerland, where she was vacationing with the children and their governess. Rainier was unable to leave Monaco at the time, consumed by business. "I am so happy to be here," Grace wrote. She then described herself as being "completely worn out and falling apart." She wrote of "tummy troubles" and other ailments brought about by "stress and just being so fed-up."

The separation from Monaco and from Rainier was a relief to Grace. "I'm feeling that I can breathe for a moment," she told her children's governess, according to a later recollection. It may have been that sense of freedom and calm that prompted Grace to reach out for counsel. While it had always been Father Tucker who had been there to offer guidance, he was no longer at her service. The Princess had even put a call in to the Villa Maria Oblate Retreat House in Pennsylvania in hopes of locating him there. However, she was informed that Tucker was unavailable to speak with her.

She later told a friend that she believed he had chosen to avoid her call, possibly wanting her to solve her own problem.

If Tucker had advised Grace during her time away from Palace walls, he might have reminded her of her allegiance to the Prince and to the people of Monaco. He most certainly would have joined her in prayer. "It's the prayerful moments that allow our problems to flow through us," he had always said. While this was well-meaning and perhaps even good advice, it wasn't the kind of counsel Grace probably needed at this difficult time in her life. It's likely that she may have wanted more practical advice, considering her next move. She sought the help of someone else in Pennsylvania: one of the Kelly family's many attorneys.

After gaining assurance that their conversation would be held in the closest of confidence, Grace asked the lawyer to do some research for her. According to what this same attorney would recall more than thirty years later, she wanted clarification of the clause in her marriage agreement that referred to divorce and to proprietary right to the children.

"I'm just curious," she said, according to his memory. "No inferences need be drawn."

The Princess told the attorney that she would be staying in Switzerland for the next few weeks. "If you have not drawn any clear conclusions by the time I must return to Monaco, there's no need for you to contact me," she said. When she was asked to clarify her oblique statement, she responded sternly, "You may reach me here until February first. After that we will have no contact. Are we clear?"

As it happened, Grace's counsel did manage to get her the information she needed before his deadline. Only Grace could say how disappointing, if at all, she found the news. He told her that that the agreement was clear: If she chose to leave Rainier and Monaco, she would also have to leave her children. She would have no legal right to them, and, moreover, it was unclear as to what extent she would be able to enter and depart Monaco, should she leave her children there. It wasn't just a question of the marriage agreement with Rainier, he explained, it was also a matter of Monaco law: The heirs to the sovereign must be raised in the principality. There could be no exceptions.

According to his memory, Grace thanked him for his time; he thanked her for the opportunity to assist her. She said that she probably wouldn't be requiring further counsel. "You have been wonderful," she said. "You'll receive an envelope at your office that I'm sure will cover your time." When he protested, she added, "I insist. We should all be compensated. However, I must clarify that our business is done, and I'll thank you for your discretion."

When the Princess returned to Monaco, it soon became clear from her actions that she had decided to resign herself to her life there.

Never a woman who shied away from conflict, Grace sprang into action as soon as she walked into the Palace. According to what she later recalled to one of her New York girlfriends, she marched into her husband's office and made it clear that she had certain needs she now wanted him to meet. For instance, she wanted the ability to plan and take trips with the children, without his "permission." She also asked to have a stronger hand in the Palace's public relations. Most important to her, however, was that Rainier *listen* to her if she had a point of view she felt he should hear.

"She came here with fresh ideas and these were not necessarily the views I always had," Rainier later explained in retrospect. "Sometimes this caused difficulties. For example, there was a traditional way of holding a reception or giving a dinner which the head butler always followed. But the Princess had ideas that clashed with these routines. After all, my staff had never done a buffet in the Palace or arranged a dinner with small tables as she suggested instead of having the big table."

If she was to be the First Lady of the Palace, Grace decided, then, she should be allowed to have some latitude to do things as she wished, especially when it came to social matters. When important dinners were held Grace's way, with the Palace's gold-and-white china and polished antique silverware set carefully on individual tables covered by hand-embroidered damask tablecloths emblazoned by the family's coat of arms, they were always successful. She also suggested that lower-wattage bulbs be used in the chandeliers so that everyone would look "nicer," as she put it, "in better lighting." Rainier would find himself pleased by such ideas. "It turned out," he would say, "that hers *were* rather good concepts. They had just never occurred to me because I hadn't imagined anything changing."

On a more serious level, Rainier and Grace strongly disagreed about some of his ongoing programs to renovate Monaco. After having lived in the principality for a few years, Grace actually began to side with National Council officials that too much construction had the potential of jeopardizing the quaint charm of Monaco. It was naturally upsetting to the Prince that his own wife disagreed with him about missions that had been vital to him for so many years, and the fact that she agreed with the conservative National Council, people he thought of as adversarial, was sometimes more than he could bear. However, Grace wouldn't budge on her view. While she was in favor of the Prince's ambitious idea of building a railroad tunnel through Monaco, she was dead-set against his pet landfill project, intended to add acreage to the principality upon which would be built office and apartment buildings. (Her opposition to this idea was one of the only things she had in common with her sister-in-law, Antoinette, though it didn't bring them any closer.)

"Some construction, yes," Grace once said in front of friends at dinner when discussing the matter. "But I think you're going to ruin the principality's intrinsic beauty with too many high-rises, Rainier. You do need to think about this."* Rainier would become incensed when she questioned his programs, especially in front of others. In the end, however, he became indifferent to her. "Why, these are problems she knows nothing about," he said publicly to writer Douglas Keay. "Hers is an aesthetic point of view. I have to be more practical than that." If he would be so publicly dismissive

---

*When a plan was afoot to demolish the historic and grand Hôtel Hermitage, an architectural landmark, Grace led a coalition against the idea before Rainier even had a chance to have an opinion about it. "I threatened to nail myself to its door if they tried to raze it," she once said.

of Grace's opinion to a reporter, imagine what he might have been like when he and Grace privately discussed such issues. She wanted him to change that. While he might disagree with her, she told him, he should take her seriously and at least be more respectful of her views. Rainier did promise to give Grace's opinions a fair airing and, more importantly, not trivialize them.

"She also said that she wished to spend more time with Albert, and not allow him to only be influenced by Rainier as a parent," Charlotte Winston recalled. "Also, she said she would one day possibly wish to take an apartment in Paris and, if so, he should not stand in her way. Rainier was concerned about the possibility of such a thing occurring, but he let it go. Perhaps he felt he would deal with it if it ever came up. He didn't put up a fight on any count. Anything Grace wanted, he would give to her. He wanted her to be happy; that had always been his intention. She had now made up her mind about her future, and was simply, I think, laying the groundwork as to how it might work for her. Perhaps she was applying to her choice the old adage, 'If you can't beat 'em, may as well join 'em.'"

While Grace had certain needs she wanted met, Rainier also had a few—and this was as good a time as any, he decided, to air them. Indeed, as he himself put it years later, "Everyone's marriage is a series of concessions."

"It would mischaracterize it to say that Grace was the only one with requirements," Charlotte Winston clarified. "It was a give-and-take discussion. They talked as a husband and wife trying to make their marriage work. They talked about commitment, and what it meant to be a Princess, and how important it was that she, once and for all, come to terms with things in Monaco. He would give her whatever she wanted, yes. But in return she had to promise to at least *try* to give her all, to him, to Monaco, and to the idea of being happy with the choice she made."

One of the things Rainier had always most admired about Grace was the way she had gone about making a life for herself in New York and Hollywood, despite an obvious lack of parental support. Antoinette Brucatto confirmed, "He often said, 'No one did anything for Grace; she did it all herself.' He was proud of that, spoke of it often. Grace obviously had great imagination; she'd applied it to her life many times in the past. Rainier now wanted her to use that imagination to create a meaningful future for herself in Monaco.

"From my understanding, he told her it was time for her to now grow up, face her regrets if she had any, and deal with them," continued Brucatto. "I don't think he meant for it to be harsh. He just meant that we don't always have things our way. Sometimes, when you have no other choice, you have to find a middle road. It's a lonely life, being a royal, difficult enough without so many regrets about it."

Of course, Prince Rainier had been raised with the protocol he was trying to instill in Grace. For a man who was, by all accounts, the most sensitive and caring of the Grimaldis, the social isolation that came with being a royal was quite a price to pay. Yet he understood that without the aura of mystery that must surround a royal family, the monarchy was sure to die a certain death. Even Rainier has said, when recalling his own ascension to power as Prince Louis's heir in May 1949 at the age of twenty-nine, "It was not an especially joyous moment for me. It meant a severe change of style in my life." That statement came from a man who was destined to be Prince from the moment of his conception.

Now Princess Grace, a woman who had experienced the joys of a glamorous civilian life, was being asked to play an endless role— one that cut her off from the independence and the spontaneity in which she had once reveled. For her, this would prove to be an ongoing sacrifice, but one she would share with generations of royals around the world who had, for centuries, been forced to compromise their lives and personal desires precisely because they *were* royal. It wasn't as if they had any choice in the matter. They were born into service; it could not be avoided.

For instance, Grace's own mother-in-law, Princess Charlotte, suffered through an arranged marriage to Prince Pierre (Rainier's father). In 1933, she wrote to her father, Prince Louis, explaining why she wanted to dissolve that union. "At the risk of being a disappointment to your hopes and aspirations," she wrote, "I believe I have accomplished my duty [to have a Grimaldi heir] which condemned me to remain in a marriage against my wishes." Charlotte was able to leave her marriage because her children were not her priority. Rather, freeing herself from her husband was the important thing. In the course of her choice, she had to renounce all rights to the throne. Making matters more startling, as soon as she divorced Pierre, her father issued an order that his former son-in-law be barred from returning to Monaco. Palace guards were instructed to eject him should he enter the principality. Prince Rainier would often speak of the loss he felt in coming from a broken home, never really feeling the love of either parent.

Indeed, there were sometimes serious repercussions when marriages ended in the Grimaldi family, and Grace was aware of much of the bitter history. She couldn't—wouldn't—take any chances when it came to her children. While she probably could have renounced her rights to the throne—and maybe she would have done so eagerly—she could never forsake Caroline and Albert. Her sister Lizanne Kelly LeVine put it best: "Once she finally made the decision that she was not going to continue to let it get her down, well, that was pretty much it. If it turned out to be just the worst thing ever, she would make the best of it—no matter what."

The Most Important Choice

Rainier and I have agreed that I don't have any choice but to just go on," said Princess Grace.

It was February 1963, and Grace was talking to Charlotte Winston, who had come to Monaco to visit her. On an unseasonably warm morning, the two longtime friends sat talking on one of the

Palace's sunny terraces while enjoying cups of milkless, sugarless tea and roasted grapefruit halves. Grace was still in her morning attire, a pale pink dressing gown with an oval neckline of marabou feathers. She also wore a knee-length satin coat. With no makeup, no jewelry, her hair whipped by sea breeze, she had never looked better—at least judging from the photograph taken of her that day by her friend.

As the two friends spoke, they took in sparkling sea and crisp city views, below and beyond. Even at this height, the dipping and soaring seagulls could be heard crying out for attention. With a sweeping hand, she motioned to the view of the principality. "And this is where I find myself," Grace said. "Why God put me here, I don't know." She mentioned that she didn't enjoy the sun, never had ("I prefer the rain"), and that she was constantly afraid that she would get sunburned in Monaco. "So, darling, what in the world am I *doing* here?" she asked, laughing. "However," she concluded, "there are worse places, I suppose."

Seemingly from nowhere, a white turtledove flew onto the glass table between Grace and Charlotte and just sat there looking up at them, as it might in a cartoon version of a storybook. Charlotte took a camera from her purse and snapped another picture. Grace laughed. "Do you *ever* run out of film?" she asked.

Charlotte recalled, "During our talk, we got onto the subject of our lives and the surprising way things had turned out for her. Back when we were living in New York, she would always say, 'Sometimes in life, you have to choose.' I was always one to be so undecided about things, about career, family. 'Choose,' she would tell me. 'At least that's a start.' Now, years later, we were dealing with *her* choices."

"What now, Gracie?" Charlotte asked.

Taking stock, the Princess noted that at least she had her children, and "my wonderful husband"—as astonished as she was, she said, that she had "found a way to get along with a Gemini." She also observed with a note of finality that she no longer had her movie career. However, she concluded, "millions of women have given up their careers for their families, and guess what, Charlotte? I'm one of them now. Time to grow up, I guess. Life isn't a picnic, is it?"

Charlotte recalled, "There was a twinge of sadness in her voice, as if a death had occurred, and in a sense it had: the death of any dream she might have had to make movies again. Oh yes, she always wanted to marry, have children, and be devoted to family ideals. She was a woman of a certain time, after all. But she was also ahead of her time in the sense that there never was anything in her that wanted to give up her career, abandon all she had worked for to become 'Grace Kelly.' However, what was done was done, and, from what I could gather, she was ready to accept it."

Grace said that, the night before, she'd had a nightmare that she'd been involved in a dreadful accident and was paralyzed for life, not able to make movies. She had awakened with a start and wondered what she would do if such a thing actually occurred. "Would I shrivel up and die?" she asked Charlotte. "And what if I went blind? Would I kill myself?"

Charlotte made a mental note of how odd it was that Grace would equate her situation as Princess of Monaco to such catastrophic events in a person's life, though she didn't mention it. Rather, she listened as Grace went on to say that, in her view, life sometimes delivered what she called "unexpected twists," and, as she put it, "either one rolls with the punches, or one doesn't. I choose to roll. I choose to trust that God has a plan for me here." Then, with a soft smile, she concluded that her father, Jack, would probably have wanted her to look at her frustrating situation in Monaco as a lesson in character-building.

Charlotte recalled, "At that moment, Rainier walked out onto the terrace with Caroline. Immediately I jumped to my feet, as you are supposed to do when the sovereign enters the room. 'Sit down, my dear,' he told me. He looked so attractive holding that little girl, practically glowing as he said to Gracie, 'I have someone here who would like to see you.'

"Gracie took Caroline into her arms. She held her close to her bosom. 'Aaah, yes, this is what it shall be about for me now,' she said, referring to the little Princess. 'I think I have always been a good mother, but now . . . well, darling, just you wait!'"

Grace held her brown-haired, blue-eyed daughter in front of her and made a funny face. Caroline laughed at her, as did Rainier.

Then the Prince turned to Charlotte and asked, "Has she always been like this? So silly?"

"Always, Prince," Charlotte answered.

The three spoke for about ten more minutes before Grace and Rainier rose, saying they had to run.

"See you later, alligator," the Prince said, using one of his wife's favorite phrases.

Charlotte smiled and gave the expected response, but the familiar words hit a nerve. Charlotte recalled that as she watched Grace and Rainier walk away, it felt to her as though it would be more than "a while" before she would once again see the "Gracie" with whom she had always felt such a connection. With the new acceptance the Princess had for her life in Monaco, it was clear: "Gracie" was gone; a new, less vulnerable woman had taken her place. However, the emotional struggle within her had somehow made a woman who was once thought of as such a flawless gem now seem slightly flawed—and, therefore, more human.

Charlotte's eyes welled with tears as the Gracie she had known and loved disappeared from view.

Many of the Princess's friends and associates would also notice a change in her from this time forth. Some were displeased by it. However, if they truly cared about her they could not justifiably mourn the loss of the old, restless Grace Kelly without celebrating the arrival of the new, more contented Princess Grace. She had finally come to terms with her choices, some for which she needed to forgive herself, others for which she deserved credit, but all of which had led her to a magical place that most women would find paradisaical. She would remain in this sun-drenched harbor for the rest of her life, even if the climate wasn't to her liking. She would say good-bye to the possibilities that awaited her in Hollywood, even if it meant the death of a dream. She would trade in her carefree youth for responsibility, for commitment to family: the children she would never leave, the man she would always love. Indeed, with uncertainty and indecision now behind her, finally Grace was home.

PART FIVE

Children Born Royal

Caroline and Albert

With the passing of the years, Prince Rainier and Princess Grace would devote themselves to trying to be exemplary parents to their children, no doubt because they had felt disenfranchised during their own childhoods. Before they even married, Grace and Rainier had discussed their backgrounds and realized that, though they had different experiences as youngsters, they both wished their parents had done things differently to make them feel more loved and accepted. They were determined to not make the same mistakes with their own offspring. Of course, they did not find themselves in ordinary circumstances. They were mother and father to children destined by royal lineage to have unusual lives, no matter what. Their goal was to be viewed not only as exemplary royalty, but as exemplary parents as well—and *that* was the challenge they would face throughout the adolescent years of their children.

Much of what Grace saw happening to her children as they grew up bothered her, even if Rainier was used to such odd occurrences. For instance, it was protocol that young girls were to curtsy in front of Caroline. Grace found the practice disturbing, particularly when at Caroline's third birthday party, all of her little friends were bowing and curtsying when received by the guest of honor. "How is she to grow up a normal child with girls her own age curtsying all about her?" Grace asked Rainier. She was told that there was no other way. In order to create a different environment for her daughter, Grace established a kindergarten at the Palace, much like the one Jackie Kennedy organized at the White House at about the same time, in 1960. There, Caroline, and later Albert, were surrounded by kids roughly their own age for play and learning time, and these visiting children were encouraged to treat the royal offspring as they would anyone else—no bowing while in the kindergarten.

The two Grimaldi children could not have been more different in temperament and personality. From the beginning, Caroline was emotional, with a fiery temper. She was dark and resembled Rainier. When Albert was born, Caroline felt jealous upon being carried in to visit her mother, who was cradling the newborn. Caroline says she remembers—though she was probably later told the story—visiting her mother after Albert was born. She was given a small bouquet of fresh jasmine blossoms and lilies to present to Grace, but she was so consumed with resentment that instead she pitched the flowers at her mother.

Though Grace and Rainier worked to make certain both children were well-adjusted—difficult under the circumstances—Caroline acted in a spoiled fashion at an early age. Madge Tivey-Faucon, who was responsible for getting Caroline to her morning lessons, recalled that the little girl would telephone her and then, with a tone of superiority, announce into the receiver, "I'm awake," before abruptly hanging up.

It became so upsetting to Grace that Caroline would sometimes bite Albert while playing, that one day she bit the little girl on the arm to teach her a lesson. Madge was aghast, and later (after she was fired) wrote about the incident in an article about her days in the Palace, inciting worldwide speculation about Grace's mothering skills.

From the age of about two, Albert—a quiet, reserved, and well-behaved boy—was trained to take over his father's role in the principality. By design, Rainier (as well as Albert's godfather, Prince Louis, Rainier's cousin) spent much more time with "Albie" than Grace did. It was as if a decision had been reached that he would become too "soft" if allowed to be coddled by his mother. "There seemed to be a concerted effort to create as much space between him and the Princess as possible," said Thomas Sartre. "It was a given that Caroline was the Princess's responsibility, and Albert was the Prince's.

"I recall that Rainier determined what kinds of nursemaids Albert should have, what kinds of books he should read, which little friends he should have in his life. The biggest concern was always that he not become dependent on his mother for advice and comfort, but that he look to his father for his every need." Considering how much Grace loved her boy, and the fact that she had given up so much to be in Monaco to raise her children, it was upsetting for her to not be able to spend more time with Albie. Sometimes Albie seemed distant to her. Once, when he was about four, he was dressed as a carabineer for a party on National Feast Day. Proudly he walked through the crowd, the little Prince in his impressive guard's uniform. At one point, Grace had to correct him about something. He looked up at her defiantly and said, "Carabineers do not come under your control, Mommy." (He was right; they didn't.)

Thomas Sartre recalled, "One day the Prince and I were discussing business by the huge Palace pool, so magnificent, surrounded by lush green lawn and exotic plants. Suddenly, the Princess appeared and angrily said to Rainier, 'I want to see my son and I want to see him *now*.' I don't know what brought it on, why she was so upset. Calmly, Rainier picked up a telephone, dialed a number and said, 'The Princess would like to see Albie. We are at the pool. Bring him.' Five minutes later, a nursemaid brought the kid to the pool. Grace took Albie by the hand, and the two of them went off. Rainier and I then continued with our business as if nothing unusual had occurred. An hour later, I stumbled upon the Princess and Albie playing in a courtyard. She apparently thought I had been instructed to fetch Albie, because she looked up at me and hissed, 'Be gone, or I'll sic the dogs on you.' She wasn't kidding."

In 1960, a well-publicized kidnapping made Princess Grace concerned about Albert's safety. Four-year-old Eric Peugeot, son of Paris automobile millionaire Raymond Peugeot, had been kidnapped from a golf course nursery outside of Paris. His kidnappers demanded a measly $35,000 for the boy's return. When the ransom was paid, the boy was returned unharmed. (Two years later, the captors were arrested and both sentenced to twenty years.) Grace asked Rainier to place sentinels in front of the nursery. He told her he was afraid the children would be frightened by the presence of such guards. "I'll take care of it," said the Princess. She then told Albert and Caroline that men dressed as toy soldiers with white gloves would be playing in front of the nursery for a few weeks, and to ignore them. Days later, however, Caroline kicked one of the sentinels on the shin for not allowing her to play with them—so hard that she actually drew blood! The guard bowed low in front of her, left his post, and then complained to his superior. The next day, Grace relieved the men of their post. At the Palace, security was tight anyway. There would have been no way for an intruder to get as far as the nursery.

To help rear the children, the Prince and Princess hired a young British woman, Maureen King, to act as governess. King—who somehow acquired the unfortunate nickname of "Killer" (supposedly because she was such a disciplinarian)—was fluent in French, which was fortunate because as the children grew older, they were taught both French and English. It was Grace's decision that they either speak one or the other around the house, lest they become confused. While Rainier wanted them to speak French, she wished for English. So on some occasions they spoke English, on others they spoke French. "Suffice it to say, it is confusing for them," Grace told one friend.

No matter how tough Killer was around the Palace ("and don't ever call her that around the children," Grace warned other staff members), it was impossible to prevent the children from being spoiled, especially since every visitor to the Palace brought them toys. Even Rainier showered both youngsters with presents, much to Grace's dismay. In terms of material possessions, as daughter of wealthy parents she had always had everything she ever wanted. However, she knew that Caroline and Albert had unique challenges ahead as adults, that they would never understand the value of earning a living, that they would go through life with a sense of entitlement. In her view, if she could teach her children not to expect that their every heart's desire would be fulfilled—every stuffed animal, every toy imaginable—it was the least she could do. However, she was fighting an impossible battle in that regard, especially since Rainier felt that the tots deserved every present they were ever given by anyone nice enough, in his view, to give to them. After all, they *were* royalty. Also, no one could be offended, meaning every gift had to be accepted. When Caroline received an elaborate dollhouse from a wealthy acquaintance of the family, Grace allowed it to be assembled in one of the Palace's rooms and permitted Caroline to play with it for just one week. She then donated it to an orphanage.

When Charles de Gaulle and his wife visited the Palace in 1960, Madame de Gaulle brought a red rocking horse for Albert. "Oh, he will simply adore that," Grace said. Then, when Madame de Gaulle was distracted, she whispered urgently to Madge Tivey-Faucon, "Goodness! Rush down to the nursery and get rid of Albie's red rocking horse." Madge raced to the nursery where Caroline and Albert were playing quietly, grabbed the rocking horse, and bolted out, leaving the children with their mouths wide open. Moments later, Princess Grace and Madame de Gaulle showed up in the nursery with the new red rocking horse. "Albie, look what Mrs. de Gaulle brought you," Grace said as she placed the gift before him. "Oh boy!" the youngster said, jumping onto the horse.

Still, Grace was devoted to both her children and to making them happy. If she spent more time with Caroline, it was only because she wasn't able to spend as much as she wished with Albert. "The problem with lavishing so much attention on Caroline was that the little girl became obstreperous, thinking she had her mother's approval no matter what," says Antoinette Brucatto, who visited the Palace many times during these years. "I'm not sure Grace could have raised her any differently, though. She was actually pretty tough on her at times. Caroline was like her mother, in the sense that she was so independent. Grace told me she wouldn't have achieved what she did in her life if she had not been so independent of her parents' opinion. The difference, I believe, not having known Grace as a youngster, was that Grace ultimately cared what her parents thought. I never got the feeling that Caroline cared what her mom thought; she was independent to an extreme."

Antoinette recalled being at the Palace one afternoon with

Grace, lunching in the library (manicotti, on this day—Grace often served Italian food and often prepared it herself), when Caroline came running into the room. As the two women were trying to review documents, Caroline began racing about, madly flinging about a rag doll apparently referred to by the family as "Pitiful Pearl." Suddenly, Pearl slipped from Caroline's hand and smashed into a vase, which then crashed to the floor. "Caroline!" the Princess shrieked, according to Antoinette's memory. "Daddy will be furious with you. That was a gift from Sir Winston Churchill." The little girl stopped for a second, looked up at her mother, and said, "So what, Grace?" Then, she darted out of the room. Grace turned to her guest, said, "Pardon me," and followed her daughter.

"A few minutes later, I heard the little girl crying and screaming at the top of her lungs," recalled Antoinette Brucatto. "When the Princess returned, we went back to our business without saying a word about any of it."

Grace's Work

Princess Grace was a traditional figurehead, just like any European country's Queen. While not a Queen reigning over a kingdom (since Monaco isn't a country, but rather a principality), she *was* royalty—a Princess whose job it was to be of service to her loyal (if sometimes not appreciative) subjects.

Princess Grace's duties included public service, establishing charities, assisting the poor, and developing health care programs for institutions such as the Monaco hospital named after her, the Princess Grace Hospital. The hospital had been a dreary place, so much so that when Grace first walked through, she didn't know whether to accept as an honor the fact that it had been renamed for her. She went about the business of redecorating the hallways and rooms with new paint colors and pictures, feeling strongly that the environment in which the patients found themselves would have an effect on their recovery. Rainier agreed, saying, "She knows what she's doing, and I want her to do it." With the Prince's full support in whatever she wished to do for the hospital, she began to host fundraisers to raise money for improvements. "She persuaded a lot of people to give help in their free time, for nothing," said Prince Rainier, "and believe me, it is not easy to get anyone to do anything for nothing down here." Her ideas were often fanciful and sentimental. For instance, after deciding that every Monegasque who gave birth at the hospital should be honored, she arranged for those women to receive medals to commemorate the important event in their lives. The practice went on for years.

Beginning in the sixties and continuing for twenty years, Grace's model would be the British royal family, in terms of emulating its philanthropic work and ability to identify with its subjects. Though Monaco was fairly well-off, it did have its poor and underprivileged. Grace focused on them. She did wonderful work, for instance, on improvements for Monaco's woeful home for the aged. She worked on establishing a volunteer program whereby a committee of people visited the elderly at the home on a regular basis, many of whom either no longer had families or had been abandoned. She would bring her children to the homes to visit the aged, and even clean the floors and paint the walls—quite an education for Caroline, Albert, and, later, Stephanie, who seldom engaged in any domestic work at the Palace. For her part, Grace got a surprising amount of joy doing this kind of work. Designer Gaia Magrelli recalled, "I went with her to the old folks' home one day, and she and Caroline were slathering paint onto the walls, getting it all over themselves and laughing so hard they could barely catch their breaths. Afterward, the Princess was trying to wash the paint off her hands and I said, 'I somehow never imagined this of you.' She said, 'Isn't it true what they say? That you can discover more about a person in an hour of play than in a year of conversation?'" (Grace was quoting Plato.)

Throughout the 1960s, she also became immersed in her new work as president of the Monaco Red Cross, a position she took over from Princess Charlotte. (Rainier has said that Charlotte came to him one day and said, "Look, I think it should be your wife who presides over the Red Cross. But of course I'll go on helping if I can." Though that seems a bit unlikely, it's the Prince's story, and he's sticking to it.) "I have had Red Cross and Girl Scout problems," Grace wrote to Prudy Wise in March 1960, "which isn't really my cup of tea, so it's twice as hard."

As part of her Red Cross work, Grace developed maternity care for expectant women, daycare centers for working mothers, and facilities for orphans. A favorite expression of hers that soon became an unofficial Red Cross motto in Monaco was, "Of course it can be done. Why not?" It served Grace well to focus on the problems of others, and she began to realize that even though she wasn't doing exactly what she wanted to do with her life, she was still blessed. She wasn't completely fulfilled, but she was busy, and, at this particular time in her life, that was important to her. She even managed to bring a touch of Hollywood to Monaco when she established the annual Red Cross costume ball, a fundraiser that always attracted the biggest names in Hollywood, many of whom were friends of Grace's. The gala, held in August at the Monte Carlo Sporting Club, not only raised terrific sums of money for the Red Cross, it afforded Grace the opportunity to catch up with show business people she might not otherwise have seen. Grace's was always the most unusual, most fantastic of costumes, her flair for glamour on full display at least on this one evening of the year. Many other causes would benefit from Princess Grace's involvement over the coming years, including the World Association of Friends of the Child (Association Mondicle des Amis de l'Enfance, or AMADE), the Garden Club of Monaco, and the International Festival of Ballet in Monte Carlo.

Tiv's Writings

As she grew more confident in her role as Princess, Grace also became less inclined to tolerate what she viewed as a lack of respect among certain of her functionaries at the Palace, chief among the offenders being Madge Tivey-Faucon. One friend of Grace's from the States recalled, "I was speaking to Grace on the telephone when Madge interrupted our conversation. Grace left the line and came back a few moments later, upset. 'That was Tiv,' she explained, annoyed. I was amazed. 'After all of these years, she's still there?' I asked Grace. 'Why, she has always disliked you, hasn't she?' Grace said that, in her view, Madge did seem envious. She was helpful, she told me, and often a part of the family. 'But then, she can also be so difficult,' she told me. 'I fear that her days here are numbered,' she concluded."

Recalled Antoinette Brucatto, "I was at the Palace with the Princess when the Prince came storming into our meeting, as irate as he could be. The Princess asked him what was wrong, and he said, 'Tiv is finished. I'm dismissing her myself.' I have no idea what happened. Princess Grace said, 'Oh no. What now?' Rainier said, 'Never mind.' He left. Grace turned to me and said, 'There are days I love that woman, and days I dislike her intensely. In six years, she has never stopped criticizing me. How I managed to re-create my mother here at the Palace, I'll never know.' It was a rare moment for us, one that seemed unusually personal. I said something about good help being hard to find, and she said, 'Luckily, one gets to choose the help, doesn't one? Would that we could choose our mothers.'"

After Madge Tivey-Faucon left the Palace, she authored a series of articles for the British media about her glory days at the Palace, parts of which are quite disturbing in retrospect. "She has a blind confidence in the stars," Madge wrote of the Princess. "The Scorpio woman, it is said, is born under the sign of sex and death, which gives her a passionate temperament—mysterious, physical, eager to seize all the good things of life, all the joys of fortune and love—for life is brief, death is at hand. The Princess once expressed her dread in this fashion, 'I have had so much luck in my life that sometimes I am afraid . . .' She has a terrible fear of dying in an airplane or a car. Cars make her uncomfortable and she rarely drives. When she does, she changes gears noisily, does not see the road well and turns the wheel erratically."

Both the Prince and Princess were distressed by Tivey-Faucon's writings, but could do nothing but ignore them. Grace wrote to her friend Prudy Wise, "Tivey has written a series of nasty, bitchy articles. Everyone in Monaco is furious with her. She's hiding out in Paris."

Stephanie

By mid-1965, Princess Grace was again pregnant. This time, following two miscarriages, she would bring the baby to full term. At about the three-month mark, she and Rainier went to Athens for the wedding of Greece's King Constantine to Princess Anne-Marie of Denmark. "Unfortunately I ate something that gave me intestinal cramps," Grace wrote to Prudy Wise, "and I was so sick. It brought on contractions and I was immediately put to bed. I have been practically immobile for a month."

While pregnant this time, Grace gained more weight than she or her doctors had expected. Also, the pregnancy was hard on her emotionally. Whenever expectant, Grace was afraid to leave the Palace. It was difficult to forget that during her first pregnancy a stranger had rushed toward her to rub her stomach for "good luck," so she rarely left home. Also, in order to avoid having to rush Grace to a hospital while she was in labor, and risk having her photographed in such a state, Rainier arranged that their children be born at the Palace in a library that was transformed into a maternity ward. (Rainier himself had been born in the Palace.)

On February 1, 1965, Princess Grace gave birth to her third child, Stephanie Marie Elisabeth. The Prince recalled, "I had seen other people's newborn children whilst making official visits to the maternity home and they had always appeared to me as being rather ugly little creatures. Probably I was biased," he added, his sense of humor at work, "but my own babies never seemed that way at all. They weren't red and they weren't ugly—in fact they have all been rather big babies, large children already when they were born and not all wrinkled and old-looking."

On the day that "Stephie" (as she would often be called by her parents) came into the world, Margaret Kelly arrived in Monaco by cruise liner to be at her daughter's side. Now that Jack was gone, Grace and Margaret continued the close relationship that had begun once Grace married and had children.

Because Grace and Rainier thought of Stephie as a "miracle baby," as Grace sometimes put it, they were determined to lavish on her as much attention as possible. They were just so grateful that she had been brought into the world successfully, considering Grace's history with miscarriages. "She shall have everything she ever wants," the Princess told Charlotte Winston of her newborn. "My mother told me at the christening that Stephanie will probably be spoiled rotten, but we're willing to take that chance."

Following her christening in March 1965 at the Cathédrale de Monaco, the same cathedral where Grace and Rainier were wed nine years earlier, Stephanie was presented to the citizens of Monaco in the Palace courtyard, just as tradition dictated and just as Caroline and Albert had been presented before her. As Grace and Rainier stood on the Palace balcony, always the setting for a royal appearance after a major event occurred in the lives of the Grimaldis, Grace held the newborn while Monegasques below, in the great square, cheered and threw flowers into the air. Little Caroline and Albert stood obediently next to their smiling parents. Flocks of pigeons were released to celebrate the presentation. "She comes to us in all her innocence and purity," Prince Rainier III said of Stephanie, "bringing us once more, as did her sister and brother, joy, happiness, and pride. Yes, indeed, pride! For she, like them, is the symbol and the bond of a family and patriotic union of which we can justly be proud. And these three children, who certainly belong to the present, also represent for us all the future."

Freedom from Onassis

A constant thorn in Prince Rainier's side for many years had been the presence of Aristotle Onassis in Monaco as chief stockholder in the Société des Bains de Mer. The two had always had a problematic relationship, friendly at times, adversarial at others. By 1966, after his marriage ended, Onassis seldom visited Monaco; he didn't hide the fact that, to him, the S.B.M. was now just a hobby, like sailing on his yacht. He even had the temerity to tell Rainier that gambling was "immoral" and should be abolished in Monaco. Coming from a man whose personal and business reputation was anything but pristine, such a disdainful judgment about one of the principality's vital income-producing activities riled Rainier. (It should be noted that even though gambling was the recreational activity that first captured the public's imagination about Monaco, at this time it accounted for only about 5 percent of Monaco's income, the remainder coming from tourism and indirect taxes on business and industry.)

"So I said, 'Really, Mr. Onassis,'" recalled the Prince, "'I don't think you're in a position to tell me what is moral or immoral.'"

It wasn't long before Rainier figured out what was really going on in Onassis's head. "I knew there must be something more behind it, and I was right," he recalled years later. "A plan emerged to split the S.B.M. into three different companies: one for games, one for auxiliary exploitation, and a third for real estate. It was the latter in which Mr. Onassis had the most interest. The value of the open land right in the center of Monte Carlo that the casino sits on, with all the gardens and greenery, is tremendous. And his idea was simple: to farm out the gambling, hotels, and entertainment activities of the S.B.M. in concessions to other businessmen, maintain control of the holding company, and concentrate on making large profits on real estate deals using the casino's land. I told Mr. Onassis flatly, 'This is never going to happen whilst I am living because it would ruin the S.B.M., and if the S.B.M. goes flunk, it would shatter the whole economy of the principality. The S.B.M. provides all the principal attractions and facilities of Monte Carlo.'"

In the Grimaldis' opinion, the question was simple: Why wouldn't Onassis simply go away and leave them alone? In fact, Rainier told him bluntly that he should just "disappear from the scene."

"I don't think that Mr. Onassis's investment in the Société des Bains de Mer of Monte Carlo is of very great importance to his overall empire," Grace said in a 1966 interview with *Playboy* magazine. "He has so many more and bigger investments than Monte Carlo. I feel that his ownership of the majority of shares, and therefore a controlling interest in the casino of Monte Carlo, has been more for his own amusement than a serious business affair. It's hard for someone to remain deeply concerned with something that was once fun but now gives him problems."

To get Onassis out of Monaco once and for all, Prince Rainier aligned himself with his brother-in-law, Jean-Charles Rey, long his foe but now an ally (at least in this particular venture), to come up with a plan that seems odd in retrospect. There are reams of documents pertaining to this strategy, but if simplified it all comes down to this: After many meetings with the National Council (which now sided with Rainier in its aggravation of Onassis) and numerous conferences with French President Charles de Gaulle, Rainier issued 600,000 new shares in the S.B.M.—all of which were purchased by Monaco. Once these stocks were purchased, Monaco once again held the controlling interest in the S.B.M. Why no one had thought of this idea before is an open question. However, such a steamrolling tactic probably wouldn't have worked in the 1950s with Onassis anyway, not when he was at his prime of ambition. By the mid-sixties, though, he was wealthy, single, and about to court President John Kennedy's widow, Jacqueline Bouvier Kennedy. He didn't have the passion for the S.B.M. he once had—though he did engage in a halfhearted battle by taking the issue to the Monaco Supreme Court, where, of course, he lost—so Rainier was finally able to seize control. Eventually, Onassis went on to sell all of his shares in the S.B.M., for which he received $10 million (an amount he felt was not nearly enough). It was to be the last fight between these two giants. Onassis then sailed his yacht out of the harbor, never to return.

Finally, after fourteen years of turmoil with Aristotle Onassis, Prince Rainier III was free of him, and, it could be argued, in a most anticlimactic way. The undisputed ruler of Monaco was now able to continue with his personal vision for the principality. He was unobstructed even by the National Council, which was now more in alignment with him than ever in his royal past. It had been a long, tough battle to truly gain control of Monaco—or at least be in a position of optimum persuasive power—but Rainier proved himself up to the task by being both patient and smart. Real estate prices in the principality would soar from this point onward; Monaco truly began to thrive. In one interview, Grace said she was proud of her husband and the way he had conducted the business of the principality. "I saw what he put up with firsthand," she said. "And I couldn't be happier about the way it has turned out for Rainier, and for Monaco. He has been through a lot, but his desire has always been to see Monaco thrive, to bring a better of way of life to the Monegasques. I think he has done that."

Of course, Rainier, in the process, also brought "a better way of life" to himself, to his family, and to generations of Grimaldis.

Along with the growth of his principality, his family's many lucrative investments doubled, tripled, and then continued to compound in leaps and bounds; he was well on his way to becoming one of the richest men in Europe. Still, it's interesting that despite his wealth and power Prince Rainier is not a world-class leader. He rules Monaco, obviously, but what occurs there really has no impact on European affairs. Monaco has no resources needed by other countries: no oil, no land, no important seaport. It has never been aggressive, has posed no threat to anyone. As long as he maintains friendly relations with France, Rainier has nothing to worry about from that country either. There's no arguing that Monaco is a rarefied world, an old-fashioned "kingdom" (or, more accurately, "princedom") in a modern world.

Happy Times (1966–1970)

In January 1966, *Playboy* published one of the most revealing interviews Princess Grace of Monaco ever gave to the media, one that gave great insight into the woman she had become since leaving Hollywood for Monaco. The writer asked if Grace ever wished she could "go back to being just Grace Kelly." "Before my marriage," she answered, "I was very much a 20th Century modern young woman. I was very independent, which I enjoyed very much. But too much independence for a woman I don't think brings much happiness."

Grace admitted that she did "miss acting at times," though she didn't miss Hollywood "at all." She said that she still received movie offers, but, as she put it, "one has to choose in life. When I was acting, I wasn't a very happy person. It isn't much fun to have success and no one to share it with. Right now, I have a full and happy life. Much too full and much too busy."*

When told that her marriage had been described as a "fairy tale romance," she responded with, "I've never seen anything fairytale-ish about it, no."

When asked to analyze herself, she gave a description that was certainly contrary to who she had been when she was "just Grace Kelly." She said, "I am a pessimist. I always expect the worst. When it doesn't happen, I have a nice surprise."

"Are you happy, then?" asked the writer. "Well, I don't expect to be," she responded. "I don't look for happiness. So, perhaps I am very content in life, in a way." When asked to define happiness, she answered, "I suppose being at peace with yourself, not anxiously seeking for something," and then, in what was probably a reference to her abandoned acting career, she said, "not being frantic about not having something."

The writer then asked if she was at peace with herself. "I argue with myself all the time," she answered, "so I guess I'm not really at peace."

The reporter was then either being facetious or truly interested when he asked if Grace had ever felt the need for a psychiatrist. "Well, for the moment, I seem to be getting along all right," she answered. "So far so good."

Princess Grace concluded on a decidedly downbeat note by saying, "I have many unfulfilled ambitions in life. God willing, I can keep my health and strength and manage to pull myself out of bed in the morning, some of them may be realized."

Prince Rainier was concerned about the article, so much so that, according to one Palace aide, he asked Grace if she was really as unhappy as she sounded in it. She explained that she was having a bad

---

*In 1966, Princess Grace made a cameo appearance in the film *The Poppy Is Also a Flower* (a.k.a. *The Opium Connection*), from an original story by Ian Fleming, creator of James Bond. Grace introduces the movie, playing herself. The film, set in Iran, tells a convoluted tale of the manufacturing and trafficking of opium and heroin. A protest against drug abuse, it features a variety of celebrities, including Yul Brynner, Angie Dickinson, and Rita Hayworth, all of whom worked for scale. Its profits went to UNESCO.

day when she spoke to the reporter, and that even though she hadn't been misquoted, she was still considering calling the writer to tell him that he could have used "more discretion" in writing about her. The Prince suggested that she not do so, saying that it was best to just leave the matter alone.

The ominous tone of the *Playboy* story set the stage for other interviews Grace would give in 1966, commemorating the ten-year anniversary of her wedding to Rainier. It seemed to her that the whole world wanted to know if she was "happy," as if a perfect outcome of her dream to be a Princess would somehow make it possible for others to realize their own aspirations. Of course, the truth was that Grace did not aspire to be a Princess, no matter how history had been rewritten, she wasn't always happy in her life . . . and she also wasn't the kind of woman to lie about it. In a television interview, Barbara Walters asked the question, "Are you happy?" Grace thought for a moment. "I've had happy moments in my life, but I don't think that happiness—being happy—is a perpetual state that anyone can be in," she said. "Life isn't that way. My life here has given me many satisfactions in the last ten years."

It was true, however, that once Grace decided to put the movie business out of her mind and focus on family and principality responsibilities, she did seem more at peace, even if somewhat less enthusiastic about the future. It had been an unexpected, defining moment in the relationship between Grace and her subjects when she abandoned the *Marnie* project. The Monegasques now had sufficient evidence of the sacrifice their Princess had made for them— as if she hadn't already given up enough!—and the principality finally began to accept her. She could feel the enthusiasm of her subjects for her, made obvious by the swarms of people descending upon her whenever she attended a public event, by the positive spin all of the press about her had taken, by the fan mail she received at the Palace. Finally, by the end of the decade, she was respected as Princess, and such validation did feel like a victory for her since she'd worked so hard, and sacrificed so much, to gain the respect of Rainier's subjects. As a public figure, few women were as celebrated. In terms of fame and publicity, her only logical equals in the 1960s were Marilyn Monroe (who died in 1962), Elizabeth Taylor, and Jacqueline Kennedy. She was much more famous at the end of the decade as a Princess than she had ever been in the 1950s as a movie star.

In 1967, thirty-seven-year-old Grace became pregnant once again. However, while at the Montreal Exposition with Rainier and their two oldest children, she became ill. Rupert Allan was with her in Montreal at the time. He later recalled being present when she was taken to the hospital. "It was the sixth time she'd been pregnant," he said. "She was devastated by the loss of that child. They said the baby, a boy, had been dead for a month inside her. She so wanted more children, but after three miscarriages in eleven years, the doctors told her that it would never happen for her. I'd never seen her more bereft in all of the time I had known her. Rainier was also deeply saddened."

After more than ten years together, Grace and Rainier recognized and understood their differences, and forged ahead with their marriage. "The Catholicism in our marriage was a very strong link between us," Grace once said. "It helped because there weren't too many other mutual bonds. Marriage is not an end in itself. It takes a lot to make it work." In another interview, she noted, "My husband refers to me as his government, and I refer to him as my leader. When he's asked something involving both of us, he says, 'I'll have to consult my government.'"

They were bonded not just by their faith, but also by that which is often responsible for the continuation of a marriage between husband and wife: their children. "I think the experience of my parents' separation when I was only six has subconsciously made me very much want my own marriage to succeed," Prince Rainier later told English journalist Douglas Keay. "So the Princess and I have always tried to minimize any sort of incident or little disagreement between us in the interest of keeping the family together—so that the children should not suffer."

When Rainier's father, Prince Pierre de Polignac, died in 1965, the loss hit him hard. (Grace was deeply saddened by Pierre's death as well, since he was one of the few of Rainier's relatives who had openly welcomed her to the principality.) After Pierre's death, and once all of the political upheaval in Monaco was settled, Rainier seemed to become more devoted to his wife and children. The family continued to do a great deal of traveling; they vacationed, had fun. They loved Switzerland during the winter months, and Paris during the spring (giving Grace an opportunity to catch up on the latest designer styles from Dior, Lanvin, Givenchy, and Balenciaga—her favorites—and to make the appropriate purchases).

In 1966, Monaco celebrated its centennial, and, with the absence of Onassis in their lives, the Grimaldis were eager to rejoice. Grace devoted herself to planning a lavish Grand Ball, an art foundation dinner, and an international ballet festival (featuring Rudolf Nureyev and Margot Fonteyn in *Romeo and Juliet*, performed at the Palace).

By the end of the decade, the Kelly family was still holding together as best it could after the death of its powerful patriarch. Lizanne was still married (and would remain with the same man, Donald LeVine, for forty-four wonderful years, until his death from cancer in December 2000). Peggy, who courageously battled a drinking problem for many years, had been divorced by the end of the decade and was facing the end of another marriage. In 1963, her fifteen-year-old daughter, Mary Lee (Grace's goddaughter), had gotten pregnant and eloped. Grace was supportive of the teenager, unconcerned about any scandal that might result of the situation, and invited the young couple to Monaco. Over the years, many of Grace's relatives would find their way to the Palace, almost as if the principality was a safe haven for them during times of trouble. Grace always made sure the gates were open to her relatives, and would pay for round-trip tickets if anyone in her family needed to "get away." When her brother Kell's daughter Lizzie (named after Lizanne) became anorexic in the early 1970s, Grace sent for her, hoping time in the principality might help. Her Uncle George, in his early eighties, was also a regular visitor; she cherished every moment with him. Also, her mother continued to visit often. Kell, however, was having problems; by the end of the decade, the troubled Kelly son had left his wife and children and was becoming somewhat notorious in the Philadelphia area for his philandering.

In August 1969, a replacement for Father Francis Tucker was finally selected; for the last few years the Palace had had a series of temporary chaplains until finally choosing another American priest, Father David Voellinger, also of Delaware, to fill the vacancy. The Oblates felt that Voellinger, who grew up in Princess Grace's home city of Philadelphia, was a perfect choice, with his fluency in English, German, and French. Father Voellinger—who would leave the priesthood in 1981 to marry—recalled that he had two months to settle in the parish house of St. Charles's Catholic Church because the family was on vacation in Switzerland when he finally showed up in Monaco. One morning he awakened to an invitation that had arrived from the Palace, asking him to celebrate Mass the next morning. The Grimaldis had returned. After arriving at the Palace chapel, he was putting on his formal religious vestments when a young boy appeared in the back of the church and began donning his red altar robe, white surplice, and cross. The youngster then walked up to the priest and casually said, "Hello, Father. My name is Albie."

Voellinger recalled, "Suddenly, it hit me. This was young Albert, eleven years old and the Crown Prince of Monaco. He was my altar boy! So I said, 'Okay, Albie, what do we do now?' He explained, 'Well, we go to the door of the chapel with the holy water and when my parents come down, you must offer them holy water and greet them. Then we go up to the altar and start Mass.' He was matter-of-fact about it. When the Prince and Princess arrived, the Princess greeted me by holding me by the elbows. Looking directly into my eyes, she said, 'Father, welcome. I hope you'll be happy with us. Will you be able to join us for lunch after Mass?' Well, what was I going to say? No?"

After Mass, Voellinger recalled, the Princess made sandwiches for lunch and served them herself, with Heineken beer, "so that I would feel at home. It was a surprising gesture. Here was Princess Grace making me a ham sandwich."

Over the years, Father Voellinger would become close to the

family, experiencing many of the luxuries of being in the Grimaldi inner circle, including swimming in the family's pool at their Roc Agel home. Because the water was purified with ozone bubbles, he recalled, "it was just like swimming in champagne." The priest said that, after a time, he became blasé about the glamour of living in the Palace, "because it was in front of you every waking moment." He said that he and Prince Albert were once playing chess in the study when Princess Grace brought a visitor through, a woman wearing a yellow miniskirt and a large diamond around her neck. "The Princess introduced her as Mrs. Burton. Engrossed in the chess game, I casually glanced at her, said, 'How do you do?' and continued my concentration. Afterward, Prince Albert cracked up laughing and said, 'Do you realize who that was? Why, that was Elizabeth Taylor.' I was stunned. Albie laughed. He loved having one up on me."

Father Voellinger also recalled that Christmas was a particularly important time to the Grimaldis. "I would serve midnight Mass on Christmas Eve. Afterward, there was a huge banquet, which lasted well until the sun rose. On Christmas Day, the Princess would then invite all of the children between the ages of three and twelve who had actually been born in Monaco—about three hundred—to the Palace. Then she would hand out sticky buns to the children, even getting the Prince to help. Then, she presented a Punch-and-Judy show to them. Afterwards, as they left, she would give each a Christmas gift. It would bring tears to your eyes every year, it was that wonderful."

Princess Grace Turns Forty

On November 12, 1969, Princess Grace of Monaco turned forty, a milestone that was as difficult for her as it often was for people of her generation, who viewed it as the beginning of the end of youth. Any former film star who had become known, in part, for her youthful, porcelain beauty, would have at least a thought or two on turning forty, as did Grace. She gave another interview, this one for *Look* magazine, in which she clarified her feelings on the subject: "For a woman, [turning forty] is torture, the end. I think turning forty is miserable . . . I'm a basket case. I can't stand it. It comes as a great jolt. It really does. It hits one right between the eyes. It's something you know is going to happen, but you think, why so soon?"

Perhaps it would have been best if she gave fewer interviews. A fundamentally honest person, Grace could only relate her feelings as she felt them—and, often these days, they weren't optimistic. She'd become a realist, pragmatic in her feeling that even though life had not turned out for her the way she had hoped, she was determined to make the best of it. Still, with the passing of years, it was clear that she had certain regrets—chief among them being that the "good old days" were behind her. Antoinette Brucatto recalls happening upon the Prince and Princess as they entered a restaurant in Monte Carlo. Both were dressed to the nines, Rainier in a well-cut black silk tuxedo and Grace in a white satin evening dress with a blue velvet stole (designed by Balenciaga). She still looked swanlike and beautiful, so many years after leaving Hollywood. With the Princess distracted by a well-wisher in the foyer, the Prince walked over to Antoinette. "She's a bit sad today because of the birthday tomorrow," he said. "Forty years. Can you believe it?"

"How wonderful," Antoinette said, according to her memory. "Why, she doesn't look a day over thirty."

"So true, but just don't tell her that," Rainier warned. He asked Antoinette not to mention the birthday to Grace at all, saying that "it'll only ruin our entire meal and, truly, I haven't had a peaceful meal in weeks." A disarming smile made it clear that he was joking.

Antoinette didn't have to mention the birthday to Grace. As soon as she finished with her conversation, the Princess rushed over to Antoinette. "Oh, darling, have you heard the news? The most awful of days is nearly upon us," she said, dramatically, the actress in her coming forth. "My fortieth. Isn't it simply dreadful?"

"Oh come now, Princess," Antoinette said. "You look marvelous and you know it."

"Bullshit," Grace said. She added that her best days were behind her, and then, with a nostalgic smile, concluded, "But, oh my! They *were* good days, weren't they?"

From a few feet away, the two women heard Rainier's voice beckoning Grace to his side. He had someone he wished her to meet.

Grace rolled her eyes. "No time to whine about the inevitable," she said as she slipped off her right glove. "Duty calls." Then, putting on a face of smiling resignation, Grace approached Rainier with her right arm extended, ready for the predictable handshake. As she greeted her husband's friend with animated expressions, the Prince put his arm around his Princess. Turning to Antoinette, he smiled proudly.

Royal Parenting

Though their circumstances would prove unique, the differences of opinion between Prince Rainier III and Princess Grace concerning the manner in which they wanted to raise their children were no different than those in many marriages. Unfortunately, these arguments between the couple would become divisive issues for years to come. With obvious dissimilarities in their own backgrounds, it was not surprising that they approached child-rearing in divergent ways.

Because Jack and Margaret Kelly had never been particularly warm and nurturing to her, Princess Grace didn't have much of an example as to how to relate to her own children. If anything, she used her parents as *reverse* role models. Though she knew that she didn't want to raise her children the way she had been raised, she didn't have an effective alternate plan. She started out being permissive with her children, and when that got out of hand, she tried to rein them in. That tactic was also ineffective because the children didn't want to give up the freedoms they had enjoyed as tots. Raising children is always a challenge, but when both parents and children live in a fishbowl, it is even more difficult. Grace and Rainier were raising *world-famous* children, babies who had been featured on the covers of national magazines from the time they were newborns. The way the Grimaldis' offspring behaved not only reflected on Grace and Rainier as parents, but on their country as well. Their children were the future rulers of Monaco: A familial drama would inevitably become a national one.

However, there was more influencing Princess Grace's parenting skills than just her history of dysfunction with her own parents. Grace expected a lot from Caroline, Albert, and Stephanie because she felt she had given a lot to them, or, more precisely, had given up a lot *for* them. It was a decision not without consequences. People who make great personal compromises often become uncompromising people as a result. Grace was no exception. As a woman and as a parent, she became implacable and strict, seemingly oblivious as to why her daughters couldn't accept the same regimented world she was forced to accept for herself. Rarely able to relax or have fun anymore, this was a different person than the Grace Kelly of old: a person divorced from the cheerful and carefree side of her youth.

"You were young once," her friends would tell her, trying to be helpful. "Can't you understand?" Perhaps she couldn't.

Prince Rainier's had been a strict upbringing, one in which he was not encouraged to express himself or his individuality. As heir to a throne, he was accustomed to rules, regulations, and protocol that governed his every decision. His choices were limited: He was going to be Prince, and that was pretty much to be the end of the story for him. In reviewing his life, Rainier is pragmatic: Though much of his childhood had been tough for him—he wished he had not come from a broken home, wished he had been able to spend more time with his parents—it had all turned out for the best, and, for the most part, he had no regrets. His practical attitude was typical of the way he looked at life as a whole: It is what it is, and there's not much use in complaining about any of it. Though one might ask what Rainier Grimaldi, born into such a privileged, entitled, wealthy world, could possibly have to complain about, even the most fortunate of people don't have perfect, carefree lives—even if it seems that way to outsiders.

Perhaps it wasn't so ironic that Prince Rainier—who never had freedom to choose as a youngster—would become the more lenient parent. Meanwhile, Princess Grace—who had always felt that freedom of choice was important to one's growth, and certainly demonstrated as much in her own life, at least until she got to Monaco—would become the strict parent.

Tough Love

Every action has a reaction," Grace Kelly told writer Curtis Bill Pepper in a 1971 cover story for *Vogue*. She had always been New Age in thinking before anyone even knew what New Age was, often talking in metaphysical terms about life's choices, about making mistakes and then "choosing again." She told him, "When you're married and have children, you realize how it is to give love and how love breeds love." The notion was easier said than done, as it would turn out for Grace and Rainier where their offspring were concerned.

For as long as the Grimaldi children could remember, their world had been regulated by obligations and protocol. Their days had started at seven in the morning—sleeping in late was never an option—and proceeded into a seemingly endless succession of studies and banal responsibilities. Weekends offered little reprieve, as they were often filled by personal appearances with their parents. The children were seldom permitted to enjoy even simple pleasures such as playing off grounds or watching television. During occasional family vacations they were allowed to relax a bit more and have fun. However, back at home, Princess Grace was inflexible: At the Palace they were expected to "toe the line," and adhere to royal standards just like everybody else.

"I was maybe fourteen when I started to see there were a lot of things my friends could do that we weren't allowed to do," Caroline recalled to writer Jeffery Robinson in 1989. "Our parents were very strict with us. They wanted us to stay home and read and take our school work seriously. We had to dress properly all the time. My mother didn't want me to wear a two-piece bathing suit when I was a teenager. She thought it would be more proper if I wore a one-piece even though other girls my age were wearing bikinis. We had to have somebody walk us to school and back. We couldn't just hang out with the kids. We didn't understand it then and I'm not sure I understand all of it now. I'm not sure all of it was necessary.

"When you're eight years old and want to play with your girl-friends and your Barbie dolls, it's not always easy to accept being told, maybe tomorrow. Mommy always used to say 'Maybe.' She said it so often that I used to imitate her telling me, 'I said, maybe, and that's final.' I guess what I'm saying is that we were a little too overprotected."

Albert had less of a problem adapting to such a structured life than his sisters. He spent much of his childhood with his father, training to be Rainier's successor to the throne. Caroline and Stephanie, on the other hand, were mostly paired with Grace. The three females were often at odds with one another, and had been from the time the girls were small—not unusual for two scrappy sisters and a fawning yet stern mother. But perhaps with this generation of Grimaldi women, the daughters sensed their mother's unhappiness, her disillusionment, and frustration.

Both of Grace's daughters had always seemed spoiled in public, with stories of their naughty misadventures often reported in the press, much to Rainier and Grace's dismay. A major reason they were so wild around others was because of Grace's resistance to public displays of discipline. After all, in terms of appearances—always a consideration to Grace—what looked worse: her daughters misbehaving or their mother losing her cool? So, many times, Stephanie and Caroline would run amok at public functions while Princess Grace simply ignored them, acting as if she was oblivious to whatever it was they were doing, or shouldn't have been doing, at the time. Privately, it was a different matter. Behind fortress walls, the daughters would be punished—often spanked, even as teenagers, their few privileges revoked.

In particular, Stephanie's behavior had been a problem from an early age. Each child had a nanny, yet Grace couldn't seem to keep one for Stephanie. She once had six nannies for her youngest child in a single year. "I really can't blame them for quitting," Grace told one friend. "Stephanie is so bossy. I hardly know what to do about her myself." However, Stephanie was so independent in her thinking that Rainier was loathe to break her spirit. He and Grace disagreed on this point. Grace thought she needed to be reined in. As she became a teenager, Stephanie turned into a tomboy: tough, aggressive, impish, and brimming with high-octane energy. She was smoking by the time she was twelve, behind her parents' back, of course. So focused were Grace and Rainier on Caroline that Stephanie somehow managed to get away with all sorts of mischief.

In 1972, Caroline was fifteen, Albert fourteen, and Stephanie seven. Each child had a distinctive personality. Caroline and

Stephanie were closest in temperament: unpredictable, fun-loving, and a bit spoiled. Albert was thoughtful and introspective, was kept close to his father, and didn't start public school until he was eight. As a teenager, he never caused any trouble—he was always sensible, and somehow seemed older than his years. He enjoyed visiting his cousins on the New Jersey shore, which Grace encouraged, hoping to expose him to youngsters his own age to whom he was related and who would not be intimidated by him.

While Grace and Rainier were proud of all three of their children, they viewed Caroline as the brightest. After her first schooling in the convent school of Les Dames de St.-Maur on the Rock, Caroline was enrolled in St. Mary's Convent at Ascot, England, another strict Catholic school, when she was about fourteen. "Catholic schools worked for me, and I know they will for Caroline," Grace had said. Caroline did thrive at St. Mary's, graduating two years later with the equivalent of a high school diploma, at just sixteen.

It would be their oldest, Caroline, who would present the first real challenge in parenting to the Prince and Princess. When she returned home in 1973, after spending two years at St. Mary's, she was brighter and more self-assured than ever, with language proficiency in Spanish, German, and English, as well as her native French. However, whereas when she was younger she had been more open to taking direction from her mother ("we have a lovely relationship," Grace wrote to Don Richardson), now she did not want to share everything with her parents, especially not with her mother. Grace was an evolved woman who understood this kind of change in a youngster, later saying to one reporter, "There's a certain point up to which a mother and daughter can share all confidences. But there are confidences a daughter will share only with friends her own age. A girl of sixteen can't have a woman of forty as her pal." However, the truth was that it hurt, and even angered, Grace that she and Caroline were no longer as close as they had been in the past.

Grace had thought it would be best if Caroline finished her studies in America, thereby balancing her European education, and also giving her the opportunity to experience a different way of life.

However, she was concerned about schools in the United States, particularly about the drug culture she thought her daughter might be exposed to, and decided against it. She and Rainier were both thrilled, then, when Caroline announced that she wanted to attend the Ecole Libre des Sciences Politiques to study government, as her father had done before her. However, in order for her to study at the Ecole Libre she would have to have her *baccalauréat,* an official French high school diploma. She decided that she wanted to obtain that diploma in Paris at the Dames de St.-Maur Lycée in the Bois de Boulogne. Immediately, Grace and Rainier were concerned.

It was Caroline's idea that she live with her grandmother, Princess Charlotte, while attending school in Paris. Charlotte enjoyed a close relationship with her grandchildren, much closer than she had with her own two offspring. Rainier wasn't happy about Caroline leaving home at all, but he realized he couldn't very well keep her in Monaco. So he agreed that if she had to go she could stay with his mother. Grace, however, didn't waste a moment vetoing that suggestion. She wasn't about to hand her firstborn over to a dowager who had never liked her and had never accepted her into the family. Though Rainier thought she was being overly sensitive to her mother-in-law's stubborn nature, Grace stood her ground. Besides, Mamou's lifestyle was a concern. She employed mostly ex-convicts at her home in Marchais, outside of Paris, part of her crusade that former prisoners be allowed to rehabilitate. It had also been reported that she had affairs with these men, though Grace knew better than to believe what she read in the press. Still, she didn't want Caroline living there.

Caroline, who was sometimes more mature and reasonable than her parents gave her credit for, then suggested that she live at the family's Avenue Foch apartment near the Arc de Triomphe with a female friend Grace approved of, and any other employee of the family selected by her parents. It was finally decided that if Caroline was so determined about going to school in Paris, Grace would accompany her and live in the city with her during the week, and then return to the Palace to be with Rainier and Albert on weekends. She would take Stephanie with her, and the three would live at the family's apartment on Avenue Foch.

"I love you so much," Grace told her daughter in front of Gaia Magrelli, who happened to be at the Palace discussing fabric for a renovation when Caroline walked into the den. "You are so special to me," she added, as she rose to embrace her. The two hugged tightly, until Caroline finally pulled away, probably embarrassed by the presence of another person in the room. When the young Princess walked away, she left her mother with tears in her eyes. "She wants to leave home, and I don't know how to deal with it," Grace told Gaia, whom she had gotten close to in the past year.

"I suppose you must let her go, Princess," Gaia told her, according to her memory. "I know it's difficult."

"But she's so young," Grace protested. "The world has changed so much. I'm scared for her."

Grace spoke to Gaia about her fear of becoming "an overprotective mother" and said that she sensed that if she didn't allow Caroline to live her life in a more independent manner she would "live to regret it." She said, "My worst fear is that Caroline will resent me for being so protective." Also, she said, "If my mother had wanted to go with me to New York, I sure wouldn't have allowed it. She bloody well would have stayed home."

"However, your father was not a Prince," Gaia reminded Grace.

"Well, not officially, anyway," the Princess said, laughing.

Though Grace expressed ambivalence about it, Prince Rainier suspected a dual agenda in his wife's decision to accompany their daughter to Paris. Obviously, Grace was concerned about Caroline's safety and well-being, but didn't she also relish the notion of, at long last, getting away from the Palace and living elsewhere? Considering her history of discontentment in Monaco, it would have been natural for Grace to view the dilemma of Caroline's schooling as an opportunity to leave the principality for a time—and maybe even her husband as well. "Rainier was as difficult as ever," said a relative of Grace's, "but, still, he loved her very much. As he got older, he became more temperamental. And as Grace got older, she became less patient. He was unhappy and hurt that Grace seemed so anxious to get away; however, he decided to approve of the plan, reasoning that maybe they really could use the time apart."

It was no big shock when Caroline objected to the notion of Grace's presence in Paris. Didn't her mother trust her? Wasn't this an opportunity for her to prove that she was an adult? "Caroline didn't want Grace living with her, watching over her like a hawk, kind of the way Grace felt when our mother went to England to keep an eye on her and Clark Gable," says Grace's sister Lizanne. "Funny how family history repeats itself, isn't it?

"Grace felt that she'd been locked up in that Palace for a long time and didn't want the same for her daughter," continued Lizanne. "She wanted her to have a full and good life, though she was worried about her, as would be any mother. In the end, she decided to let her go to Paris. 'I have to let her go,' she told me. 'After all, I left home—though I was a little older. I went to New York, and it was an important part of my life, Lizzie. So I know I must let her go.'"

Exodus from the Palace

In late summer 1974, young Princess Caroline left the Palace of Monaco for a flat in Paris where she would live with family friends Roger and Micheline Crovetto. She enrolled in school, and all was well—at least for a few days, which was how long it took the paparazzi to find the young Princess and to begin stalking her. Grace's daughter was now on her own in a major metropolis, ill-equipped to deal with the media's scrutiny of her. "Why do I have to be a Princess?" she cried to the Crovettos.

"I would kill those people if I could," Rainier said of the paparazzi after seeing some of the photographs, especially the headlines alluding to "secret affairs" and "wild parties." In fact, while Caroline was going out on weekend evenings to friends' homes for parties, and certain nightclubs as well, it wasn't surprising that she would want some freedom the first time she was truly on her own. She was sixteen, however, and anything but worldly.

Not surprisingly, Grace was pained by the screaming headlines about Caroline. The sensational reportage hit emotional hot buttons with Grace, not only implying that she hadn't been a good mother in allowing her daughter to be on her own in Paris, but also harkening back to a time in her life when she was under the same kind of scrutiny. She had felt at the time that she could handle the paparazzi, but she'd been accustomed to being on her own in New York by the time she was famous enough to generate such interest. Caroline was younger than Grace had been when she was being tailed by photographers, and also much more innocent.

Within weeks, Grace decided she now had no choice but to move to Paris, as originally planned, and be with her daughter. "It was Rainier's opinion that they should just drag Caroline home," said Gaia Magrelli. "However, Grace didn't want to pull the girl out of school. She decided that she should take Stephanie with her and that they would just do the best they could in Paris. Predictably, Stephanie didn't want to go. Grace might have taken Albert too, if she had been able to do so, but Rainier put his foot down. 'Absolutely not,' he said. 'Albie stays.' This decision really did divide the family, but it wasn't made without long deliberation."

The rule where young Prince Albert was concerned was clear: hands off—especially after the effects of Grace's parenting skills on Caroline and Stephanie were clear. Even though one of the Princess's requirements for devoting herself to her station in Monaco back in 1962, after the disillusionment of *Marnie*, had been that she be allowed more influence over Albert, she never got it. It was always understood that the next occupant of the throne on which Rainier sat would be a son shaped by his persuasion, not his royal wife's.

In the fall of 1974, Grace, Caroline, and Stephanie moved into the apartment on Avenue Foch in Paris. "It was a defining moment, as I recall it," said Gaia Magrelli. "It changed everything. It made everything . . . worse."

When Grace, Caroline, and Stephanie arrived in Paris, there was no way for the ravenous paparazzi there to contain their enthusiasm for such juicy new prey. Now these aggressive photographers had *three* Princesses to stalk, and they did not disappoint: Immediately, photos of the women became a daily fixture in the press, with comprehensive reports on their every movement.

Though Grace seemed unhappy, and more so than ever, she wrote to one friend of feeling as if she were now living in "a retreat within a fortress" and there was little she could do about it. She may have even wished she were back in Monaco, immersed in her royal duties. After all, Grace's life at the Palace had sometimes been so busy that she hadn't been able to keep track of what was going on there. In the early 1970s, she told a reporter that she had no idea how many people were employed at the Palace; there were so many butlers, maids, footmen, valets, housekeepers, laundresses, and chauffeurs that she'd lost count. "You see, whole households with children live inside the walls," she explained. "It's a whole world unto itself." In 1972, she wrote to Don Richardson that she was so busy in Monaco, she felt like "a one-armed paperhanger."

Now Grace had little to do but obsess over her daughters' safety and reputation. She spent her mornings outraged over the press coverage of whatever the girls had done the day before in the outside world. She began to argue with them over their rights to even leave the apartment except for schooling, and demanded that their security be beefed up to include more than one plainclothes bodyguard at all times. She couldn't just keep them in the apartment; they were young and full of life, and she had to let them out on weekends.

For her part, Caroline already felt that she would never live up to the standards of being a Princess, let alone to those of her mother, the highly principled Grace of Monaco. It would seem as if Caroline had made a conscious effort to do exactly as she shouldn't; her free-time activities as a "Playgirl Princess" had not been exaggerated by the media. She *did* enjoy dancing and frequenting discos all over Paris. She *was* photographed smoking, kissing boyfriends, and drinking. Her classmates *did* call her "Max," as widely reported, after a comic-strip character named Max the Menace—much to Grace's utter dismay.

Caroline's life in Paris became especially wild during the summer of her seventeenth year. Grace had taken part in so many screaming matches with her rebellious daughter that, as one of their housekeepers put it, "Both of them were hoarse from the shouting." As is common in the raising of teenagers, there were constant bids for power in the household. After years of practice, Caroline was skilled at wearing her mother down. "It was hard to tell who was the mother and who was the daughter," said that same housekeeper. "Caroline was not easy to deal with."

A schoolmate of Caroline's recalled one incident the teen Princess shared with her. As she told her friend, Caroline had been out until the sun came up, against the rules. When she walked in the door she found her mother in the parlor, seeming calm. "Aren't you going to ask what I did last night?" Caroline asked. "No," answered Grace. "If you had been here an hour ago I would have, but since the morning paper beat you here, I've seen a two-page spread on your entire evening." (Actually, Grace was probably reading a report of Caroline's activities the previous evening.) The conversation became heated, with Caroline claiming that her mother couldn't understand the pressures on her to prove that she wasn't *vaniteuse* (conceited). She said that she was doing everything in her power to blend in with her peers, lest they think she felt superior to them. "You're a Princess," Grace shot back. "You're supposed to be conceited." When this exchange fizzled out, Grace did the thing that infuriated her daughter the most. She picked up the recent copy of the *Almanach de Gotha*, described by its publishers as "the nearest thing there will ever be to a royal trades union when it comes to questions of dynastic disputes, successions or who's who in the extended royal and ruling families of Europe." Grace had been referring to this reference book from the time Caroline received her first Holy Communion, in hopes that a prospective husband for her daughter would be found in its pages.*

Many royal parents over the course of history have done exactly as Princess Grace in hopes of arranging the perfect marriage for their offspring. Caroline has spoken of her mother's fondness for the book: "She used to leaf through the *Gotha* to find a husband for me," she recalled, "and I felt so strongly that this was a constraint. And this was not supposed to be a priority in my family anyway. My father did not marry someone titled, did he?"

Grace was frustrated by her daughter's lack of interest in her role as a royal figure. "You have an undeniable place in history," Grace was once overheard telling Caroline. "Why not try to shape it so you're remembered fondly, so we're *all* remembered fondly?" Caroline's priorities were a mystery to her mother. She was a daredevil; she took flying lessons, drove a motorcycle, skied, swam, rode horses, and played tennis, all under the watchful eye of the press. Hoping possibly to instill more domestic values in her daughter, Grace suggested that she attend the fashionable six-week cooking course offered by Maxim's restaurant. "Why, I don't need that, Mommy," said the young Princess. "We've got slaves for that."

As speculation arose over whether or not the chestnut-haired Caroline was to be linked in marriage to Prince Charles or Prince Henri, heir to Grand Duke Jean of Luxembourg, Grace became immersed in the daily ritual of pouring through her *Gotha* to see if there was someone out there better suited than those rumored to be under consideration.

Imagine if Margaret Kelly had moved into Grace's apartment in Hollywood after Grace became famous and, with nothing else to do with her time, spent her Monday mornings reviewing sensational press coverage of Grace's activities the previous weekend,

---

*The *Gotha* is considered an indispensable tool for royal scholars. It was first published in 1763 in Saxe-Coburg, the court that, under Duke Friedrich III and later Duke Ernest II, attracted the likes of Voltaire. Today, as in centuries past, the *Gotha's* own familiar crown is stamped on the cover of what is considered, according to the publisher, "the ultimate power register of the ruling classes. Unmoved by government decrees or bribes, those not included in its pages found themselves thwarted, Pretenders' claims left in ruins, by the publisher who would not compromise itself for either inclusion—or exclusion."

then demanding an explanation for each report. It wasn't long before the real problem, at least in the Grimaldi daughters' view, was not outside the Avenue Foch apartment, but inside. It was their mother. The toll that this time—about a year—took on the relationship between Grace and her daughters cannot be overstated. Grace would pay a devastating price, in terms of erosion of trust and breakdown in communication between herself and Caroline and Stephanie, in order to be what she viewed as the best mother she could be under the circumstances. Years later, Caroline would remember of this time, "There were days when we truly could not take it. It was an awful, awful time for us as a family, and I felt terribly responsible."

Rainier's Jubilee

On May 8, 1974, Prince Rainier and Princess Grace celebrated the twenty-fifth anniversary of Rainier's sovereignty, his Silver Jubilee. (Though his official coronation had not been until April 11, 1950, Rainier became de facto Prince upon his grandfather's death on May 9, 1949.) During one of the first events of the two-week celebration, Grace unveiled an impressive bronze bust of her husband in the Centenary Gardens. As the Monegasques cheered on, Grace kissed Rainier on both cheeks, as did his daughters. Albert came forth with a firm and manly handshake.

Rainier intended that the Jubilee be a celebration not only of his reign over Monaco, but also a recognition of Grace's seventeen years there. She had worked hard for acceptance in the principality, and he felt strongly that the time had come for his subjects to grant her unconditional loyalty. The timing could not have been more propitious; it happened that it would be during his Jubilee that the Monegasques would finally form a strong alliance with their Princess. An important and, for Princess Grace, image-shaping gala would be the Texas-style barbecue, which had been Grace's idea, and which was held on the Louis II Stadium's soccer field. All of Monaco's 4,529 citizens were invited to attend. During the festive occasion, Grace wore what was described as "the official national costume" for the first time—white bodice and lavishly embroidered black silk apron over a red-and-white-striped skirt. (Caroline and Stephanie wore similar outfits.) If there was ever a noticeable turning point in Grace's relationship with her subjects, it occurred during that afternoon. Though royal in her demeanor, she presented a more accessible persona than ever—perhaps the straw hat with flowers was a great equalizer—giving undivided and sincere attention to every Monegasque who presented himself. She seemed to make a favorable impression on all present, including members of the media. Everyone ate, sang folk songs, and had a wonderful time. After that barbecue, Monegasques generally stopped referring to Grace as *"la Princesse américaine"* and began calling her simply *"la Princesse."* Also, while it never received any publicity in the States, Grace's subjects were well aware from local press reports that she had recently renounced her American citizenship to become a Monegasque. That decision, not particularly difficult for her to make since she had lived in Monaco for seventeen years, went a long way toward Grace's acceptance as Monaco royalty.

Another anniversary celebration, this one for the wealthy international crowd, was the Red Cross Ball. Both Rainier and Grace had always lent their support to the Red Cross, which is not only an organization for good works in Monaco, but also one of the most prominent social groups in the principality. Six hundred and fifty guests were invited to a sit-down dinner in the new marble and blonde wood Sporting Club (which would, in years to come, become a playpen for the nouveau riche as well as for those who like to watch them lose their money in the gaming areas). In anticipation of Rainier and Grace's arrival, guests mingled and drank "pinkies" and "blue sharks," two cocktails created for the evening. Finally, when the orchestra struck up "True Love" (from Grace's film *High Society*), the Prince and his Princess made a grand and royal entrance, then led their guests into the dining room for an elaborate dinner, beginning with Grace's favorites—caviar and champagne. (Three hundred and fifty bottles and twenty magnums of champagne were consumed that evening.)

The only glitch in the evening occurred when Sammy Davis, Jr., who had been scheduled to perform, refused to participate. A few hours before showtime, he sailed off in the yacht he had been loaned as partial payment for his services. Later, Sammy held a news conference in Beverly Hills to explain his actions. He claimed that he and his wife, Altovise, had not been invited to the same parties as the white entertainers. According to the *New York Times*, Davis said, "The Princess thought I was just another jig in the woodpile." Hopefully, Sammy had been misquoted, because any inference that Princess Grace was prejudiced was absurd.

It was Josephine Baker who came forth at the last minute to replace Sammy, with a dazzling show of her own; she also recruited Bill Cosby, Desi Arnaz, and Burt Bacharach to perform.

Grace and Josephine had been friends for several years. Baker, the stunning black singer and dancer, was an American expatriate from St. Louis, who had become the toast of Gay Paree in the 1920s. After settling in France, she gained fame not only as an accomplished performer but also as a humanitarian. She adopted twelve orphans of various nationalities and religions—ten boys and two girls, which she called her "rainbow tribe"—and then began to raise them in a vast French chateau, Les Milandes. In 1969, Josephine went bankrupt and lost her home—but not without a fight: With the heat and water turned off, she and her "tribe" lived in one room with a fireplace. When Grace and Rainier heard about the dire situation, they sprang into action and arranged for Josephine and her children to relocate into a large Riviera villa near Monaco. By working with the Red Cross, Grace also organized a fund that would enable Baker to become financially solvent. Josephine and Grace then became good friends.*

After midnight, the retractable ceiling of the Sporting Club rolled open. As the guests continued to dance, Grace and Rainier presented a glorious display of fireworks over Monaco. "It was a grand night," Rainier later recalled, "truly memorable."

While the Grimaldis may have had the same kinds of private challenges raising their children as other families—probably, many other Monegasque families—when it came time to present the royal image, the Prince and Princess of Monaco always acquitted themselves admirably. Celebrations such as the one commemorating Rainier's twenty-fifth Jubilee were commonplace in Monaco. During these extraordinary galas, the principality's denizens were invited to socialize with their Prince and Princess, shake their hands, speak to them, and laugh with them, all the while illustrating an unusual, mutual affection.

It's been said that Prince Rainier is the only sovereign who knows all of his subjects personally. Though it's an exaggeration, it's not far from the truth. Still today there exists an unusual camaraderie between the ruling family and its compatriots. By any stretch of the imagination, Monaco is an unusual place in which to live. Think of what it would be like in an American neighborhood if the Fourth of July occurred four or five times a year, and each resident was invited to the best block party imaginable in order to celebrate the day—hosted by the wealthy family that lives on top of the hill. Then add the glamour of royalty to the mix and, to make it even more interesting, a ruling family that makes itself accessible to "the little people." What kind of crazy world is that? "We call it Monaco," Prince Rainier would answer.

---

*About a year after Rainier's Silver Jubilee, on April 8, 1975, Josephine premiered at the Bobino Theater in Paris. Grace was in attendance to see the sixty-eight-year-old legend perform a medley of routines from her astonishing fifty-year career. The reviews the next day were among Baker's best ever. Just days later, she slipped into a coma. On April 12, she died from a cerebral hemorrhage. Grace led the funeral cortege; Josephine was buried in the Cimetière de Monaco.

Whatever Happened to the Old "Gracie"?

Princess Grace of Monaco was, by the mid-1970s, a very different woman than Grace Kelly had been in the 1950s. Grace of days gone by had lived her life as a renegade, dating whomever she pleased without discretion or much regard for what other people thought about her private affairs. She was optimistic, full of life, ready to take on the world. Grace wasn't just a budding free spirit, she was a woman who felt *entitled* to her freedom. She had done it her way, becoming a respected actress and realizing her dreams on her own, and during a time when success, respect, and autonomy weren't an entitlement for women; they were an anomaly. Going so far as to refuse financial support from her parents even when she might have needed it, Grace did everything she could back then to be both unconventional and to be her own woman. She seemed fearless, powerful.

Princess Grace was much more tame and old-fashioned, a consequence of living in the Palace for almost twenty years and conforming to so many strict regulations. She was often negative in her thinking, fearful of the world around her from which she had become so isolated. There was still a metaphysical woman beneath the present façade, and occasionally she did appear—but for the most part, she was buried beneath layers of pragmatism and realistic thinking. After all, hers was now a life of responsibilities. There were children and family; there was procedure. She no longer had the luxury of being unconventional. Grace had found herself in restrictive circumstances, and just like many do, she eventually conformed to them.

The frustration for her had always been clear: No one had forced her to choose Monaco over Hollywood, or over any other life, for that matter. Perhaps if the only thing at stake had been the marriage and the principality, she would have eventually changed her mind. However, it was ultimately the fear of losing her children that compelled her to stay the course. As far as Grace was concerned, she had chosen her fate, and now she had to live with the consequences. Should it be such a surprise, then, that she was now ambivalent about women's rights? About freedom of choice, independence, and free will? About defying convention?

For instance, Grace had no time or patience for the popular women's liberation movement of the 1970s, though she did openly support the idea of breast-feeding and was a spokesperson and honorary member of La Leche League (literally translated from Spanish as the Milk League). Many writers over the years have pointed to this endorsement as proof of Grace's alignment with a feminist cause. However, her link to the League actually had more to do with the notion of family nurturance than it did with women's lib. In Grace's view, nothing threatened the family more than the concept of a woman being liberated from it. However, her speeches regarding La Leche League were so poorly written that they did little to enlighten, and much to confuse, her audiences.

"I will not be the first to compare life to a never-ending relay race," she said to one packed house, "a handing over by us of the torch of life, out of the past to be carried into the future by our children. The act of breast-feeding, the giving of food and security from within our own persons, is an integral and vital moment in the passing of that torch."

Plus, Grace's support of La Leche League also had a fascinating tie-in to self-control and self-denial, concepts about which she was all too familiar. In another speech, she said, "Breast-feeding calls for discipline on the part of the mother. Sometimes it can be painful and discouraging. There is help of many kinds for these, but the greatest of all in overcoming them is the determination of self-control sparked by concern and responsibility for the child . . . and a well-being that comes from the natural act of unselfishness. The breast-feeding mother is living for the happiness of another beside herself." It's safe to conclude that Princess Grace's endorsement of breast-feeding was not an endorsement of the women's movement.

When her friend Rita Gam tried to engage Grace in a discussion about the women's movement as a whole, Grace was quick in her appraisal of it: "I think those women are disgusting," she said.

"For them to put a name on it, 'women's liberation,' well, it's the right thing to do," Rita offered, "to have a label on what we're working toward, what we've suffered from a lack of."

"Suffered from?" Grace asked, exasperated. "What in the world are you talking about?"

"Doing our own thing, Gracie," Rita tried to explain, using the lingo of the time. "That's what I'm talking about."

"Oh, for heaven's sake," Grace said. "It's so self-indulgent for women to do their so-called own thing. It turns women away from what is right and natural. I'm sick of hearing about it, really. So narcissistic!"

Years later, Rita said, "She just didn't know what I was talking about. It was ironic, because she was one of the first independent women in show business. She left her home, she earned her own living, she made her bed . . . but she was also trapped by her position, so I guess it was natural that she felt this way. However, for her to now be so closed-minded was a surprise. I couldn't help but to ask myself, 'Whatever happened to "Gracie"?'"

Many people thought Grace just sounded unenlightened, especially when she would throw off reductive one-liners such as one to John Bainbridge, a reporter for her hometown's *Philadelphia Inquirer*: "What we need today are more square people." Or, worse, when she told Joyce Winslow of *Holiday* magazine, "Some women may be able to cope with politics, but most cannot."

"My mother is beautiful but rather reserved," said Caroline of Grace. "She is a marvelous housewife, full of self-control, always impeccable down to the smallest detail. I sometimes find it difficult to do the things Mother expects of me."

When she was younger, Grace had had a number of relationships with older and married men and exhibited a certain amount of sexual freedom, unusual for the times. However, as an older woman she didn't seem to have much of an evolved perspective on sexuality—and when it came to pornography, she definitely had a strong and conservative viewpoint. "Take things like pornography and the sex magazines you see being sold everywhere," she told writer Roderick Mann in September 1974. "How must it be for a young girl walking past, seeing them? Either she'll turn into a sex maniac or become completely frigid. When I pass a newsstand selling those magazines, I go and talk to the seller. I tell him exactly what I think."

Many people who had known Grace for years—sometimes even her own husband—were confounded by her puritanical viewpoints. Rainier could probably be considered a chauvinist—he certainly never gave a second thought to women's liberation. Not only was he not nurtured as a youth to think of women as equal to men, the question of such equitability rarely ever came up in discussion. Still, he certainly remembered how spirited Grace had been when he married her and how she challenged him when, prior to their marriage, he told her she would have to abandon her career. She was a different woman by the mid-seventies, that much was certain. Sometimes her narrow-mindedness exasperated him, especially where their daughters were concerned. "They're girls," he once told her, in front of friends at a charity event. The subject of Caroline and Stephanie's upbringing had come up in casual conversation. "They'll be immature and irresponsible, we can count on that, my dear. It's our job to help them along; however, to frustrate ourselves over it is just pointless."

"In my view, it's not a frustration to insist that our children have self-control," Grace said, her tone adamant. "We don't always get to do exactly what we want to do in this world," she concluded, an observation painfully ironic to anyone who knew Grace's story. "Sometimes," she added, "you have to be told what you can and cannot do."

Prince Rainier, perhaps wisely, quickly changed the subject.

Antoinette Brucatto was present at the function. "Grace then turned to me and said, 'To be honest, Caroline and Stephanie have him wrapped around their little fingers. It's so frustrating. I hardly know what to do about it.' I said, 'Well, Princess, we were all young once,' to which she responded, 'Not me. I was never young.' Her comment rendered me speechless. As she walked away, I thought to myself, 'How ever did this happen to her?' Then I thought, 'Well, of course she would turn out this way, strict and rigid as she approaches middle age, now blind to the independence she had in her youth. Look at what she was forced to give up. Look at how her choices were limited for her, at how she was constricted by her circumstances. If I had been her husband, I wouldn't have had the gall to challenge her, under the circumstances. He was wise not to do so.' "

When one paparazzo caught Caroline during a particularly unfortunate moment, Grace became incensed. The photo showed the seventeen-year-old Princess dancing in a nightclub while wearing a provocative dress, a deeply plunging neckline accidentally revealing one breast. After its publication, Grace gave an interview and—as often happened when she spoke to the press—probably said more than she should have: "There was nothing wrong with that dress. It was the way that she wore it—or rather the way she didn't watch how she was wearing it. It may have been dark in the nightclub but she should have kept an eye on what the photographers were doing. That ugly and upsetting picture went around the world. We were distressed and so was she. She learned her lesson the hard way."

Domenic Forlini, an Italian friend of Caroline's who also lived on Avenue Foch and who dated the Princess from time to time, recalled Caroline's unhappiness with her mother at this time. "She felt, simply, that there was no pleasing Princess Grace," he recalled.

"I must say that the times I was in the presence of Caroline's mother and father were often not unpleasant. I once went to their apartment and both Grace and Rainier came to greet me. Imagine the intimidation factor of that. But, really, they were typical parents. 'Where are you going?' 'What are you planning?' 'When will you be bringing her home?'

"Prince Rainier was fairly amiable, but Princess Grace was chilly and unwelcoming. In front of the others, she said, 'If there are any unflattering photographs of Princess Caroline in the papers tomorrow, we shall hold you personally responsible.' The Prince then turned to his wife and said, 'My dear, if such a thing should occur, it would not only be this young man who would be held responsible.' I thought he meant Caroline would also be blamed, until I saw the way he looked at Princess Grace. She shot him back a warning stare. It was uncomfortable.

"When we walked out the door, the last thing I heard was Princess Grace shouting out, 'And you'd bloody well better not smoke, Caroline.' Caroline turned to me and said, 'How embarrassing!' We weren't even to the sidewalk yet when she pulled a thin cigar from her purse and asked me for a light."

Crossing the Line

Charlotte Winston, Princess Grace's longtime friend, was one of many people in her life who had noticed significant changes in her personality by the mid-seventies. "It was interesting, having known Grace for so many years, to see how, over time, she took on many of the more stringent characteristics of her mother," she recalled. "I visited her in Paris during a period when she was confused as to what to do about Caroline. 'All I am trying to do is protect my daughter,' she said, 'and if that makes me my mother, well, so be it.'

"I tried to reason with her, telling her that if she were overprotective of Caroline, it was only because she cared so deeply about what happened to her. I further observed that since we all knew her own mother didn't care enough, there was no similarity between them. Even though we had discussed Margaret's parental skills countless times over the years, Grace lashed out at me. 'First of all, that's not true of my mother,' she said. 'She only wanted what was best for me. I refuse to speak ill of my mother and would appreciate it if you didn't.'"

Suddenly, Charlotte was talking to the Grace Kelly who cared what people thought, and who never wanted anyone to think poorly of her parents, except with one difference: In speaking critically about her mother, Charlotte was also, in a sense, now speaking critically about Grace—that's how much Grace seemed to be identifying with Margaret.

Charlotte recalled another conversation she had with Grace while having breakfast with her one morning at a Parisian sidewalk café. In a futile attempt to be incognito, Grace wore a beige turban and large Jackie-O sunglasses. As she ate her meal of *oeufs en cocotte*—individual servings of eggs, each baked in a crock—she complained about the recently published photos of Caroline in her scandalously low-cut dress. "How can she allow photographers to take such photos?" Grace asked. "What was she thinking?"

"Gracie, do you remember when you and that gorgeous Jean-Pierre Aumont were photographed, right here in Paris, many years ago?" Charlotte asked, according to her memory. "You were holding hands and kissing. Remember?"

Surely Grace remembered that time with the French actor. It was right after she met Rainier at the Palace, in 1955. Her public romance with Aumont had been caught by photographers. Pictures of the two appeared in the very same *Time* magazine that now, almost twenty-five years later, had published the "offensive" photograph of Caroline.

Back then, Grace had been so anxious about Margaret's reaction to the photos of her and her French lover that she sent a telegram to her in Philadelphia: "I'VE LOST NEITHER MY HEART NOR MY HEAD." She then telephoned her mother to tell her not to believe everything she read in the press. "Even pictures?" Margaret had asked. "Yes," Grace had answered. "*Especially* pictures, Mother. They can be doctored! You would be *amazed* at what they can do these days!"

Now, decades later, Grace didn't seem eager to discuss Jean-

Pierre. "I don't see the relevance," she said. She took off her sunglasses and stared at Charlotte, slowly narrowing her gaze.

Charlotte continued, "As I recall it, you sent a telegram to your mother because you were afraid of what she was thinking."

Grace wasn't about to start drawing ironic parallels between her past and her daughter's present. She straightened her back, adopting a regal posture. "All I know is that Caroline needs to toe the line, *today*," Grace said angrily. "And what I did one hundred and fifty years ago has no bearing on it whatsoever." She also noted that "the times are too permissive, anyway," veering slightly off subject. "Whatever happened to manners, anyway?" she asked, giving Charlotte a sharp look.

Many years later, Charlotte recalled, "I thought that the Princess role she had been playing for so long had taken over. Not only did Caroline have to toe the line, after that brief conversation, I felt that I did as well. *Princess* Grace had been . . . well, *royal* with me."

Charlotte Winston says that she suspected Grace's bad mood had much to do with fear. She had been in her Monaco tower for so long, Charlotte theorized, she had forgotten what it was like in the real and contemporary world, and she was scared of it—for herself and her children. Also, Charlotte felt that her friend had worked for so long to be considered a "real" Princess, it was likely that she feared Caroline's behavior would reflect poorly on her. Moreover, even if she was finally being viewed by her subjects as a good Princess, the rebellious nature of her daughter perhaps meant that she had been a bad mother. "But, in the end," Charlotte concluded, "what really hit me was that she seemed somehow . . . *bitter* about the whole thing, and that was so unlike the Gracie I knew and loved."

Charlotte recalled that a heavy silence hung between the longtime friends, making it clear that she had crossed the line of propriety with Grace. "Somehow, when it's your own daughter, I suppose it is different, isn't it?" Charlotte said to Grace, hoping to hit a conciliatory note.

"Indeed," Grace said, her tone still icy. "One would suppose so, wouldn't one?"

The Princess flagged down the waiter and asked for the check, signaling to Charlotte that breakfast was over. The two women rose. Grace leaned over and kissed Charlotte on both cheeks. "Gracie, please don't be mad at me," Charlotte said. Through a frozen smile, Grace responded, "Why, darling, perhaps you should have thought of that *before* you decided to throw my past in my face." After delivering her parting shot, she turned and began to walk away.

"See you later, alligator?" Charlotte asked weakly, hoping for the "crocodile" response. She didn't get it. Grace never stopped walking.

What to Do about the Past?

It's likely that Princess Grace feared she would one day be forced to deal with her youthful Hollywood indiscretions, and that such confrontation might even occur in an embarrassingly public way—especially in the 1970s when tell-all books about celebrities came into vogue. While there had always been a sensational element to the media's coverage of celebrity lifestyles, going all the way back to the advent of show business scandal magazines such as *Confidential* in the 1950s, the permissiveness of the 1960s and '70s allowed for even more freedom in writing about the private lives of public figures. Movie magazines such as *Photoplay* and *Modern Screen* reached their zenith in popularity and circulation during the forties, thanks to the 50 million Americans attending movies every week. After World War II, as movie-going began to wane, so did the circulation of the fan magazines. Their coverage of the new television medium helped to recover some of their popularity in the fifties. But it remained for Jackie Kennedy, the Queen of Camelot, to commandeer the covers of the magazines in the sixties that had been dominated by the stars of television and movies. Today it is the supermarket tabloids that have taken over from the movie magazines.

In the seventies, all bets were off where the notion of privacy for public figures was concerned. The Woodward-Bernstein investigation of the Watergate break-in (and their subsequent book, *All the President's Men*, in 1974) launched a feeding frenzy among Americans for their kind of investigative reporting and the secrets that such reporting engendered—even if it meant bringing down the Presidency. The public's thirst for warts-and-all nonfiction made possible such biographies as *Mommie Dearest* by Christina Crawford, about her own mother, Joan, in 1977, considered by many in the publishing business as the first truly sensational tell-all celebrity best-seller. (It's not likely that Joan Crawford's image as a child abuser will ever be rehabilitated after that book and the movie based upon it: "No more wire hangers, ever!") A year later, *Jackie Oh!* by Kitty Kelley became one of the biggest-selling books of the decade.

At about this same time, in 1975, the respected New Zealand author Gwen Robyns was preparing what she intended to be a full-fledged biography of Princess Grace. Such an undertaking had not been previously attempted, the only publication close to it being Grace's friend Gant Gaither's 1957 book *Princess of Monaco*. Although Gaither's book was sweet and nostalgic in tone, it upset Grace. She actually banished the author from Monaco for a number of years, before finally reconciling with him. ("Rainier says the greatest quality a friend can have is discretion," Grace wrote to Prudy Wise, "which Gant certainly has not shown with this. It is terribly disappointing.")

Robyns, a scrupulous researcher and writer who had previously written about Vivien Leigh and Agatha Christie, did attempt to obtain Grace and Rainier's cooperation with her book. However, when she was unable to do so, she proceeded with her research anyway. Finally, she did obtain the cooperation of the Kelly family in Philadelphia, including Grace's mother and sisters—and then she was exposed to Grace's friends in Hollywood. The story she got from Grace's show business peers was nothing like the one she had envisioned she would be writing when she began the work. Details of Grace's Hollywood romances came forth in a way that promised big sales for Gwen Robyns, but also a complete reevaluation of Princess Grace in the public eye. Torn about how to now present Grace in light of all of this new information, Robyns says, "I just wrote it all up, and sent it to her at the Palace, and held my breath. I wanted to give her a chance to respond, though I didn't think she would."

When Grace received the manuscript, she discussed it with Rainier. According to a source who worked for Rainier at the time, "He wanted to read it, but she said, 'Absolutely not.' She said that some of it wasn't true and that she didn't want to have to go over it with him and separate fact from fiction. He became concerned. 'Well, if it's not true, then we must stop it,' he said. 'We'll sue.' Grace was smarter than that. 'You can't sue until *after* it comes out,' she said. 'And by that time, the damage has already been done. Believe me, I have been down this road many times.' The Princess said that because people in her office had told her that Gwen Robyns was a reasonable woman, she'd decided to deal with the matter personally with the author. 'I'm tired of fighting with the press,' she said. 'For once, I wonder what it would be like to just sit down with one of these people and explain my problems to them.' Rainier said, 'I can tell you what will happen: They will then write about your problems.' Grace laughed. 'Well, that does make sense,' she said."

Gwen Robyns recalled, "One day my telephone rang, one of Grace's secretaries calling. The Princess had summoned me, wanting me to meet her in Paris. Of course, I said I would be happy to go."

When Gwen Robyns flew to Paris to see Princess Grace at the Avenue Foch apartment, she feared that their meeting would be a contentious one. To the contrary, however, Grace was polite, unassuming, and surprisingly anxious. A smart woman, and a media-savvy one as well, the Princess must have realized that sitting before her was a journalist who knew many, if not all, of her secrets—and that such knowledge gave Gwen Robyns a certain power over her, understandably daunting to any former movie star with a colorful past. "She was playing with her hands, wringing them, appearing to be almost frightened," said the writer. "She seemed vulnerable."

It's difficult to know whether or not Grace was "acting" the afternoon she met with Gwen Robyns, primarily because she dressed for the occasion in a way that implied virginal innocence—not the way the Princess dressed under ordinary circumstances, especially for a business meeting with a stranger. "She had no makeup on," said Robyns, "and she was wearing a simple, pleated skirt and a little silk blouse. Her hair was pulled back. My God, I thought, she looks like a schoolgirl. I was astonished. I kept saying to myself, 'This can't be Princess Grace, it just can't be. Can it?'"

The two entered Grace's well-appointed dining room, filled with French antiques and framed photographs of her family. A floral arrangement of soft peach roses and light blue delphiniums graced the table, which was set with fine white china edged in silver. Pale pink napkins folded in the shape of swans sat at the two place settings, opposite each other. In the center of the table was a silver tea service from which would be poured Earl Gray tea. A butler brought a silver tray of food: open-faced tea sandwiches of cream cheese and watercress, scones, crumpets, and tea cookies with jam and butter, as well as other high tea delicacies, such as *petits-fours* and chocolate-dipped strawberries. The two women sat down and, after a few pleasantries, Grace got to the matter at hand.

"First of all, I must tell you that I respect your work," Grace began, according to Gwen's memory. Grace conceded the difficulty of writing about another person's life and said that she had always enjoyed biographies. "I think this is a good story," she said, "even if it is my own life." She laughed, tilting her head back girlishly. "However, I am a little worried about a few things."

Gwen recalls having held her breath.

"You see, I have two daughters," Grace began carefully. "And they are my primary concern here." She said that she couldn't care less about what people thought of her as a result of Gwen's book, and said that she wanted the writer to not only know as much "but believe it, because I swear to you it's the truth." She then went on to say that she'd "already been through the mill many times," and therefore understood "the way the media works." "I have always lived my life in the spotlight," she said, "and I have taken my lumps because of it. So be it. I always knew what I was doing and I'm not ashamed of any of it. Not one second of it." However, she added that things were different in her life now, because she had children to consider, "and the problem I have, frankly, has to do with what you have written about my life before Monaco."

"Fine," Gwen said, immediately impressed by her subject's candor. "Then we shall go through the book together, and deal with it."

"I don't want to spoil your book," Grace said, seeming surprised.

"Well, I don't want to spoil your marriage," Gwen said with a smile.

"Then, while drinking tea and eating strawberries, we went through the entire manuscript," recalled Gwen Robyns. "She didn't deny any of it, any of the romance stories. She was very forthcoming. 'Oh, Oleg, I simply adored him,' she said. 'But my mother now, darling, *that* was the problem there.'"

"You see," Grace told Gwen at one point, "my dilemma is this: How can I tell my daughters not to have affairs with married men when that's exactly what I did when I was young?" She said that she was having "enough problems with Caroline already," and that if her elder daughter were to read the book in its present form, "there'll be no dealing with her." Then, pointing to the first page of a chapter about her romance with Ray Milland, Grace said that reading details of it after so many years would prove embarrassing because the Millands—still married—now resided in Monaco. She felt it would be unfair to embarrass them by calling to mind an extramarital relationship from a time long ago. "It's so unfair," she said. "They're lovely. Besides," she confided, "I really thought their marriage was over back then. I had no idea I was just one of a long string of affairs he'd had. I was only twenty-four," she added. "What did I know?

"And this business about me and Bill Holden," she said, flipping to another chapter. Grace suddenly looked sheepish. "You see," she said, "Rainier doesn't even know about me and Mr. Holden . . ."

"Then I will reconsider it," Gwen offered. "All of it."

"I would so appreciate it," Grace said. "What can I do to help you?" She then offered to introduce the author to friends of hers who could assist her in her research. "I wouldn't think to try to stop you from writing about me," she concluded, "and I know you will do what you have to do."

Gwen now says, "I was completely seduced by her, I admit it. I knew she had problems with her girls, and I knew she had certain issues with Rainier, and I wouldn't have hurt her for the world. I'm not that kind of person, so, yes, I deleted all of it: Holden, Gable, Milland, Aumont, Cassini . . . all of it."

The absence of material about Grace's affairs altered Gwen Robyns's book considerably, making it not as comprehensive but certainly a great deal more upbeat. When it was published in the spring of 1976, the author sent a copy to Grace in Monaco. Not long after, she received a telephone call from her. "I can't believe you did it," she told Gwen. "But, somehow, I knew you would. Please come see me so I may thank you." She then invited the author to the Palace. In the end, Gwen Robyns's acceding to Grace's wishes would lead to a long and close friendship with the Princess and her husband. Over the next few years, Gwen spent a great deal of time with Grace—who was thirteen years her junior—at the Palace and also at Roc Agel, and Grace reciprocated with visits to Robyns's farmhouse home in Oxfordshire, England. Gwen would also collaborate with Grace on My Book of Flowers for Doubleday in 1980.

"I can't say that I regretted my decision to censor that biography," she now says. "I did get a wonderful friend out of the deal. Besides, I spent many hours soul-searching at the time and I believed then, as I still do, that Princess Grace was more concerned with protecting her family from her past than she was in trying to rewrite it for her own benefit. Her daughters, in particular, were her concern.

"I remember her saying, 'They'll get all of this startling information soon enough. If at all possible, I'd rather them not have it now while trying to raise them. God knows I have my hands full as it is.'"

Rebellion

In the fall of 1975 after obtaining her *baccalauréat*, Princess Caroline entered the Ecole Libre. However, the strain of the last year had taken its toll on the young woman, who was now even more stubborn than she'd been in the past when it came to exerting her independence from her parents—her mother in particular.

By this time, Princess Caroline was an attractive and shapely eighteen-year-old and already one of the most popular figures in pop culture, thanks to making fashion expert Eleanor Lambert's annual "Best Dressed" list that year, as well as a cover story in *Time*. Less than twenty years earlier (in January 1956), Grace had appeared on the cover of *Time* with the accompanying headline, "Gentlemen Prefer Blondes." Annoyingly, at least for Grace, gentlemen also seemed to prefer brunettes in the seventies, at least judging from the long line of suitors at Caroline's door. "I would like to get this straight," said Caroline, in one of the interviews marking her eighteenth birthday, this one to the *New York Times*. "I don't spend my life on the social scene, and those romantic stories annoy me. I seem to keep reading all the time about myself with people I haven't met. I have to do homework every moment I have free."

Not only had the constant media scrutiny under which she had lived since moving to Paris to attend school embittered Caroline, but what Grace feared most when she decided to go to Paris with Caroline had also happened: Caroline resented her for it. Rainier's relationship with his girls mirrored that between many doting fathers and their daughters: He attempted to be firm, but he was actually a softie when it came to Caroline and Stephanie, especially Caroline. Very often, when the first child is a daughter—even though a son might have been wanted—she becomes "Daddy's girl" and remains Daddy's darling throughout her adult life. It certainly was true in the Kelly household, where Peggy was clearly her father's favorite. Rainier had a miserable mother who had forced her husband out of Rainier's life. However, Rainier was much more involved with his children when they were young than his forebears had been. As they grew older and more difficult, he was happy to turn over the parenting bit to Grace because that was her "job," while his was to be a father figure to the whole country. So he left it to Grace to reprimand them, thereby making her their adversary in many instances. "My mother was the disciplinarian in our family," Grace noted in an interview with Curtis Bill Pepper for McCall's in 1974. "My father was very gentle, never one to spank or scold. My mother did that. But when my father spoke, boy, you moved. I believe the father teaches authority, and the mother sees that it's done. It's that way with Rainier and myself."

The battle lines were soon drawn between Caroline and her mother, with Stephanie siding with her sister. It went deeper than Grace's feeling that her daughter, now eighteen years old, shouldn't wear so much makeup, or smoke. It became a philosophical difference about what was "proper behavior for a Princess," as Grace often put it, and what was Caroline's right to live her life as she wished. How ironic it was that Caroline was the spitting image of Grace's mother-in-law, Princess Charlotte, with her aquamarine blue eyes, brown hair, and olive skin. Charlotte had never approved of Grace and had not set foot in the Palace since the day her daughter-in-law showed up there in 1956!

Rainier had come to believe that Grace was being too strict with their daughter—with both of them, actually—and his lack of support of his wife's position began to cause a wedge between them as well. Caroline knew she could override many of her mother's wishes by going directly to Rainier. If Rainier caved, as he often did, Grace couldn't help but be angry at him for undermining her actions. Whenever children play one parent against another, it creates dissent in the entire household.

Luckily for Prince Rainier and Princess Grace, they had few problems with young Albert. He was athletic, intelligent, reasonable—literally a Prince of a boy, good-looking and personable, especially as he entered his teen years. He attended secondary school in Monaco and then took his *baccalauréat* at a lycée named after Albert I, his great-grandfather. During the summers, he sometimes attended camp in New Hampshire, giving him the opportunity to visit with his American relatives—all of whom were inevitably impressed and charmed by the well-behaved, disciplined lad. He was an interesting combination of both parents: generally outgoing and demonstrative like his father, but at times reserved and seemingly unknowable like his mother. His parents didn't feel the need to worry about Albert. He would attend Amherst College in Massachusetts, after Rainier rejected Harvard (too liberal) and Princeton (too competitive). After college, Albert would serve in the French navy, stationed on the warship *Jeanne d'Arc*.

By the time Stephanie came along, Rainier already had fathered his heir to the throne and was more than happy to leave this child's rearing to Grace. After going through a series of miscarriages, Grace knew this was the last child she would bear and was even more indulgent because of that fact. "When Caroline was little, it seemed as if I spanked her every other day," Grace admitted at the time. "Albert didn't need so much. A sharp word to him was enough. Stephanie? Well, I should have been beating her like a gong long ago. You get a little tired with the third one and give in to keep the peace."

Indeed, worn out by Caroline's demands, Grace threw her hands in the air and figured if she loved Stephanie enough and kept the door open, it would suffice. It didn't. Stephanie was spoiled as a child and seemed to get even worse as she aged. "I thought she spoilt the little one too much," confirmed Grace's sister Lizanne. "She was so thankful to have Stephie that she spoilt her. She would call her 'my baby' and really give her anything she wanted, let her do anything she wanted. I would say, 'Grace, maybe you'd better watch that one,'" Lizanne recalled with a laugh. "'That one is trouble,' I would tell her. And she would say, 'Who? My baby? Why, no, Lizzie, she's just spirited,' and we would laugh. But, oh . . . we knew. We knew."

Like her sister Caroline, Stephanie began her education at the convent school of Les Dames de St.-Maur on the Rock. More athletically inclined than her sister, she was interested in gymnastics and was good at it as well. She also attended ballet classes at Marika's Academie. One always knew one's standing with Stephanie, a vastly sensitive and deeply emotional teenager. Whereas Albert and Caroline had their mother's sense of diplomacy as they became older, Stephanie had her father's more direct approach to communication: She said exactly what she felt in frank terms, and left it to the listener to determine how such information should be digested. She was candid, sometimes to the point of seeming arrogant. Still, while her parents tried to teach her to be less blunt, they admired her direct approach to life. She was true to her convictions, stubborn though they may have been at times. Rainier and Grace decided early on that their youngest daughter would go far in life because no one would ever be able to cow her, or pull a fast one on her. Still, when remembering her as an adolescent, Rainier has had to admit, "she was quite the holy terror."

Carlos Caprioni, one of Princess Grace's assistants during 1975, recalled, "It seemed to me that Stephanie was given more latitude than the other children, though I don't know why. Some on the Princess's staff felt that it may have been because she'd had so many miscarriages prior to Stephanie's birth. Many times, I saw Stephanie push Princess Grace beyond the limit of all endurance.

"Once, I was with the Princess in London on business in a hotel suite when Stephanie came bursting in, screaming at her mother about a boy who had called and whose message she hadn't been given. In a stoic manner that was all her own, the Princess just took it all, smiled faintly, and said, 'I'll make sure you get your messages in the future, dear.' Stephanie said, 'See to it that you do, Mommy,' and then stormed back out. It was ugly, and embarrassing. I wanted to chase her down and smack her myself. However, Princess Grace acted as if it had never occurred; we just went on with our business.

Later, in an offhanded manner, she said, 'Dear Stephanie. A royal pain in the ass, isn't she?' I didn't feel it appropriate to agree. 'Well, she'll soon be going to the Galapagos Islands with her father on a cruise,' she said, adding, 'thank goodness.'"

At the end of her semester at the Ecole Libre, Stephanie's sister, Caroline, made an announcement: She did not wish to continue with her studies. It was a rash decision made by a rebellious teenager, but an understandable one when viewed in light of the repressive and heavily ritualized life she had led up to that point.

"This rebellion business has gotten out of hand," Grace decided. She packed up her two daughters and took them back to the Palace.

When imagining Princess Grace leaving Paris to take her daughters "back to the Palace," perhaps the image comes to mind of her bringing the girls to a giant old castle, and then locking them away in a dungeon where they will be forced to do their homework while sitting cross-legged on a stone floor. Perhaps she would even allow a tray of food to be slipped into their dungeon, if they completed their tasks. Actually, nothing could have been further from the truth about the way the Grimaldis lived.

By this time—the mid-1970s—Grace was in the middle of a dramatic remodeling of their living space in the Palace. In doing some research on the history of the royal home of Monaco, she happened upon architectural plans that indicated that there had once been a wing on the west side of the Palace's main entrance. When she learned that it had been destroyed during the French Revolution and then turned into a hospice, Grace became intrigued. She decided that she wanted to restore the area as the royal family's new home. During the course of the work, she managed to locate some of the original pieces of furniture, as well as paintings. Her vision was as an open, airy, and contemporary motif, but with a touch of the classic. When completed, the large apartment was home to the Grimaldis from the mid-seventies into the eighties; today, Prince Albert lives there.

The living room—called the Grand Salon (only Princess Grace would dub her living room the Grand Salon!)—is a strikingly large room that boasts golden Italian marble floors and a fireplace that Grace designed of sea stones from Monaco and from Grimaldi, the family seat in Italy. A double white sofa is one Grace picked up while in New York. An eighteenth-century Chinese screen stands behind a monk's refectory table. Cages with birds are suspended all about, with hanging plants and giant palms. Above the living room is a study loft where, today, Prince Albert works. A smaller study is next to it, where Grace once performed her office duties as Princess. When visiting, Princess Caroline now uses this space. Outside, on a patio that overlooks a courtyard, is an extravagant steel-and-brass balustrade, which Grace found in Paris. The apartment also has a dining room, kitchen, and family room on the bottom level. Upstairs is a master bedroom, his-and-her dressing rooms, and a large bath. The three children had two-room suites upstairs as well, separated by another large family room in which each had a desk for schoolwork. Today, Caroline's children—and sometimes Stephanie's—can often be found in these rooms.

Prince Albert shows this living space to guests proudly because it remains largely the same as it did when his mother remodeled it to her exact specifications. (He often refers to his mother as "Grace" when discussing her household activities, and "Princess Grace" when talking about her work in the principality.)

Once back at the Palace, Grace and Rainier showed a united front in addressing Caroline's education, even though they disagreed as to how to proceed. Grace wanted Caroline to go back to school in Paris, whereas Rainier wanted her to go to Princeton, now feeling she needed to be as far away from metropolitan Parisian influences as possible. Since they had previously tried it Grace's way, they agreed to send her to Princeton. Caroline wasn't consulted, she was told what she would be doing, which did little to align her to her parents' point of view about her education. However, the notion of being in America—far away from her mother—did intrigue her enough that she agreed to enroll in Princeton; she was scheduled to begin attending school there in the fall of 1976.

Grace's Brother in Trouble

As if Grace and Rainier didn't have enough distractions with their daughters, another unsettling family matter concerned them at this same time, the fall of 1975.

Back in America, Princess Grace's brother, John Brendan Kelly, Jr., "Kell," was considered the logical Democratic candidate to run for Philadelphia mayor against the headline-grabbing incumbent, Frank Rizzo. Many observers thought Kell had grown as a politician and speaker, so much so that his chances to win a mayoral election would be favorable. Previously elected to the city council three times, he was at the peak of his persuasive powers. It was also thought that his late father, Jack—gone for fifteen years by this time—had been robbed long ago, in the 1935 election, and that Kell would once again balance the scales of justice, just as he had done with the Diamond Sculls at Henley. However, Margaret Kelly had another idea: She didn't want him to run.

Much to Margaret's dismay, Kell had left his wife, Mary, six years earlier after twenty-five years of marriage. They had six children. He said at the time that his thinking about the notion of monogamy had changed—which it had, but not in any way that was healthy for a marriage. Instead of choosing to be faithful to his wife, he admitted that he was a philanderer, and simply left it at that. He was no longer going to act as if extramarital affairs did not exist in his life—everyone interested could know about them, and then deal with it. Margaret, of course, was aghast. "Do what you have to do, but do it like your father," she told him, according to Cathy McKenna, who was Kell's councilman administrative assistant. "Keep up appearances. It worked for us, didn't it?" Kell told his mother that he would no longer tolerate a marriage such as hers, "where the couple acts as if the husband is faithful when everyone knows he's not."

When Kell finally confessed all of his indiscretions over the years to his wife, she was crushed, saying she had not known about any of them. He too was amazed, thinking she *had* known all the time, but was being quiet about them, just as his mother had done for so many years. Mary filed for divorce, but, because she was pressured by Margaret to withdraw it, ended up just being separated from Kell for eleven years.

Kell then made the rebellious decision to become publicly associated—though not romantically—with a popular blonde transsexual performer, twenty-eight-year-old "Rachel Harlow," formerly Richard Finocchio. His mother was incensed. Jules Lavin, who was Margaret's escort after Jack's death, told Kelly family biographer Arthur H. Lewis, "Ma Kelly had it on good advice that one of the posters being prepared, should Kell be selected as the primary candidate, would read, 'Will the First Lady be Harlow?'" Lavin felt that Margaret did not want to expose her family, and especially the Princess, to such controversy. She was determined to put an end to the campaign before it began.

While she may have been concerned about any scandal that might affect Princess Grace, Margaret was also angry with Kell for ending his marriage, for not heeding her advice regarding appearances, for reminding her that her own marriage had sometimes been a sham—and also, maybe more importantly, for making her look like a less than perfect mother. Using her influence with the president of the city council and the chairman of the Democratic Committee, she made her move on the evening before the official announcement that he had received Democratic backing for his mayoral campaign. She threatened that if her son—whom she referred to as "Junior"—ran for mayor, *she* would be the one to air his dirty laundry, and on television. "I know more about him than anyone else," she said, "and I'll be more than happy to reveal it." She also said that she would financially support his opponent, Frank Rizzo, in his campaign. The party decided that nominating Kell promised nothing but heartaches from Margaret Kelly, and decided against it.

Few people in positions of power in Philadelphia were unaware of what Margaret had done to her son. "He had defied her, so she fixed him . . . and she fixed him good," said Cathy McKenna. "He was devastated by what she'd done to him, and completely destroyed in city politics. I think he could not believe she'd done it. When I spoke to him afterward, he was a changed man." The forty-eight-year-old son of Jack and Margaret Kelly would never again be thought of as a serious candidate for any local political position. "He had so much to give, and all he wanted to do was give it," said his sister Lizanne. "Looking back on it all these years later, I can't say I really understand what happened, or why. I truly can't. I'm a little perplexed by it. I loved my mother, that's all I can say. We all did."*

As much as they loved her, both Grace and Rainier were taken aback by Margaret's actions. Grace had been so supportive of her brother's political aspirations and had even gone to Philadelphia to assist him in the campaign by making a special appearance at the city council. Cathy McKenna recalled, "It was chaos when she showed up. Never had I or anyone there seen anything like it . . . sheer bedlam. She went with Kell to each and every councilman's desk, shook his hand, spoke to him, asked about his family, gave autographs, posed for pictures. What an impression she made! There wasn't enough she could do for Kell. Watching the two of them together was so heartwarming."

---

*Kell divorced Mary in 1979 and remarried in 1981. Despite the fact that he never again ran for an election, he would remain a popular Philadelphia fixture, known for playing the role of George Washington in the annual Philadelphia re-creation of Washington's Christmastime crossing of the Delaware River. In excellent shape, he jogged every morning and spoke frequently of his personal dedication to fitness. He would continue to run the family's brickwork business until selling it in 1985 to begin a four-year term as president of the U.S. Olympic Committee. Tragically, he had held his new post for only three weeks when, on March 2, 1985, he collapsed and died of a heart attack at the age of fifty-seven. He was survived by his second wife, Sandra; a son, John B. III, and five daughters; his mother, Margaret (in a nursing home by this time); and sisters Peggy and Lizanne. Prince Rainier, Prince Albert, and Princess Stephanie attended his funeral service.

Not only did Grace and Rainier feel badly for Kell, they were astonished by Margaret's vengefulness toward him. Though Margaret and Grace had forged a more peaceful relationship since Caroline's birth, Grace still saw the side of Margaret that was demanding and unreasonable. However, what Margaret had done to Kell was a harsh reminder to Grace that her mother could be malicious, and this awareness scared her. "She was heartbroken for Kell, scared for her mother, and for herself," said Antoinette Brucatto. "'I can't believe she did that to him,' she said. 'Could that be me?' she kept asking. 'Am I turning out that way? Do my girls think of me that way?' What her mother did really hit Grace hard. It made her wonder about her own ability to raise children. Rainier kept telling her, 'Look, you bloody well are *not* your mother. Caroline is not you. Stephie is not you.'"

Some wondered if, perhaps, there had been something physiologically wrong with Margaret that might better explain her treatment of her son. A few months later, she suffered a severe stroke. Distraught, Grace rushed to Philadelphia to be with her, but Margaret had lapsed into a near-vegetative state. It was impossible for anyone to reconcile any of it, with so much left unsaid, so much unsettled. A sorrowful Grace returned to Monaco praying that the doctors were wrong, that her mother would somehow recover. She never did.

Margaret Kelly would remain mentally impaired until her death at the age of ninety-one in January 1990, never even aware that her daughter Grace, or son, Kell, had died. Shortly after Margaret's death, on November 26, 1991, Peggy Kelly Conlan—Grace's elder sister—passed away after a long and courageous bout with alcoholism. Lizanne Kelly LeVine is the last surviving member of her generation of Kellys. "They all died and left me, the dirty sons-of-guns," she said in 2002, her sense of humor, such a Kelly family trait, still intact.

Philippe Junot

Princess Grace and Prince Rainier were relieved that their daughter Caroline was leaving Europe to attend college at Princeton in the United States. However, their respite from melodrama was short-lived, for, in the summer of 1976, Caroline met a man whose presence in her life would dramatically alter the course of events.

Princess Caroline met Philippe Junot one night at Regine's, the famous nightclub in Paris. At thirty-six, good-looking, with lots of wavy dark hair, a muscular body, and a gleaming smile, he was seventeen years older than Caroline. He possessed such a worldly, refined veneer that some of Grace's less enlightened friends made comparisons between him and Oleg Cassini. In truth, Junot and Cassini were both jet-setters, but that was where the similarity ended. Whereas Oleg was a passionate, motivated man with a booming career as a fashion designer, Junot, at least at this time in his life, was frivolous and free-spirited. He loved to dance, have fun, and live in a way that seemed to be, at least to most observers, irresponsible.

Philippe Junot was witty, charismatic, and entertaining. (If not also perhaps a bit gauche: He referred to Caroline as "fatty" upon first meeting her at that disco, though, oddly, she didn't seem to mind. Maybe it was the *way* he said it.) He was usually trailed by a posse of friends who acted as if they adored him and depended upon him to organize their good time. Described by some as a "ringleader," he was loyal to the people in his circle, almost to the point that he seemed to feel obligated to keep them entertained. Perhaps betraying a deep insecurity about himself, he was the one who organized social gatherings, he was the one who felt responsible for the enjoyment of all participants—though he often wasn't the one who picked up the tab—and he was the one who felt it a personal failure if the evening had not gone well, as if the success of a night on the town for his friends was part of some job description for him.

Actually, as it happened, few, if any, seemed to know what Philippe Junot actually did for a living, though there was talk that he was involved in "investments." There were also stories—which Philippe didn't deny—that he was a descendant of Andoche Junot, the first Duke of Abrantes. (Andoche Junot got his title from Napoleon after conquering the Portuguese town of Abrantes.) The French version of *Who's Who* had Philippe's father, Michel, listed as a direct descendant of the old warrior, but when Rainier checked that claim further, he found it to be untrue, though the name Michel Junot did sound familiar to him.

Also, Philippe Junot said that he had graduated from the New York Institute of Finance, but it wasn't long before the press learned that the Institute was not issuing diplomas at the time he said he graduated. There was simply too much mystery surrounding this young man's background for the Prince to be comfortable about him. When Charlotte Winston met Philippe, she recalled that he struck her as the "type of man Grace might have had in her life way back when—a little too slick for his own good but, oh, so sexy."

Junot today dismisses the word "playboy," widely used to describe him at the time he was dating Caroline, saying, "I was a man who wanted to have a good time like anyone else. The difference between me and other people was that I actually did it. I worked a lot, but when I was finished, yes, I played tennis, I went out with fun people, I went dancing in clubs. I'd get to bed at four or five in the morning, and then at 8:30 A.M. at the latest, I would awaken and get on with a new and exciting day. There was nothing wrong with the way I lived, for a young man. More people wished they could do it. Caroline loved my energy, my zest for life. I did live. I *loved* living. I still do. More people should try it."

At the time he was involved with Caroline, Philippe Junot would often cite as his greatest annoyance the inevitability of the first question asked of him: "What is it you do?" Being pressured to answer what he called "that question" was inappropriately invasive of his privacy, he said. How he earned a living was nobody's business, he insisted. While that may have been true where the public was concerned—and considering that he had become so quickly involved with as public a person as Princess Caroline of Monaco, it is debatable—it certainly wasn't a response Prince Rainier and Princess Grace appreciated when they posed "that question" to their daughter in regard to her new beau.

It wouldn't have taken a psychology major to discern that Rainier and Grace would not be happy about the presence of this older man with no discernible employment in the life of their nineteen-year-old daughter. His enigmatic nature did nothing to ingratiate him to them. At worst, they feared, he was a fortune-hunter. To some, Grace began to refer to Junot as being "from café society," meaning he was shallow and not of royalty or the aristocracy.

"They simply wished I would go away," Philippe recalled. "That was no secret, and no surprise."

In the view of Rainier and Grace, Philippe was the worst kind of influence, and for many obvious reasons, not the least of which was that he actually seemed to court and even enjoy the kind of sensational media attention his whirlwind assignation with Caroline generated. When the couple went vacationing in St.-Tropez, they told Rainier and Grace they were in Paris. How they thought they could get away with such a ruse was a mystery, especially considering the hungry, predatory pack of paparazzi following their scent.

After photos of Caroline sunbathing in the nude surfaced in the press—with her new boyfriend nibbling at her breasts—Grace's response was predictable. She was angry and embarrassed. Rainier's reaction was more fascinating. Of course, he wasn't happy. However, as he put it to one confidant, "Royal scandal is as old as the notion of royalty itself. Check the history books. Worse has happened, and worse will in the future." While Rainier certainly realized that, for royals, the notions of discretion and sexual restraint were to be adhered to as principles, he also realized that they often were not—such is the nature of royal scandals. After all, his own family history held some rather vivid examples of royal indiscretion. While he accepted it, Grace could not do the same. In some ways, it could be said that she had become more "royal" than her husband, at least in terms of rigid thinking. So when she demanded that Rainier give Caroline and Philippe a "good talking to," he did. The Prince summoned Caroline and Philippe into his office to express appropriate outrage.

Indecent photography aside, the bigger issue for Rainier was that Caroline had, at nineteen, made the choice to link up with an older man who appeared to be a playboy with not much going for him. While Grace was not surprised, Rainier was taken aback by his daughter's decision. He had imagined her to be too savvy to allow herself to be taken in by someone just because he was colorful and exciting. He had thought of Caroline's years of rebellion as being just an annoyance, natural in her maturation to womanhood. He hadn't taken her insurgence as seriously as had Grace. Because he hadn't been living with her in recent years, he hadn't been a first-hand witness to much of the drama that involved his daughter.

While Grace often expressed annoyance that Rainier hadn't taken his elder daughter's actions more seriously over the last couple of years, he had accused her of overreacting to Caroline's attempts to exert her independence. However, now that Caroline had become involved with a man he perceived as a true ne'er-do-well, Rainier didn't know what to think. A Palace source overheard Princess Grace expressing little patience for her husband's bewildered state. "Why you are so astonished at the situation as it now stands is a true mystery," she told him. "Darling," she concluded, "a Philippe Junot was *inevitable* in Caroline's life, in all of our lives."

Caroline knew that although Albert was the heir apparent, it would probably be many years before he became ruler. In the meantime, she had almost no official obligations; Grace took care of most of the ceremonial duties and at least appeared to enjoy them. To Caroline they were chores and she didn't bother to hide her feelings. Smart and attractive, Princess Caroline could have gone far in academia or the business world. But, being a Princess, and a stunningly beautiful one at that, she was tracked by the media. They invaded her privacy. They exaggerated. They invented news when there was none. Once Caroline starting dating, Grace began to strictly curtail her activities. It would have been more helpful, though, if she had given her lessons in how to handle the media. Surely, from her Hollywood days, Grace knew the value of cooperating with the press, the art of giving them just enough of an approved story so she could then control what she'd rather not see in print.

Domenic Forlini, who had dated Caroline in Paris but had never really become involved in a serious relationship with her, received a surprising telephone call from Princess Grace asking for his assistance. "Never had I heard from the Princess about anything," he recalled. "We were strangers in every way, other than experiencing the inevitably awkward meeting that occurred whenever I had to collect Caroline at the front door. Once, I saw her at the Monte Carlo Beach Club and she snubbed me in a way that embarrassed even the waiter. However, Princess Grace was now different toward me. 'Why did you stop seeing Caroline?' she asked me in a pleasant voice. I told her that it just hadn't worked between us."

"Have you heard about this young man she is now dating?" Grace asked, according to Forlini's memory.

He said he had read about Philippe Junot, but had never met him. "Seems like a nice chap, though," he offered.

"That he does," Grace concurred, her tone careful. However, she added that she and Rainier were concerned about the sudden romance that had developed between their daughter and Junot. "I am telephoning some of Caroline's good friends to inquire about him," she said casually. "For instance, have you any idea what this nice chap does for a living?"

"Isn't he in investments?" Forlini answered. "At least, I think that's what I've read."

There was a long pause. "Hmmm. I've read that as well," Princess Grace said. "Fascinating," she stated. Then, after another silence, she added, "Mr. Forlini, I want to thank you for speaking to me. Have a wonderful day." After saying good-bye, she quickly hung up.

"I was beside myself," recalled Domenic Forlini. "I felt badly for this mother, who, I presumed, had decided that resorting to calling Caroline's friends was the only way to learn about Junot. She was a celebrated person, a Princess, a star—yet in the end, she was just a worried mother trying to get information on her kid's activities any way she could get it. I fantasized that if Caroline had kept a diary, Princess Grace was looking for it under the bed. I also felt badly for Caroline that she and her mother had this kind of difficulty between them, this lack of communication. I thought 'My God, what a shame this is.' I also decided never to tell Caroline that her mother had called me. Knowing her as I did, I suspected that such a revelation would only lead to trouble."

Caroline may not have told her mother much about Philippe, but she really didn't need to provide too many details. Grace was well-acquainted with the Philippe Junots of the world; she'd come across plenty of them in her Hollywood days. Since she'd dated a number of men like him, she could understand Caroline's attraction to someone like Philippe. He was sexy and exciting, obviously. But was he husband material for a Princess of Monaco? How many girls had already fallen at his feet? How many hearts had he already broken? His easy success with the opposite sex gave him a confidence Grace found completely unappealing.

Would he be faithful to Caroline in marriage? Grace doubted it. Certainly women would find him irresistible for years to come. Would he be a stimulating mate, a person who might broaden Caroline's horizons? Grace doubted that as well. He was shallow, unworthy of Caroline—at least in her estimation of him. While Philippe Junot would probably have objected to such reductive thinking about him based purely upon the superficial, he offered little else upon which to base any evaluation.

To think, after all of those hours of Grace poring over the *Gotha*, Caroline ended up with this guy, Junot. "I guess that serves me right," Grace told Gwen Robyns, the irony not escaping her. "Remind me to throw that damn book away."

One afternoon, Gwen and Grace were shopping at Harrod's in London. "I know I don't like him," Grace said, "and I know why. But you don't like him either. Why is that?"

Without missing a beat, Gwen said, "Well, his remarks are too trite. His teeth are too bright. And his crotch is too tight."

Grace laughed so hard, she could barely catch her breath.

Grace then told Gwen that she could see in what she called "my mind's eye" that Caroline would marry Philippe, that the marriage would last less than two years but would be miserable for her daughter. "And there's nothing any of us can do about it," she concluded. "It's already written."

Show Business . . . but Not Really

In 1976, Hollywood again beckoned Princess Grace when her former agent, Jay Kanter, presented her with an opportunity to once again become involved in show business. By this time, Kanter and Alan Ladd, Jr., were heading up the studio and production departments of 20th Century-Fox. When a position on the ten-man board was vacated Alan, Jay, and Dennis Stanfill, chairman of Fox at the time, thought of Grace. Though they believed it to be a far-fetched idea, they decided that Jay should ask if she would be interested. Kanter recalled, "When I telephoned her, she was surprised and honored. She asked that she be allowed to think about it for a few days. She then called back and said she would like to do it." As the first woman on the board of 20th Century-Fox, Jay Kanter says, "Grace performed the normal duties of a board member, to look after the stockholders' position, make certain [budgetary] approvals, that sort of thing."

For Princess Grace, one of the advantages to being on the Fox board was that her position would afford her the opportunity to travel in luxury four times a year to meetings in New York or Los Angeles. Often, the trips were at Fox's expense, but sometimes not. David Voellinger, chaplain at the Palace at the time, recalled, "She was planning a trip to America for a board meeting. The Prince asked her how she was going, by Air France or another commercial airline. She shook her head and said that Cary Grant was sending his private plane to pick her up. Rainier just raised an eyebrow."

These trips allowed her to leave Monaco—"a gift from heaven," as she put it to Kanter—and reconnect with old friends and relatives in the States. (Whenever she did make it to the States, it was always the cause of great chaos, with police and other security forces lining the streets.)

Dennis Stanfill has said that Grace became much more than "just a token" Fox board member, even if that may have been the board's intention upon approving her position. She took her role seriously, studying reams of material before every meeting, showing up prepared to do business. She would use the Fox screening room in Paris to stay updated on current films, and then make her conservative position clear at meetings: "too much sex and violence, not enough storyline." At one point, the Princess criticized a particular director for what appeared to be his free-spending ways, warning the board that if they didn't put a stop to his excesses they would go over budget. It was unusual for the board to criticize specific directors; no one listened to Grace. Sure enough, the movie came out and lost a bundle. "See that," Grace told Dennis Stanfill. "I knew it. Oh, I still do love being in this business, even if it's not in front of the camera." (Princess Grace would remain on the board for four years, until the studio was sold in 1980. Today it is owned by Rupert Murdoch's News Corporation.)

That same year, 1976, Jay Kanter proposed a return to films for Grace in the Herb Ross movie *The Turning Point*, written by Arthur Laurents, author of the musicals *West Side Story* and *Gypsy*. The story involves two women whose lives are dedicated to ballet: Dee Dee, who abandoned her promising career to marry and have children, and Emma, who went on to become a ballet star, though she is about to retire—and is not happy about it. Both want what the other has, and now face middle-age conflicts together.

Herb Ross recalled, "We wanted Princess Grace for the Dee Dee role, but thought maybe it was a bit too close to home, what with the character having abandoned her career and not being happy about her lot in life as a result. I, personally, had no idea if Grace was happy in Monaco or not, but on the off-chance she wasn't, I didn't want to offend her. However, we thought, what the hell? Let's give it a shot, she could do *either* role for all we cared. When she read it, she loved it, thought it was well written, very good, but also thought she should play the Emma role so that people wouldn't identify her so much with the character of Dee Dee. My view was, hey, whatever she wanted to do, we would do. I felt she would win an Academy Award for it, whichever role she ended up playing. She was interested, and told Jay Kanter that she would discuss the matter with Rainier and then give him a final decision. I was excited, very hopeful."

When Rainier and Grace discussed it, it became clear that Grace wanted to do the movie. It wasn't the first time in recent years that she had been approached. In 1970, Hollywood producer Sam Spiegel had offered Palace chaplain Father David Voellinger complimentary use of his 250-foot yacht, as well as the services of its crew for the entire summer, if he could persuade Princess Grace to play the lead role in Spiegel's motion picture *Nicholas and Alexandra.* The priest had to tell the producer that he didn't have that kind of influence over Grace, but word got back to her about the offer anyway. She turned down that role, mostly because she didn't like the script.[*] She didn't want to reject this movie as well. "How many more chances will I get?" she asked.

Unfortunately, Prince Rainier was adamant that Grace should turn down the role, especially given what was going on with Caroline and Philippe Junot. The Prince felt that Caroline needed Grace's undivided attention. Decorator Gaia Magrelli recalled, "Grace knew that Rainier was right. The timing was off. 'How could I concentrate?' she had asked. It hurt her to have to turn down that film. She would chalk it up to yet another sacrifice for her family and the principality. It was disappointing, so unfair.

"They ended up having a benefit premiere [for the film] in Monaco, which was so like Princess Grace to suggest such a thing,

---

[*]Actress Janet Suzman took the role in the film, which was released in 1971. She was nominated for an Oscar in the Best Actress category, as was the film for Best Picture. Neither would win.

to swallow her frustration and put on a happy face. She must have been heartbroken."*

Though deeply disappointed, Princess Grace had other work to do and couldn't spend much time dwelling on any unhappiness.

On August 2, 1976, the Forty-first Eucharistic Congress opened in Philadelphia for eight days, before 6,000 attendees. The theme of the Congress was "Hungers of the Human Family," with each day emphasizing a different physical, moral, or spiritual hunger—that is, a hunger for God, for truth, for peace, for family. Between Ella Fitzgerald and Dave Brubeck performing religious jazz, and Mother Teresa of Calcutta acting as keynote speaker, there were so many activities that *Time* dubbed it the "Catholic Olympics." (Although Pope Paul VI was scheduled to attend, ill health kept him in Rome.) Almost two million communion wafers were consumed.

On August 3, the *New York Times* reported, "In another conference on family life today, Princess Grace of Monaco, a native of this city, warned against permissiveness in child rearing and declared that 'the Christian family is of utmost importance and can be a strong and vital force in today's society. But we need help,' she continued, 'and we look hopefully to the church for encouragement and guidance.' The Princess was accompanied by her husband, Prince Rainier, who also spoke, and their two children, Princess Caroline and Prince Albert. They received a long respectful ovation when escorted to their places with other dignitaries, including Cardinal Krol of Philadelphia, host to the congress."

Meanwhile, back in France, when Grace's friend Gwen Robyns heard that the 1976 Edinburgh Festival was searching for an American with a good speaking voice to read poetry at the event, she suggested Princess Grace. "John Carroll, the organizer of the poetry recital, mentioned the opening to me, and when I told him Grace was perfect for it, he was thrilled," Gwen recalled. "I telephoned her and told her that this was just what she was looking for. Though

---

*The movie starred Shirley MacLaine as Dee Dee, and Anne Bancroft as Emma. It received eleven nominations—a record at the time—including nods for MacLaine and Bancroft, but would go winless in every category.

she couldn't go to Hollywood and make movies, this could be a good outlet for her to express herself in front of an audience. Mr. Carroll had worked with some of the best of British actors, such as Peggy Ashcroft and Ralph Richardson. Grace was excited. 'Do you think I can do it?' she asked me. I told her, 'My dear, you are a movie star. What do you think?' She thought it over, spoke to Rainier, and got back to me quickly with a yes."

In September 1976, Grace appeared with American actor Richard Kiley, and British actor Richard Pasco of the Royal Shakespeare Company, in four recitals at Edinburgh's St. Cecilia's Hall, reading poetry to sellout crowds and also to the delight of critics who attended. The trio's reading of American poet Elinor Wylie's "Wild Peaches" (which Grace performed with a southern accent) would go on to win the BBC's Pick of the Year as the best poetry reading of 1976. For the next six years, Grace would appear in arts festivals reading poetry for sellout crowds in cities such as London, Stratford-upon-Avon, Dublin, and Chichester. ("This work has rejuvenated me in a wonderfully surprising way," she wrote to Antoinette Brucatto. "What sheer joy it is!")

Francesco Greco was a fan of Grace's who would become a friend of hers in the late seventies, following her to many of her poetry readings in the States. He refers to himself as having been a "Groupie de Princess Grace." Greco recalled, "The American International Poetry Forum brought her to the States [in 1978] for twelve performances, and I was lucky enough to see the Princess at Princeton in her presentation called 'Birds, Beasts and Flowers.' [Grace's fee was donated to the World Wildlife Fund.] When she walked out in a beautiful silk gown, her hair pulled back in a chignon, and stood in front of the microphone, you could hear a pin drop. She took my breath away, she was so moving as she did her marvelous reading of Wallace Stevens's poem about flowers. She had the right tone for poetry, the right presentation, so poised. The applause was deafening, and she just stood there and soaked it all up, tears running down her face. I so wished the Prince had been there to see it, but he wasn't. Later, she sadly told me he had never [up until that time] seen her do a reading, which I thought said a lot about their relationship.

Prince Rainier recognized Grace's unhappiness when she finally settled into the Palace. He would do anything in his power to help her adjust to her new life, with no career and no friends. She didn't even speak French—and, to make matters worse, her mother-in-law and sister-in-law disliked her! (PHOTOFEST)

On January 23, 1957 (just nine months after the wedding), Princess Grace gave birth to her and Rainier's first child, Princess Caroline Louise Marguerite. Caroline's birth guaranteed the continuation of the Grimaldi lineage and freedom of Monaco from France, as per the terms of the 1918 treaty. (PHOTOFEST)

On March 14, 1958, Princess Grace gave birth to Prince Albert Alexandre Louis Pierre, a son and heir for Rainier. The Prince and Princess pose with their children, Princess Caroline, one year old, and Prince Albert. (PHOTOFEST)

Thirty-one-year-old Princess Grace with her three-year-old son, Prince Albert, in New York in April 1961. Even as a young boy, "Albie" was level-headed and reasonable, unlike his more recalcitrant sisters. (PHOTOFEST)

A meeting of icons: While in America in April 1961, Prince Rainier and Princess Grace met with First Lady Jackie Kennedy and President John F. Kennedy. (PHOTOFEST)

On February 1, 1965, Princess Grace gave birth to Princess Stephanie Marie Elisabeth. "I think Grace spoiled Stephanie because she became so exhausted by the difficulties of trying to raise Caroline," Rainier would later say. (PHOTOFEST)

The proud Royal Family of Monaco in 1967, standing on the balcony of their Palace; note father and son in similarly royal uniforms. "I think the experience of my parents' separation when I was only six subconsciously made me very much want my own marriage to succeed," Prince Rainier has said. "The Princess and I tried to minimize any disagreement between us in the interest of keeping the family together—so that the children would not suffer." (PHOTOFEST)

By 1974, Grace and her mother, Margaret, had put aside their differences and were closer. Margaret marveled at the way her daughter eventually adapted to life as Her Serene Royal Highness. Here the two chat during the Princess's visit to Philadelphia that year. (PHOTOFEST)

After leaving Hollywood, Princess Grace tried to keep up with old friends such as her former director Alfred Hitchcock, seen here with her in New York in 1974. Twelve years earlier, Grace had been forced to turn down a role in his film *Marnie* because her subjects so vehemently objected to the idea of her returning to films. (RETRO-PHOTO)

The Grimaldis—(clockwise from lower left) Caroline, Albert, Stephanie, Rainier, and Grace—pose in April 1976. That year Grace went off to live with Caroline and Stephanie in Paris, ostensibly to watch over them as they attended school there. However, Rainier suspected that Grace secretly relished the idea of, at long last, getting away from the Palace. (PHOTOFEST)

The Prince missed his Princess when she was in Paris and greatly anticipated her return to the Palace. Grace's quiet serenity, her willingness to listen, and the fact that she made no demands on him made him appreciate her more than ever before. Here Grace and Rainier, forty-eight and fifty-four, make one of their many official appearances in 1977. (REPORTERS ASSOCIES/RETRO-PHOTO)

For Princess Grace of Monaco, along with age came wisdom. She realized that she had forced twenty-year-old Caroline into the arms of an unsuitable husband. Perhaps remembering her own impassioned youth, the Princess concluded: "I suppose Caroline must obey her heart at that age. I know I always did." Here Grace poses with one of her pets while on vacation in Switzerland in February 1977, at the age of forty-eight. (RETRO-PHOTO)

On June 27, 1978, Princess Caroline married playboy Philippe Junot. Grace had suggested that Rainier issue an official ban of the wedding, but the Prince thought better of it. "Princess Grace and myself saw it as a mistake," Rainier later said of his daughter's marriage. "But there was no use opposing it. I think that's why there wasn't more harm done, because we didn't wave our fingers at her, saying, 'See, we told you this was wrong.'" (PHOTOFEST)

By August 1980, Princess Caroline's marriage was all but over, and Grace suggested a divorce. After all, how many times over the years had she wished she could have changed her own circumstances? She was happy that her daughter had the freedom to choose. Here Caroline (on the right), with Prince Albert, Grace, and Rainier, arrive at the Monaco Red Cross Ball that year, two months before the final decree. (PHOTOFEST)

In March of 1981, Princess
Grace met the troubled
Princess Diana of Wales.
When Diana asked for
advice on how to adjust to
her new life as a Royal,
Grace put her arms around
her and patted her on the
shoulder. "Don't worry,
dear," she said with a
gentle smile. "You see, it'll
only get worse."
(THE ACADEMY OF MOTION
PICTURE ARTS AND SCIENCES)

On April 19, 1981, Princess Grace and Prince Rainier celebrated their silver wedding
anniversary at the home of Grace's former *High Society* costar Frank Sinatra and his
wife, Barbara. Left to right: Princess Caroline, Frank, Barbara, Grace, Rainier, Princess
Stephanie, and Prince Albert. (PHOTOFEST)

Mother and son, Grace and Albert, share a dance at a Palace ball on October 8, 1981. Never would anyone have believed that, in less than a year, Grace would be gone. (PHOTOFEST)

On September 18, 1982, Prince Rainier buried his wife, Princess Grace. "My life will never be the same," he said after the service (which took place in the same Monaco cathedral in which he and Grace were married). Here, Albert and Caroline flank their deeply grieving father. Stephanie was still in the hospital, due to injuries suffered in the accident that claimed her mother. (BETTMAN/CORBIS)

Twenty years later, royal life goes on for Prince Rainier III and his family. This photo was taken in 1999 when Rainier, seventy-four, celebrated his Fiftieth Jubilee. Prince Albert, forty-one, stands at his side. Seated is Princess Caroline, forty-two (left), and Princess Stephanie, thirty-four (right). An oil painting of Grace in the background is a reminder of the glory days of yesteryear. (HERIBERT BREHM/ CORBIS SYGMA)

Though he is not one to look back, Prince Rainier III can't help but miss his wife of twenty-six years. "We were very close and discussed and debated everything—problems or plans or decisions," he said of Princess Grace. "That is now a void, a great and awful emptiness. We worked as a team . . . and the team was split up, forever. Since then, it's never been the same." (CORBIS)

"Poetry is what saved Princess Grace, I believe," Greco said. "It was what gave her life again. It was show business, but not really. Leave it to her to find a way, I thought. She had fought for years to not get completely swallowed up by Rainier's world, and now she was finally creating one of her own again."

Afterward, Francesco Greco went backstage to visit Grace, who was sitting at her vanity, surrounded by elaborate displays of red and yellow roses. Behind her, on the mirror, she had taped telegrams from well-wishers, just as one would expect a star to have in her dressing room. "Oh, *dah-ling*," she said, exaggerating the word comically when she saw her fan. Then, motioning grandly to her surroundings, she said, "Well, it's not my dressing room at MGM, but it is magic just the same, isn't it?" Francesco agreed. "So, tell me the truth. Was I good?" she asked urgently, as if his opinion truly mattered, though she'd just received two standing ovations.

"*Dah-ling*," he said, "you were wonderful."

The Princess laughed, tilting her head back in a way that was all hers. "You know," she concluded, "I *was* rather good, wasn't I?"

An Official Ban of Caroline's Wedding?

After a few weeks of living with the subject of the enigmatic Philippe Junot on his mind, Prince Rainier III of Monaco finally conducted his own investigation into the background of his daughter's suitor. He soon learned that Philippe's father, Michel Junot, had been a member of several ministerial cabinets and was, at the time, a deputy mayor of Paris under (current President) Jacques

Chirac, and also president of the French branch of Westinghouse Electric. Rainier also learned that Philippe supposedly held stock in shopping malls in North America, though he was unable to verify such holdings. The name Junot had sounded familiar to him, he had said, and once the young man's background was confirmed he did feel more at ease, though he wondered about the purpose of the mystery Junot had created about himself.

Finally Caroline told her parents the disappointing news that she had changed her mind about attending Princeton. Instead, she wished to enroll in the Sorbonne in Paris and study for a *licence* (bachelor's degree) in psychology. She explained the obvious: She wanted to remain close to Philippe Junot.

In early 1977, Philippe asked Caroline to marry him. She accepted his proposal. She was twenty. He was thirty-seven. Rainier and Grace were distraught. A romance was bad enough, but marriage? Lizanne LeVine recalled that her sister feared that Philippe Junot, a practiced seducer in their view, would not change his ways after marriage. "Oh, he was a playboy, let's face it," she said, "a real son-of-a-gun. Grace and Rainier did everything to rationalize it for themselves. Grace said to me, 'You know, Lizzie, maybe because he's older he'll be a good influence on her.' That didn't wash. Then, later on, she said, 'Lizzie, maybe Caroline will be a good influence on *him*.' Well, that didn't wash either. None of us wanted her to get hurt, and we all felt it was going to happen. Finally, Grace said, 'What do you do, Lizzie, when you know your child is headed for disaster and you can't stop it from happening?' I told her, 'You let her get hurt, Gracie. There's no other way. Then you just have to be there to pick up the pieces.'"

Still, Grace and Rainier pleaded with their daughter to delay any wedding for a few months so that she could focus on her studies. Reluctantly, Caroline agreed. However, in the fall, she decided that she wanted to marry as soon as possible. Many years later, she explained to writer Jeffrey Robinson that she decided to marry in order to have more freedom. "I was twenty or twenty-one, and didn't really want to get married. But I wasn't allowed to go off on vacations with him or even spend weekends with him, except at his parents' house, which was all very proper. Getting married was simply the correct way out."

Princess Caroline assured her parents that she would not marry Philippe Junot if they continued to disapprove of the union. Instead, she would simply live with him. It would have to be the lesser of two evils for Grace and Rainier: Should they allow their elder daughter, age twenty, to "live in sin" with a man who seemed to have no job—and how would that look to the principality?—or should they allow her to legitimize the affair and marry him?

For Princess Grace, the decision was an easy one. She was more sophisticated in such matters than her devoutly Catholic husband, having come from a Hollywood ethos. She would rather Caroline simply live with Junot, rather than risk a bad marriage to him. She reasoned that Caroline didn't really love Philippe anyway, that she was just rebelling against her parents, and that it wouldn't take long for her to realize that she had made a mistake. While Grace agreed that it would be terrible for the principality to have one of its Princesses living openly with a playboy, public relations could not be her primary concern at this time. Her daughter's future was more important.

Caroline was Grace's firstborn; Grace had poured herself into the making of this young woman, sacrificed for her from the time she left America for Monaco until the time she left Monaco for Paris (maybe even putting her marriage in jeopardy in the process). Was she now supposed to relinquish her daughter to someone she didn't know or trust? She didn't know how she could do it, but said that, lately, she was feeling more "clueless" as a parent than ever before—especially after what had happened between her own mother and her brother back in Philadelphia. Antoinette Brucatto recalled that Grace "was grasping at straws trying to figure this thing out, trying not to be her own mother, trying not to ruin her daughter's life the way her mother had ruined Kell's."

In Rainier's view, since Caroline had been living with Junot in his apartment anyway, she already knew him pretty well. If his appeal hadn't diminished in her eyes by this time, it never would. Still, Rainier didn't know what to suggest, what course of action to take. At a loss as to how to deal with the matter, he did what he usually did in such situations: He deferred to his wife. Still, he seemed more sensitive than ever to what the press was reporting about his daughter, even though she had certainly not presented herself as the most conservative Princess in history. When a few months earlier, in October 1976, a young, wealthy, but obscure playboy named Francisco Scarpa, Jr., had suggested in a TV interview in Rio de Janeiro that Caroline had been one of his lovers, Rainier heard about it and was livid.

Maybe the Prince was having a bad day, because much worse had been said about Caroline by this time. Or perhaps the incident was the proverbial camel's-back straw for a protective father—or maybe he was just hoping to scare off other rumormongers—because Rainier decided to sue, which he did in January 1977 (just in time for Caroline's twentieth birthday, on the twenty-third). Grace's and Rainier's spokeswoman, Nadia LaCoste, explained, "Look, we're not going to let this young man get away with murder." Rainier asked for $4 million in damages. Then, when the editors of *Pan*, a Belgian satirical magazine, made fun of Rainier's suit, he sued *them*. (The suit against Scarpa was later dropped when he apologized; however, *Pan* ended up paying damages of $3,300 to Rainier and $1,650 to Caroline.) It was all a silly business; Caroline may not have known the one playboy, but she certainly knew another, Philippe Junot, and it's doubtful that she was a virgin since she was living with him. She was getting ready to marry him, and no court of law was going to prevent that from happening.

Finally, Grace came up with a plan: Her husband should use his princely powers to issue a formal ban against the marriage, meaning that Caroline would not be permitted to marry in the principality of Monaco. Moreover, her parents would boycott the wedding, no matter where it took place. Also, if because of the ban Caroline chose to live with Philippe Junot rather than marry him, "it will look worse for her than it does for us," Grace reasoned, according to Antoinette Brucatto, "because if she'll do that with the world knowing we have forbidden it, then I don't know what to think of her myself." In her "ruling," Grace sounded eerily like her own mother, a comparison that didn't escape many people in her circle. No one would dare bring it to Grace's attention, however, since her friends knew how sensitive she would be to such an association, especially with her mother now so unwell.

Prince Rainier thought that Grace's plan was too extreme, feeling that if they took such drastic action against her they would lose their daughter forever. She would never forgive them for the humiliation caused by a public veto, he said, and she would be gone from their lives forever. "Still," recalled one source at the Palace, "he wasn't completely against the notion, feeling that it might be dramatic enough to actually discourage Caroline from marrying Junot." Rainier and Grace remained undecided for some time—a more difficult personal decision they'd never made in their twenty-year marriage.

After a few weeks of such irresolution, Princess Grace was close to an emotional breakdown. Finally, she seemed to get ahold of herself; she began to reevaluate her position about Caroline's future. In the end, the question of banning the wedding and all that such an action would entail—the public humiliation and the damage it would cause to the family—was more than she could handle.

How ironic, Grace may have thought, that her daughter was probably marrying someone for reasons other than love and romance. How alike the patterns of their lives were, mother and daughter. Was Caroline madly in love with Philippe? She didn't seem to be, any more than Grace had seemed madly in love with Rainier so many years earlier. In fact, Grace had seemed more enamored of her Prince at that time than Caroline did of her playboy now. Indeed, both mother and daughter had reasons for entering into marriage, which had more to do with parental defiance than with marital bliss. One of Grace's motivations had to do with impressing her uninterested father, while one of Caroline's seemed to be to gain independence from her overbearing mother, or, as she put it, as a means to "the correct way out."

Charlotte Winston recalled Grace's sudden change of heart where her daughter's marriage was concerned, and the onslaught of guilt she felt about the way she had handled Caroline's rebellious years. The two women had mended their relationship after Charlotte's difficult visit to Monaco during which Grace became peeved with her for bringing up her Hollywood past in order to illustrate a point about child-rearing. Since that time, Charlotte had divorced her second husband; she'd also just buried a twelve-year-old daughter who'd died of leukemia.

Grace visited the United States in 1977. While in New York, she lunched with Charlotte in a lovely outdoor café at a table shaded by maple trees. "She was resigned to what had occurred with Caroline," recalled Charlotte, "feeling now that she was responsible for it, and determined to change things."

"I pushed her into this," Grace stated while picking at her chicken salad and analyzing the role she might have played in molding such a mutinous child. She was wearing the kind of beige turban headdress she favored at that time, rather than have to deal with the styling of her hair, along with a beige-and-brown caftan that concealed her recent weight gain. ("Too much caviar," she joked.) Her complexion was still flawless, though she had aged since last seeing her friend. Her expression was grim.

"I've been sick about it," she said of the way Caroline had so far conducted her relationship with Philippe Junot. She added that she should have known better, after what she had been through with her own mother. She now believed her intransigence where Caroline's freedom was concerned had been the catalyst for the young woman's rebellion, she said, and had forced her into the ultimate defiance: marriage to an older and completely unacceptable man. "I could kick myself for being so stupid," Grace concluded.

"Grace, for years you have had to play the bad guy, giving Caroline advice she hasn't wanted to hear," Charlotte offered. "That takes courage. You've tried to protect her."

"The way my mother was protecting me from Oleg?" Grace countered. She lowered her voice and asked, "Do you realize that if my mother hadn't been so difficult about Oleg Cassini, I probably would have married him?" Grace further noted that if she had wed the European fashion designer, she would have been able to continue with her career, and would still be an actress. "How many wonderful roles might I have played by now?" she asked, wistfully. "How might my life have turned out? That one decision," she observed, "changed my entire future." She concluded that she was pushed into making it "by my own mother."

Charlotte recalled, "I was stunned to hear her say this. Many of her friends had expressed this sentiment among themselves over the years, but no one would ever have said it to Grace. It would have been too cruel. To now hear her come to such a conclusion broke my heart."

"Your child is not you," Charlotte reminded Grace. "And you are not Margaret." Charlotte noted that Grace had to "learn things your mother didn't know, deal with things your mother never dreamed of."

Grace agreed. Her biggest mistake, she observed, was in not allowing Caroline to move to Paris alone and attend school there. She said that she now realized that her daughter wanted her to, as Grace put it, "get off her back." Grace had left home for New York at a young age to study there. Why hadn't she allowed Caroline to do the same thing, leave home for the big city? Of course, she knew why: Caroline was a Princess and, as such, faced challenges with the media the likes of which Grace, as an unknown actress, never knew. Still, Grace concluded, "I've learned my lesson: Push too hard and you push your child away."

Charlotte told Grace that she had to "make it right" with Caroline, and not oppose the wedding. However, Grace was ahead of her; she said that she'd already told Rainier that she no longer wanted him to place an official ban on the marriage.

Grace also said that she had called upon Father David Voellinger, who had been the Palace chaplain until July 1971, to counsel Caroline. She had always liked and respected the priest, who happened to be in Monaco at about the time they were planning to announce the engagement. When Voellinger suggested to Caroline that Philippe's age might be a problem for her down the road, she was unconvinced. If that was the best he could do, it was pretty weak. However, Grace felt he had done his all. "If the Lord

Himself materialized in the Palace garden and pleaded with her, I'm not sure He'd be able to get through to her, either," she joked.

The ceremony would occur, Grace revealed, in less than a year. "For me, it's time to accept that I may have pushed my daughter into a bad marriage, and then pray for a merciful ending to it." Perhaps remembering her own impassioned youth and lack of caution so long ago, the Princess then concluded, "I suppose Caroline must obey her heart at that age. I know I always did."

PART SIX

Life Changes

"What Happens to a Marriage?"

On August 25, 1977, Prince Rainier and Princess Grace announced that their daughter Caroline would wed Philippe Junot, who was described in the official press release only as "a financial and investment adviser to international banking establishments" with "offices in Paris and Montreal." The evening before the statement was made, author Gwen Robyns visited Grace at Roc Agel, at her request. "There was a lot of tension," she recalled many years later. "Grace called and said, 'Please come. We need you here. We need friends with whom to commiserate. We can press some flowers, together.'" Grace had recently taken up the hobby, from which she derived great contentment. However, many of her friends found her new venture somewhat depressing, and maybe even metaphorical for her life: She'd begun creating designs from dead flowers by drying the blossoms and then pressing them into scrapbooks and collages.*

Gwen recalled that as soon as she arrived at the Grimaldi home, Prince Rainier bolted from his study to greet her. "Come with me," he said urgently, putting his arm around her shoulder. They walked out to the garden. "So what do you think of this Junot character?" Rainier asked.

"Why, sir, I think he's a playboy," Gwen answered, according to her memory.

"Do me a favor, won't you?" asked the Prince. "You're a journal-

*In 1977, Princess Grace exhibited some of her designs at a gallery in Paris and attended the opening, selling all of her works—with much fanfare from the media. She donated all of the proceeds to the Princess Grace Foundation. A year later, she designed a line of bedding featuring her designs.

ist. Take Junot out for a walk and grill him. Find out what he does for a living."

Gwen recalled being stunned. "Why, sir, you mean you still don't know?"

"No, I don't," Rainier answered. "Can you believe it?"

Gwen didn't respond.

"Well, I can't either," concluded the Prince, ignoring her silence.

"From the expression on his face, it was as if he felt the world was spinning the wrong way on its axis," she later recalled of Rainier. "What I never understood, frankly, is that with all of the resources available to him in terms of secret service investigations, why this was all still a mystery. I now think Rainier was just too upset to think straight, which tells you how upset he really was."

Indeed, while it was difficult for Princess Grace to accept Philippe Junot as husband to her daughter, it seemed even more heartbreaking for Prince Rainier. Caroline, as his firstborn, obviously held a special place in his heart. Though he had for years been training his son, in terms of education and example, to one day take over the sovereignty, his daughters were also important to the Prince. They had always projected such enthusiasm and strength; he couldn't help but view them as powerful and self-reliant. He'd always been reluctant to constrain them in any way, from the time they were young girls. In some ways, the manner in which Caroline was handling her whirlwind romance with Philippe Junot was not surprising to him, even if it was disappointing: She was leaping feet first, in that strong-minded, confident, dramatic way that had always been hers, right into the arms of a man who enjoyed breaking all the rules just as much as she.

Grace wrote to Don Richardson that "Rainier went into a decline" after he realized that the wedding was definitely going to take place and that "there was nothing we could do about it, but smile." She added that "he has taken it very personally, and very hard." As he grew older, Rainier became a more sentimental person. However, because he also had a tough exterior, few were aware of his sensitivity. In a letter to Charlotte Winston, Grace noted that, in the past, Rainier had always been best at expressing himself through correspondence, and had written his daughters letters "even when we're living [in the Palace] together!" However, she observed that recently her husband had been communicating with Caroline in a more personal manner, with long talks in his study. "Better late than never," she noted, adding that she was "proud" of Rainier for "growing so much, as a result of this trial. I only hope it will help us, he and I," she wrote, though she didn't elaborate.

In another letter to Charlotte Winston, Grace wrote of Rainier's emotional state of mind. "I wish that more people knew how deeply Rainier feels such things," she wrote. In her lengthy missive, dated June 16, 1978, about two weeks before the wedding, Grace thanked Charlotte for her advice not to ban the wedding, "though I think Caroline should thank you, as well," she noted. She also said that she had been feeling "closer to Rainier through all of this business," because "when he shows the depth of his true feelings, he is all the more wonderful." (She also wrote that she wished her mother, Margaret, was well so that she could be aware of what was going on with Caroline. "I'm sure she would have a thing or two to say about it," she observed.)

The marriage between Grace and Rainier had not been particularly happy for some time. "Some of us sign on for a run of the play contract—no options," is how Grace explained her relationship to the Prince to one of her show business friends. "I do not have the luxury you have."

Not surprisingly, all of the talk of Caroline's upcoming wedding brought forth the strengths and weaknesses in the Grimaldi parents' union. One of their strengths was that, when it came right down to it, they could communicate and try to provide a united front when dealing with their children.

Prince Rainier once recalled a conversation he had with his wife the night before Princess Caroline married Philippe Junot in June 1978. The two took a long walk in the Palace gardens to discuss the future of their eldest child. Earlier, at a party for Caroline, someone had asked the Prince what his future son-in-law did for a living. "I think he has something to do with investment counseling," the Prince said, his tone disheartened. Rainier now told Grace that he had hoped for someone "better" for their daughter, and that his heart was breaking because, as he put it, "I know this marriage will end in tears." According to his memory, he also said, "We have taught her not to steal, cheat, lie, or take drugs, and I guess that's the best any parent can do in today's world, isn't it?" Grace had to agree. Then, trying to lighten the mood, she told her husband, "Well, perhaps this wedding is for the better, darling. After this experience, she's bound to have a successful *second* marriage." He laughed. Together, it seemed, they could handle anything.

However, the marriage of Rainier and Grace was always a puzzlement to their friends because he never seemed to be outwardly supportive of her—one of the weaknesses in their union, no doubt. For instance, in 1978, Princess Grace was scheduled to give a poetry reading at St. James's Palace in London for the Queen Mother. Rainier had not seen her read yet, which was a disappointment to her. "One would think he would be interested," Grace told Antoinette Brucatto, "however, one would be wrong."

"But you must make him go," Antoinette told Grace.

"Darling, if he has to be *made* to go, then why would I want him there?" Grace asked.

Perhaps because the Queen Mother was to be present, Rainier decided to accompany Grace to London for her performance. She walked onto the stage to deafening applause from the black-tie audience. For a short time, Rainier seemed transfixed by the vision of his beautiful wife bathed in blue and white stage lights. However, as the reading neared the thirty-minute mark, he began to doze. Soon he was sound asleep, snoring.

Later, when Rainier's lack of interest was brought to Grace's attention, she tried to brush it off. "Oh, he always sleeps when the lights go out," she said. "I suppose I now join the endless list of actors who have put my dear husband to sleep."

"They didn't communicate that well physically after they had the three children," said family friend Bill Hegner. "She fulfilled her commitment and they stuck it out because it was mutually beneficial."

There were even rumors that both Grace and Rainier took on

lovers during the last years of their marriage, as if they would have been able to have secret trysts without paparazzi eventually supplying photographic proof to a Paris newspaper. Biographies about Grace over the years have also reported that she had affairs with young men, all in their early thirties, while she was in her late forties. So titillating had been some of the reports that a few of her loyal New York girlfriends actually hoped they were true. One said, "If anyone deserved a middle-aged fling, Grace did. However, it never happened. That wasn't Grace, not at that age."

There is no persuasive evidence to prove rumors of infidelity on either Grace's or Rainier's part. However, their friends do agree that the Grimaldis had grown apart in their marriage by the end of the 1970s.

In the early years of his marriage, Rainier had confided a great deal in Grace, and such sharing had made them close. After the children came, she couldn't give him her undivided attention, which seemed to bother him, and sometimes even made him angry, at least according to some who worked around the Prince and Princess at the time. Ironically, considering the tough time she had had in the beginning and how much he had wanted her to be accepted by the Monegasques, the more popular Grace became in the principality, the more uneasy Rainier seemed. It was as if she, not he, were the star of the show; he was "second banana," which didn't do much for his ego. Maybe, consciously or not, he stopped sharing with her as he once had, and instead began pushing her into the background—not at ceremonial events, where her presence was absolutely necessary, but certainly at home where she had once given advice about the day-to-day running of the government. It was his loss. Grace was shrewd and a good negotiator. He could have trusted her not to have any hidden agendas the way his ministers often did. She could have provided another point of view and was more knowledgeable than he about certain cultural matters. His neglect of her drove a wedge into the marriage as Grace looked for other things to do and spent more time away from him.

In the spring of 1978, Princess Grace and Gwen Robyns began work on Grace's *Book of Flowers*, spending a great deal of quiet time at Gwen's farmhouse in Oxfordshire. "Once we were talking about a couple that had recently ended their marriage with both parties left in great despair," Gwen recalled. "Grace said, 'Well, you know, when those two review their marriage, it will be the love they most remember, not the pain. Pain goes away,' she said. 'Why, look at childbirth. Would we ever do it again if we remembered the pain? But love,' she concluded, wistfully. 'Oh, yes, love remains. Love never dies.'"

One morning, while walking among fragrant and colorful roses in Gwen's sumptuous garden, Grace opened up to her friend in an unexpected way.

"I can't help but notice that you are spending more time in Paris with the girls, and much less in Monaco with Rainier," Gwen began, carefully. She asked if everything was okay.

After a moment's reflection, Grace answered, "Actually, I have come to feel quite sad being married to Rainier. It's not what I had hoped for."

Gwen was taken aback by Grace's candor and wondered why she felt that way.

"Because he's not really interested in me," Grace responded. After a long pause, she asked, "What happens to a marriage, anyway?" She had hoped for more out of her union with Rainier, she said, though she hastened to add that she didn't know why, "especially when I think of my own parents' marriage."

Gwen recalled that, because she didn't know what to say to the Princess, she said nothing. She smiled politely.

"Oh my," Grace said, turning to her friend with a mischievous grin. "Have I shocked Gwen Robyns, author extraordinaire? How delicious," she exclaimed. "At least you won't think of me as a big bore."

"No," Gwen said. "Nothing could shock me, Grace. I wrote about Vivien Leigh, remember?"

Grace laughed heartily. "Well, I bet I *am* a big bore next to Vivien Leigh," she remarked happily. She then linked her arm into her friend's as the two continued their stroll through the rose garden, enjoying the silence. About five minutes later, Grace suddenly said, "I so appreciate those times in my life when I was madly, desperately, and hopelessly in love. *Those* were the best of times."

Again, according to her memory, Gwen simply didn't know what to respond.

In her reverie, Grace continued. "I don't know that I ever had that with Rainier. However, I did have it with a few others. And it was *marvelous.*" She smiled with serene contentment.

"There was such sadness about Princess Grace," recalled Robyns many years later. "She had given up so much for Rainier and the children, and I knew it, of course. But I didn't realize until that day that she had also given up passion. That loss, for a true romantic like Grace Kelly, had to have been the biggest sacrifice of all. Look at how she felt about the men in her life before she met the Prince . . . the joy, the tears, the deep feelings she had for Clark Gable, William Holden, Ray Milland, Oleg Cassini, and the rest . . . she was so alive, so full of passion. To then settle into something less had to have been difficult."

That day, as the Princess and the author walked along verdant garden paths, Grace observed, "I've made compromises to make my marriage work, just as I have to make my life work. However, I have always known exactly what I was doing. And," she concluded, thoughtfully, "I suppose it's all worked out for the best. Don't you agree?"

"Yes, I'm sure it has," said Gwen. What else could she say?

When Grace left Gwen's home, she gave the author an assemblage of pressed and dried flowers as a gift. In the lower right-hand corner of her creation Grace had written the initials "GPK"—her initials *before* she became the Princess of Monaco.

Caroline's Wedding

While there were many thrilling parties and joyous dinners in honor of Princess Caroline's wedding, the festivities in no way compared to the storybook union that had transformed her mother, Grace Kelly, into a real-life Princess some twenty-two years earlier. Many observers noted that the primary reason for such downscaling was because her parents did not want to put Caroline through the same ordeal they'd been through, with paparazzi and media descending upon the principality to ruin the day. "She still speaks of her marriage as the worst event of her life," said Jacques Sallebert, head of Tele-Monte Carlo, the principality capital's television station. "The Princess has an awful memory of her wedding, invaded by photographers and TV cameramen who pushed her around. She was determined not to let that happen to her daughter."

However, the truth was that Rainier and Grace were half-hearted about the marriage of their daughter to Philippe Junot, a man who had recently pulled his pants down at a nightclub and then poured a bottle of Johnnie Walker over his body, all for attention. Bravely, they did their best to get through the pomp and circumstance of it all, knowing in their hearts—according to what they told friends—that "this too shall pass." Making matters worse, perhaps, no members of the British royal family decided to attend the ball held the night before the wedding, nor did anyone from the Norwegian, Swedish, Belgian, or Dutch royal families. Just as it had been with Grace's wedding, the rest of the world's royalty didn't think of Monaco as a major player in world affairs and didn't pay the principality, or its Prince or Princess, the respect that would otherwise have been accorded them.

Grace's press secretary, Nadia LaCoste, said, "Obviously they have busy lives and many commitments and it appears they were unable to fit Caroline's wedding into their respective schedules." She also reasoned that Caroline's was not "a state affair"—a grand state ceremonial would be reserved for Albert, she said—but, rather, a private affair. Therefore, she said, the Prince and Princess required the presence of only close friends anyway. She said that she couldn't understand all of the controversy surrounding the marriage: "I don't understand why anyone would write negative things," LaCoste told the *Washington Post* in June 1978. "For most people, Monaco is a fairyland with a Prince and a Princess. It's a land of hope and sunshine. It's so nice to know that a Princess can marry a commoner. Caroline could have married a King. It's like becoming president of the United States. It can happen to any boy or girl. Fairy tale things can happen and people want that image of Monaco. In this world that's so drab, so full of violence, Monaco is like a Christmas tree. So let's see it all trimmed."

On June 27, 1978, a ball was held at the Palace to celebrate the upcoming union of Caroline and Philippe. Eight hundred guests attended, including celebrities such as Frank Sinatra, Cary Grant, David Niven, Gregory Peck, and their spouses. One of Grace and Rainier's frustrations this evening was that thirteen-year-old Stephanie was not present. She had refused to wear a dress for the occasion. Grace had said that if she insisted upon wearing pants, she would not be permitted to attend. "So she's not here, and that's that," an exasperated Grace told guests. For her part, the bride-to-be looked elegant in a white tulle gown designed by Marc Bohan of the House of Dior, along with a diamond necklace that was a family heirloom. A touching moment occurred at the beginning of the ball when Caroline made her entrance on the arm of her father to the sound of Neil Diamond's hit record "Sweet Caroline," to which the two then danced.

During the ball, Michel Junot seemed annoyed by the suggestion that Philippe was not of solid stock. He told one guest, "Look, my son is respectable," and then, to prove his point, produced a piece of Philippe's official-looking letterhead stationery. Princess Grace, who happened to be walking by at the time, was seen rolling her eyes as she passed the scene. As much as she tried to assume the posture of the loving and approving mother, it was difficult for her at times to appear an approving mother-in-law-to-be.

"He says he's an investment banker, but he seems to have no money—and no bank," said Princess Grace to Frank Sinatra's wife, Barbara, according to Barbara's memory. "So, what can one make of that?" Grace asked as she sipped champagne. Barbara shook her head, and shrugged. "Not much," she answered. Then, holding up her own flute of bubbly, she said, "A toast to ignorance. May it be as blissful for your daughter as it once was for us." The two older women clinked glasses, perhaps remembering their own youthful naiveté. Princess Grace forced a smile.

The next day, David Niven hosted a pre-wedding luncheon at the Palace. Frank Sinatra sang "My Way" during the luncheon, which somehow seemed appropriate at an event honoring such a strong-minded bride-to-be. Veronique Peck, Gregory's wife, watched with tears running unchecked down her face. Later, holding her husband's hand, she remarked, "Isn't young love beautiful?"

Then, in the same Palace Throne Room in which her parents had been married twenty-two-years earlier, Princess Caroline was wed to Philippe Junot in front of thirty members of the bride's and groom's immediate families. Standing in front of the throne, Rainier gave his assent so that the marriage could proceed. Both Prince Rainier and Princess Grace seemed to fight back tears during what turned out to be a lovely ceremony. Philippe Junot's mother and stepmother sat side by side, along with his father, looking searchingly at the Prince and Princess, as if to detect their approval or disapproval.

The next day, Caroline and Philippe were married again in a Palace courtyard ceremony presided over by the Bishop of Monaco, Monsignor Gilles Barthe, who had also married Grace and Rainier. The bride was lovely—exquisitely slim, her long hair parted in the middle and pulled into a chignon under a fragile white veil. Her olive skin was flawless, just as her mother's had always been. Her gown by Dior was simple, white organza and delicate embroidered lace. She appeared ebullient, her young, eager face seeming now somehow more fragile than ever. She looked unspoiled, innocent.

After the ceremony, Rainier took Caroline into his arms and held her tightly. The poignant exchange was broken only when a teary-eyed Grace tapped her husband on the shoulder and said, "My turn." She then whispered something in the new bride's ear, kissed her on both cheeks, and hugged her, seeming not to want to let her go. After a few moments clutched in a tight embrace, Grace pulled away and held her daughter's hands. Then, with photographers' flashbulbs popping all about them and guests beaming at them, father, mother, and daughter seemed somehow able to reconcile private hurts without saying much, yet saying all that mattered. All three were heard declaring, "I love you," and using other expressions of affection, reaffirming their true feelings for one another.

Wiping away tears, Caroline suddenly looked a bit unsteady, perhaps overwhelmed. A photographer came in for a closer shot. Philippe rushed up to her and took her by the arm, as if to steady her.

Between Philippe and his new in-laws there was an awkward moment of silence. Finally, Grace embraced him. It's not as if she had much choice: The lensmen seemed anxious for the moment, as did the guests. Rainier smiled broadly, shook his son-in-law's hand, and then smacked him on the back heartily. As he walked away, the Prince shook his head back and forth, as if thinking it odd that he'd just relinquished his daughter into the care and protection of a person who might or might not have a job. Later, at the outdoor reception, Rainier pulled Grace close and kissed her on the lips. "It's settled," he announced, as if a deal had just been struck and there was nothing anyone could do about it now. "That it is," said the Princess with a tone of resignation. When Rainier turned away, he took off his sunglasses and seemed to be wiping tears from his eyes.

Later, the entire Monegasque citizenry were invited to the Palace to celebrate the wedding. Thousands of people filled the courtyard, tossing flowers, cheering, dancing, and eating custard-filled tarts topped with peaches. It would turn out to be a wonderful party, dutifully presided over by Monaco's Prince and Princess, both of whom were accessible and kind to any subject who wished to share a moment with them.

Christian de Massy, Caroline's cousin, recalled, "We all gathered at the top of the double staircase after the ceremony to have a toast, with the Monegasques gathered in the courtyard. I nudged Philippe, whispering to him, "Welcome to the club. You are now to submit yourself to your father-in-law's authority. You must be looking forward to it." Always humorous no matter the circumstances, Philippe winked at me and said under his breath, 'Like hell!' "

Moments later, the Prince addressed his subjects: "I invite you to unite with the Princess, with myself and my children in the affectionate wishes that we make for the young couple. In a moment, we will lift our glasses to their happiness: That they build a solid and happy family under the protection of Sainte Devote" (the patron saint of Monaco).

Toward the end of the exhausting, emotional day, Antoinette Brucatto asked the Prince how he was faring. He smiled a thin smile. "The Princess may be the acclaimed actress in the family," he whispered, "but I must say that I am learning quite a bit about that particular profession today." Then, so typical of his wry sense of humor, he added, "Perhaps I shall call Mr. Hitchcock to see if there might be a part for me in one of his pictures."

The Inevitable Divorce

The marriage between Princess Caroline of Monaco and Philippe Junot did not last long. While a book could probably be written about their tempestuous relationship—reported upon in meticulous detail by the media every step along its sure way to divorce court—

suffice it to say that tears were shed all around. Over the course of the short marriage, neither could accept the other's ways and temperament. Confused by and dismayed with each other, the newlyweds weren't willing to compromise in the way Grace and Rainier had once done to make their own marriage work. Within months, paparazzi *not* hired by Junot caught him in the company of others, in assignations that seemed romantic. Soon after, Caroline was doing the same thing.

Grace and Rainier decided to allow Caroline to go through the experience on her own, offering her little advice about any of it. Not only did their daughter have a right to claim her freedom, they decided that she must also have a right to fail, to make her own mistakes—as difficult as it probably was for them to watch her do it. During the entire time of Junot, Grace gave interviews to reporters all over the world for cover stories in magazines about her "perfect" husband and her "perfect" children—"Don't say I'm an expert because I'm not," she cautioned a writer for *Good Housekeeping*. This kind of interview was public relations work Grace once called "the dreariest duty of my life." To that same reporter for *Good Housekeeping*, she quoted Kahlil Gibran's *The Prophet*—one of her favorite readings—when speaking of Caroline: "Children are living arrows that the parents send into the world."

In April 1980, Gwen Robyns was assigned a story on Caroline's happy marriage for *Ladies' Home Journal*. "When she married Junot, Rainier gave Caroline a villa, Clos St. Pierre, three minutes or so from the Palace, as a gift. I went to the new home ready to write about how well things were going, and who should greet me at the door but Princess Caroline, in tears. 'My dear,' I said, 'what's wrong?' She said she was miserable and that things were not going well. I did the interview with her and Philippe; it was dreadful. Then Philippe said, 'Listen, I will pay you if you'll just write that we are happy. This is a bad day, that's all. Don't characterize the whole marriage by this bad day.' I said, 'Look, as a family friend I'll put a nice spin on the story. But, again as family friend, I have to tell you that I am not at all happy about any of this.'"

As soon as Gwen left Caroline, she telephoned Grace. "Your daughter is absolutely unhappy," she told the Princess, according to her memory. "You must do something."

Grace said she was well aware of Caroline's misery. "And it's killing me," she said. However, she said that she and Rainier had discussed the matter and agreed that they had to wait for Caroline to ask them for assistance. "It's the only way we will ever get back on track with her."

Finally, in May 1980, Caroline did come to her parents for advice, after a loud and public argument with her husband at the Monte Carlo Grand Prix. Rainier wrote to Rupert Allan, "Poor Caroline's marriage is not going well. She's been hurt and—God be blessed—she came to mum and dad and told them of her unhappiness."

As soon as Grace felt she had her cue, she raced over to Caroline and Philippe's and had a loud confrontation with him. "Oh, she let me have it," Philippe recalled. "She was the protective mother, what can I say? Whatever I had to say was meaningless. Her daughter was her Princess. That was that. She told Caroline, 'Pack your bags. You are coming with me. Do it. *Now*.' Then, without questioning it, Caroline packed her bags, and off they went. That was the end of my marriage. I think we could have worked it out if her parents hadn't been so involved. Their interference made it impossible."

"Mommy said, 'You have to get divorced,'" Caroline later recalled. "I didn't dare to divorce or even mention divorce because Catholics don't divorce. You're supposed to just make the best of it. I said, 'How can you talk like that? We're a religious family.' But Mommy said, 'Religion is there to help people, not make your life miserable.'"

Grace's position was not surprising. She was not about to counsel her daughter to remain in an unhappy marriage. How many times over the years had she wished *she* could choose again? She might actually have left Rainier . . . if only she had had the choice. At least Caroline had the luxury to change her mind, and to move forward in her life—without Philippe.

While Grace was unhappy about the end of her daughter's marriage, and continued to blame herself for, in her view anyway, pushing her into it, Rainier was downright angry about it, and blamed Philippe for it. "I knew better than to try to explain myself to him," says Junot today. "That wasn't what our relationship had been like, anyway. In all of the time I knew the Prince, I don't think I ever had an in-depth conversation with him about anything—just small talk about racing cars and boats. Word got back to me that he blamed me for the end of the marriage, as if Caroline hadn't been unfaithful to me when, actually, she had been the first of us to be unfaithful. My cheating was only as a reaction to hers, but what father wants to hear that, I suppose."

Countered Rainier, "Princess Grace and I saw it [the marriage] was going to be a mistake, as a father, there was no use opposing it. [Here, he seemed to be alluding to the notion of the "official ban" that Grace had suggested.] I think that's why there wasn't more harm done, because we didn't wave our fingers at her, saying, 'See, we told you this was wrong.' I think that was why she was so ready to come back home and talk it over with us."

Many years later, after Grace was gone and Caroline had children of her own, she was able to review her first marriage in an analytical way. She recalled that, at one point during all of the back-and-forth about Philippe, Grace even resorted to reverse psychology—as if *that* would have worked with Caroline, who by that time had become a master of manipulating her mother. "When I met this seducer," Caroline recalled to interviewer Louis Pawels, wryly referring to Philippe, "my mother said to me, as a challenge, 'Leave him, or marry this man who is not made for you.' So . . . I married him! I admit, of course, that it was all out of a spirit of contradiction, rebellion. And, as for him, well, I think he wanted a solemn wedding just so as to have one more big party. I think it was as simple, and as stupid, as that."

The official divorce was granted on October 9, 1980.

In 1981, Prince Rainier appealed to Pope John Paul II to grant his daughter an annulment by the Roman Catholic Church. "Article 1405 of canonical law makes it obligatory for heads of state, either for themselves of their children, to appeal directly to the Vatican in order to avoid local pressures," Princess Caroline has explained. Because Rainier was Head of State, the plea for an annulment would have to be made directly to the Pontiff. John Paul refused to commit himself, but said he would take the matter under advisement.

Stephanie's Turn

While Princess Caroline attended school and then married unsuccessfully, Prince Albert completed his studies at Amherst College in Massachusetts. Catharine Rockwell, a student at Amherst at the time, recalled, "We dated a few times. He was Al Grimaldi, that's how he introduced himself. He was honest and sincere, the kind of boy who would never have sex with you because it just wouldn't be 'right.' Handsome beyond belief, so good-looking. Thin, sexy, beautiful eyes, great teeth—a bit of a stammer when he spoke. When, after about six dates, he finally told me who he was, I was floored. Princess Grace's son! After I got to know him, he spoke a lot about his father, not much about his mom. I felt he was closer to the Prince. On and on he would go about him—how wonderful a tennis player he was, what a boatsman he was, what a car enthusiast he was, the best dad in the world—never said anything about him being ruler of a principality. He loved his father very much, no doubt about it.

"Finally after about four months, Al and I were intimate. Afterward, he was concerned about me, hoping he hadn't taken advantage of me. He said, 'What matters to me is that you have a good memory of me and of what we did.' I did, and I still do.

"Then he went off to the French navy, where he spent about six months as an ensign aboard the *Jeanne d'Arc*. I never heard from him again, but I didn't expect to. It was a college fling, but how fortunate I was to have had it."

There had been few problems with the sensible, level-headed Albert over the years. Even though Grace sometimes wished Caroline had been more like Albie, some suspected that Rainier wished he was a tad more like Caroline, that he had some of Caroline's ambition and drive, her spunk. Rather, Albert had always been passive and agreeable, a nice guy. Even today, a popular joke has it that if Rainier lives to a ripe old age, the still-single Albert may be known as "His Senile Highness" rather than "His Serene Highness" by the time he finally reaches the throne. Rainier will never hand it over, and Albert doesn't have the ambition or cunning to encourage him in that regard.

Princess Stephanie was another story. Grace called her "difficult but sensational" in a letter to Don Richardson—and that she was, and still is today.

At the beginning of 1981, Princess Stephanie turned sixteen. For years, as her parents focused on the melodrama of raising Caroline, Stephanie had, perhaps, more latitude than was best for her. She had always been spoiled as a youngster, but by the time she was sixteen she was even less likely to listen to her parents' advice than Caroline had been at the same age. Perhaps she resented all of the attention her sister got as a result of her sensational lifestyle, and "acted out" in a way that she hoped would shift some of the attention to her. Whatever the case, Grace—and to a lesser extent because of the way the family was structured, Rainier—had a major challenge in raising the teenage Princess Stephanie.

"I remember when I was sixteen thinking to myself, why are my parents giving me such a hard time? I always thought they were after me," Stephanie would recall, many years later. "Of course, every teenager goes through that. I didn't realize until lately how lucky I really was." Then, perhaps romanticizing her teen years just a bit, she went on to say, "We were raised to respect each other and to be honest with each other, and above all to communicate with each other. We were raised to understand that we were a family.

When any of us had a problem, we'd bring it out, we'd talk about it with each other instead of just keeping it inside. We do it to this day. We've always done that."

Antoinette Brucatto recalled, "I was at the Paris apartment lunching with Grace one afternoon and Stephanie, who was about fifteen or sixteen, came tearing into the living room wearing blue jeans and a little T-shirt with the word "REBEL" across it. In a scene that struck me as one from a middle-class American family, Grace said, 'Young lady, you go right upstairs and change into something more appropriate for company.' Stephanie looked at her mother, then at me, and spat out in the most bitter of tones, 'That woman's not company. She's here all the time. If I have to get dressed up every time *she* walks in the door, I'll run out of frilly little Princess dresses—and we wouldn't want *that* to happen, now would we, Mommy?' Then she skulked away. We both acted as if we didn't smell the strong scent of tobacco left in the girl's wake. Grace put both hands to her forehead and said, 'I used to be her best friend. Now I'm her worst enemy. My God, when did it become Stephanie's turn to cause chaos?' She seemed exhausted. 'Well, what else is new?' she asked with a sort of resigned detachment."

Princess Grace was still living, for the most part, at the Paris apartment, with Stephanie now in school in that city at the Institut St. Dominique and under the supervision of her mother. While it seemed to some observers that Grace was using Stephanie's schooling as an excuse to stay away from Monaco, and even Rainier, the truth was that when she did return to the principality, it was better than ever between her and Rainier. In some ways, they were closer because they did not need to make demands on the other for emotional sustenance. A long marriage, even one where one or both partners are always unsatisfied, brings a certain comfort because each knows what to expect of the other. Grace knew she could always count on Rainier. In his own way, he had lately provided support as no one else could for her.

"We love each other," Grace told Antoinette Brucatto. "We have an understanding, like a lot of couples our age."

"But are you happy?" Antoinette asked her.

Grace laughed. "Oh, please!" she said. Then, turning serious, she said that when she was with Rainier, she was happy, "and when I am not, I miss him so. The last two years have, somehow, been good for us."*

Grace also spoke about her recent weight gain, saying that no matter how many diets she had tried, she could "not lose an ounce." She concluded, "Now I know why they call it 'the change.' *You change*." Because menopause had not been easy for her, she had been taking heavy doses of hormones to counteract some of its effects. The medication served to bloat her and make her face appear puffy. (Later, biographers would account for the added weight by claiming that she'd become an alcoholic. It simply wasn't true. While she enjoyed champagne and an occasional brandy, she was actually a light drinker.) She also said that she would soon be cutting back on her medication and had therefore promised herself to be fifteen pounds thinner by this time next year, so help me God." The weight gain did depress her, no matter how hard she worked to fight despair about it. "I'm a Princess," she said, "and they expect me to look a certain way. It's very, very difficult for me."

At about this time, Grace gave an interview to *People* in which the reporter questioned her about her children, her daughters in particular. When asked how the girls differed, Grace said, "Caroline is perhaps more literary, Stephanie more mathematical. Both are warm, bright, amusing, intelligent, and capable girls. They're very much in tune with their era. Besides being good students, they are good athletes—excellent skiers and swimmers. Both can cook and sew and play the piano and ride a horse. But, above all, my children are good sports, conscious of their position and considerate of others. They are sympathetic to the problems and concerns in the world today."

When asked if Grace felt that Caroline had made certain mis-

---

*In an interview with *McCall's* in 1981 for a story on Grace and Rainier's twenty-fifth wedding anniversary, the late Ava Gardner—a good friend of Grace's—was asked if she saw a happily-ever-after story in Grace's life. "Grace is like me, a realist," Ava said. "You take what life dishes out and grab what goodies you can for yourself along the way. She's grabbed quite a few—a husband, three kids, all the money in the world. I say, good for her."

takes in life, Grace was firm: "I am not going to discuss my children, or their lives, or their mistakes."

Pushing, the reporter asked if she had "any reflections on the failure of Caroline's marriage to Philippe Junot?" Standing firm, she answered, "Again, I've just told you: No."

Then he asked about reports that an annulment was being sought. Grace reiterated: "No comment."

The writer then changed tactics and asked about an upcoming TV movie of her life starring former "Charlie's Angel" Cheryl Ladd, of which Grace said she did not approve. When told that "one of the producers has said what they plan is actually a kind of fairy-tale story," Grace observed, "That sounds rather icky and revolting. I certainly don't think of my life as a fairy tale. I think of myself as a modern, contemporary woman who has had to deal with all kinds of problems that many women today have to deal with. I am still coping—trying to cope."*

Princesses: Grace and Diana

In March of 1981, Princess Grace, accompanied by Gwen Robyns, flew to London to give a poetry reading at Goldsmith Hall, a gala event on the seventh, at which Prince Charles was guest of honor.

---

*As it happened, Grace handled the ABC-TV movie, *The Grace Kelly Story*, in the same sensible way she dealt with Gwen Robyns's biography of her: She became involved, saying that she thought the idea of suing over it was "demeaning." She invited the movie's producer, Brian Russell (who would go on to marry the film's star, Cheryl Ladd; they are still married today), to the Palace for two days of script consultation. After Brian made the changes Grace asked for, she gave the movie her blessing. Grace would die just two days before production was scheduled to begin. At that time, Cheryl Ladd said she couldn't conceive of going ahead with the project. She was about to pull out of it when Prince Rainier sent word from the Palace that he would like for the movie to go on, as planned . . . and as Grace would have wished.

He and Diana Spencer had just become officially engaged; this was Diana's first public appearance as his bride-to-be. That evening, the swanlike Diana wore a black, very décolleté, strapless evening gown. Even if she had appeared in a high-necked and long-sleeved muumuu, she would have created a sensation. However, dressed as she was, the paparazzi went wild at the sight of her. "Her breasts were on display, and she was quite a wreck," recalled Gwen Robyns. Diana's panic was still evident at a reception afterward at Buckingham Palace. Concerned for her, Grace asked if she would like to accompany her and Gwen to the ladies' room for a chat.

Both Princess Grace of Monaco and Diana, Princess of Wales, were, in so many ways, Princesses of our imaginations, icons of beauty and elegance whose storybook lives seemed to open limitless possibilities in the lives of millions of observers around the world.

Diana, Princess of Wales (not "Princess Diana," as she is often called, in that only someone born a Princess may use that style), was the daughter of an earl, descended from the Stuart kings, and thus a member of the aristocracy. Her family, the Spencers, was one of the more illustrious in England. She was in the royal periphery long before she married Prince Charles in July 1981. Of course, Grace had no such ancestry. Whereas Diana was a Princess who became a star, Princess Grace was a star who became a Princess.

However, similarities between the two women do abound: both blonde and beautiful; both younger than their husbands; both chosen (in part) because they appeared to be capable of bearing children (and both having to be physically examined to ascertain the fact); both receiving little assistance about protocol from their royal in-laws; both devoted mothers; and both meeting untimely deaths in automobile accidents.

There were also differences. For instance, Grace was far more worldly than Diana, even as a young Princess. Diana was a kindergarten teacher. Grace was a star, financially independent, widely traveled, and prone to moving in sophisticated circles.

Like Diana, Grace was a romantic, but she was also strong-minded and resolute, not prone to the kind of dramatic dysfunctions that plagued Diana, such as bulimia. As an actress, Grace faced the biggest challenge of her life in her role as a royal and was determined to turn in an award-winning performance. Unlike Diana, Grace was not a consciously stylish woman. Even as a movie star, she often dressed more for comfort than for glamour once she was offstage. After she married Rainier, for her public appearances she would transform herself from dowdy housewife to radiant Princess by a change of clothes, carefully applied makeup, and skillfully arranged hairstyles. However, no matter the dress she wore, her overall regal bearing was what made the first impression. Though Diana certainly won no prizes for elegance when she was first engaged, fashion soon became her signature. Whenever she made an appearance, what she wore was the first thing the media noticed.

Although Princess Diana's funeral would bring a great outpouring of grief in 1997, it is probably Princess Grace's memory that will prove the more indelible. In a way, that is an irony, because while Diana immediately received an outpouring of love from the British people, Grace had been viewed by her subjects as an interloper, an outsider, a rich and spoiled American who couldn't speak their language properly. However, Grace worked to burnish Monaco's image by bringing to it cultural events—an excellent symphony orchestra, an outstanding ballet school, competitive flower shows—which generated tourist revenue for the principality; she also raised enormous amounts for charities by sponsoring fetes attended by the rich and famous from all over the world; she looked after the Monegasques by seeing to it that a first-rate hospital was built and that facilities for the elderly were upgraded.

Even if Diana had remained married and had wanted to emulate Grace's philanthropic works, she still might not have been able to do so. Whereas Grace was married to a de facto ruler, head of a principality, Diana was married to the heir to the throne. As long as Charles remained Prince, whatever Diana may have wanted to do in terms of making an impact—short of graciously visiting children's hospitals and giving of her time to certain charities—would have had to have been approved by her critical mother-in-law, Queen Elizabeth II.

According to Gwen Robyns, who was present, it was during her talk with Princess Grace while touching up her makeup in front of the ladies' room mirror that Princess Diana burst into tears. The dress she was wearing was so revealing, she explained, because it was two sizes too small; the intended outfit had not arrived in time—an unnerving situation to occur for her first formal appearance. She also said that she now realized more than ever how unbearable it would be to have so many people jostling for her attention, asking questions, not only of her, but of anyone who knew her. She foresaw a life totally devoid of privacy. She was frightened. What could she do? She was certainly asking the right woman for advice. Grace had always known how to use her celebrity to her advantage, whereas Diana seemed to shrivel under the spotlight's glare. No matter how troubled her private life, once the spotlight shone upon her, the former Grace Patricia Kelly transformed into Her Serene Highness, Princess Grace—the greatest role of her life. Now Diana Spencer looked to Princess Grace for solace and, perhaps, a bit of advice.

The elder Princess put her arms around the distraught young woman and patted her on the shoulder. She then put one hand on each of Diana's cheeks, cupping her face. "Don't worry, dear," she said with a gentle smile. "You see, it'll only get worse."

Princess Diana later told her biographer, Andrew Morton, that she found Princess Grace to be "wonderful and serene. But there was troubled water under her," she concluded perceptively. "I saw that."

In July 1981, Princess Grace not only attended the wedding of the Prince and Princess of Wales at the baroque St. Paul's Cathedral in Great Britain, she was one of the featured luminaries. Because the parallels between herself and Princess Grace had not escaped Diana, she thought it appropriate that the Grimaldis lead the procession of royals during the ceremony. Because nearly all of the reigning sovereigns of Europe would be in attendance, Diana's request of the Grimaldis was a great honor and a validation—if one was even needed by this time—of Prince Rainier's and Princess Grace's rightful place in the royal landscape.

On that summer day, 700 million television viewers around the world witnessed another "fairy tale come true" scenario: the handsome Prince Charles in naval uniform marrying the winsome Diana Spencer, twenty-year-old daughter of an earl, amid the sort of splendor the modern world hadn't seen since the so-called Wedding of the Century in Monaco almost twenty-five years earlier. At precisely 10:14, a fleet of black Rolls-Royces carrying nearly all of Europe's crowned heads left Buckingham Palace. Grace's car led the procession. Sadly and, no doubt, a huge frustration for him, Rainier was under the weather and, at the last moment, could not attend. However, he was proud to have Prince Albert stand in for him at Grace's side.

The royal procession led by Princess Grace and Prince Albert included the Netherlands' Queen Beatrix, Denmark's Queen Margrethe, Sweden's King Carl XVI Gustaf, Norway's King Olav, Belgium's King Baudouin, Grand Duke Jean of Luxembourg, Prince Franz Josef of Liechtenstein, and many others. The distinguished assembly traveled down the red-brick Mall through Admiralty Arch, across Trafalgar Square, down the Strand and Fleet Street, finally climbing Ludgate Hill to St. Paul's. While leading the royals into the cathedral, Grace looked cool and elegant in a broad Breton straw hat. Albert was dignified in a conservative tuxedo. That night (and the previous), the royal mother and son stayed as guests of the Queen at Buckingham Palace.

The gifts Diana and Charles received from royalty and heads of state as well as lesser-known people were valued at $7.2 million and took up seven rooms in St. James's Palace, a royal residence in central London. The United States' gift to the Prince and Princess of Wales was a Steuben glass bowl decorated with kings, noblemen, and crusaders. Nancy Reagan, President Reagan's official representative to the wedding, selected the bowl, valued at $75,000 but sold to the U.S. government for $8,000. The Crown Prince of Saudi Arabia gave Diana large diamonds and sapphires set in a watch, bracelet, pendant, ring, and earrings. He gave Charles a box the size of a telephone book, encrusted with gems. Grace and Rainier, however, decided to be a bit more modest with their gift—*surprisingly* modest, in fact: They decided upon a simple silver picture frame, which Grace thought was "quite lovely" and which could not have cost more than a few hundred dollars, if that. However, it was a better gift, or a least a more sentimental one, perhaps, than Queen Margrethe of Denmark's: a set of canvas garden chairs.*

"While We Dream, Time Flies"

In the spring of 1981, Princess Grace found herself in New York for a benefit for the documentary *The Children of Theatre Street*. She and Charlotte Winston had dinner with a group of friends. Afterward, Grace pulled Charlotte into a hallway for a private chat. She mentioned that she was taking an apartment in New York because she was tired of staying with friends whenever she was in town, which was often these days. She then tried to catch Charlotte up on what was happening with Stephanie.

Sixteen-year-old Stephanie had become romantically involved with a twenty-one-year-old Italian socialite, Urbano Barberini, a brief romance that ignited a firestorm of press coverage, not to mention frustration for her parents. "Stephanie and Urbano were seen kissing and groping one another on a beach, which is when Princess Grace hit the roof," said Dragonet Andenet, a friend of Barberini's. "She came down hard on her, said she wasn't even allowed to go to the beach any longer. Most people felt that Stephanie's mother was overdoing it with her because she thought she'd not been so successful raising Caroline. Even Stephanie said,

---

*Ironically, Princess Grace's funeral was the first official function that Diana would attend as Princess of Wales, just a little more than a year after her wedding to Charles. "I hope she was happy at the end," Diana reportedly said of Grace after the service. Little did Diana know that she too would lose her life in a horrible automobile accident.

'I'm always being punished because they're still mad at Caroline for Philippe Junot.'"

Now, shortly after having ended with Urbano Barberini, Stephanie was involved with handsome, seventeen-year-old Paul Belmondo, son of French actor Jean-Paul Belmondo.

"Stephanie is driving me crazy," Grace said, according to Charlotte's memory. She said that she feared she was repeating some of the same mistakes she had made with Caroline, and that she didn't know whether to be lenient or strict with her youngest child. "The kid has me walking on eggshells, second-guessing everything I say or do." She also mentioned that at the 1981 Red Cross Ball, Stephanie refused to wear the designer dress Grace had selected for her and, as a consequence, was banned from the ball—just as she had been from Caroline's pre-wedding gala. "She sat in her room and cried, preferring that over wearing the dress," said Grace, adding that it was a "constant battle of wills" between her and Stephanie, "and, God help me, but lately I think she is winning. It's hard to keep a step ahead of her," she concluded. "I am just happy if I can keep a step behind."

When Charlotte asked what Rainier thought about the matter, Grace laughed. "My poor darling Rainier," she said. "He never dreamed it would be like this." She noted that her husband was able to run a principality, but when it came to his own daughters, "forget it." She added that whenever Caroline or Stephanie did something outrageous, Rainier would say, "Well, at least Albie hasn't shocked us yet." Then she observed that if Prince Albert ever decided to rebel and cause a principality scandal, "it'll do both of us in."

Grace also mentioned that, a few months earlier, she had been tested at Duke University's Institute for Parapsychology in Durham, North Carolina, to determine if she were psychic. The Institute is noted for its vast contributions to psychic research. Its founder, the late J. B. Rhine, is credited with turning parapsychology into a true laboratory science. In fact, Rhine invented the term "parapsychology."

For many years, Grace had felt that she possessed ESP. Of course, she had always been interested in astrology and in the occult, and had always felt intuitive. Some of her friends still insist that she purposely sabotaged her chances to appear in *Marnie*, in 1962, because she sensed that she would have a problem with Alfred Hitchcock, and as it happened, Tippi Hedren did have her hands full with the eccentric director when she replaced her in the film. Just before Grace's mother suffered her stroke, she had told Rainier that she was concerned that something was about to happen to Margaret. At the time, he felt that what she was probably referring to was the karmic effect of what Margaret had done to Kell's political career—Grace was also a strong believer in karmic law. Shortly after she and Rainier had the conversation about her mother, Margaret suffered her stroke. Over the years, there had been many other instances pointing to the strong possibility that Grace was psychic; Rainier often joked that if he were allowed to gamble in the Monte Carlo casino he would sure to be a consistent winner with his wife at his side cueing him. When an administrator from the Institute for Parapsychology vacationed in Monaco, he contacted Grace and said that he had heard through a mutual friend that she might be "gifted." He suggested she be examined.

When she was tested at the Institute, it was supposedly determined that she did indeed have psychic ability. However, as Grace told Charlotte Winston, she wasn't impressed with the testing process, which involved her choosing the winner between four horses in a computerized horse race. Tested more than a hundred times, she chose the correct horse in 65 percent of the cases. Grace, who was always open to new ideas when in came to parapsychology, was disappointed in the process. "I just don't think it proves anything," she said, "except that I'm a good guesser."

Before she and Charlotte parted company, Grace noted that she and Rainier had just celebrated their twenty-fifth wedding anniversary. "Where has the time gone?" she asked. "It seems like just yesterday I wore that ridiculous hat!" (She was referring, no doubt, the wide-brimmed hat she wore when she first arrived on the shores of Monaco, the one that kept photographers from seeing her face.) "While we dream," she said, "time flies, doesn't it?" She also said that she and Rainier intended to be in New York again in June to see *Amadeus* on Broadway, "and I pray he will stay awake for it," she added, laughing.

"The marriage was still going strong because they had a great relationship," said Grace's sister Lizanne. "They liked separate things. When they were apart, they had their individual lives to lead. By this time, they were even financially independent of each other. Our family's money had been invested well. Grace was well-off, separate and apart from Rainier, because of her inheritance—which had nothing to do with any joint money they shared as a couple."

During the spring, Princess Grace spent a couple of weeks at historic Holker Hall, the stately home and extensive (twenty-five-acre) formal gardens owned by Lord and Lady Cavendish of Furness near Grange-over-Sands, Cumbria. Grace was a big fan of Holker Hall, winner of the prestigious Christie's/Historic Houses Association Award. She often visited the gardens when feeling depressed, and this year was asked by the Cavendishes to open the Rose Show of their annual Garden Festival.

Alan Selka, who was the Cavendishes' butler, recalled Grace as seeming somewhat introverted. "I was disappointed when I met her," he said. "There was little personality there. She seemed to hate it, the public appearances and everything associated with it."

Delores Bingham-Hall, a friend of the Cavendishes, recalled, "She told me she was tired of being a figurehead and wanted to go back to acting, that she had some things in the works but wasn't at liberty to say what they were. She also said she was dismayed by her daughter Stephanie, that the girl was having trouble with her studies, and that she and Rainier were thinking of enrolling her elsewhere just to get her through high school. Princess Grace seemed distracted. She wasn't as scintillating a personality as I had hoped she would be, and seemed to have the weight of family problems on her mind."

In fact, when Princess Stephanie was about to be held back her sophomore year at the Catholic school, Institut St. Dominique in Paris, because of poor grades, Grace and Rainier decided to enroll her in a more liberal, and coed, Catholic school, Cours Charles de

Foucauld. She graduated in the spring of 1982. That summer, Grace insisted that Stephanie return to Monaco, feeling she was spending too much time with Paul Belmondo. The argument that ensued between mother and daughter was as fierce as any Grace had ever known with Caroline—and maybe even a little more painful because Stephanie was more obstinate than even her sister at that age. Distraught, Grace returned to Monaco. Once there, she turned to the only person who knew firsthand what she was going through: her husband. She wrote to Don Richardson, "My darling Rainier, he is here for me when I need him most, which seems to be this summer."

The summer of 1982 found the Grimaldi clan buckling under family feuds.

Stephanie, feeling suffocated, was still struggling with Grace and Rainier over the parameters of her freedom. She was serious about Paul Belmondo, she said, and was threatening to run off and marry him. Was it even possible for a Princess to elope? Grace and Rainier would not have put it past Stephanie. "I just have a love of life that is very big and I just don't want to miss anything," said Stephanie, sounding so much like her mother when Grace was a young Hollywood actress.

Caroline, now twenty-three, was resentful that her mother was trying to micromanage her life. Caroline, who now held a degree in psychology, wished to further her studies in London and live there with a female friend. However, Grace believed Caroline needed to be protected. At this juncture, she was torn between her desire that her eldest experience life at its fullest, and her urge to protect her from heartache on a par with what she had experienced at the hands of Philippe Junot. She didn't trust Caroline's judgment and decided not to allow her to go off to London. Rainier disagreed with Grace and tried to intervene on his daughter's behalf, but Grace felt strongly about the matter. She might feel differently, she said, in six months.

Albert, meanwhile, was stuck playing the even-handed referee, now trying fruitlessly to help everyone reach a compromise.

So far, the 1980s had been better for Grace and Rainier as a couple. They had begun to find harmony in their marriage in the last two years, and could be even happier—if only their daughters would give them a break. Still, Grace seemed to be unable to resist a certain nostalgia about her life in Monaco, as evidenced by an essay she wrote at this time. Her friend, painter and flower enthusiast Fleur Cowles, had asked her to join a host of celebrities to write a composition about which plant life she might include to create a perfect fantasy island, for Cowles's book *The Flower Game*. After writing of roses, irises, apple blossoms, and gladioli, Grace noted, "I would try to find a fresh water pond on the island for my water lilies with the hope that their large leaves will attract frogs. Who knows? One might turn into a handsome prince who would be decent enough to whisk me off this lonely island and take me back to civilization."

The Grimaldis may have been royalty, the most revered family of Monaco, but at the end of the day, they were a family, nothing more, as vulnerable to the dysfunctions and trivial conflicts that can contaminate any household, regardless of the members. Still, there was no reason to think that the hurt feelings would be anything but temporary. As with many families, the jousting and arguments that seem so catastrophic in the moment fade into levity with the passing of time, becoming something people laugh about, stories they recount to each other later on with a knowing shake of the head. While time may not heal everything, it often gives people the space to eventually appreciate each other for the things they share rather than focus on their differences—not to mention the hindsight to see their own silliness. There was no reason to think the same wouldn't happen for the Grimaldis once the children matured and grew up.

However, unbeknownst to any of them, time was running out . . . for Grace.

Rainier's Change of Heart

The inevitable passing of time saw Rainier's feelings for Grace intensify, especially during the last two years. He would miss her when she was in Paris, greatly anticipating her return to the Palace. The Princess's quiet serenity, her willingness to listen, and the fact that she made no demands on him, had made him appreciate her more than ever before. As they aged together, he knew he could always depend upon her. Words seemed unnecessary between them. They had been through so much, they knew how to communicate with just a look, a smile—they had an intuitive intimacy accessible only to people who have been in long-term relationships. "'It's wonderful to be loved by her,' he told me," said Antoinette Brucatto. "I think that the time she had spent away from him in Paris in recent years had made him hunger for her. If it's true that absence makes the heart grow fonder, that's what it did for the Prince where his wife is concerned. He planned a vacation for them, time away together."

A little more than a year earlier [in April 1981], during a dinner in celebration of their twenty-fifth wedding anniversary, the Prince made his feelings for his Princess clear. The Grimaldis celebrated the occasion in California at Frank and Barbara Sinatra's home. Before the meal, Rainier rose to speak about his wife. Seeming to hold back tears, he talked of Grace's devotion to him, as well as to the principality in which they had lived for a quarter of a century. "My life and the lives of so many have never been the same since the day this wonderful woman entered my world," he said, looking at Grace lovingly. "I adore her more today than ever before. She is my Princess," he concluded, "and I salute her." As he raised his glass in her direction, it was difficult for Grace to maintain her composure; tears ran down her face, unchecked.

Rainier planned for him and Grace to take a cruise to Norway on the French cruise ship the *Mermoz* in August 1982. As it happened, Grace thought it would be nice if the children joined them. While Albert and Caroline went, Stephanie stayed behind with Paul Belmondo. They had a fun time without her; Grace and Rainier dressed as pirates for one of the costume balls. Later, Caroline joined a magician's stage act without her parents' knowledge, stunning them when the magician asked for a volunteer from the audience to cut in half and she stood up and joined him onstage. "The look on their faces was perfect," she later recalled. "He [the magician] cut me in half, and put me back together. My father was on his feet, cheering."

When they returned from that cruise, Prince Rainier III was working in his study when his wife presented him with a book for his review. She said that it had been sent to her with the idea that it could possibly be a film vehicle. Though Rainier's thoughts are not known, they were probably along the lines of, "Oh no, here we go again." He smiled indulgently, however, and told her he would read the volume.

It had been twenty years since the Prince encouraged his wife to appear in Alfred Hitchcock's suspense/thriller *Marnie*. Since that time, he had had mixed emotions about her return to the screen—especially when offers came in that conflicted with her principality duties or with child-rearing responsibilities. However, it would be untrue to say that he remained as closed-minded about a movie career for his wife as he had been before he married her—though he still couldn't fathom how such a "return" would be orchestrated since she was and would always be a Princess. Also, Grace was fifty-two at the time, an age at which most actresses see plum roles dry up.

The book Grace had asked Rainier to read was the historical novel *A Search for the King*, written by the venerable Gore Vidal in 1950 when he was about twenty-five. It tells the fabled story of the twelfth-century English king Richard the Lionhearted, kidnapped by the Austrians and rescued by his faithful court poet, Blondel. Actually, the story of Richard's capture ended with a large ransom being paid for his return. However, Vidal turned the legend into a lyrical and compelling story of friendship and male bonding. In the midst of the relationship between the King and his troubadour was a love story that would involve a character played by Grace. It had been submitted to her by Robert Dornhelm, the young director with whom she'd worked on *The Children of Theatre Street*. Because Rainier had enjoyed the documentary and was proud of Grace's work in it, she thought he might take an interest in another of Dornhelm's ideas.

Prince Rainier read the book in just two days. Afterward, he told Grace that he enjoyed the work, even though Gore—notorious for his caustic wit—did take a negative view of royalty in it. Rainier also said he would be interested in reading any script based on it. In the end, he gave Grace his approval, should she decide to make a movie based on *A Search for the King*—a huge step for Rainier and one, as he told an associate, that was the result of significant soul-searching.

That associate recalled, "Rainier told me that he had certain regrets about not being as supportive of Grace's film aspirations as he might have been. In his view, he never really stopped her. He would often point to *Marnie* as an example of his willingness to let her make movies. 'Still,' he said, 'when one speaks of regrets in life, I do regret not encouraging her more to find fulfillment in pictures.' He felt that there was time to rectify that mistake, and was happy that she might now, finally, make a movie. It was big news for anyone who knew the Prince and Princess that she might actually do such a thing, and at the age of fifty-two. Actually, it seemed impossible, yet it was definitely on the horizon. 'If it makes her happy,' Rainier told me, 'then it does the same for me. A lot of things have seemed impossible,' he said, 'yet were also achieved.'"

Four months earlier, Princess Grace had been honored in Philadelphia by the Annenberg Institute of Communications for her film work—a gala affair during which many film clips of Grace's work were screened to an appreciative audience. Rainier was not able to attend. Though much media speculation pointed to his absence as another sign of his lack of interest in his wife's activities, the truth was that he had unavoidable principality business. Over the years, Rainier had felt that he was being underestimated when Grace and others accused him of not being interested in her work that didn't have to do with the principality. Of course, the reason he had such a reputation was because he often *did* seem uninterested in her endeavors. The fact that he only went to one of her poetry readings and fell asleep during it "is still being used against me," he joked. However, now at the age of fifty-nine, the Prince seemed to be taking stock of his life and marriage. "I'm turning sixty next year," he told one associate. "Maybe it's time for me to change some things. I'm not saying it is time," he added cautiously, "I'm just saying that maybe it's time."

The Prince was regaled by Grace's anecdotes about the tribute and about Frank Sinatra's and Jimmy Stewart's participation in it when she returned to the Palace. He said later that the expression on his wife's face was "priceless" as she went on about all of the show business elite who had attended the function. After all of the passing years, and despite so many disappointments along the way, the Princess still found delight in show business, and in her chums from that world. "I am overwhelmed and so filled with love," she had said to the celebrity-packed audience at the tribute. "I would just like to hug every one of you."

Whereas Rainier had once felt cold toward Grace's famous friends, he now thought of them as his friends as well—he and Sinatra, in particular, got along famously. A running gag between the Grimaldis and Sinatra was that Grace had been awarded a gold record for a million copies sold of "True Love," her duet with Bing Crosby from *High Society*. "She got one before I did, and she ain't even a singer," Sinatra would say. Grace would tell him not to feel slighted because, as she joked, "it took me eighty takes to sing that goddamn song." Rainier had a phony gold record made of "True Love," and presented it to Sinatra as a gift, saying, "Now you have one as well, so I don't want to hear another word about it."

The recently opened Monte Carlo Théâtre de Princesse Grace was a further testament to Grace's devotion to acting and her continued involvement in theater, possibly as a producer of productions she hoped to bring to the principality. Moreover, this theater named after Grace was also evidence of Rainier's open-mindedness where her career was concerned. Whereas there had been a time when he didn't even want her movies shown in Monaco for fear of reminding the Monegasques of her connection to show business, now he had actually encouraged a theater in the principality named in Grace's honor, and was proud of it.

"In the end, despite all of the separations over the years, they were getting back on the same track again and truly thinking like a married couple with a future," said Barbara Tuck Cresci, widow of Frank Cresci, Rainier's longtime Consul General. "He had become very supportive to her and was now focusing on what might make her happy. That was his concern: What did Princess Grace want, and how could he give it to her? Personally, I'm not sure he ever would have allowed her to star in a full-length movie, but who knows? He would have worked, I think, to find a way, some compromise, perhaps."

It appeared that Rainier had come to terms with Grace's never-ending love affair with show business. For many years, the Prince had seemed to view the influence of Hollywood on his wife as a threat. He may have felt that it was always lurking, waiting to call her away from him, from their life together. Yet, somehow, during this tender time in their relationship, Rainier saw the joy that his wife got from just the simplest of involvements in the dramatic arts. The Prince's evolving support for Grace and her endeavors was not lost on her. In fact, she was quite moved by it, as she told one confidante: "The Princess said that she was surprised by Rainier's 'patience' with her, when it came to acting. She said that he used to change the subject when she would start telling Hollywood stories, but something had changed. They started eating supper out on the west veranda, just the two of them. Grace would often stand up from the table to do an impression of some star or another. There was more laughter between them at that point than there used to be."

A mutual respect and appreciation between Rainier and Grace had blossomed from so many years together, and the level of comfort the two shared was apparent to all observers. They had begun to settle into a simpler routine, with intimate dinners becoming more frequent. The royal couple would sit together for hours, each evening meal lit by a setting sun until candles would become necessary to illuminate the garden. It was clear to all who witnessed this magical time that the Prince and his Princess were falling for each other again, but, this time, without the anxiety that had characterized their first years together. In many ways, Grace and Rainier were coming together in a whole new way—falling in love again . . . but for the first time.

"So Little Time"

In late August 1982, Grace was finally putting a number of health issues behind her. The previous weeks had been difficult. She had been suffering from a lingering case of bronchitis, which she believed was the result of powerful air-conditioning on the cruise to Norway. She'd also been having migraine headaches, which had become practically debilitating. "As I get older, I really am falling apart, aren't I?" she jokingly told her sister Lizanne. Now, though, as summer was coming to a close, her problems were falling away. It seemed that Grace was entering a period of renewal—she was aglow with glorious possibilities; life once again was magical. "She got so busy all of a sudden, 'so much to do,' she would say. She seemed to have the energy of a schoolgirl again," recalled Lizanne. Her interest in acting was sparked again as well. After obtaining her husband's approval, she wrote an enthusiastic letter to Robert Dornhelm to tell him that she thought Gore Vidal's book had "all of the elements I can handle" and that he should "work on the love story"—she was speaking of a script that Dornhelm intended to co-write, based upon the book. She then began telephoning friends with the good news.

Charlotte Winston recalled, "She called me and said, 'You know, I think Rainier may be softening in his old age.' She said that he had read the Gore Vidal book in record time, and that she should proceed with caution. 'I just may make a movie based on this book,' she said. 'Wouldn't that be marvelous, at my age?'

"We talked about whether such a thing would be possible, a Princess making a movie. It was the age-old question, after all, wasn't it? To this day, I'm not sure that it could have happened, but at the time it seemed at least a possibility. She said that if not a movie, perhaps she and Dornhelm would find a way to do the book as a theatrical production, 'maybe a rock musical,' she said, very excited. [It's doubtful that Grace would have appeared in it, if Vidal's book was produced as a 'rock musical.']

"I asked her if she had enjoyed Vidal's work in the past, and she said that she had. In this particular one, she said, the love story was weak. 'I'm not sure he knows what love is,' she said of Vidal. 'But I do, and I think I can work with this, either as an actress or a producer.'

"I hadn't heard her so energized in ages. She said she had another tour of America planned in a few weeks, more poetry readings, and she would be meeting with the young man [Dornhelm] about the movie while she was here."

Charlotte and Grace spoke about Caroline and Stephanie, and the ongoing crises relating to them. However, Grace didn't criticize her daughters. Rather, she spoke about how "tough and smart" they were, and how such characteristics would serve them well, later in their lives. "At least no one will ever be able to convince those two not to follow their hearts . . . except maybe a Gemini," she said. She didn't have to remind Charlotte that Rainier was a Gemini. Then Grace concluded, "They are both their mother's daughters, aren't they?"

"I had to laugh," Charlotte Winston said, "because Grace knew it, and I knew it: Those girls were the combination of everything she had been when she was young—full of life, impulsive, independent, refusing control, eager to choose . . . and demanding the freedom to choose again—just like you-know-who. Laughing, Grace said, 'Caroline and Stephanie, they're me . . . for better or worse, God help them both . . . they're me. What fun they shall have!'"

Grace told her friend that she was on her way to Roc Agel, and would telephone her in a few weeks with her New York schedule. Meanwhile, she said she was mailing a copy of the Gore Vidal book to her. "Oh, darling," she said, in that breathless way of hers. "So much to do, and so little time."

When Charlotte hung up the telephone, she felt hopeful for Princess Grace's future: "I kept hearing her words ringing in my head: 'So much to do, and so little time.' It made me smile for days afterward whenever I thought of it."

"You're coming back to Monaco with me, aren't you, Lizzie?" Grace asked. It was the first week in September, 1982; Princess Grace was on the telephone with her sister Lizanne in Ocean City, New Jersey. The two were making plans: Grace was soon to arrive in New York, and Lizanne and her husband, Don LeVine, were to return to Monaco with her for a vacation there. Lizanne would later recall her sister's mood as being "real upbeat, completely happy." She told Grace that she and Don were looking forward to seeing Rainier and the Palace. "I can't wait to get there," she told her.

With their parents gone, Grace, Lizanne, Peggy, and Kell had made a concerted effort to remain close, speaking to each other as often as possible. Lizanne was in the process of organizing a small family reunion once Grace got back to America, probably at her and Don's beach house, in Ocean City.

Grace said that she planned to stop in Ireland before going to the United States, for she had just purchased the original Kelly homestead there, where her father's ancestors were raised. "They said it was an old estate," Grace said, laughing. "However, it's actually quite rustic, to say the least. It needs a lot of work, Lizzie. After that, I'll be in America and then I have to get right back to Monaco. I can't stay away too long," she cautioned, according to Lizanne's memory. "I must get back to Rainier as soon as possible."

"But Grace, he's so well taken care of when you're gone," Lizanne said, laughing. "Look at all the help you have at the Palace. Don't you think he can survive for a few weeks without you?"

"No," Grace said firmly. "I know what he needs, Lizzie. He needs *me*."

"Just as he always has," Lizanne observed.

Lizanne and Grace seldom talked about the past. "We lived through the past," Lizanne explained later. "There wasn't much reason to dredge it all up, was there? I knew that Gracie didn't live the life she had originally dreamed of for herself, but I also knew that, along the way, she changed her dreams. So, we didn't spend a lot of time analyzing it." On this day, however, Grace seemed somewhat reflective as she spoke of Rainier, of Caroline, Albert, and Stephanie . . . of her life. Perhaps it was because she had the possibility of a new movie on her mind, the notion of which did, in many ways, bring her life full circle.

"You know, I was thinking the other day about how lucky I am," Grace told her sister. "It would be nice, I suppose, to say that I have no regrets. But how ridiculous would that be? I *do* have regrets, Lizzie. However, I came to terms with them long ago and, today, I must tell you, I feel absolutely wonderful."

The two Kelly sisters spoke a few more moments about their families, the challenges presented by raising teenagers in contemporary times, and how, in the end, it all somehow seemed worth it to them. "I love my husband," Grace said. "I love my children. I do think I made all of the right choices . . . at least, for me." After a pause, she added, "Maybe my one regret is that I took so long to accept certain things. But in the end it all worked out, didn't it, Lizzie?"

"Well, that's because you worked it out," Lizanne told her.

"That I did," Grace agreed. "I sure did."

The two spoke a few more minutes. "I love you, Gracie," Lizanne said before hanging up.

"I love you too, darling," Grace told her sister, "more than anything."

Those were her parting words.

September 13, 1982

Monday morning's dawn on September 13, 1982, brought with it the end of a difficult weekend for the royal family of Monaco. The time away from the Palace had been spent at their vacation retreat, Roc Agel in the Maritime Alps. Rainier, Grace, Caroline, Albert, and Stephanie were joined there by Rainier's niece Elisabeth (an adult daughter of his sister, Princess Antoinette), as well as two of his young nephews. Also present that weekend was Robert Dornhelm, who had been so excited about Grace's interest in the Gore Vidal project that he decided to fly to France and meet with her about it, rather than wait for her to get to New York. It was hoped that everyone would have a relaxing time at Roc Agel, perhaps even enjoy a cookout or two. However, an unexpected family drama was caused by the impending wedding of Christian de Massy (Princess Antoinette's son), which pretty much ruined the weekend for everyone.

Princess Antoinette, who was estranged from her son, Christian, and had only recently seen him briefly after more than two years, was adamantly opposed to his marriage. Of course, she didn't like his intended. When she telephoned Rainier to ask that no one in the royal family attend the imminent ceremony, he agreed to officially embargo it. According to an old 1882 law of the land, no one in the immediate royal family was allowed to marry without the sovereign Prince's permission; therefore, Christian would risk sure banishment should he do so. Desperate to salvage his relationship, he telephoned his Aunt Grace to ask that she sway Rainier on the matter. "She was the only member of our bizarre family who had both compassion and consideration," he later explained. "She was completely truthful and trustworthy, qualities some in our family did not possess."

Though Grace had a pleasant, and sometimes even close, relationship with her nephew, she loathed being caught in the middle of another Grimaldi family dispute. A few years earlier, when Christian (who the family called Buddy) became involved with a married woman, Grace had been concerned enough to take the matter up with Antoinette. "Oh well, these things happen," Antoinette had said, refusing to admit that the relationship might be inappropriate. Clearly, it was only because Grace disapproved of what was going on with her nephew that Antoinette approved of it. "Buddy is having an affair with a married woman, and I just don't appreciate your indifference about it," Grace told her sister-in-law. The two Princesses then had words, one proverbial "thing" leading to another until, finally, they weren't speaking.

Though the matter eventually blew over, it did serve to remind Grace that she should not become involved in the personal lives of Antoinette's children, or have to tough it out with her difficult sister-in-law. However, since Christian seemed so sad about the events surrounding his upcoming nuptials, Grace decided to at least try to change Rainier's mind about the embargo.

In fact, Rainier had ambivalent feelings for Christian, this nephew of his who was often used as a pawn in his sister's ongoing attempts to dethrone him. However, as he put it, "what's right is right"—and it was "right" that Antoinette be the one to decide whether or not Christian was ready for marriage, not Grace. Therefore, until Christian secured his mother's approval, he would not have Rainier's. Since Christian's sister, Elisabeth, was also at Roc Agel that same weekend, the tension there concerning this matter was thick—of course, Elisabeth sided with Rainier against Grace.

"Oh, fine," Grace told an American friend of hers on the telephone. "This is all I need."

Grace knew not to push Rainier any further. She was sorry she had even broached the subject, especially in that it had caused tension between her and her husband over a matter that actually had little to do with them anyway. Indeed, they had their own problems, namely a new one involving the ever-difficult Princess Stephanie.

Earlier in the week, Stephanie had suffered a serious waterskiing accident in Antigua, which required her to have fifteen stitches in her head. Grace's chauffeur drove her from Monaco to Roc Agel to be with her family. Grace was, of course, concerned, wanting further x-rays to be taken. However, Stephanie seemed fine and, the next night, stood in the middle of the sprawling living room to make a startling announcement to her parents: She wished to drop out of the Institute of Fashion Design in Paris and become a race car driver. She hoped to enroll in race car driving school with her boyfriend, Paul Belmondo..

Because the young Princess had barely squeaked through high school, Grace had called upon influential contacts in order to get her enrolled in the prestigious fashion school. Now it seemed the idea of fashion designing was passé for Stephanie, race cars being her new passion.

Saturday night and all day Sunday, Grace and Rainer argued with Stephanie about her plans. Was she thinking straight? Her new interest made no sense to either of her parents. How ironic: Grace didn't even like to drive, and now her daughter wanted to race cars for a living. For his part, Rainier had been involved in a serious car accident in 1953, one that had nearly cost him his life. He too was not a big fan of racing, and the idea of a woman doing it—let alone his daughter, the Princess—was more than he could fathom.

Grace would continue to do her best to talk Stephanie out of her latest scheme, of course . . . but later. How much more could she deal with in one weekend? Therefore, the matter was left unresolved, with Princesses Grace and Stephanie barely speaking to one another.

On the afternoon of Sunday the twelfth, Grace said good-bye to Caroline, who was off to London and then to Forest Mere, a spa in the Hampshire countryside. Afterward, Robert Dornhelm also left Roc Agel, headed for Paris. Once there, he planned to meet up again with Grace in a day or so to continue discussions about the exciting upcoming movie. He would later say he was glad to get away from Roc Agel, it had been that tense a weekend there.

That Sunday night, Princess Grace fell into a restless slumber.

Monday dawned optimistically enough, despite the weekend's royal squabbles: At least a glorious sun shone down upon Roc Agel. Perhaps the worst was over, and the week ahead would be less emotionally taxing for the Grimaldis. The week's schedule was a busy one. Grace planned to drive back to Monaco with Stephanie, where the two would remain for just a night. Then they would be off to Paris, where Stephanie would attend the first day of school—though how long she would remain enrolled was undecided. On Wednesday, Grace was to be in London, where she would give a poetry reading for the Queen Mother at Windsor Castle. While there she would also visit a doctor. Her friend Gwen Robyns had arranged for her to see a specialist to get a second opinion on the medication she was taking for menopause, which might have been contributing to her severe headaches. When Gwen had spoken to Grace the previous night, she had been concerned at how depressed Grace sounded. The headaches—along with everything else going on—had caused the Princess to feel dreadful, thus the doctor's appointment.

That Monday morning, at about 8:15, Rainier said good-bye to Grace and was driven by his chauffeur away from Roc Agel and down to Monaco, ready for the busy week of Palace business ahead. An hour later, Princess Grace and her maid loaded the backseat of her eleven-year-old brown Rover 3500 with so many dresses and hat boxes (for a later appointment with her couturier) that there would only be room enough for two in the automobile.

Despite the urgent protests of a chauffeur who begged her to leave the dresses behind, saying he would return for them later, Grace decided that she would drive herself and her daughter back to the principality. Though she disliked navigating the treacherously winding road that snaked its way down the mountain and back to the Palace, and seldom did so, this time her mind was made up about it. "However, you may run behind us if you like," she told the chauffeur, joking with him.

At about 9:45 in the morning, an exhausted Princess Grace along with her cranky daughter, Princess Stephanie ("Why did I have to wake up so early?"), bid Prince Albert, Princess Elisabeth, and her two nephews good-bye. They then got into Grace's Rover and pulled away.

The "Stephanie Theory"

D37, the snaking road that leads into the principality of Monaco, is particularly difficult to maneuver. It's just two narrow lanes that wind up and down a mountain at awful angles, with sharp turns and steep bends. One curve in particular—two miles from the monument at La Turbie where the road veers 150 degrees to the right—is the worst of all. Here the road cuts inland sharply and then disappears below a slope, appearing again atop another slope beyond. "Darling, one day someone is going to have a dreadful accident here," Grace had once told Gwen Robyns when the two women were driving this awful stretch. "Someone will die. I can see it."

On this Monday morning, as Grace and Stephanie made their way along the serpentine stretch of road, something went terribly wrong, something that would horribly fulfill Grace's prophecy. Thirty minutes into the drive, for some reason, the automobile did not successfully negotiate one of the most treacherous of hairpin turns. The car careened across the road, and then off it. After crashing through a retaining wall, it sailed about a hundred feet down the hillside, slicing off the top of a tree and then flipping over several times. Finally, it landed on its roof near a vegetable garden, leaving one of its occupants injured, and another near death.

What had happened, and why? To this day, the chain of events leading up to the tragic accident that morning outside of Roc Agel remains the subject of great controversy and speculation.

Some facts are indisputable, such as that Princess Grace had never liked to drive, and had never been very good at it. Over the years, she had become even meeker behind the wheel, especially as her vision deteriorated with age. She had often said that she'd had premonitions of perishing in an automobile accident. "Back in the early days, when she first went to Hollywood, I flew out there for a time to be with her just to drive her around," said her sister Lizanne. "We all [the Kelly family] agreed it was best if she didn't drive."

Years earlier, Grace had driven Hollywood columnist James Bacon and actor William Holden so recklessly over the winding Laurel Canyon road from Hollywood to the San Fernando Valley that "we were both scared to death," said Bacon. "She spun around those curves like a stunt driver. I once went a hundred miles per hour, with Holden driving, on Wilshire Boulevard in his Ferrari. So for him to be scared while being driven by Grace was telling."

Perhaps that was true of Grace when she was a young starlet, but as an older Princess she was far more cautious. "She was a slow, careful driver," noted Rainier. "If she said to her children, 'Come, I'll take you in the car,' they'd say, 'No, we'll go by foot. We'll get there quicker.'"

According to Barbara Tuck Cresci, "A few years earlier, Grace broadsided the car of an Italian tourist at the intersection that led up to the hill to the Palace [Rue Grimaldi and the Place d'Armes]. No one was hurt, but she was shaken by it. She said at the time that she would stop driving, and from then on, as far as I know, she was usually chauffeured."

The accident Barbara spoke of occurred while Grace was driving a converted taxi she used to own, an odd choice for an automobile but one that allowed her plenty of room in the back for packages, dresses, and whatever else a Princess might need for a busy day.

Usually she would sit in the passenger seat while her chauffeur would drive. Sometimes, though, she liked to drive it herself. However, the day that she careened into the tourist's car proved most embarrassing. The angry Italian she hit had no idea who she was and began screaming out, "This bitch ran into me! This bitch ran into me!" As Grace assured the driver that she would take full responsibility, a police officer threatened to arrest him if he continued to insult the Princess. It was awful.

"[In August of 1982] Grace was absolutely forbidden by the Prince to drive," Barbara continued. "Something else had occurred—I don't recall what it was—and Rainier put his foot down and said, 'That's it. No more driving. From now on, you will be driven.'" Other sources say that Grace had almost become involved in another accident in Monaco on a day she wanted to be alone and took the car out for a spin, which worried the Prince enough for him to issue his edict against her getting behind the wheel.

Generally speaking, the Princess was chauffeured about, and her stints at hopping in a car for quick trips were few and far between. So seldom did she drive, in fact, that many Palace observers thought her license had expired. She certainly rarely made the treacherous drive from Monaco to the mountaintop Roc Agel or back, because Rainier was against her doing so.

For many who remember the horrible accident that claimed Princess Grace's life—and even for those who don't recall all of the heart-wrenching details but, rather, have just a vague concept of the tragedy—there remains one single, big question: Was Stephanie driving? Truly, the speculation that the royal daughter, not her mother, was behind the wheel that morning is almost as popular a bit of conjecture as whether or not Lee Harvey Oswald was solely responsible for the murder of JFK in Dallas . . . or whether or not Sirhan Sirhan actually acted alone in assassinating Robert Kennedy . . . or whether or not Marilyn Monroe truly committed suicide (or did the Kennedys have something to do with her death, or even the Mob?) . . . or whether or not the auto death of Diana, Princess of Wales, was caused by stalking paparazzi, or a drunk chauffeur . . . or whether or not the plane crash that claimed the life JFK Jr. was the result of poor flying conditions, or pilot error (or even if he was distracted, arguing with his wife during a time when he should have had his attention on the control panel). The sudden and unexpected demise of a popular, well-loved figure is often followed by rumors, theories, and speculation, all of which envelop the deceased in a kind of mythology that, in some ways, guarantees his or her immortality.

That Princess Stephanie had been pleading for her mother's permission to attend race car driving school is not contested by the Palace, and many who are firm believers in the "Stephanie Theory" point to this fact as evidence that she may have wanted to get behind the wheel that day and demonstrate to her mother that she could negotiate a tricky drive. Clearly, Stephanie had somehow gained enough experience as a driver to lead her to believe that racing was a passion she intended to pursue. No doubt her boyfriend Paul Belmondo had at least familiarized her with the thrill that comes from speed and risk.

Princess Stephanie did drive on the property of Roc Agel, even though she didn't yet have a legal license. Though one must be eighteen in order to hold a driver's license in France, all three Grimaldi children were permitted to drive the substantial distance from the garage to the house at Roc Agel before they had licenses; all three also practiced their driving skills on the estate's expansive grounds. Grace and Rainier had a strict rule that, though the children could drive on the private property, they were not permitted to drive on public roads without licenses. Ordinarily, Stephanie would have even pulled the car up to the front of the property and then allowed someone else to take the wheel.

Some believe that Princess Stephanie continued a campaign that morning to convince her mother that she was meant to race cars and that, after much persuasion, Grace caved and allowed her daughter to sit in the driver's seat. Princess Grace, though, was concerned with appearances—say the theorists—so she may even have pulled away from the villa as the driver of the doomed Rover, and then allowed her daughter to later take the wheel. However, when would this switch have happened? Grace's car crashed only a mile and a half from Roc Agel, a distance that took less than ten minutes to travel. Would she have driven just a few yards (or even a mile) on a narrow, twisting, single-lane road, then stopped the car, exited, allowed Stephanie to shift over into the driver's seat, and gotten back in on the passenger's side? Perhaps. Who knows, but maybe Grace felt faint and asked Stephanie to take the wheel.

However, Yves Phily, a truck driver, testified to the police that he had been behind Grace's automobile for much of its journey down the hill—and that it never once stopped. He also testified that the Rover was being driven so erratically, though, that at one point he became alarmed enough to blow his horn in warning. The car straightened out for a few moments, he said. Then it began to approach a hairpin turn, where, from his view, he should have seen its brake lights go on. However, they didn't. Instead the car accelerated dangerously. "The moment I saw it going faster, my heart leapt into my throat," he said. "I knew there was no way it would make the bend. It was just going too fast. The car took off, and then I literally saw it fly over the side. My breath was taken away for whoever was inside of it."

Exactly what had occurred that morning would become the immediate source of great and morbid fascination—especially to the tabloid press. For instance, a contingent of nine *National Enquirer* reporters flew in on the Concorde to Paris, where they met up with nine more reporters from Europe and Africa. The team then descended upon Monaco in search of unique story angles to the tragedy. Tens of thousands of dollars were paid to Sesto Lequio, who said he witnessed the accident and in whose backyard Grace's car landed, for his "exclusive story" and the right to take photos on his property. Lequio, who owned the property and was renting it out at the time, said that when he found Grace in the car, she tried to speak to him, whispering the names of her family members.

"Soon my garden would be buzzing with police and white-coated medical attendants," he said. "But I would hear none of the commotion. All of my senses were numb. All I saw was the horror of the crash, and all I heard was the sound of Grace's voice, whispering to me the names of her loved ones."

Of course, it's difficult to know if such a scene actually took place, especially since the *National Enquirer* purchased an exact replica of Grace's car (same make and model) in order to restage the accident for a cover photo. The story cost $150,000 (equivalent to almost double that much in today's money), but was worth it to the *National Enquirer* in that it sold close to six million copies of that issue. Lequio ruined his story, as sensationalists often do, by going just one step too far with it. He said that, "with her last breath," Grace told him, "I want you to believe that I was driving." Would she have the presence of mind to say such a thing at that moment? A woman so close to death? (Not only that, but she didn't die on the scene.) Still, Lequio's account of what he saw and heard that day was the spark that ignited flames of controversy that, to this day, continue to burn. Or, as Prince Rainier himself put it, "Based on the information supplied by the wretched gardener who says he found the car, rumors spread very quickly."

One of the most crucial bits of evidence that seems to support the theory of Princess Stephanie having been the driver of the car is the "wretched gardener's" account of her point of exit from the vehicle. He said that Stephanie—bleeding heavily from a head wound—kicked out the driver's door, and crawled from the car to plead for aid for her mother. Grace was, apparently, lying on her back, her head resting against the back window, her feet toward the windshield. Medics, when they finally arrived, smashed the rear window to extract the badly injured and bleeding Princess from the wreckage. Buttressing Sesto Lequio's account is one given by his neighbor Michel Pierre—but even his provides a contradiction. Pierre says that he took to the driver's door with a sledgehammer and, out, he says, came a staggering and bleeding Stephanie.

However, Stephanie hotly disputes both accounts, insisting that she remembers "every minute of it." She recalled that after the accident, "I found myself huddled under the space below the glove compartment." She said that she "thought the car was going to blow up . . . and so I bashed down the passenger door with my legs. It wasn't hard because the door was half gone anyway."

Therefore, to this day, it remains Sesto Lequio's and Michel Pierre's word against Princess Stephanie's.

Another story had it that mother and daughter had been arguing as Grace drove, and that it was this disagreement that led to Grace's losing control of the car. "I have no idea whether Stephie was arguing with her mother," said Grace's sister Lizanne in 2002. "She could have been, but who knows? Stephie is the only one who knows and she hasn't said. I have never questioned her about it. If she wanted to talk to me, she would. I would never bring it up: It would upset her too much."

The problem with the investigation surrounding the death of the Princess of Monaco is the same one that often plagues matters that involve touchy public relations: When people in powerful positions are not completely forthcoming out of fear that certain disclosures will further claims they hope to dispel, it usually serves to make them appear to be guilty of something, even when they are not. A strong case of that kind of PR misfire is found in the Palace's official version of Rainier's actions on that terrible day, an account repeated and published countless times over the years. Supposedly, Prince Rainier rushed directly to the hospital when he heard the bad news about Grace and Stephanie. However, this now turns out to be untrue. According to Captain Roger Bencze, the officer in charge of the accident investigation, Rainier first stopped at the crash site.

When Bencze arrived on the scene at 10:35, about thirty-five minutes after the crash, the Prince was already there, along with his private secretary, the chief of the Palace guards, and the chief of the Monaco police force. Bencze, acting as liaison between the local French police and the Monaco police force, says that, based on his questioning of others present, the Palace contingent showed up on the scene about five minutes prior to his own arrival. Rainier was present when Grace and Stephanie were loaded into two ambulances. The anxious Prince and the rest of the stunned royal coterie then followed the ambulances to the Princess Grace Hospital.

Of course, the presence of Prince Rainier at his wife's crash site could very well have been without any ulterior motive. He may have simply and understandably wanted to be with her and Stephanie, and was able to get there in time. However, the fact that his presence there is information that has been withheld for decades only makes it appear that someone is covering something up—and, if nothing else, what that may or may not be lays the groundwork upon which a conspiracy theorist can then build a strong foundation for any hypothesis.

Seeming to make matters even more suspicious is the fact that the French police never officially questioned Princess Stephanie. They were unable to do so because protocol between France and Monaco exempts members of the royal family from being questioned by French police officers during an official investigation. That Stephanie could not, maybe would not, be interviewed by the French authorities would not make matters any easier for the Palace in its effort to be clear that Grace, not Stephanie, had been driving the car. However, Roger Bencze says that he was satisfied enough with his own investigation to determine that, in his opinion, Stephanie had not been driving the car. "Princess Grace was driving," he says. "I have no doubt about that."

Meanwhile, Stephanie's immediate recollections of what had occurred that morning were given only to immediate family members. According to the Prince, his daughter told him, "Mommy panicked. She didn't know what to do. She lost control."

However, even how and when that statement was made by the young Princess seems to be in question, because she never actually discussed the accident with her father. She says she did not do so "because I know it hurts him and I don't want to do that." Rather, the statement Rainier says Stephanie made to him was actually one she made to Caroline when the two sisters later discussed what had happened. Caroline recalled, "Stephanie told me, 'Mommy kept saying, "I can't stop. The brakes don't work. I can't stop."' She said that Mommy was in a complete panic. Stephanie grabbed the handbrake. She told me, 'I pulled on the handbrake but it wouldn't stop. I tried but I just couldn't stop the car.'"*

---

*According to official crash investigation documents the car's handbrake was "functioning, not engaged," and the automatic gear was "set in Drive." These documents also indicate that the driver had utilized the wrong gear in going down the hill: "Standard" instead of "Mountain." The "Mountain" gear would have slowed the speed of the car had it been used while in such a steep descent; that's the purpose for which it was created. It would seem that, since Grace had owned the car for a number of years, she would have known how and when to use it. Or was she really that inexperienced a driver?

"I know that I did everything that I could do for it to not happen, for the car to not go off the road," Princess Stephanie told Diane Sawyer years later in a television interview. She reiterated that she had tried to grab the emergency brake just before the Rover hurtled off the steep ridge. Instead, she said, she only managed to put the car in park, though it continued moving. Stephanie also theorized that Grace, acting in a confused state, may have gotten the brake and gas pedals mixed up.

"I don't know how many times we've had to say that Grace would never have allowed Stephanie to drive her down to Monaco," Prince Rainier has said, "especially on that road, as dangerous as it is. Yes, Stephanie did drive the car from the house to the garage at Roc Agel, but she never drove that car off the property."

Aside from all the accident inquiries, police investigations, eyewitness accounts, conspiracy theories, and royal contradictions, one thing is fairly certain: Princess Grace would have had a better chance of surviving such a terrible accident had she just done one simple thing before departing from Roc Agel that fateful morning: used her seat belt.

"The Unthinkable Has Happened"

By the time Prince Rainier got to Princess Grace Hospital, his cousin Prince Louis de Polignac was already there, pacing back and forth and biting on his lower lip, perhaps to stop the quivering. Others began showing up, including Prince Albert, but, maddeningly, there was no information for anyone. Finally a doctor emerged to say that Princess Stephanie had suffered a concussion and a cracked vertebra. Though in great pain, she would recover and be home within two weeks. Grace, he said, had broken her collarbone and leg, and also suffered lacerations. It didn't sound serious; in fact, Caroline, when she heard the news, decided that she could put off leaving London for Monaco until Tuesday morning.

Immediately, Prince Rainier telephoned Frank Cresci in New York, to tell him what had happened to the Princess. Barbara Tuck Cresci recalled, "My husband was the first person in America that Rainier called. He said that Princess Grace had broken her leg, that they were at the hospital, and that he should get over there immediately in case there were other developments. However, there wasn't a lot of concern. She had broken her leg, that's what we thought."

Rainier then had one of his secretaries call Lizanne Kelly LeVine at her beach home in Ocean City, New Jersey. The injuries were minor, she was told; the doctors believed that both Grace and her seventeen-year-old daughter would be fine.

However, within an hour, things changed: It was clear that there was more damage than had been thought, and that Grace would need surgery—four hours of it, as it happened—perhaps demonstrating that the hospital may have been ill-equipped to accurately diagnose her injuries. In fact, she had sustained damage to her thorax, had a collapsed lung, and also internal bleeding. Within hours, Grace had slipped into a coma. Rainier again telephoned Frank Cresci: "The unthinkable has happened," he said.

The doctors, now suspecting that Grace had suffered a brain hemorrhage, ordered a computerized axial tomography, a CAT scan. Her head was shaved in preparation for brain surgery. However, the facility did not have the proper scan equipment for a CAT scan—an enormous metal machine that looks like a large donut (called the gantry) standing on its side with a table going though the center of it. The patient lies on the table as it is moved slowly into the gantry where the body—in this case the head—is then x-rayed in great detail.

(Over the years, reports about the absence of such important medical equipment have been laced with cynicism, making it seem as if the Princess Grace Hospital was poorly prepared. Today, of course, most hospitals have computerized axial tomography apparatus, technology that was actually invented only two-and-a-half years before Grace's accident. Many European hospitals had not yet been equipped with it.)

Rainier suggested a Swiss clinic, but Grace was too weak to make the flight. She probably wouldn't even survive a drive to another hospital. Instead, now thirteen hours after the accident, she was taken by ambulance to a nearby doctor's office, where the CAT scan was performed.

The news was not good: A doctor who, to some witnesses, seemed somewhat pale, announced to family members and a few friends that Princess Grace had suffered two brain lesions—one, it was suspected, before the crash, which had probably caused her to faint, and then another after the incident. Had the first one occurred at any time other than while Grace was driving a car, it might not even have been a problem. She would have passed out, perhaps, and then been treated for a mild stroke. It was the second lesion, a result of the impact of the accident itself, that had been so devastating. There was no hope; Grace would have had to be in treatment within a half hour of the accident in order for her to have survived such damage, and even then she would probably have been severely paralyzed.

At the news, Caroline, her eyes dark and shadowed in pain, drew in a sharp, horrified, and audible breath. Albert appeared to struggle with it, perhaps trying to comprehend the meaning of the doctor's words. Rainier went weak in the knees, nearly having to be held up by his son.

Once back at the hospital, Princess Grace was put on life support as family and friends, including Nadia LaCoste, official spokeswoman for the Palace, stood vigil.

On Tuesday evening, September 14, Rainier, Caroline, and Albert conferred with the hospital doctors and learned the final, awful truth: Grace could not be saved. The only choice was the most agonizing of all: to take her off of life support so that, free from earthly binds, she could drift from them peacefully. Though it seemed unfathomable, it was the only sensible course of action—as if any aspect of the unfolding nightmare made sense. "Let my wife die,"

Rainier told the doctors. He then went into Stephanie's room to tell her the news.

"Stephanie was asleep when we entered her hospital room," said Nadia LaCoste, who accompanied .the Prince. "Rainier gently shook her shoulder to wake her. He leaned down, kissed her cheek, and said, 'Darling, Mommy is dead.' Never in my life have I seen a man more completely torn apart by emotion. He was shaking and crying, utterly desolate."

From the other side of the door, Stephanie's scream could be heard, loud and blood-curdling, a horrifying sound that expressed better than any other the deep emotion shared by Grace's loved ones.

After Rainier emerged from Stephanie's room, he and Caroline and Albert went into Grace's to say good-bye to her. Soon after, Caroline and Albert walked into the hallway, leaving Rainier with the still-beautiful woman who had sacrificed so much to marry him more than a quarter of a century ago—his Princess. When he finally came out, it was with tears running down his face. Visibly trembling, the Prince now appeared much older than his fifty-nine years. As he walked slowly down the corridor, supported on either side by his son and daughter, he shook his head in despair and disbelief. "This can't be true," he was heard to say. "Please, dear God. This can't be true."

Calling Her to Glory

On September 18, 1982, an intense sun bathed Monaco in golden light. It was a warm, fragrant, and lazy day, one so typical of the principality. Long ago, Monegasques had taken to dubbing this kind of weather "Princess Grace Weather," calling to mind the way the rain had stopped when the *Constitution* docked outside Monte Carlo, and Grace Kelly crossed to the *Deo Juvante II* as part of her journey to the principality's shores. They also remembered the way the sun shone on Grace's wedding day—more "Princess Grace Weather." Ordinarily, such weather was the promise of a great day. Today, however, a dull and overcast sky would have been more appropriate; this was the saddest, most depressing day. The principality seemed to have lost all of its charm. Thousands of Monegasques lined the streets from the Palace on the Rock to the Cathedral of St. Nicholas, many crying, some silently praying, others seeming to be in a kind of trance. Shop windows displayed photos of Grace, draped in black.

All of Monaco seemed numbed by the tragedy of losing not only its Princess, but a huge part of its history, and in such an unexpected, dreadful way. For the Monegasques, their Princess had been a strong figurehead, one with natural grace and unswerving dignity who had *earned* their affection. For the rest of the world, she represented a fairy tale: the beautiful actress who had relinquished her career at its height in order to marry a Prince and help him govern his people. It was destiny that had transformed her into royalty, a station more unique than she ever could have achieved had she simply continued as an actress. Not since President John Kennedy's assassination in 1963 had the world seemed so joined together in international grief over the loss of a public and beloved figure. Ironically, along with JFK's widow, Jacqueline Kennedy Onassis, Her Serene Highness Princess Grace of Monaco had perhaps held the public's fascination longer than any other celebrity of her time.

For two days, Grace had lain in state in the Palantine Chapel of the royal Palace surrounded by white flowers and candles, in order that every Monegasque who wished to could view her body. Though some witnesses have romanticized her as having been as beautiful in death as in life, such was not the case. Actually, the face in the casket was a pale reflection of Princess Grace's classic beauty. Something wasn't right—perhaps it was the odd wig that had been pulled lower on her forehead than Grace ever would have worn it, ostensibly to cover a wound. In the coldness of death, no one looks as they did in life, and especially not a woman who had been so vital in life. "Virginia Darcy would never have allowed this," one good friend recalled thinking to herself when she later viewed Grace's body at the family's chapel in the Palace. Peggy and Lizanne were visibly upset by their sister's appearance; Peggy, in particular, couldn't believe how the makeup artists and hairstylists could have done such a dreadful job.

It didn't matter. Grace was gone, and nothing would ever bring her back to them. For her loyal friends and loving family, the tragedy that had occurred was deeply personal and life-altering. Grace's death would leave an irreplaceable chasm in their lives.

Grace's sister Lizanne recalled, "I'll never get over it. For half a day I was left believing that she was going to be okay. Then, Rainier called. [Her husband] Don was talking to him on the phone, whispering to him. My knees went weak. I thought, 'Oh my God, what's happened?' I knew something was terribly wrong, just from Don's tone. When you're expecting death, it's a different experience—the death of my mother or father, for instance, I was prepared for; one had a stroke, the other cancer. But Gracie? Having her taken from us that quickly, that suddenly? It was awful. The shock of it was immeasurable."

Grace's good friend Rita Gam recalled, "We had always said that when we were seventy-three, we would be together—two little old ladies on the Côte d'Azur, she with her hair blonder than blonde and me with mine now blue-tinted, basking in the Mediterranean sun, looking at the fishing boats pass by, listening to the putt-putt of the motorbikes and proudly talking about our grandchildren's report cards. I can hardly believe I won't again hear that clear mountain-stream voice of hers: 'But, Rita, *darling* . . .'"*

Perhap Charlotte Winston put it best: "It was as if the natural order of events had been cruelly shifted for all of us. We knew, then, that nothing would ever again be the same."

As an estimated worldwide television audience of 100 million watched, a bugle call at 10:30 A.M. signaled the funeral procession

---

*Grace would have been seventy-three on November 12, 2003.

as the Princess's bier was brought from the west wing of the Palace. Twenty members of the local penitent society, dressed in white robes with black capes, carried their burden through the main gate to the majestic great white cathedral of St. Nicholas, six hundred yards away. Prince Rainier, dressed entirely in black, walked directly behind the coffin, draped with a white banner bearing the Grimaldi coat of arms. His head hung low, he looked like a man who had been shattered by loss. Many wondered how he would ever be able to endure the rest of his life without his Princess.

Princess Caroline, dressed in black and her head covered with a black mantilla, walked to the right of her father, Prince Albert to his left. Grace's siblings, Peggy, Kell, and Lizanne, followed directly behind. From her hospital bed, Stephanie watched the ceremony with Paul Belmondo at her side; at one point, she became so distraught that she lost consciousness. Until the last of the eight hundred mourners were seated in the great cathedral, Rainier and his children stood beside the coffin. The cathedral steps were strewn with flowers. The bell tolled slowly. A black cloth canopy hung from the cathedral's highest point, draping soberly to the altar. To some of the mourners, the church seemed warm and sticky, even claustrophobic despite its enormity.

The High Requiem Mass began with the solemn invocation, "We weep for our good Princess, Her Serene Highness Princess Grace. Savior, Savior, we are sure You are calling her to You and Your glory." Music from Bach, Haydn, and Barber accompanied the service. Rainier had no great love for classical music; he would often begin to doze almost as soon as a concert started, and would start snoring if not for Grace's persistent nudges. So immersed was he in his grief, it's likely that the Prince didn't even hear the notes that now filled the cathedral. Twenty-six years ago, he and Grace had knelt before the altar to begin their life together, almost where she now lay. He'd been unhappy then that most of European royalty and other heads of state had shunned the wedding. They were here today. From Presidents to Princes, from Duchesses to Princesses—including Diana, Princess of Wales—from Presidents' wives to an Archbishop representing the Pope, they came to mourn: Prince Philip of Liechtenstein; Prince Fuad of Egypt; Princess Benedicte of Denmark; former Empress Farah Diba of Iran; Prince Albert of Belgium; King Baudouin and Queen Fabiola of Belgium; Queen Anne-Marie of Greece; Princess Feriad of Jordan; Prince Karim Aga Khan and Begum Salima; Prince Betril of Sweden; Prince Bernhardt of Holland; Princess Paola of Liège; Grand Duchess Josephine-Charlotte of Luxembourg; and Madame Claude Pompidou, widow of the former President of France. Some of Grace's Hollywood friends were also present, including Cary Grant, Sam Spiegel, Mrs. David Niven, Mrs. Frank Sinatra, and, of course, Grace's former agent, Jay Kanter. First Lady Nancy Reagan walked into the cathedral in such grief that she couldn't stop repeating, "It can't be true. It can't be true." When she saw Princess Caroline, she hugged her and broke into a deep sob. She then sat with Madame Danielle Mitterand, wife of the French President, in the front row of the congregation.

The presence of so many dignitaries was a tribute to what Rainier and Grace had done together to transform Monaco's image; a quarter of a century earlier it had been considered a playground for rich gamblers. Now it was a cosmopolitan principality, headquarters for a number of multinational corporations that enjoyed tax-free advantages, home of Jacques Cousteau's Oceanographic Institute and Museum, site of the world-famous auto race, known for its many cultural events—garden shows and ballet and symphony performances, glittering galas that attracted people from all over the world and made huge sums for charity. Unlike most of his predecessors, Rainier not only lived in his own country, but took an active part in ruling it. Grace had improved Monaco's image in her own way. At first she had been looked upon by the Monegasques as an American actress, beautiful but cold, and certainly not one of them. Somewhere along the way, Her Serene Highness had stopped being called the "American Princess" and had become "our Princess." They had come to love her, and in return she had come to love them, love Monaco and also its history.

"Lord, we weep for our Princess Grace," intoned Monsignor Charles Brandt, an old family friend. "The brutality of her death adds to our pain. She was such a good person, so beautiful and so loved. She was an exemplary Christian. Not only are her husband and children crushed by this tragedy, but a whole people. *Au revoir*, Madame. You have perfectly fulfilled your contract. Signed, Monaco."

After a prayer for Prince Rainier, during which the congregation stood while His Highness remained slumped in his chair, the Archbishop swung the censer of burning incense over the coffin, then holy water. Finally, Rainier, Caroline, and Albert stepped forward to touch the coffin and then pause for a moment of silent prayer. They then followed the Archbishop out of the cathedral, where a waiting car took them back to the Palace.

"My life will never be the same," a shattered Prince Rainier told his Consul General, Frank Cresci, after the service. "Without Princess Grace, none of it matters for me now," he concluded, clinging to Frank for support. "It's all meaningless. My God, it's all meaningless." Rainier then buried his face in his hands and wept.

Life after Grace

After Princess Grace's solemn burial alongside other royal family members on a peaceful promontory overlooking the Mediterranean, her friends attempted to celebrate her life by proceeding to post-funeral gatherings at the Palace. Their pained and rigid smiles were evidence of both their courage and their grief. Some told stories about the good times, while others said nothing at all. A New Age woman before it was fashionable, Grace may have wanted those close to her to rejoice in her life, not wallow in mourning over her death. However, no one was ready to do that yet. The loss was too great, the emotion too strong.

Grace's immediate family—her husband and children—were

powerless to do anything but reconcile themselves to a sudden, shocking twist of fate. The Grimaldis of Monaco certainly had had their share of times, both good and bad, over the years, but nothing could prepare them for a tragedy of this magnitude. In a moment, everything that had ever been was all there would ever be: trips that were or were never taken; arguments that were or weren't resolved; a greater capacity for tenderness and understanding that was or was not displayed. With the Princess's death, the good times and bad, the conflicts and differences, all became permanent and irrevocable. In the breath of an instant, the present became the past, and the future what might have been.

The inequity of the loss would drive the family to feel as much anger and resentment as they did grief. The challenge for the Grimaldis, as for any family facing such loss, would be to learn to accept what had happened and live on, and without bitterness or regret. The greatest tribute they could give to the memory of Princess Grace would be to celebrate life, not condemn it.

Today, the memory of Princess Grace is still strong in Monaco; souvenir shops all over the principality specialize in memorabilia featuring her image. A bronze statue of her overlooks 3,500 rose bushes and 150 varieties of the blooming flower in the Princess Grace Rose Garden in the Fontvieille section of Monaco. The stunning monument was inaugurated by Rainier in June 1984, an everlasting tribute to his Princess, a woman considered by many Monegasques to be on a par with the sainted. "When my husband and I went over there [in 1999] we were just amazed at how strong Grace's presence still is in Monaco," said her sister Lizanne Kelly LeVine. "You mention her name, and my goodness! It's as if she was a saint. And to me, well, she was just Gracie, you know?"

Indeed, Grace's legacy is forever immortalized in the hearts and minds of fans everywhere—not just in Monaco—who miss the star she had been and the icon she represented. Many people around the world had for years been invested in what they perceived to be the fairy tale of Grace Kelly's life. They counted on her to live happily ever after, embodying the dreams of a generation. It was difficult to reconcile that such tragedy could occur in the life of a woman for whom everything had always seemed so perfect. However, for Grace's family, there is no legend or icon, no Cinderella story. She is just a woman who lived twenty-six and a half years in the United States with one family, and twenty-six and a half years in Monaco with another. She didn't have unattainable goals in life; rather, hers were basic, modest, and human. As she told Pierre Salinger, who conducted one of the last TV interviews with her shortly before her death, "I would like to be remembered as trying to do my job well, of being understanding and kind. I'd like to be remembered as a decent human being and a caring one."

"I think she was truly happy at the end," concludes her sister Lizanne. "I look back on her final days, her last weeks and months and, yes, I feel in my heart that she was content. She had so much more to give, though . . . so much more living to do. It seemed unfair then; it seems unfair now."

Prince Rainier has said that he misses his wife as much today as he did twenty years ago; his children have said the same. For them, Grace Kelly was, once upon a time, not a Princess or a fable, but a mother and wife—like any mother and wife, as capable of flaws as she was of perfection, with the same dreams and disappointments as anyone else. She was as tender as she could be domineering, and as understanding as she could be uncompromising. She was as caring and inspiring as any person who contributes to the lives of those around her, and it is that contribution to the people she knew and loved that is perhaps her greatest achievement.

Epilogue: Rainier

On Sunday May 9, 1999, His Serene Highness Prince Rainier, seventy-four at the time, celebrated his Golden Jubilee, the half-century anniversary of his sovereignty. Had it really been twenty-five years since the Texas-style barbecue that Princess Grace had hosted for the Monegasques in honor of her husband's twenty-fifth? It seemed like only yesterday; Grace had been so alive and vigorous, wearing the traditional red, black, and white costume and straw hat, mixing with her subjects as their beloved Princess, no longer an outsider in the principality but someone they loved and cared about as they would one of their own. What had happened to the time? The years had just fallen away; Grace had been gone for all but seven of the last twenty-five. So much had changed, her beloved children were now adults—Caroline forty-two, Albert forty-one, and Stephanie thirty-four.

Had the Princess lived, she would have known and loved six grandchildren, three from Caroline and three from Stephanie. She would also have seen Caroline through the sudden death of a second husband, Stefano Casiraghi, and then marriage to a third, Prince Ernst, whose child she was now carrying.

Might Grace also have been able to convince Stephanie not to bear two children out of wedlock before finally marrying their father, Daniel Ducruet, a man who would publicly betray her with another woman? What influence might she have had on Stephanie's choice to then give birth to a third child without benefit of marriage?

No doubt she would have been proud of Albert, still the level-headed, sensible young man of his youth. Honor, duty, and loyalty had been inculcated in him since birth, sometimes at the expense of his being able to bond with his mother as a young child; she would be proud of his continued dedication to the principality (though she would probably raise an eyebrow about his ongoing bachelorhood).

In appraising the range of experiences of her children in the past seventeen years, Princess Grace would no doubt take consolation in the fact that, whatever their mistakes, all three have lived independent lives. While they have sometimes made unpopular choices, they have also felt free to "choose again," as she would have put it, whether that meant marriage, divorce—or no union at all. She has left her imprint on each of them. They are Grace's legacy, her immortality. None would ever be stuck in any situation or forced to submit to a life devoid of passion. Rather, all have found strength in adversity and the freedom to move forward, even when doing so was not popular in the principality—or with their father.

For his part, Prince Rainier refused to dwell in the past and seldom questioned what might have been had his wife lived a fuller life at his side. "Life is for the living," he had said. "We have no choice but to go on."

The royal celebration of Prince Rainier's fiftieth milestone began with a solemn morning Mass at Monaco's cathedral during which a personal message from Pope John Paul II was read to the sovereign by His Eminence, Cardinal Paul Poupard, president of the Pontifical Council for Culture. The festivities would conclude many hours later with a carnival of music and fireworks at the principality's Hercules port. However, without doubt the most emotional part of the day occurred in the afternoon when Rainier and his family appeared before thousands of their subjects in the Place d'Armes, the Palace square, dotted with red-and-white flags and similarly colored medieval-style canopies in honor of the festivities.

As the sun shone intensely upon them, the Grimaldis walked onto the scarlet-carpeted platform. The Prince appeared confident and pleased, though physically weakened, while flanked by his children, as well as Caroline's husband, Prince Ernst, eldest son of Prince Ernst Augustus von Hanover, Duke of Brunswick-Lüneburg, and Princess Ortrud Bertha of Schleswig-Holstein. (With Caroline's marriage to the handsome Ernst a few months earlier, in February, she had stepped into the higher echelon of European royalty, becoming a Princess of Hanover—a distinction that carries with it the title Her Royal Highness, which outranks her previous title of Her Serene Highness.) Other family members, including several Grimaldi grandchildren, as well as dignitaries and other governmental officials, were also present.

On this day, Prince Rainier was somberly but impeccably attired in a navy blue suit with a sky-blue tie over a gray shirt, his snow-white, wavy hair smoothly combed back. Dark glasses shielded his eyes from a brilliant sun. Albert and Ernst were also dressed conservatively, sporting red and blue ties, respectively. Stephanie, in a double-breasted white ensemble, looked more approachable than she did royal, with her chestnut-brown hair pulled back casually into a ponytail. Caroline, seven months pregnant, was more matronly than glamorous in a lavender two-piece satin jacket and calf-length dress. Each took his or her seat on a red velvet chair: Princess Stephanie to the far left, then Prince Ernst, Princess Caroline, Prince Albert, and Prince Rainier.

After brief introductory remarks by Prince Albert, Prince Rainier stood and walked to a lectern.

"It is difficult for me to express my emotion and joy at being here among you, with my children and my family, to celebrate my fifty years of rule," he told the Monegasques and assembled media. Despite his advancing years, Rainier's voice was still deep and melodious as he talked about Monaco, how proud he was of the principality and of its subjects. He made note of the opportunity another Monaco celebration afforded "to bring us all together once again in a feeling of profound unity and affection." Pausing for a moment, he then said, "I want to take advantage of this exceptional day to pay Princess Grace the homage she so richly deserves for the part of the path she walked at my side."

At the mention of Grace, the crowd fell silent.

"How can we ever forget the exceptional qualities of heart and spirit which made her such an admirable Princess and mother,"

Rainier asked, "and which brought such light to the principality whose dynastic continuity she guaranteed?"

The elderly Prince paused again, seeming confused, perhaps lost in a sweep of memories. As he leaned forward on the lectern, he looked vulnerable, unsure of himself yet stubbornly determined not to show it. Albert—always Rainier's good right hand—leaned forward in his seat at the ready, in case his father needed his support. However, with a subtle hand gesture, Rainier motioned for his son to remain in his chair.

"Yes, this is difficult," Rainier admitted, his voice now softer. "I still feel her absence, you know? It was a marriage of love, it truly was." While Prince Rainier would ordinarily not allow himself such a public display of emotion, in this case of celebrating his fiftieth Jubilee without Grace at his side, he seemed not to be concerned with propriety. It was a bittersweet day; certainly, no one missed her more than he did.

Stephanie and Caroline were unable to contain their sadness. Stephanie in particular was overcome; tears spilled down her cheeks. She finally lowered her head and wiped her eyes with a handkerchief.

"God bless her," Rainier said of his late wife, his voice breaking. "God bless her," he repeated.

Quickly regaining his composure, the Prince then went on to speak of his son, Prince Albert. "My heir sees the third millennium opening up before him," said Rainier as he looked behind him at Albert. "He, together with all of us, will have to face that challenge. It's a proud principality, altruistic and confident in its future, that I would like to leave for him," he added, his voice getting stronger. "His active participation in state affairs is preparing him for this, and you are there to assure me and to assure him of your support, your faith, and determination."

After a few closing remarks, the Prince's short speech, just twenty minutes in length, was over. As soon as he backed away from the lectern, Rainier's subjects burst into spontaneous cheers, filling the Place d'Armes with jubilance. In unison, Rainier's children and his son-in-law rose and also applauded, his daughters wiping tears from their eyes. One by one, they all approached Rainier, kissed him on both cheeks, and hugged him. Each time one of his offspring embraced the sovereign, the applause from thousands of Monegasques grew more robust, as if in recognition of the bond that particular child had with Rainier and, by extension, with Grace.

As Prince Ernst gave a firm handshake to his father-in-law, people began tossing roses onto the platform. Stephanie picked one up, walked over to her older sister, and handed it to her tentatively. Smiling, Caroline took the offering. The crowd roared its appreciation, perhaps thinking of it as a peace offering between sisters. It was well-known that Caroline had not approved of Stephanie's life in recent years, and that Stephanie had not attended Caroline's wedding to Ernst. The sisters were estranged; how sad this separation would have made their mother, and how happy she would have been at the simple gesture of détente.

Graciously, Ernst took a few steps backwards and joined the dignitaries behind him to give the immediate Grimaldi family some time with their loyal subjects. There they stood side by side, Stephanie, Caroline, Albert, and Rainier, under a clear sky, polished blue and radiant with sunlight.

It may have been the tribute the Prince had offered to his fallen Princess that softened certain hearts, for on that day after the long procession of Monegasque citizens had ended and the bustling crowds had filed out, the royal family remained together. With the Prince's grandchildren playing tag and the sound of laughter echoing from the Palace, it looked to many as if this day might mark a new beginning for the Grimaldis: a chance for each to make the same decision Grace had once made—to accept disappointments, forgive misdeeds, and celebrate the moment. That evening, Rainier raised a glass to his children, all gathered in a vine-covered arbor under the night sky. "To my Princess," he proclaimed, "whose laughter I hear in every child, whose comfort I feel in every embrace, whose beauty I see more clearly each day."

Rainier misses his Princess. He also misses Grace Kelly, the young, strong-minded woman who took his breath away with her flawless face, and stole his heart with her undying loyalty. As in many fairy tales, the Prince, after a soulful search, had found his Princess. She had taken his hand and left the world she'd known behind. Together they created a stronger sovereignty and carried forward a legacy. The years melted away. Now he lives with the memory of his Princess, alone in the Palace: the place he met her; the place he loved her . . . the place he'll never leave behind.

APPENDIX

PRINCE RAINIER'S MONACO TODAY

Today, Prince Rainier of the Principality of Monaco (Principauté de Monaco) is head of state over about 35,000 residents, about 6,000 of whom are bona fide citizens. Not only is Rainier monarch of the oldest reigning family in Europe but, with the death of Hirohito—Emperor of Japan from 1926 until 1989—the longest-serving monarch in the world. However, the image one might have of the elderly Prince sitting on a throne and unilaterally passing into law his every whim is far from accurate.

Actually, Prince Rainier rules through a Minister of State (whom he nominates from a list of three French diplomats submitted by the French government), and a cabinet of Monegasque councilors. (Since January 1, 2000, the post of Minister of State has been held by Patrick Leclercq, who succeeded Michel Leveque.) All laws are approved by the eighteen-person National Council, elected by Monegasque citizens once every five years.

Despite Monaco's autonomy, France is still involved in its business affairs—too much so as far as Rainier is concerned. For instance, the judiciary is largely staffed by French citizens on secondment, and the Bank of France controls the Monegasque banking system. Monegasques follow the French education system. The French presence, however, is reviewed once a year by a joint commission to make sure that it is not too intrusive. Still, Rainier has for years been trying to break free of French involvement, for instance trying to overturn the law that he pick his Minister of State from a list provided by the French government. Such disagreements with France have been going on for decades, at least since the major 1962 showdown with de Gaulle.

In March 2000, a report produced by the socialist-dominated French National Assembly accused the principality of encouraging tax evaders (who allegedly use Monaco to hide and launder money) while still profiting financially from its close ties with France. (Larger countries such as Switzerland and Luxembourg also faced similar criticism.) As it's been since 1962, apart from the French who live in Monaco, none of the principality's residents pay income tax. Many of those residents—including certain celebrities, race car drivers, and tennis players—obviously live there to escape high taxes in their home countries. Thousands more non-residents also have investment and tax-free bank accounts in Monaco.

In response to the report, an angry Prince Rainier pointed out that Monaco's prosperity was important to the French region around it (about 25,000 people a day commute from France into Monaco to work). Again, he said, it was time for his country to reassert its sovereignty. "France must respect us," he said in one interview. "We are a sovereign state. For too long, I believe, we have allowed our sovereignty to be limited."

The outcome of subsequent negotiations was that Monaco agreed to tighten up its anti–money laundering procedures. Like other offshore financial centers, it is also presently considering European Union demands that it introduce a withholding tax on savings. However, Rainier remains firmly opposed to full disclosure of bank accounts, which would mean the end of banking secrecy there.

Though obviously not omnipotent, Prince Rainier is no mere figurehead. He proposes all legislation voted upon by the National Council. He has the power to exile people, if he chooses to do so. He can rewrite the constitution. He has final authority over the daily lives of Monaco's residents, and he does it all without a real army. (It's been said that there are more musicians in Monaco than soldiers.)

In the year 2001, crime statistics in Monaco comprised four auto break-ins and a few burglaries. Rainier's police force, 300 uniformed and highly visible policemen—that is, one for every 115 or so inhabitants and one of the highest ratios in the world—continues to keep a tight watch over the streets of the principality. Surveillance is high-tech and extreme in order to protect wealthy visitors. After all, where there are jewels, there are often jewel thieves, and Rainier has made it a personal mission to see to it that tourists are safe in Monaco. For instance, seventy-five cameras watch over an area just a bit less than a square mile. "It should only be a problem if you're doing something you shouldn't be doing," he has said. The Prince can point to one of the lowest crime rates in the world as evidence that his security systems work.

Because newspapers and magazines are monitored, with offensive material often banned, some have found it odd that, after all of these years, Prince Rainier can't find a way to keep paparazzi out of the principality. In fact, Rainier, always as much a realist as a shrewd businessman, realizes how vital publicity has always been to Monaco's tourist trade. He doesn't want to squeeze out coverage of his family's lives—he just doesn't want the local Monegasques to have to read about the always-unfolding melodrama in the grocery stores.

Rainier is a Prince who has always pushed ahead with vision and enterprise, seldom accepting the notion of limitations. For instance, decades ago, "the Builder Prince" (as he is sometimes called in Monaco) decided to expand the principality's physical size. However, there was simply no room for such growth on the cliffs that horseshoe around the Mediterranean, with mountains on three sides and ocean on the fourth. In a feat of engineering that took years to complete, Rainier decided to build on the ocean—by reclaiming land from the sea. By layering rock in 131 feet of water, he added nearly 55 acres, enlarging the country by nearly 20 percent with its new Fontvieille area.

Though it has had fiscal setbacks over the years, Monaco still prospers, boasting more millionaires per square foot than any other place on earth. The principality counts on tourism for about 25 percent of its revenue. There's always something going on in Monaco to keep the tourists busy, annual events such as the Feast of Sainte-Devote, patron saint of Monaco; the Monte Carlo Grand Prix; the Saint Martin Gardens Ball; the Bonfires of Saint John; the Monte Carlo International Circus Festival; the Monte Carlo International Fireworks Festival; and the World Music Awards.

Prince Rainier considers himself, in effect, the CEO of a small but diverse company forced to compete in the world market for its survival. He says that such work requires intuition and nerve, both trademarks of the Grimaldis. Today, in tribute to Rainier's business savvy, income from gambling constitutes just 3 percent of Monaco's economy, the bulk of which is driven by environmentally correct businesses, tourism, and banking. More than one hundred industries have settled in Monaco. "I think I've built a solid, active, and modern principality," he says. "When I first came to the throne, my priority was to get rid of the image Monaco had of being an operetta set, a tax haven enjoying a permanent carnival. The living in Monaco is good, that's true, but we work hard, too."

It's interesting to note that, despite his wealth and power, Prince Rainier has never been a world-class leader. Though he is the sovereign of Monaco, his decisions regarding the principality and what occurs there really have no impact on important European affairs at all. Certainly, Monaco doesn't possess any resources needed by other countries: no oil, no land, no important seaport. No one in the tiny principality has ever been aggressive—at least not in the past few centuries (except, for a time, Aristotle Onassis). It poses no threat to anyone, anywhere. As long as its Prince maintains friendly relations with France, he has nothing to worry about from that country either. Indeed, Monaco is a rarified world in and of itself, an old-fashioned "kingdom" (or, more accurately, "princedom") in a modern world, populated by people who, by some crazy luck of the draw, found themselves living the good life there—and paying no taxes!

Seldom is a critical word about the much-beloved Rainier ever uttered, at least publicly, in the principality. Not only is he the Monegasques' Prince, he is considered the "father of Monaco," a symbol of the past, present, and also, due to his reliable longevity, the future. Though he has been sick in recent years with heart-related illnesses, he seems to always rebound, each visit to the hospital ending with a press notification of his release. "He is nothing like what one might expect," says Gwen Robyns, Princess Grace's biographer. "He's not sophisticated, but rather funny. One of my fondest memories is of mixing dry martinis with Rainier, and then filling the vodka bottles with water so Grace wouldn't know how much we were drinking. Over the years, he has aged, of course, but he is still interested in sports and western movies. He's also still not interested in ballet or poetry. He's beloved. When he passes away, it will be as sad a day in the principality as it was when we lost Grace."

Prince Rainier doesn't focus much on what he lost when Grace died twenty-one years ago. "There is a lot to say about her, of course, because we were very close and discussed and debated everything—problems or plans or decisions about what to do and how," he has said. "That is now a void, a great and awful emptiness. She was always present and ready to do things either with me or for me, if I couldn't do them. We worked as a team . . . and the team was split up forever. Since then, it's never been the same." In another interview, he recalled "the Irish in her, a mixture of good-heartedness and kindness, combined with strong will."

Remarrying, however, has never been a serious consideration for the Prince. He has said that he could "never replace" Grace in his life, and was also afraid that attempting to do so could mean his children would "become distanced from me at a time when they needed me most." As he once told Diane Sawyer, "I've never, never had the urge to wed again. I've never spoken about it to my children, nor have they spoken about it to me. It's been a sort of understanding. And, you know, they've given me enough troubles. I wasn't going to add new troubles . . . a better solution was to keep it as it was."

Rainier is still in communication with Lizanne Kelly LeVine, Grace's sister and, at seventy-one, the only surviving member of that generation of Kellys. "I speak to him often," she says. "I always call him on his birthday. 'Happy birthday, Old Thing,' I'll say. He's really a great guy. I do love him." Lizanne also remains in close contact with Grace's children, her nephew the Prince and nieces the Princesses.

Some feel that Monaco's future seems uncertain because Rainier has not yet entrusted his son, Prince Albert, with any real power in the principality—either because he feels Albert is not ready for it, or that he doesn't want the responsibility of it. "I suppose I'll know it's time when people start telling me that I'm not making sense," says Rainier, his sense of humor still intact.

Though Prince Rainier has included Prince Albert in all major principality decisions in recent years ("His ideas give me energy," he has said), until Albert is put to the test of actually ruling over the principality, his persuasive power will not be recognized. However, those who know Rainier well insist that he will never willingly abdicate. "Though ill, he's still a strong and powerful man who has the unconditional love and devotion of his son," says Lizanne LeVine. "I would be surprised to see him hand over the throne; in fact, I doubt he will. I would also be surprised if Albert ever wanted it prior to his father's death."

A NOTE ABOUT SUCCESSION

No doubt as a reaction to Prince Albert's continued bachelorhood, an amendment to Monaco's constitution was enacted on April 2, 2002, allowing power to pass from a reigning Prince who has no descendants, to his siblings' children—a move that will keep the Grimaldi family on the throne even if Albert never has children of his own. Under the old constitution, succession was restricted to a monarch's children (thus Rainier's determination, in the 1950s, to marry and have an heir). However, now Albert's nieces and nephews can also succeed him if he dies without heirs.

In recent years, there have been numerous press reports that Rainier had taken Princess Stephanie and her children out of the line of succession. This is not true. At present, the order of succession is:

Albert Grimaldi as Hereditary Prince;

Princess Caroline, widow of Stefano Casiraghi (killed at the age of thirty in a boating accident in 1990); her children by Stefano: Andrea Casiraghi (born on June 8, 1984); Pierre Casiraghi (born on September 5, 1987); Charlotte Casiraghi (born on August 3, 1986); and her child by her third and present husband, Prince Ernst August of Hanover, Alexandra of Hanover (born on July 20, 1999).

Following in line of succession would be Princess Stephanie, then her children by her former husband Daniel Ducruet: Louis Ducruet (born on November 26, 1992) and Pauline Ducruet (born on May 4, 1994). Although Stephanie's children were both born before her marriage to Daniel Ducruet in June 1995, Monegasque civil law, like French law, provides that natural children are fully and completely legitimized by the marriage of their parents.

Since Stephanie has not disclosed the name of the father of her daughter Camille Marie Kelly Grimaldi (born on July 15, 1998), that child is not yet considered legitimate and thus is the only descendant from the immediate family not in the line of succession.

PRINCESS CAROLINE

Her Serene Highness Princess Caroline of Monaco has a recollection of her mother that, while somewhat disconcerting, is typical of the experience of a girl raised by a beloved, much-sought-after celebrity such as Princess Grace. "There's sort of a vision, as a small child, of seeing someone incredibly beautiful and well-dressed going out, with a trail of perfume behind," she recalled of Grace, "and this woman saying to me, 'Don't! Careful! Don't mess my hair and makeup.'"

Caroline is today a mother with three children of her own and can probably relate to Grace's harried schedule as Princess. After her mother's death, many of Grace's principality duties then fell to Caroline as Monaco's new First Lady. With the passing of the years, she has brought both charm and intelligence to her role, and is a popular and well-loved figure in Monaco. Not only has she handled Princess Grace's cultural responsibilities—as well as instituting many of her own, such as Les Ballets de Monte Carlo, which she founded twelve years ago—Caroline is also president of the Princess Grace Foundation of Monaco, which, among other things, awards scholarships to musicians, and provides financial support for three French hospitals. Princess Caroline insists, however, that she is simply filling in until her brother marries, for, when he does, his wife will then be Monaco's preeminent Princess. Perhaps learning from her Aunt Antoinette—Rainier's sister who grudgingly stepped aside when he married Grace—Caroline has said, "If I was too much of a presence, it would be ghastly for Albert's wife."

Because of her royal position, Caroline's personal life has, of course, always been the subject of great public scrutiny. In April 1983, she began seeing a lot of Robertino Rossellini, son of Ingrid Bergman. Because his mother had died of cancer two weeks before Grace's fatal accident, it seemed to some that their mutual grief brought Caroline and Robertino together, and for a time it did appear that they were romantically involved. The two, friends since childhood, remain close to this day. By the summer, Caroline was romantically interested in someone else: Stefano Casiraghi, twenty-three-year-old heir to a Milanese oil-refining fortune.

At first, Casiraghi seemed cut from the same cloth as Caroline's former husband, Philippe Junot. Viewed by many observers as a playboy, Stefano was nicknamed "Fancazzista" by friends (which means, "he doesn't do a fucking thing"). A gentle man who seemed to understand Princess Caroline's needs, he offered her unwavering support as she grieved over her mother's death, though most royal observers still insisted that he would be no good for her in the long run. In the fall of 1983, when Caroline became pregnant with Stefano's child, a concerned Prince Rainier summoned the young man to the Palace to learn of his intentions. It was then that Casiraghi asked the Prince for his eldest daughter's hand in marriage. Rainier agreed to the marriage.

On December 29, 1983, Caroline and Stefano were wed in a private and simple twenty-minute civil ceremony at the Palace, in front of just twenty guests. Because she was pregnant—and it was her second marriage—it was decided that the less attention the wedding received, the better off the principality would be for it. On June 8, 1984, Caroline gave birth to Rainier's first grandson, Andrea Albert Pierre. Though the birth was also downplayed by the Palace, Rainier was filled with joy about the birth, though he did tell friends that his happiness was bittersweet. "If Grace was here for this, she would love this grandchild like no grandchild has ever been loved," he said. On August 3, 1986, Caroline and Stefano welcomed a daughter, Charlotte Marie Pomeline, named after Rainier's mother. On September 5, 1987, the couple had a third child, Pierre Rainier Stefano.

"Stefano was a humble guy," said television producer Gary Pudney, a close friend of the Grimaldis. "He would always step back when the rest of them were having their picture taken. He never forced himself into that world." Pleased by his son-in-law's devotion to Caroline, Rainier bestowed upon Stefano the title Duke of Monaco.

In 1988, Caroline was compelled to give a painful and embarrassing sworn statement to the Sacra Rota, the Vatican's marital court, in the ongoing proceedings having to do with the annulment of her marriage to Philippe Junot. She said, "The day of my marriage [to Junot], I was flying on a cloud of happiness. Then we went on honeymoon [to Tahiti] and I got a real shock. Waiting at the airport was a friend of Philippe's whom he had invited. All three of us went on our honeymoon together. (In his defense, Philippe says that the gentleman Caroline spoke of was a photographer he had hired to take photos of the honeymoon, which is true. However, the fact that he didn't tell Caroline he was intending to sell photos of their honeymoon to the press did not bode well for him.) Caroline also outlined in great detail numerous cases of infidelity on Junot's part, in order to illustrate her view that he had never been committed to the marriage. "I admit that we had intimate relations before our marriage," she said, "but have nothing else to say about it."

As the years passed, Princess Caroline found herself content in her second marriage, to Stefano. He continued to prove his critics wrong; he became a successful businessman, amassing great wealth and becoming involved in the business of building a $160 million housing complex in the principality.

It was once said of Monaco that it's a country small in size but epic in anguish, and never did the sentiment hold more truth than on the morning of October 3, 1990. Just as it seemed as if Caroline had settled into a happy marriage to a successful, well-adjusted spouse, she fell victim to the so-called curse of the Grimaldis. Her husband, thirty-year-old Stefano, a world powerboat champion, was killed in a boat race.

Shocked when he heard the news, Rainier—who by this time considered Stefano a son—collapsed in tears. Later, it would fall upon the elderly Prince to tell his grandchildren of their father's sudden death. Caroline, who had left for Paris the night before the tragedy, returned to Monaco to face her grief.

The funeral Mass for Stefano Casiraghi was overwhelmingly sad, occurring almost exactly eight years after Princess Grace's and in the same cathedral, St. Nicholas's. Caroline, dressed in black with a long mantilla and dark glasses, seemed numb as Rainier assisted her into the church. Now the widowed mother of three, she would mourn her husband's death for years. Somehow, though, she would find a way to go on, for her children. "Strength comes when you're in a very narrow alley, and have no way of turning back. You just have to choose to live your life," she recently said, expressing a sentiment that sounds so much like one her mother might have made. "I had to go on."

On June 21, 1992, a year after Stefano's death, the Tribunal of the Holy Rota, the ecclesiastical court, finally granted Caroline the annulment of her first marriage, to Philippe Junot. A Vatican spokesman explained that the Church "recognizes circumstances in which the vows taken by the couple are not efficient, and so the marriage does not exist right from the beginning, whether the couple are aware of it or not."

The Vatican's official ruling stated that Philippe Junot was "incapable of giving the essentials in a good marriage." He was alleged to have made a bet with a friend that he would "win Caroline." He was not "psychologically a good husband," according to the court, "and continually cheated on the Princess; there was evidence that he had a six-month relationship with an ex-lover while with Caroline." In the end, the absence of parental stability, according to the ruling, and especially the absence of his mother while he was growing up, "drew him to a playboy lifestyle."

Underlining its opposition to divorce, the Vatican also issued another statement with its decision, pointing out that an annulment is not a divorce but merely a ruling that the marriage never actually existed. The spokesman added that the church could recognize that a marriage was null and void when there were "impediments to the marriage, technical problems or lack of consent." Or, as Caroline's grandfather, Jack Kelly, might have put it, "There's a way around everything. You do what you have to do." (By this time, Philippe Junot was happily married [in the Protestant church] to Nuna Wandelboe Larsen, with three young children. He was not officially informed of the annulment by the Vatican. Instead, he read about it in the press.)

In April of 1993, Pope John Paul II legitimized the births of Caroline's three children with Stefano (a union that had not previously been recognized by the church since it had occurred before the annulment of her marriage to Philippe Junot).

Meanwhile, Caroline had begun dating French actor Vincent Lindon, well-known in France, with an impressive list of credits. It wasn't long before the international press began to speculate that the couple would wed. However, by this time Caroline was no longer the outrageous, publicity-generating Princess she had been in her youth. She had become removed, enigmatic, rarely giving interviews, always conscious of how to best present herself as Monaco's Acting First Lady. "I may be a Princess," she said. "but gossip is the 'king.' And he's a tyrant."

Caroline and Vincent Lindon lasted for nearly five years, their romance helped by their decision to move out of Monaco and live in seclusion in St.-Rémy-de-Provence in France. They never married. It is said by those close to the Grimaldis that, because Rainier feared another failed Grimaldi union, he issued upon Lindon a list of "marital conditions." Accustomed to giving orders, and accustomed to having them obeyed (at least by anyone but, it would seem, his daughter Stephanie), Rainier composed a list that included Lindon's renouncing Judaism and converting to Catholicism, awarding custody of any children from their marriage to Caroline and her father only, waiving all claims to maintenance, and allowing the Palace to veto his acting roles. Lindon apparently found the list intolerable and left Caroline in 1996.

Caroline was so upset by the end of that relationship and other family matters (including the scandal caused at this same time when Stephanie's husband, Daniel Ducruet, was videotaped having sex with a stripper) that she lost her hair—a case of nervous alopecia, as she explained to her Aunt Lizanne. For a time afterward, the Princess would wear a turban in public. Eventually, however, she just went about bald, not caring what people thought of it, and prompting the issuance of one of the oddest official statements from the Palace: "Caroline is suffering from a condition which is not serious or life-threatening. She does not have cancer, nor is she receiving any treatment which has caused her hair to fall out. We are not prepared to discuss the matter but we are hopeful her hair will grow back one day." (It did.)

In the spring of 1996, Princess Caroline turned to Prince Ernst von Hanover, who was, ironically, a man Grace had had in mind for her daughter many years earlier. Grace had hoped that Caroline would leave Philippe Junot for Ernst. Of course, that never happened. Now, years later, Caroline was fulfilling her mother's wish, though by this time it's likely that Grace would have had second thoughts about Ernst.

Born into a world of wealth and royalty, Prince Ernst is the eldest son of Ernst Augustus von Hanover, Duke of Brunswick-Lüneburg, and Princess Ortrud Bertha of Schleswig-Holstein. He is directly descended in the male line from England's King George III's fifth son, Ernest, Duke of Cumberland.* At the time he began dating Caroline, he was married. He

*The House of Hanover began its long rule of England in 1714 with the accession to the throne of George I and continued for the next 203 years to 1917, when George V changed its name to Windsor, his reason being that the hostilities with Germany in World War I demanded it, since the Hanovers' roots were German.

also seemed to court controversy. However, he was the man who made Princess Caroline happy for the first time since Stefano's death.

Because Ernst's wife, Chantal, was reluctant to grant him a divorce, the proceedings made splashy tabloid headlines for almost a year before finally concluding in March 1997. Nearly two years later, on Caroline's forty-second birthday, January 23, 1999, she and Prince Ernst were married in the Salon des Glaces at Monaco's Royal Palace. After her marriage, Caroline was officially Her Royal Highness Caroline, Princess of Hanover, Duchess of Brunswick and Lüneburg. She now outranked everyone in her family except for her father, the Prince.

On July 20, 1999, Caroline gave birth to the couple's first child, daughter Alexandra.

In recent years, Prince Ernst August of Hanover has generated media attention for his flamboyant behavior and famously bad temper. After being convicted of physically and verbally attacking two journalists, a photographer, and a restaurant owner, he was fined $228,000 and given an eight-month suspended sentence. The Prince did confess to one of the three incidents: making abusive telephone calls to two German tabloid editors after they published photographs of him urinating against the Turkish pavilion at the Hanover Expo. (Last year he took out an advertisement in the *Frankfurter Allgemeine Zeitung* to defend his behavior at the world fair. "I did indeed relieve myself during my visit to Expo 2000, but neither against the wall of the Turkish pavilion nor on the soil of the Turkish state," he said. To be fair, the photographs do show him urinating on the orange fence of the pavilion, not *on* the pavilion.)

Ernst August, referred to these days by the German press as "the pugilist Prince," was also recently convicted over a brawl with a restaurateur on the Kenyan resort island of Lamu, as well as for kicking a photographer at the Salzburg opera festival back in 1999, another incident that was well-documented by the media.

"I think it's a form of reassurance for people to look at others who supposedly have everything and all the luck and then have incredible misfortune and behave badly," Princess Caroline told writer Sarah Mower. "I guess it makes people safe and comfortable in their lives."

Whatever the state of mind of her husband, Princess Caroline seems "safe and comfortable" with him—though it is a bit disconcerting to know that she can watch silently while he lets loose a brutal tirade against a paparazzo. "I have been taught to avoid any expression when a camera is present," she has said in explaining the publication of so many pictures of her recently in which she appears . . . blank. "People will just add what they want to the caption, anyway."

Still, as she raises her family, Caroline tries to keep her children out of the spotlight as much as possible. She now feels that her own parents kept her and her siblings too much a part of the public forum. "We were over-exposed as children," she says, "so that people in the media thought we belonged to them at a very young age. Yes, I think there was overexposure, certainly. I wouldn't go so far as to say it was using children as props, but we were part of the picture. My children hate the press. They see them as the bad guys."

They may "hate" the press, but much of the press seems to adore them: In particular, Andrea and Charlotte have captured the imagination of the world's media with their charismatic personalities and good looks. If Albert does not have children, it is Andrea who will follow his mother as third in line of succession. (He made his first official public appearance when he was just three years old, wearing a royal guard's uniform and white gloves, while waving to the Monegasques from the Palace's balcony.) Pierre, fifteen, has also been photographed while playing sports such as soccer, smiling cheerily at the camera, ready for his own close-up. Who knows how three-year-old Alexandra will turn out, but chances are her life will be one also under great scrutiny. However, Princess Caroline hopes to not overprotect her children and, no doubt, won't be moving with them to whatever city they end up living in while furthering their studies, as Grace did when Caroline moved to Paris. With her children, the young Princess hopes to not make the same mistakes Grace may have made in raising her—which were, perhaps, the same ones her grandmother, Margaret, had made with Grace.

"The thing to remember is that children are not ours. They don't belong to us. They come through us," Caroline has said, paraphrasing Grace's favorite philosopher, Kahlil Gibran. "So you can just show them the doors and maybe try to give them keys, if you have them, but they've got to choose the door and use the key. Protection has its limits. It doesn't mean stifling or smothering people. In the name of love, a lot of damage can be done."

PRINCE ALBERT

As of this writing, His Serene Highness Prince Albert of Monaco is forty-five years of age. After the death of his mother, Princess Grace, Albert took over her work with the Monaco Red Cross. He also worked in New York as an intern for the Morgan Guaranty Trust, and then at the Rogers and Wells law firm as a paralegal. A determined young man, he said he would do whatever necessary to obtain the background in business he felt he would need in order to take over management of the principality. He also studied public relations in Paris at Moet-Hennessy. Amiable and good-natured, he was never caught by photographers having a bad moment, unlike his sisters, who were often photographed during the worst of times for them. He lived his life in New York and Paris with discretion, conscious of his image, protective of his legacy.

In 1985, Albert was elected to the International Olympic Committee as its youngest member. Today, he is a world-class bobsledder and has often been a contender at the Olympics—following in the footsteps of his grandfather, Jack, and uncle, Kell. Albert has imbued Monaco with his passion for sports, bringing annual (and money-making) events to the principality, such as the Monte Carlo Tennis Open, the Monaco Grand Prix, the Monte Carlo Grand Prix Track Meet, the World Push Championships, and the Laureus World Sports Awards.

Of Albert, Gary Pudney, who produces the annual Laureus World Sports Awards from Monaco, said, "The reason for his popularity is that he treats everyone the same way, whether ball player or king, you have his attention and direct eye contact. He's much beloved in Monaco, much like Grace—he has her blue eyes and disposition, that outstanding likeability. People practically genuflect in his presence. He drives his own little electric car around, but then you notice there are two squad cars behind him, Palace guards." (When he is home, Prince Albert has two bodyguards with him. And when he drives down a street in Monaco, he is followed by his bodyguards in a car close behind.)

In 1989, Albert headed up the first World Music Awards from Monaco, now an annual—and popular—showcase event for Monaco, televised globally and featuring the biggest names in popular music of the year.

In 1993, Monaco was accepted into the United Nations, with Albert heading the UN delegation for the principality.

With a receding hairline and a dignified but invariably friendly and gentle manner, Albert has, over the years, been linked with actresses such as Brooke Shields, Donna Mills, and Catherine Oxenberg, and supermodels Claudia Schiffer and Naomi Campbell. He has also apparently enjoyed many high-profile relationships with women who are not well-known but who have gleefully shared alleged details of their lovemaking to reporters. Additionally, a couple of frivolous paternity suits have been filed against him—none have been successful in the courts. His failure to marry remains a mystery to many Monegasques, and there has been a great deal of speculation about it. Remaining committed to his bachelorhood, he shrugs off long-standing rumors of bi- and homosexuality.

Gary Pudney observed, "I've said to Prince Albert, 'You know, the two things I get asked all the time are, "Number One, when are you going to get married, and, Number Two, are you gay?"' He just laughs. My guess is he'll meet the right girl and, when he does, it'll probably be right-on-the-nose casting. It would be nice if he married an American girl, a movie star. But the truth is, whoever he does marry becomes the Princess of Monaco. So, forget about career, if that's what she's doing. There's no way she could have a career. There's a lot going on in Monaco; there's big business going on, and it's a close family."

In 1997, Albert noted, "I would love to have a wife and kids, but it will be a tremendous problem for her. The inevitable comparison to my mother will be there. She'd have to be a strong woman to withstand such comparisons and pressures, mainly put on her by the press." (Grace's shadow does continue to loom large; Rainier has also stated that her memory was of concern whenever he thought of his future with another partner. "Apart from thinking of the children," he has said, "I was afraid that people would compare a new wife with Princess Grace. That would be difficult for any woman to put up with.")

When Prince Albert will take over the throne seems to be anyone's guess since Rainier does not seem interested in abdicating at any time in the near future. "I think I'll be ready when the time will come," Albert has said. "When that time will be, I cannot tell at this point."

PRINCESS STEPHANIE

In the years after her mother's death, Her Serene Highness Princess Stephanie of Monaco became the Grimaldi child to generate the most controversy. Stephanie, already a headstrong youngster, seemed to become even more rebellious after Grace's death, causing some in royal circles to speculate that the emotional trauma of the accident served to strengthen her resolve to live her life to the fullest—regardless of the consequences of her choices.

It didn't last long between Stephanie and Paul Belmondo, the man she had been dating when Grace died. Much to her father's despair, Stephanie entertained the attentions of a number of suitors after Belmondo, causing the French media to refer to each of her new beaux as Stephanie's *"Nouvel élu,"* meaning her "new chosen one."

When she was twenty, Stephanie signed a modeling contract with a Paris modeling firm, posing for fashion spreads in *Elle*, *Vogue*, German *Vogue*, *Rolling Stone*, and many other international publications. In March 1985, she signed with the top American modeling agency Wilhelmina, against her father's wishes: Princesses, as a rule, do not have modeling careers. Ten days after signing her contract, however, Stephanie entered a detox program at the Belvedere Clinic in Boulogne, complaining of the pressures of her new career. Her father, brother, and sister rushed to her side to offer support and convinced her to abandon her modeling aspirations. Stephanie then went on to design a line of swimwear.

The swimwear business did not last long for Stephanie; by the time she was twenty-one she was a recording artist. Her bad-girl image propelled her first single release, "Irresistible," a dance song recorded in English and

French, to million-selling status in France. Despite its success, Rainier was unhappy about the song, especially after seeing its provocative music video. However, there was no controlling Stephanie by this time; he knew it and accepted it. An album was equally successful in Europe, though none of Stephanie's recordings at this time, or later, would ever cause a ripple in America.

Unlike her sister Caroline, who was intensely interested in Monaco and in her royal position at the Palace, Stephanie shied away from it. Her public behavior remained controversial, as she often appeared in public seeming to be inebriated or under the influence of drugs. In the mid-'80's, she became involved in a highly publicized romance with actor Rob Lowe (who later showed a lack of chivalry when he said of Stephanie, "she kisses like a boy"). "It is obvious that Stephanie is going through a bad and difficult period," wrote Rupert Allan to Prince Rainier in 1986, "but I am confident, as she is an intelligent girl, that she will pull herself together soon. Her human environment at this time is so awful and really trash-bad."

In late 1986, Rainier asked some of Grace's New York and Los Angeles friends to keep an eye on the deeply troubled Stephanie, now in Los Angeles and dating French-born Mario Oliver, who had once been arrested and charged with the rape of a nineteen-year-old. (He received a suspended sentence after pleading no contest to sexual battery.)

In early 1987, Stephanie was photographed topless and in an embrace with Mario in Mauritius; soon after, they moved into a mansion in the Benedict Canyon area of Beverly Hills. At that time, Stephanie began studying acting with drama coach Nina Foch. When she began implying that she and Mario might soon marry, Rainier became concerned enough to summon her to a family summit at the St. James Club in Antigua. He threatened to take away her title if she married Oliver, later writing to Rupert Allan that he and the family had "some hard and grave talks" about her romance, which he termed as "painful but indispensable. She is warned," he wrote, "and of course mad at me. In the doghouse am I. But it will pass."

With Caroline also opposed to her sister's romance, Mario Oliver was not permitted to visit the Palace. As Rainier pointed out, it was not easy for Stephanie to take the advice of her older sister in making life choices.

"It's a hard passage to go from the mother's authority to the sister's," he observed. "Caroline resents that . . . there are clashes."

"I'm afraid that within five years of Grace's death, it could be said that the family fell apart," said Grace's friend Gwen Robyns. Grace would have been terribly upset, though I'm not sure how much would have happened had she been there to stop it—but at what cost of heartache?"

By the summer of 1988, Mario Oliver was out of the picture (and Stephanie had to undergo painful laser surgery to remove a tattoo of his initials from her buttocks). She then became involved with Ron Bloom, a producer hired by Sony to produce her first American album; they bought a home together in the suburban San Fernando Valley of Los Angeles and settled there in quiet domesticity. Rainier approved of Bloom, feeling that the producer might have a settling influence on the young Princess. One day, Rainier showed up unexpectedly at Stephanie's doorstep; the two had a tearful reunion. After inspecting his daughter's modest $200,000 house, Rainier made a list of things he felt she might need, and then sent an assistant to a nearby mall to purchase the items (which included a microwave oven).

By the beginning of 1990, however, Stephanie had ended it with Ron Bloom, moved back to Paris, and become involved with young and handsome Frenchman Jean-Yves Lefur, who, like many of the men who courted Caroline and Stephanie over the years, was described by the press as a playboy with no income other than what was provided by the generosity of wealthy friends. By April, Stephanie and Jean-Yves were officially engaged. However, amid stories that he had lied about his background and a published report that he had spent five weeks in jail for fraud, that romance followed all of the others in failure.

Soon after Lefur, Stephanie fell in love with the handsome, dark-haired, and heavily tattooed Daniel Ducruet, a former Palace guard hired by Rainier, at first as Albert's bodyguard, then as Stephanie's. The previously married Ducruet was from a working-class, broken home in Marseilles. When he met Stephanie, he was living in a two bedroom apartment in Beausoleil, outside of Monaco.

In May 1992, Stephanie announced that she was having Daniel Ducruet's baby—out of wedlock. There was little that Prince Rainier, who would turn sixty-nine in June of that year, could do about her decision. His daughter's relationship with Ducruet, and the resulting pregnancy, was hard on the elderly Prince. He found that distancing himself from his youngest daughter was the only way he could deal with her choices. Clearly, she didn't care about his opinions or feelings, and would continue to indulge her excesses.

In the spring of 1992, Rainier changed his will by placing the Grimaldis' wealth into a trust in order to prevent his children's spouses from being able to inherit it without significant complications. In November of that same year, Stephanie gave birth to a boy at Princess Grace Hospital, a child she named Louis after Rainier's grandfather. Most telling was that none of her family members visited her in the hospital, making the estrangement between her and her father and siblings obvious to any observers. On May 31, 1993, Rainier turned seventy; Stephanie was not present at the celebration.

Stephanie's estrangement from Rainier did not last long. Within a year, the two had warmed to one another; the Prince even began to accept Ducruet and his grandson. "Grace would have been proud to know that he never closed the door entirely on Stephanie during this terrible time," said Charlotte Winston. "Their children are still an important part of his life, though God knows they have not made it easy on him."

In early 1994, Stephanie announced that she was expecting another child, with still no plans to marry the baby's father, Daniel Ducruet. On May 5, she gave birth to a daughter, Pauline Grace.

In March 1995, Daniel finally asked Rainier for Stephanie's hand in marriage; he agreed (as if he had any choice). Finally, after having lived together for four years, Stephanie and Daniel were married on July 1, 1995, in a low-key service on the terrace of the touristy Loews Hotel in Monte Carlo. The press noted that the wedding did not occur at the Palace. However, Rainier, Caroline, and Albert did attend the ceremony.

By the summer of 1996, Daniel Ducruet and Stephanie had been married for a year; he was considered part of the royal family, seen with Caroline at all of the official gatherings. Rainier, Caroline, and Albert had finally accepted him, recognizing the calming effect he had on Stephanie. She did seem to have matured since falling for Daniel, and now was more accepting of her royal position in the Grimaldi family, and a doting mother as well. Stephanie and Daniel offered many press interviews about their relationship, both seeming happy and in love. "Things are completely changed," she told *People* magazine in June 1996. "It is a happiness of such intensity, there are no words to express it. He really loves me for myself. He has proved to me that I am the one who counts." Sadly, Stephanie's marital bliss would not last. Just a few months after that interview, Daniel was caught on video making love to a Fili Houteman, a stripper who held the distinction of having been the previous year's "Miss Bare Breasts of Belgium."

Apparently, Ducruet had been entrapped by certain enemies of his, with the cooperation of the stripper, and photographers at the ready. When the explicit video and accompanying photos were sold to the tabloid media, the resulting scandal was bigger than anything that had ever hit the Grimaldi family. While royal watchers worldwide seemed aghast by Stephanie's latest problems, Monegasques were more forgiving. "The personal problems confronting the Grimaldis sometimes add a bizarre touch to Monaco," admits Archbishop Joseph-Marie Sardou of Monaco, "but Monegasques care very much for the Grimaldis and, like me, tend to forgive and forget their problems."

Heartbroken by her husband's grievous betrayal, Stephanie turned to her father for support. He was there for her, as he had been so many times in the past. "I think my children should know that I am not a judge waving my finger at them telling them, 'See I told you so,'" said Rainier later.

Though Stephanie still loved Daniel, there seemed nothing left for her to do in her position but divorce him, which she did in October 1996. "My mistake has destroyed me," a repentant Daniel Ducruet told a reporter for an interview with *Hello* magazine. "I have betrayed my wife, I have betrayed her love and I have betrayed my children. I have humiliated Stephanie in the eyes of the whole world." He said he was certain that his drink had been "spiked," and that the drug had instigated his bad behavior. "I curse the day I met her," he said of the woman he claimed entrapped him.

Daniel Ducruet still seems to love Stephanie and, according to most who know him, would be grateful for another opportunity to prove himself to her, and to her family. He remains close to his children, seeing them as often as possible. He and Stephanie have become friendly, and are often seen together at family outings.

Stephanie would give birth to a third child, Camille Marie Kelly, on July 15, 1998. However, the identity of the father of this baby is not publicly known.

In May 1999, Camille Marie was baptized in a small private ceremony. Prince Rainier and Prince Albert were present, as was Jean-Raymond Gottlieb, the Palace security man widely believed to be little Camille's father.

After all of these years, Prince Rainier has had little choice but to reconcile himself to the fact that he and Princess Stephanie don't adhere to the same traditional family values. As he said in 1999, "Children are often born before marriage these days. It's a shame because children born into free relationships sometimes become lost. Family stability is compromised. For me, family is a value that has to be respected and preserved. The lack of concern about the breakup of the family idea is terrible."

Though Caroline was pregnant before marrying Stefano Casiraghi, that was almost twenty years ago. Today, she is stately, more conservative—unlike Stephanie. Stephanie had two children before marrying Daniel Ducruet, and is not now married to the father of her third child. One wonders, perhaps unfairly, what Princess Grace would think of the unfolding of such circumstances in her youngest daughter's life . . . or if they ever would have happened, had she lived.

While Rainier and Albert try to tolerate Stephanie's extreme personality, Caroline simply does not accept it. She feels that Stephanie has made too many mistakes, against her advice, and, as she told one friend of hers in Monaco, finds it "painful to watch as my sister goes through life testing the limits. It's too much," she has said, "and as much as I love her, I can't go through it anymore. I just can't." Though they try to always be there for their father when he is ill, the sisters have been estranged for years. They sometimes show up at public functions when required (such as Rainier's fiftieth Jubilee, which they would never have missed), but, mostly, they have nothing to do with one another. Stephanie did not attend Caroline's wedding to Prince Ernst; Caroline did not attend the christening of Stephanie's daughter Camille Marie. "I would have preferred them to put aside their differences for these events, but it wasn't possible," Rainier explained to reporter Didier Contant, when pushed on the matter. "Prince Albert gets on well with both his sisters and doesn't want to get involved for fear of hurting one or the other."

Caroline certainly must have had a few private thoughts the day she found out that Stephanie had run off with the circus . . . with Franco Knie, an Italian circus performer she met in the summer of 1999 at the International Monte Carlo Circus Festival.

For many years, the Circus Festival had been an important date on Monaco's social calendar, with Prince Rainier acting as honorary ring-master. Rainier had created the festival in 1974 as an annual event in which performers came from around the world to compete against each other in an eight-day marathon.

As a boy, Rainier fantasized about running off to the circus to escape his preordained future as Prince. Today, he sometimes uses a drawing of a clown as part of his signature (though he is not related to the famous Ital-ian clown Grimaldi, as has been rumored). Circus ties to the Grimaldi family are so strong that the only time the festival was canceled was in 1982, when Princess Grace was killed. Rainier had often joked that, upon his retirement, he might drive off in his custom-made camper and follow the circus. He probably never dreamed that his daughter would actually make such a whimsical notion a reality in her life.

During the Circus Festival, Princess Stephanie presented Franco Knie, co-owner of the famous, eighty-two-year-old Circus Knie, with the Silver Clown Award for Best Animal Trainer. A few months later, they began a relationship, finally going public with it in March 2000. Finally Stephanie was able to live out her fantasy of being someone other than a Princess of Monaco when she and her children moved into a twenty-foot trailer (which, ironically, bore the brand name "Palace"). Stephanie and the young ones then spent almost a year traveling with the circus in the trailer they shared with Franco, pulled along by a red pickup truck (which she drove). Stephanie even allowed her daughter, six-year-old Pauline, to make appearances under the big top—with a three-ton elephant holding his immense foot over her, and then wrapping his trunk around her tiny body. The little Princess insisted that she wanted to be a trapeze artist when she got older. Meanwhile, eight-year-old Prince Louis learned to juggle. From time to time, photographers would catch Stephanie chain-smoking while sitting on the steps of her trailer, wearing an old white robe and pink slippers, her hair bleached and unkempt. To say that she appeared less than royal would be an understatement. (And to think, Grace didn't even like it when she wore jeans!)

Twice-married Franco, forty-seven, had left his second wife (of fourteen years), Claudine, fifty-one, to be with Stephanie, thirty-six at this time. Claiming that Stephanie had once been a friend, Claudine refused to grant Franco a divorce, adding fuel to the flames of controversy that were sure to ignite whenever Stephanie decided to explore new romantic frontiers.

"I am happy in my own skin and my own headspace," said Stephanie at the time. Then, sounding so much like Princess Grace when she finally learned to accept her position in Monaco, she added, "I can't say I'm happy twenty-four hours a day because happiness is not that permanent. But I've stopped trying to change the game, stopped trying to change people. Now I think about myself and my children. Fortunately, I am strong. I am a fighter and I believe in destiny. You build your own way in life with everything that is thrown at you, and make what you can from it. That's my philosophy. I don't look back anymore and I don't have any regrets." As outraged as Grace might have been by some of her daughter's recent actions, she would no doubt be proud of Stephanie's "philosophy," for, really, it had been hers as well.

In August 2001, Stephanie showed up for the Red Cross Ball at the Monte Carlo Sporting Club, her first official appearance since the revelation that she had joined the circus. Escorted by Rainier, she looked nervous and drawn. Princess Caroline barely even acknowledged her sister's presence. She went so far as to take a separate table from the rest of the family in the Salle des Etoiles ballroom, joining them only for the official portrait (and then standing as far away from Stephanie as possible).

In the spring of 2002, Princess Stephanie's relationship with Franco ended and she returned to Monaco, happily for Rainier, who still insists that "the family's anchorage is in the Palace." She also enrolled her children, Louis, nine, Pauline, seven, and Camille, three, in prestigious Monaco schools. Stephanie does what little she can to protect her offspring from media scrutiny, and becomes anxious when they are photographed going to or leaving school.

Gary Pudney said, "Princess Stephanie once told me, 'I've been stared at since I was born.' Everywhere I go, people point at me and say, 'Look, there she is.' I wish my kids didn't have to go through that, but I guess it's their curse too. Mom, of course, had the same problem.'

"Stephanie talks a lot to me about her mother," he continued. "She adores her, still. They were close, despite whatever problems they may have had when Stephanie was a teenager. Or, as Stephanie put it to me, 'What kid doesn't have issues with her mother?' It's unfair, she thinks, to characterize the relationship based only on teenage angst."

The terrible accident that claimed her mother on a treacherous Monaco highway more than twenty years ago haunts Princess Stephanie still. "It's hard enough, you know, losing your mother, and then being blamed for it," Stephanie said. "I'd like people to try and put themselves in my skin. Can't you just leave people to their pain?

"There was so much magic that surrounded Mom," Stephanie concluded. "She almost stopped being human. People figured I must have caused the accident because she was too perfect to do something like that. After a while you can't help feeling guilty. Everybody looks at you and you know what they're thinking—how come she's still around and Grace is dead?"

Prince Rainier perhaps put it best about Stephanie when, in a 1999 interview, he noted, "I believe that she was deeply traumatized by the accident, and I think she is the one who has needed the most family support. She has a very strong character and has always known what she wants in life, though maybe hasn't always gone about getting those things in the best way possible. But I have always given her my opinion, even when it wasn't asked for. Of course, my advice hasn't always been followed. However, one of the most emotional moments of my life was when she said, 'My father is the only man who has never betrayed me.'"

A NOTE ABOUT THE ROYAL FORTUNE

In 2000, Prince Rainier redrafted his will, decreeing that the bulk of his estimated $1.7 billion fortune (very little of which is actually liquid) go to his two oldest children, Princess Caroline and Prince Albert. The catalyst for Rainier's decision occurred in August of that year when Tunisian-born Eskander Laribi, a twenty-five-year-old suspected cocaine dealer, was gunned down in Nice. As detectives examined the murder scene, a red Chevrolet Jeep appeared, driven by Laribi's girlfriend, Virginie Tereberrou. It was Stephanie's car. Virginie happened to be staying at Stephanie's home in the Alpine ski resort of Auron when she heard about her boyfriend's death.

Though police hoped to interview Stephanie as part of their investigation, they were prevented from doing so because of diplomatic immunity. Through lawyers, the Princess said that she would be willing to answer questions, but not at a police station. In the end, she cooperated fully; she had nothing to do with the murder and didn't know the victim. However, Rainier was distraught by even his daughter's tangential involvement, fearing that she could one day lose her inheritance by association with the wrong kinds of people.

As now written, Rainier's will stipulates that Albert will inherit the bulk of the Grimaldi assets along with his father's title. As well as the 235-room Palace Princier de Monaco, there is the chateau at Marchais, just outside Paris, with extensive hunting grounds, which will also be Albert's. Also stipulated for Albert will be Rainier's private jet and yacht, as well as his collection of 180 vintage cars. Rainier's stamp collection, regarded as the second most valuable in the world, as well as artworks and furniture and millions of dollars' worth of shares in the Monte Carlo casino, will also be inherited by Albert.

As well as splitting her father's financial wealth with her brother, Princess Caroline will inherit La Vigie, the family's forty-room villa at Roquebrune-Cap-Martin, and most of the jewelry that belonged to her late mother, Princess Grace.

Stephanie will not want for much after her father's death, even with his new will in place: She will receive 1 percent of $1.7 billion, which amounts to $17 million. Instead of inheriting the money as a lump sum, however, she will receive a monthly allowance of $50,000. She will also inherit a six-bedroom chalet in Auron as well as an apartment in New York and a ski chalet in Gstaad, Switzerland.

At his death, Prince Rainier's wealth will be administered by the law firm of Henri Rey, whose family has acted as notaries for the Monegasque royal family for generations. According to sources, it is understood that the Prince is willing to allow Stephanie control over her own finances "if she shows greater maturity."

A NOTE ABOUT ROYAL STATUS

Though the family of His Serene Highness Rainier Grimaldi III, Prince of Monaco, has ruled the small principality of Monaco for more than seven centuries, making it the oldest family of continuous rule in Europe, there has been some argument among American journalists as to whether or not longevity of rule qualifies the family to be called "royal." Also questioned: Does the size of the domain, Monaco in this instance, somehow mitigate the family's right to be referred to as royalty?

As Art Beeche, editor of the *European Royal History Journal*, explains, "Monaco is a Sovereign Principality and, as such, the Grimaldis are royalty in the broader sense, just as much as are the Sovereign Prince of Liechtenstein and the Grand Duke of Luxembourg." Mr. Beeche goes on to cite the definitive authority for determining royal status as being the *Almanach de Gotha* and confirms that the Grimaldis are indeed included in the First Section, as are the ruling families of Liechtenstein and Luxembourg.

Further arguments for the Grimaldis' so-called right to royal status, which would seem to be the final word on the matter, are the genealogical searches conducted by Frank H. Mann and others—including William Addams Rietweiser, Tim Powys-Lybbe, and Leo van de Pas—which track a familial linkage between King Henry II, a Plantaganet, and Prince Rainier Grimaldi of Monaco. Since the Plantaganets' royal status is unquestioned, the Grimaldis' connection to that ruling house places Prince Rainier in that same royal company, according to Mann's *Henry II of England to Rainier Grimaldi of Monaco*.

Perhaps the most compelling case for royal status for the Grimaldis, however, would be the social acceptance they received from other royals after Grace Kelly married into the family and became Princess Grace. As mentioned earlier in this text, it was Princess Grace and Prince Rainier who were asked by Diana Spencer not only to be a part of but to *lead* the impressive procession of international royals at her wedding to Prince Charles in 1981. (Albert substituted for Rainier, who was ill on the day of the ceremony.) If reassurance of Monaco's recognition as a principality on a par with the kingdoms of Europe was ever necessary, then this was it. Also, considering all of the royalty that appeared for Grace's funeral, it becomes clear that she and Rainier do hold the respect and admiration of other royals.

Acknowledgments

First of all, I must acknowledge those readers of mine who have followed my career over the years. The reason that I write about noteworthy people such as Princess Grace and Prince Rainier is to bring about an exchange of ideas about how others have lived in the hope that we may learn and even be influenced by their choices. Never did I dream that I would have a global audience for such communication. I am indebted to every reader who has stuck by me over the course of ten books, and who has let me know that what I do has impacted, in whatever small way, on how they may think and feel about the world. In that I believe we're all one, I can't ask for anything more than to feel so connected.

I would like to thank my venerable editor, Maureen Mahon Egen, president and COO of the AOL Time Warner Book Group, who had the idea for *Once upon a Time*. This is our second book together, the first being *Jackie, Ethel, Joan: Women of Camelot*. Never have I worked with a more encouraging editor, and also a person with such great heart. I look forward with anticipation to our next project.

Special thanks to Stephen Gregory, not only for so many years of friendship but also for his invaluable input into this work. It would be a very different book if not for his vision. His desire to see this project through and to help me present Grace and Rainier in an honest, fairminded fashion was incalculable. I'm grateful to him.

My deepest appreciation also goes to Mitch Douglas at International Creative Management (ICM). He is an important person in my life and career, and I thank him for his constant and enthusiastic encouragement.

Dorie Simmonds of the Dorie Simmonds Agency in London is always there for me when I most need her during the development and writing of any of my books. As well as being my capable representative in Europe, she is a good and trusted friend. I appreciate her dedication to me and to my work. She's a woman who can get *anything* accomplished for me.

I am so proud to have this book published by Warner Books, and I owe a debt of gratitude to a number of people who have contributed to this work. First of all, my thanks to Jamie Raab, my publisher, for always being so wonderful to me and for distinguishing Warner Books from the rest as the publishing company that truly cares about its authors. Editorially, I am grateful to Bob Castillo, the managing editor. Also, I am grateful to the wonderful production team behind *Once upon a Time,* including the talented Jackie Meyer, Thomas Whatley, and Jim Spivey. Thanks also to those in publicity, including Emi Battaglia and Jimmy Franco; and to those in the Rights department, including Nancy Wiese, Rebecca Oliver, and Erika Riley. Also, once again, I was happy to work with Warner's counsel, Heather Kilpatrick, a dedicated and precise attorney.

As an editor and a friend, Paula Agronick Reuben has been a source of strength to me for many years and through five books—every one of which has been a best-seller, which says a great deal about Paula as my private editor. I thank her for her good sense and direction.

Every author has a team of people upon whom he depends for research. I've had so many investigators and researchers over the years, but none who have been as consistent as Cathy Griffin. Cathy is also a fine journalist in her own right. It would be easy with a subject as popular as this one to simply re-interview those people who have told their stories to others, and hope for an occasional new angle. However, Cathy always manages to locate people who have new, previously untold stories. I thank her for her assistance over the years, her tenacity, and, most of all, her friendship.

Without my extremely capable fact checker and editor, James Pinkston, I shudder to think of how this book might have suffered. An author in his own right, Jim is tireless in his quest for accuracy. He also dedicated himself to a significant amount of library research, and I thank him for that as well. As always, Jim went the extra mile on this, our third book together, and I am grateful. I wouldn't think to take on another book without Jim in my corner.

Without a keen-eyed copy editor, a book does suffer. I had the best in Roland Ottewell, and I thank him for his dedication.

My thanks to Jonathan Hahn, fellow author, personal publicist, and also close friend. Jonathan was important to *Once upon a Time* in many ways, not the least of which was by making himself available to me at a moment's notice to answer the all-important question: "How does this sound to you?" He also has a positive outlook, which I can rely on during moments when I'm about to lose my head over something that won't make a bit of difference in a week's time. I thank him for all he does on a daily basis for me.

I thank, as always, Al Kramer, my trusted friend and writing colleague who has, for years, been there for me. Thanks, Al, for your continued friendship.

I must thank Juliette Burgonde, Cloe Basiline, and Maxime Rhiette, who translated many hundreds of pages of French interview transcriptions and other documents for me. There is no way I could have managed all of that material without them.

Also, I would like to thank Babette Valmonde, who conducted many important interviews for me in Monte Carlo and in Paris. Babette was determined to find just the right people to help me tell this story, and her persistence paid off in many ways. I thank her for her amazing work.

Clarette Olsen-Smith also conducted interviews for me in Monaco, and traveled to Rome in search of credible sources—which she found. I appreciate her work on this project, and congratulate her on her marriage to Frederico.

Not only did Suzalie Rose comb libraries in Paris verifying information for me, she also translated all of her notes, more than a thousand pages, into English. Who could ask for more? I thank her for her time and consideration, not to mention her keen eye for accuracy.

I must also thank Thomas DeWitt in the United Kingdom for his work there, and also Teri Donato for her research in Italy. I am also indebted to Nick Scotti, for providing me with all the video material I reviewed regarding Grace Kelly's life and career, as well as footage of her wedding to Prince Rainier.

A special thanks to the fine folks at Photofest for providing so many of the wonderful photographs that are found in this book. I go to Photofest first when selecting pictures to illustrate my books. They always come through for me, and I thank them for that.

As I have often stated, without a loyal team of representatives, an author usually finds himself sitting at home writing books no one reads. Therefore, I thank all of those on "Team JRT" who mastermind the activities in my office during book production: attorneys Joel Loquvam and James Jimenez; accountants Ken Deakins, Rae Goldreich, Teryna Hanuscin, and Harold Stock of CBIZ Southern California, Inc.; advisers Mike Johnston of Capital Lending and Doris Duke of Common Cents, Inc.; and West Coast literary and TV agent Ron Bernstein of International Creative Management (ICM). I also owe a debt of gratitude to Buddy Thomas at ICM, who always manages to cut through so much red tape for me.

I want to thank Jeff Hare for being such a good and trusted friend, and for always understanding and appreciating the work that I do.

I also want to acknowledge Iake and Alex Eissinmann for years of unwavering support and encouragement—and also for all of the fun times we have shared.

Thanks also to Brian Evan Newman for sharing with me his positive, joyful outlook on life.

It means the world to me to be blessed with so many good friends, some of whom I would like to acknowledge here, including:

Richard Tyler Jordan, Steve Ivory, George Solomon, Jess Cagle, David Shofner, Paul Adler, Michael Puopolo, Hazel and Rob Kragulac, Barbara Giampappa, Bob Meyer, Lisa Reiner, Sven Paardekooper, Andy Skurow, Daniel Coleridge, Randall Friesen, Billy Barnes, Roby Gayle, Sonja Kravchuk, Scherrie Payne, Lynda Laurence, Barbara Ormsby, Rick Starr, John Passantino, Linda DeStefano, Mr. and Mrs. Joseph Tumolo, Daniel Tumolo, Charles Casillo, John Carlino, David Goldberg, Peter Martocchio, Wayne Brasler, Tony and Marilyn Caruselle, David Spiro, Mr. and Mrs. Adolph Steinlen, David and Frances Snyder, Abby and Maddy Snyder, Maribeth and Don Rothell, Mary Alvarez, Mark Bringelson, Hope Levy, Tom Lavagnino, Anthony Shane, Anne McVey, Bethany Marshall, Billy Masters, Valerie Allen, Michael Bentkover, Millie Wolski, and, of course, Yvette Jarecki.

My thanks to Andy Steinlen for being such a great influence on me, for teaching me so much about life, for being my "sounding board" . . . and my ever loyal, ever true friend.

I have always been so blessed to have a family as supportive as mine. My thanks and love go out to: Roslyn and Bill Barnett and Jessica and Zachary, Rocco and Rosemarie Taraborrelli and Rocco and Vincent, and Arnold Taraborrelli. And also to Rydell and Dylan.

Special thanks to my father, Rocco, who has always been my inspiration, encouraging me in ways too numerous to mention.

This book is dedicated to my mom, Rose Marie, who so admired Princess Grace of Monaco. I believe she would enjoy this work; her influence on its author is, I hope, evident throughout its pages.

Source Notes and Other Information

First of all, I would like to extend my appreciation to Lizanne Kelly LeVine, Grace's sister and the only remaining member of that generation of Kellys, for her time and consideration, and invaluable personal memories. Lizanne has, throughout the years, dedicated herself to the accurate preservation of not only her sister Grace's memory, but also her beloved family's. Having written about complicated families in the past, such as the Kennedys, I recognize that nothing is ever simple when it comes to familial dynamics. I did my best to try to understand and relate the Kelly experience, and I hope my affection for them is clear in my work. I think it's safe to say that there is no one alive who knew Princess Grace better than her loving sister Lizanne, and so I am pleased and honored that she was involved in this project.

Prince Rainier and his royal family no longer cooperate with the writers of biographies about them, which is perhaps understandable. Staff members at Rainier's office explained to me that the Prince and his children have often felt betrayed by the media and mischaracterized by the writings of once-trusted journalists. Still, despite lack of approval—or perhaps even because of it—I certainly did not feel a lack of cooperation from those who have been intimates of the Grimaldis over the years.

I must also thank Grace's good friend Charlotte Winston, who so warmly received me and shared decades of memories about her close friendship with Grace. The time Charlotte spent with Grace spanned many years, and I am so grateful to her for the years of interviews that went into the research for *Once upon a Time*. Charlotte now intends to write her own book about Grace, and I think that anyone who reads her stories as told here would enjoy reading more . . . and so I hope she takes on the challenge of that book.

It is impossible to write accurately about anyone's life without many reliable witnesses, such as Lizanne Kelly LeVine and Charlotte Winston, to provide a range of different viewpoints. A biography of this kind stands or falls on the cooperation and frankness of those involved in the story. Over the years, a great number of people went out of their way to assist me in this endeavor: Hundreds of friends, relations, journalists, royal watchers, socialites, lawyers, celebrities, show business executives and former executives, associates and friends, as well as foes, classmates, teachers, neighbors, and archivists, were contacted in preparation for this book.

I and my researchers had the opportunity to interview a wide range of sources. However, as always with my books, we decided to focus on those who had not previously told their stories. These people were interviewed for this work over the past three years either by myself or my researchers, Cathy Griffin in the United States; Juliette Burgonde, Cloe Basiline, Maxime Rhiette, Suzalie Rose, and, especially, Babette Valmonde in Monte Carlo and Paris; Clarette Olsen-Smith in Monaco and Rome; and Teri Donato in Italy.

I would also like to thank Harlan D. Boll, Marvin Paige, Ed Lozzi, and Pierre Salinger, who conducted one of the last TV interviews with Grace. Also, the interview with Virginia Gallico, widow of writer Paul Gallico, was conducted by Jill Evans in 1975. I thank her for sharing it with me.

Whenever practical, I have provided sources within the body of the text. Some people were not quoted directly in the text but provided observations that helped me more fully understand Grace and Rainier and their lives.

Also, in writing about a person as powerful and as influential as Prince Rainier of Monaco, a biographer is bound to find that many sources with valuable information prefer to not be named in the text. This is understandable. Throughout my career, I have understood that for a person to jeopardize a long-standing, important relationship for the sake of a book is a purely personal choice. Nevertheless, I appreciate the assistance of many people close to Rainier and Grace who, over the years, gave of their time and energy for this project. I will respect the wish for anonymity of those who require it, and as always, those who could be identified are named in these notes.

Because of their voluminous nature, I have made the choice not to include complete listings of the scores of magazine and newspaper features that were referenced. It would simply be impractical to do so. Those mentioned within these source notes are included because I felt they were important to recognize.

Since chapter notes are usually not of interest to the general reader, I have chosen a more general—and practical for space limitations—mode of source identification, as opposed to specific page or line notations. The following notes are by no means comprehensive but are intended to give the reader a general overview of my research. In some instances, I included parenthetically the year(s) interviews were conducted.

Library Research

I must thank, in particular, Thomas DeWitt and Marybeth Evans in London for their diligent work in the Manchester Central Library reviewing reams of documents for me that have been reposited in the Monegasque Collection of the library. The Monegasque Collection, donated to the library in the nineteenth century by Alfred Beaufort Grimaldi, contains correspondence, documents, photographs of the Princes de Monaco, and their reigns. For anyone researching the Grimaldi family, this collection is indispensable.

Thanks, also, to the staffs of the Hans Tasiemka Archives in London, the Special Collections Library of the University of California in Los Angeles, and the Special Collections of the Temple University Library in Philadelphia.

Numerous other organizations and institutions provided me with articles, documents, audio interviews, video interviews, transcripts, and other material that was either utilized directly in *Once upon a Time*, or just for purposes of background. Unfortunately, it is not possible to thank all of the individuals associated with each organization who were so helpful and gave of their time, but I would at least like to express my gratitude to the following institutions:

American Academy of Dramatic Arts; American Film Institute Library; Associated Press Office (New York); Bancroft Library (University of California, Berkeley); Beverly Hills Library; Brand Library Art and Music Center; British Film Institute Library Archives; Born Free Foundation; *Boston Herald* Archives; British Broadcasting Corporation; University of California, Los Angeles; California State Archives (Sacramento); Corbis-Gamma/Liason; Glendale Central Public Library; Hartford Public Library; Hayden Library, Arizona State University; Hollywood Library; Houghton Library (Harvard University); Hulton Picture Library; Kobal Collection; Lincoln Center Library of the Performing Arts; Los Angeles Public Library; *Los Angeles Times*; Manchester Central Reference Library; Margaret Herrick Library (Academy of Motion Picture Arts and Sciences); *Michigan Chronicle*; Museum of Modern Art (Film Study Center); Museum of the Film; National Archives and Library of Congress; Neal Peters Collection; New York City Municipal Archives; *New York Daily News*; *New York Post*; New York Public Library; *New York Times*; New York University Library; Occidental College (Eagle Rock, California); Philadelphia Free Library (Theater Collection); Philadelphia Historical Society; *Philadelphia Inquirer* and *Philadelphia Daily News*; Philadelphia Public Library; Photofest; Princeton University (William Seymour Theatre Collection).

Five others having to do with the research for this book whose kindnesses should not go unacknowledged are Maxwell Taylor, Stephen Rossdale, Irene Roberts, Susan Taylor, and Geri Thomas. These five researchers typed many of the notes and other minutiae that were unearthed during library research, saving me and others involved with this book so much time and energy. I am indebted to them.

What goes into the production of a book of this nature boggles the mind (even my own, and this is my tenth!). I could never do it alone, and if I forgot any single person who contributed in any way to the library research of this book—particularly those who are employed by my researchers and who I may not have even met—I am truly sorry. It does take a team of professionals, not just a single author, to tackle a project such as *Once upon a Time*, and I am eternally grateful to all of the players.

The History of the Kelly Family

Interviews: Lizanne Kelly LeVine; Martin Gruss; Jim Lang; Oleg Cassini; Rachel Martin; Pierre Kitson; Barbara Seymour; Susanne Marschok; and Al Kramer.

Thanks also to Thomas Ludlow, a close friend of George Kelly's, who provided so many memories of the family, as well as his own unpublished manuscript, *The Kelly Family*, from which I was able to draw so much information.

Thanks to Jane Lieberman, a close friend of the Majer family, who provided me with her scrapbook of memories from which to draw material about the Majers and the Kellys. Mrs. Lieberman also introduced me to many people who knew both families in the Philadelphia area. I could not have done my research without her assistance.

Thank you to the staff of the Philadelphia Public Library for allowing me access to archives chronicling the Kelly family, and also to the staff of the Philadelphia Historical Society. I also used as source material "Are We Becoming a Nation of Weaklings?" *American* magazine, March 1956.

Thanks to Emmet Bridges, nephew of Godfrey "Fordie" Ford, for his assistance, and for his memories of his uncle and of Ford's close working relationship with the Kelly family.

The staff of Special Collections at Temple University in Philadelphia was most helpful in assisting my researchers there with the reams of tapes, transcripts, and other material created and utilized by Arthur H. Kelly (and then reposited at the library) for his excellent book *Those Philadelphia Kellys*.

Volumes reviewed: *Those Philadelphia Kellys*, by Arthur H. Lewis; *That Kelly Family*, by John McCallum; *Princess Grace*, by Gwen Robyns; *Princess Grace: An Interpretive Biography*, by Steven Englund; *Grace*, by Robert Lacey; and *The Bridesmaids: Grace Kelly, Princess of Monaco and Six Intimate Friends*, by Judith Balaban Quine.

Video reviewed: *The Grimaldi Dynasty: Life with Grace* (Meridian TV).

Grace Kelly's Early Years as an Actress in New York

Interviews: Dominick Dunne; Don Richardson; Allan Kramer; Dr. Michael Hunter; Jay Kanter; Charlotte Winston; Mary Berolzheimer; Robert Ritchey; Stanley Kramer; Vidal Lacoste; and Rita Gam.

For this section, and others in this book, I also relied on correspondence from Grace to Prudy Wise, some of which was published privately in the book *With Love, Grace: Personal Letters from Grace Kelly, Actress & Princess 1949–1969*, by Terry Kinsella and Angelika Kinsella. (The April 13, 1949, letter from Grace to Prudy Wise, describing the weekend when Don Richardson visited her in Philadelphia in April 1949, was published in full in *Paris Match* on March 24, 1994, as well as in the catalogue *Heroes, Legends, Superstars of Hollywood & Rock*, published by Superior Auction Galleries, March 1994.)

Thanks to Darlene Hanover for providing me with transcripts of her interviews with Carolyn Scott and Sally Parrish, which I utilized for the section of the book relating to Grace's years as an actress, as well as for other sections.

I want to thank Delores Newman for her transcripts of interviews with Don Richardson, which were used throughout this book. Though I interviewed Mr. Richardson in 1995 for my own research regarding Princess Caroline of Monaco, it is Delores who has the better and more thorough material on Richardson's relationship with Grace over the years, and I thank her for allowing me such complete access to it. Don, who was a wonderful, thoughtful, and gregarious gentleman, died in January 1996 of heart failure.

Features reviewed: "Grace Kelly—Her Biggest Gamble," by Maurice Zolotow, *American Weekly*, April 29, 1956; "A New Princess in Monaco" (no byline), *Look*, June 1, 1965; "The Prince and I," by Graham and Heather Fisher, *Ladies' Home Journal*, November 1961; "The Other Princess Grace" (no byline), *Ladies' Home Journal*, May 1977; and "Monaco: The Years of Grace—Part One," by Hugo Vickers, *Royalty*, vol. 8, no. 8.

Volumes reviewed: *Grace: The Secret Lives of a Princess*, by James Spada; *Those Philadelphia Kellys*, by Arthur H. Lewis; *Grace*, by Sarah Bradford.

Grace Kelly in Hollywood and Her Romances before Rainier

Interviews: Tippi Hedren; Janet Leigh; Dominick Dunne; Don Richardson; Allen Kramer; Virginia Darcy; Dr. Michael Hunter; Jay Kanter; Fred Zinnemann; Charlotte Winston; Celeste Holm; Stanley Kramer; Vidal Lacoste; and Rita Gam.

Thanks to Oleg Cassini for his interviews regarding his romance with Grace Kelly. Also, Oleg's entertaining autobiography, *In My Own Fashion,* proved helpful.

Thanks to Juliette Auteur, cousin of Jean-Pierre Aumont, for her interviews and assistance where Grace's romance with Jean-Pierre was concerned.

I reviewed all of the press clippings, press kits, and other studio-related material, biographies, and releases for each of Grace's films, which are on file at the Margaret Herrick Library. I thank the staff of that library for their assistance, not only on this project but on all of my books.

The videocassette *Grace Kelly: The American Princess* (Brighton Video, New York) is an excellent documentary that proved very helpful.

Of course, I reviewed all of Grace's movies, but it was my trusted researcher and editor James Pinkston who truly helped me analyze Grace's work. Jim is one of the most well-respected film historians in Hollywood, and to have him on my team made all of the difference with this work.

I relied heavily on my research for my book *Sinatra: Behind the Legend* (also known as *Sinatra: A Complete Life*) for material relating to Grace's work on *Mogambo* and her friendship with Ava Gardner (who was Frank's wife at the time). I would also like to thank Tom and Lorraine Banks and Doris Rollins Cannon at the Ava Gardner Museum in Smithfield, North Carolina, who assisted my researchers with the Sinatra book, and also this one.

There are so many Alfred Hitchcock historians, and so many books about the famous director, upon whom I relied for this work. I would like to thank James Ellis for all of his research relating to Hitchcock, and also Maureen O'Donnell and Benjamin Goldberg for all of their transcripts and other notes having to do with Hitchcock and his many stars, including Grace.

Thanks also to Grace's biographer Gwen Robyns for her insight.

I would also like to thank James Ellis for the use of his many interviews with Rupert Allan. During his years in public relations, the formidable Rupert Allan represented many top international stars, including Marilyn Monroe, Bette Davis, Steve McQueen, Rock Hudson, Marlene Dietrich, Gina Lollobrigida, Jeanne Moreau, Catherine Deneuve, and Melina Mercouri, as well as Grace Kelly, both before and after her marriage to Prince Rainier. His successful handling of some of the potentially disastrous situations involving the wedding between Grace and Rainier made him a friend of the ruling Grimaldi family for life. Rupert was a founding partner in two firms: Allan, Foster, Ingersoll and Weber; and ICPR. In 1978 he became a principal in the prestigious international public relations firm Stone Associates (later Stone/Hallinan Associates) and continued to serve as a director of the company until his death on August 24, 1991. Reporter James Ellis met Rupert while at Stone Associates and interviewed him many times for magazine articles and television programs involving the royals of Monaco. His transcripts of those interviews were absolutely invaluable to my research for this book, and I cannot thank him enough for making them available to me.

Features reviewed: "The Girl in White Gloves" (no byline), *Time*, January 31, 1955; "My Daughter Grace Kelly: Her Life and Romances," by Mrs. John B. Kelly as told to Richard Gehman, *Los Angeles Herald Examiner*, January 15, 1956 (Parts 1 through 10); "Exclusive Royal Portfolio" (no byline), *Ladies' Home Journal*, May 1973; "That Special Grace," by Rita Gam, *McCall's*, January 1983; "Rita Gam: The Starlet Who Could," by Peter Marks, *New York Times*, February 24, 2002; "Monaco: The Years of Grace—Part One," by Hugo Vickers, *Royalty*, vol. 8, no. 8.

Volumes reviewed: *About Grace: An Intimate Notebook*, by Jeannie Sakol and Caroline Latham; *Grace Kelly's Men*, by Jane Ellen Wayne; *Grace*, by Robert Lacey; *Grace: The Secret Lives of a Princess*, by James Spada; *The Grimaldis of Monaco*, by Anne Edwards; *Princess Grace: An Interpretive Biography*, by Steven Englund.

Papers reviewed: "The Hedda Hopper Papers/Grace Kelly File" (Academy of Motion Picture Arts and Sciences).

Videos reviewed: *Grace Kelly: The American Princess* (MPI Video); *E! True Hollywood Story: The Curse of the Grimaldis* (E! Channel).

Grace and Rainier's Relationship prior to Their Marriage

Interviews: Gwen Robyns; Virginia Darcy; Jay Kanter; Don Richardson; Charles Fish, Jr.; Charlotte Winston; Rita Gam; Thomas D'Orazio; Leanne Scott; James Bacon; Melvin Shiffle; Marianne Dressler; Jeffrey Trent; Laurence Lanier; Howell Conant; Paul Renquist; Dolores Donato; Dominick Dunne; Don Richardson; Kathy McKinnon; B. Dale Davis, Jr.; Frances Martyn; Al Kramer; Stanley Kramer; and Rita Gam.

Thanks to Michelle Betrand for the transcripts of interviews conducted with Pierre Galante in June 1993. This material was extremely important in putting together the pieces of the puzzle having to do with Grace's first meeting with Rainier.

I relied heavily on: "Where Will the Prince Find His Princess?" by David Schoenbrun for *Collier's* and "My Daughter Grace Kelly: Her Life and Romances," by Mrs. John B. Kelly as told to Richard Gehman, *Herald-Examiner*.

Thank you to Steven Ormandy for supplying me with, and also transcribing, Prince Rainier's address on Radio Monte Carlo, October 11, 1955.

Mrs. Anne Evans of Philadelphia, who died in 1996, was a dedicated fan of Grace Kelly's. She maintained three meticulously compiled scrapbooks of Grace's life from the time she met Rainier, through their marriage, and up to the birth of their first child, Princess Caroline. I am so grateful to the Evans family for allowing me access to Anne's scrapbook of hundreds of cuttings, too many to detail here, most from the *Philadelphia Bulletin* daily newspaper. It seems fitting that Anne's dedication to Grace's life so many years ago could now be utilized in this biography of her and Rainier.

Features reviewed: "The Prince and I," by Graham and Heather Fisher, *Ladies' Home Journal*, November 1961; "A New Princess in Monaco" (no byline), *Look*, June 1, 1965; "Life with Grace: An Exclusive Interview with Prince Rainier," by Douglas Keay, *Ladies' Home Journal*, May 1974.

Volumes reviewed: *Prince Rainier of Monaco: His Authorised and Exclusive Story*, by Peter Hawkins; *Royal House of Monaco*, by John Glatt; *Grace*, by Howell Conant; *Monte Carlo Casino*, by Peter A. Polovtsoff;

Inside Monte Carlo, by Stanley Jackson; *Princess of Monaco* by Gant Gaither; *That Kelly Family*, by John McCallum.

Videos reviewed: *Grace Kelly: The American Princess* (MPI Video); *E! True Hollywood Story: The Curse of the Grimaldis* (E! Channel); *Grace Kelly: A Portrait* (WinStar).

Prince Rainier's Life and Times prior to His Marriage to Grace Kelly, and also the History of the Grimaldis of Monaco

Interviews: Gwen Robyns; Virginia Darcy; Charles Fish, Jr.; Thomas D'Orazio; Leanne Scott; Mary Carol Mueller; Frederick Kelly; Louis Rothstein; James Bacon; Howell Conant; Paul Renquist; Dominick Dunne; Don Richardson; Ricardo Gardner; Michel Kelly; and Rita Gam.

I relied heavily on documents found in the Monegasque Collection in the Manchester Central Reference Library, including *Princes of Monaco: Remarkable History of the Grimaldi Family*, by François de Bernardy (trans. Len Ortzen); and *History of Monaco*, by H. Pemberton.

Ann Edwards's assistance was invaluable, as was her insightful book, *The Grimaldis of Monaco*.

Maureen Molnar, a Monaco historian, was very helpful in laying out the history of the principality for me, and also of Rainier's family. Also, Ms. Molnar was a personal friend and confidante of Gisele Pascal's and was able to illuminate for me the facts surrounding Pascal's romance with the Prince.

Steven Ormandy is a fine writer with an unpublished manuscript about Princess Antoinette of Monaco, Rainier's sister, to which he allowed me access. I am indebted to him for providing me with so much information about the complex relationship between the Grimaldi siblings. I never would have been able to put the pieces of the jigsaw together without the benefit of his many years of research into the life and times of Princess Antoinette. I pray that he one day sees his work about her published.

Features reviewed: "Grace, She Looked Cool . . ." (no byline), *Life*, April 11, 1955; "Prince Rainier Tells of Our Life Together," by Prince Rainier and Peter Hawkins, *Good Housekeeping*, March 1967; "A Life of Grace" (no byline), *People*, September 27, 1982; "The Legacy of Princess

Grace," by Richard B. Stolley, *Life*, March 1983; "Amazing Grace" (no byline), photographs by Howell Conant, *People*, September 21, 1992; "The Truth about My Sister, Grace," by Andrew Wilson, *Daily Mail*, June 27, 1998.

Volumes reviewed: *Prince Rainier of Monaco: His Authorised and Exclusive Story*, by Peter Hawkins; *The Grimaldis of Monaco*, by Anne Edwards; *Grace*, by Howell Conant; *Princess Grace: An Interpretive Biography*, by Steven Englund; *Princes of Monaco: The Remarkable History of the Grimaldi Family*, by Arthur Baker (trans. Len Ortzen); *The Wizard of Monte Carlo*, by Caesar Egon Corte; *Round about Monte Carlo*, by Elizabeth Croly; *Bibliograpy of Monaco*, by Geoffrey Handley-Taylor; *The Big Gamble: The Story of Monte Carlo*, by Charles Graves; *The Money Spinner: Monte Carlo Casino*, by Xan Fielding; *The Courts of Europe*, by A. G. Dickens; *Palace: My Life in the Royal Family of Monaco*, by Baron Christian de Massy and Charles Higham; *Princess of Monaco*, by Gant Gaither; *Caroline and Stephanie: The Lives of the Princesses of Monaco*, by Susan Crimp and Patricia Burstan; *The Big Wheel: Monte Carlo's Opulent Century*, by George William Herald and Edward David Radin; *Histoire de la Principauté de Monaco*, 2nd ed., Archives de la Principauté de Monaco, 1934.

Videos reviewed: *America's Castles: Prince's Palace in Monaco* (Arts & Entertainment); *E! True Hollywood Story: Grace, Caroline and Stephanie* (E! Channel).

Prince Rainier's Friendship with Father Francis Tucker

My thanks to Joseph A. Tucker, Sr., and Joseph A. Tucker, Jr., Father Tucker's brother and nephew, for their assistance. Joseph Tucker, Jr.'s book *Miracle at Monaco* was privately printed by Signatran, and includes correspondence between Father Tucker and Prince Rainier, from which I drew for my own research. This book is a moving tribute to Father Tucker, and if the reader would like to learn more about the priest's life before and after Rainier, he or she should certainly look to this work for information. The book is a companion to *God Was Not a Stranger*, another small-press biography of Father Francis Tucker by his nephew Joseph A. Tucker, Jr.

Because neither book may be purchased in bookstores, point your browser to:

http://www.galaxymall.com/site/343680

Interviewed: Mirielle Anglade; Chantal de La Haye; Marie-Paule Doniné; Françoise Boudet; Nathalie Danjou; Achille Junca; Clarisse Vignon; and Lisette Chauagnat.

Thanks also to Father Tucker's good friend Father James McGinnis, who provided me with so much insight.

Features reviewed: "Grace Kelly's Biggest Gamble," by Maurice Zolotow, *American Weekly*, April 15, 1956; "Farewell, Friend: A Tribute to Canon Tucker," by Monsignor Paul J. Taggert, *Delmarva Dialog*, November 10, 1972.

Princess Grace and Prince Rainier's Wedding and Early Years in the Palace

Interviews: Lizanne Kelly LeVine; Bettina Thompson Campbell; Chantal de La Haye; Charlotte Winston; James Bacon; Nathalie Danjou; Virginia Darcy; Gaia Magrelli; Barbara Tuck Cresci; George Walter Smith; Patrick Frommeyer; Oleg Cassini; Thomas Sartre; and Antoinette Brucatto.

Thanks to royal watcher and writer Augustus Leonard for his extensive file on Madge Tivey-Faucon, which was vital to my research. Augustus offered me such consistent kindness . . . and for so many years during the course of my research! I am grateful beyond words.

Features reviewed: "Hollywood's Queen Becomes a Princess," by Martha Weinman, *Collier's*, March 2, 1956; "And Now, Here Comes the Bride . . ." (no byline), *Life*, April 9, 1956; "The Princess and the Palace," by William B. Arthur, *Look*, August 18, 1959; "A Tour of Monaco—Your Guide: Princess Grace" (no byline), *TV Guide*, February 16, 1963; "Inside the Palace with Princess Grace," by Madge Tivey-Faucon, *Cosmopolitan*, March 1964; "Princess Grace: After Five Years," by William B. Arthur, *Look*, April 11, 1961; "Princess Grace: A New Role," by Jack Hamilton, *Look*, February 12, 1963; "A New Princess in Monaco" (no byline), *Look*,

June 1, 1965; "Prince Rainier Tells of Our Life Together," by Prince Rainier and Peter Hawkins, *Good Housekeeping*, March 1967; "Princess Grace of Monaco," by Curtis Bill Pepper, *Vogue*, December 1971; "Life with Grace: An Exclusive Interview with Prince Rainier," by Douglas Keay, *Ladies' Home Journal*, May 1974.

Volumes reviewed: *The Bridesmaids: Grace Kelly, Princess of Monaco and Six Intimate Friends*, by Judith Balaban Quine; *Princess of Monaco*, by Gant Gaither; *Grace*, by Robert Lacey; *Monte Carlo Casino*, by Peter A. Polovstoff; *Histoire de Monaco*, by J. B. Robert; *Rainier and Grace: An Intimate Portrait*, by Jeffrey Robinson; *Princess Grace*, by Gwen Robyns; *Monaco and Monte Carlo*, by Adolphe Smith; *Royal House of Monaco*, by John Glatt; *Those Philadelphia Kellys*, by Arthur H. Lewis; *About Grace: An Intimate Notebook*, by Jeannie Sakol and Caroline Latham; *Grace*, by Howell Conant.

Videos reviewed: MGM filmed the ceremony of the wedding of Grace and Rainier and copies are available for viewing from the archives of the Academy of Motion Picture Arts and Sciences, and the Museum of the Film; Movietone News (newsreels); *Once upon a Time Is Now: The Story of Princess Grace* (NBC-TV documentary, 1977: Lee Grant, presenter); *Grace Kelly: The American Princess* (MPI Video); *E! True Hollywood Story: The Curse of the Grimaldis* (E! Channel); *Grace Kelly: A Portrait* (Win-Star).

I also relied on archival material from United Kingdom newspapers: the *Times*, the *Sunday Times*, the *Daily Express*, and the *Evening Standard*.

"Rainier Stages a 'Coup,'" "A Crisis in Monaco," and "Freedom from Onassis"

Interviewed: Digby Kelly; Jules C. McDonald; Frances Regen; Philip Longo; Francis Shea; Aleen Klein; Chantal de La Haye; Thomas Sartre; Georges Anglade; Jean-Paul Boniface; Philippe Dacremont; Yves-Marie Griscot; Salomon Brocheré; Joseph Canrobert; Pascal Derrey; Cecile Blanche; Cecil Rochut; Corinne Millet; Ilinca Gaubert; Regine Voirol; and Sophie Vignon.

Features reviewed: "Grace of Monaco," by Maurice Zolotow, *Cos-*

mopolitan, December 1961; "Will Princess Grace Lose Her Throne?" by William B. Arthur, *Look*, July 31, 1962; "Inside the Palace with Princess Grace," by Madge Tivey-Faucon, *Cosmopolitan*, March 1964; "Playboy Interview: Princess Grace" (no byline), *Playboy*, January 1966; "Prince Rainier Tells of Our Life Together," by Prince Rainier and Peter Hawkins, *Good Housekeeping*, March 1967; "The Prince and the Paupers," by Don Katz, *Rolling Stone*, March 10, 1977; "A Family Affair with the Whole World Watching," by Thomas Sancton, *Time*, January 20, 1997; "Monaco's Royal Anniversary," by Marco R. della Cava, *USA Today*, April 29, 1997; "First Official Photographs to Mark the Golden Jubilee . . ." by Anne Saint-Jean, *Hello*, January 9, 1999.

Volumes reviewed: *Prince Rainier of Monaco: His Authorised and Exclusive Story*, by Peter Hawkins; *Princess Grace: An Interpretive Biography*, by Steven Englund; *The Fabulous Onassis*, by Christian Cafarakis; *Onassis*, by Willi Frischauer; *Aristotle Onassis*, by the (London) *Sunday Times*: Nicholas Fraser et al.; *The Greek*, by Pierre Ray; *Ari*, by Peter Evans; *Onassis*, by Frank Brady; *Monte Carlo Casino*, by Peter A. Polovtsoff; *Inside Monte Carlo*, by Stanley Jackson; *Monaco Cool*, by Robert Westgate; *Le Régime International de la Principauté de Monaco*, by Jean-Pierre Gallois.

Papers reviewed: *Monaco Papers*, National Archives (Washington), Reference Number RG59; *Constitutions of the Countries of the World* [the text of the Monaco constitution is dated 1986], by Albert P. Blaustein and Gisbert H. Flanz; *Codes et lois de lag principauté de Monaco* (Jurisclasseur), Imprimerie du Sud, 1958–79; *Monaco au point de vue international* (doctoral thesis), by Maurice Lecomte-Moncharville; *La Principauté de Monaco et le Traité du 17 juillet 1918*, doctoral thesis by Michel Pret (Nice: Imprimerie de l'Association du Patronage Saint-Pierre, 1920).

Marnie and Text Relating to Grace's Turmoil over It

Interviews: Lizanne Kelly LeVine; Bettina Thompson Campbell; Thomas Sartre; Rita Gam; Francis Lacey; Martin Hay; Robert Ducruet; Thomas DeLongpre; Father James McGinnis; and Charlotte Winston.

Thanks to Emily LaCoste, a close friend of Princess Ghislaine's, for her memories of Ghislaine's relationship with Princess Grace. Her generous assistance was invaluable.

Again, transcripts of James Ellis's interviews with Rupert Allan were crucial.

Features reviewed: "Princess Grace Turns 40," by William B. Arthur, *Look*, December 16, 1969; "The Prince and the Paupers," by Don Katz, *Rolling Stone*, March 10, 1977; "Princess Grace of Monaco," by Curtis Bill Pepper, *Vogue*, December 1971; "Grace," by Brenda Ralph Lewis, *Royalty*, vol. 11, no. 10.

Volumes reviewed: *Grace*, by Sarah Bradford; *The Bridesmaids: Grace Kelly, Princess of Monaco and Six Intimate Friends*, by Judith Balaban Quine; *The Dark Side of Genius: The Life of Alfred Hitchcock*, by Donald Spoto; *The Art of Alfred Hitchcock*, by Donald Spoto; *Hitch: The Life and Times of Alfred Hitchcock*, by John Russell Taylor; *Hitchcock*, by Francois Truffaut.

Papers reviewed: "Alfred Hitchcock Papers/'Marnie' File" (Academy of Motion Picture Arts and Sciences).

Grace and Rainier as Parents to Caroline, Albert, and Stephanie

Interviews: Lizanne Kelly LeVine; Gwen Robyns; Thomas Sartre; Antoinette Brucatto; Sarah Callaghan; Andre Powers; Lucy Eringer; Neil Innicenti; Father David Voellinger; Jay Kanter; Gaia Magrelli; Howell Conant; and Francesco Greco.

Features reviewed: "Grace of Monaco," by Maurice Zolotow, *Cosmopolitan*, December 1961; "Will Princess Grace Lose Her Throne?" by William B. Arthur, *Look*, July 31, 1962; "A Tour of Monaco—Your Guide: Princess Grace" (no byline), *TV Guide*, February 16, 1963; "Inside the Palace with Princess Grace," by Madge Tivey-Faucon, *Cosmopolitan*, March 1964; "Princess Grace: How She Lovingly Raises Her Children," by Maureen King as told to Serge Fliegers, *Good Housekeeping*, February 1966; "Playboy Interview: Princess Grace" (no byline), *Playboy*, January 1966; "Prince Rainier Tells of Our Life Together," by Prince Rainier and Peter Hawkins, *Good Housekeeping*, March 1967; "Princess Grace Turns

40," by William B. Arthur, *Look*, December 16, 1969; "Life with Grace: An Exclusive Interview with Prince Rainier," by Douglas Keay, *Ladies' Home Journal*, May 1974; "Tales That Could Melt the Myth . . ." by John P. Hayes, *Philadelphia Inquirer*, May 3, 1987; "Amazing Grace" (no byline), photographs by Howell Conant, *People*, September 21, 1992; "The Truth about My Sister, Grace," by Andrew Wilson, *Daily Mail*, June 27, 1998; "Former Priest Tells of Duties . . ." by Bob Wittman, *Morning Call*, November 16, 2001; "Days of Grace: Part One," by Hugo Vickers, *Royalty*, vol. 13, no. 1; "The Years of Grace: Part Two," by Hugo Vickers, *Royalty*, vol. 8, no. 2; "Amazing Grace," by Anne Edwards, *Majesty*, vol. 17, no. 3.

Papers reviewed: "The Hedda Hopper Papers/Grace Kelly File," (Academy of Motion Picture Arts and Sciences).

Volumes reviewed: *Prince Rainier of Monaco: His Authorised and Exclusive Story*, by Peter Hawkins; *Grace: The Secret Lives of a Princess*, by James Spada; *Those Philadelphia Kellys*, by Arthur H. Lewis; *Palace: My Life in the Royal Family of Monaco*, by Baron Christian de Massy and Charles Higham; *About Grace: An Intimate Notebook*, by Jeannie Sakol and Caroline Latham.

Videos Reviewed: *Grace Kelly: A Portrait* (WinStar).

Princess Caroline's Relationship and Marriage to Philippe Junot, as Well as the Material about the Princess in the Appendix

My research included extensive interviews conducted over a six-month period between January and June 1993 for a full-length biography of Princess Caroline of Monaco, which I intended to write at that time, including interviews with: Philippe Junot; Howell Conant; Francesco Greco; Giuseppe Pesaresi; Carlos Caprioni; Domenic Forlini, James Bacon, Gwen Robyns, Jean-Pierre Aumont; Don Richardson; and Antoinette Brucatto.

Features reviewed: "Princess Caroline at her Christening" (no byline), March 25, 1957; "Princess Grace's Problems as a Mother," by Curtis Bill Pepper, *McCall's*, December 1973; "Grace's Girl" (no byline), *Life*, January 1984; "Princess Caroline's Husband Killed . . ." (no byline), Associated Press, October 4, 1990; "Monaco's Modern Princess," by Sarah Mower, *Harper's Bazaar*, October 1996; "Caroline in Italy . . ." (no byline), *Hello*, October 12, 1996; "Princess Caroline—Dazzling . . ." (no byline), *Hello*, October 19, 1996; "A House Divided," by Michelle Green, *People*, May 12, 1997; "Princess Caroline of Monaco and Prince Ernst of Hanover" (no byline), *Hello*, November 1, 1997; "Princess Caroline and Prince Ernst" (no byline), *Hello*, April 25, 1998; "The Private Monte Carlo Wedding of Caroline of Monaco" (no byline), *Hello*, February 6, 1999; "Ernst Goes to Monaco," by Kim Hubbard, *People*, February 8, 1999; "The Rebel Prince, Round Two," by Margaret Morrison, *Scotland on Sunday*, February 6, 2000; "Princess Caroline Lashes Out at Mom, Grace . . ." (no byline), Associated Press, March 1, 1988; "Is Princess Caroline the Victim . . . ?" by J. D. Heyman, *US Weekly*, July 17, 2000; "The Importance of Being Ernst," by Judy Bacharach, *Vanity Fair*, January 2001; "A Tale of Two Sisters," by John Glatt, *Australian Women's Weekly*, October 2001; "A New Day Dawns for Caroline of Monaco," by Mandy van Zuydam, *Royalty*, vol. 2, no. 9; "The Real Princess Caroline, Face to Face," by Louis Pawels, *Royalty*, vol. 7, no. 10; "The Tragedy of the Grimaldis," by Peter McKay, *Royalty*, vol. 10, no. 2; "Caroline: Comeback to Public Life" (no byline), *Royalty*, vol. 11, no. 4; "Princess Caroline: Quiet Days in Provence (no byline), *Royalty*, vol. 11, no. 11; "Caroline's Spring of Joy," by Fiona Florence, *Royalty*, vol. 12, no. 4; "Disco Noise Makes Prince Ernst Lose His Cool" (no byline), *Royalty*, vol. 16, no. 5.

Videos reviewed: *Primetime Live* (ABC-TV), January 8, 1997 (Diane Sawyer with the Grimaldis); *E! True Hollywood Story: Grace, Caroline and Stephanie* (E! Channel).

Princess Stephanie's Teenage Years, as Well as the Material about Her in the Appendix

Interviews: Lizanne Kelly LeVine; Gary Pudney; Carlos Caprioni; Gaia Magrelli; Charlotte Winston; Domenic Forlini; Gwen Robyns; Robert Sorbet; John Richard Carroll; Judith Wood; and Antoinette Brucatto.

Features reviewed: "A Princess Reborn," by Michelle Green, *People*, June 15, 1992; "Son Born to Monaco Princess, Boyfriend," Associated Press, November 29, 1992; "Princess Stephanie Shows Her Inner Strength . . ." (no byline), *Hello*, October 5, 1996; "Daniel Ducruet: An Exclusive Interview," by Jose Antonio Olivar, *Hello*, September 28, 1996; "Stephanie and Daniel Officially Divorced" (no byline), *Hello*, October 19, 1996; "Stephanie: The Latest in a Line of Unfortunate Monegasque Princesses" (no byline), *Hello*, December 31, 1996; "Princess Stephanie's Pain," by Liz Smith, *Los Angeles Times*, January 7, 1997; "Princess Stephanie on Holiday" (no byline), *Hello*, February 23, 1997; "Princess Stephanie Marks her 32nd Birthday" (no byline), *Hello*, March 8, 1997; "Princess Stephanie Finds Romance" (no byline), *Hello*, April 12, 1997; "Princess Stephanie: Exclusive" (no byline), *New Weekly*, March 24, 1998; "Princess Stephanie Spends Time with the Two Men . . ." (no byline), *Hello*, April 25, 1998; "Princess Stephanie: Monaco Mystery" (no byline), *People*, August 3, 1998; "Rainier's Wild Child Grows Up," by Neal Travis, *New York Post*, July 30, 2000; "Circus Princess" (no byline), *Australian Women's Weekly*, June 2001; "Monaco's Princess Stephanie . . ." by Neal Travis, *New York Post*, June 17, 2001; "Stephanie Runs Away from the Circus," by Janice Gregory, *Woman's Day*, April 2002; "Stephanie: Motherhood and Marriage," by Monica Guignard, *Royalty*, vol. 10, no. 8; "Stephanie: Comes Motherhood, Comes Maturity?" by Victoria Austin, *Royalty*, vol. 11, no. 12; "The Wild One at 30," by Victoria Austin, *Royalty*, vol. 13, no. 9; "The Downfall of Daniel Ducruet" (no byline), *Royalty*, vol. 14, no. 6.

Volumes reviewed: *Rainier and Grace: An Intimate Portrait*, by Jeffrey Robinson; *Grace: The Secret Lives of a Princess*, by James Spada.

Videos reviewed: *E! True Hollywood Story: Grace, Caroline and Stephanie* (E! Channel); *Grace Kelly* (Learning Channel).

Prince Albert, as a Young Man and Presently

Interviews: Gary Pudney; Catharine Rockwell; Howell Conant; Guy DiMario; and Lizanne Kelly LeVine.

Features reviewed: "Inside the Palace with Princess Grace," by Madge

Tivey-Faucon, *Cosmopolitan*, March 1964; "Princess Grace's Problems As a Mother," by Curtis Bill Pepper, *McCall's*, December 1973; "A Life of Grace" (no byline), *People*, September 27, 1982; "The Legacy of Princess Grace," by Richard B. Stolley, *Life*, March 1983; "Allentonian Fondly Remembers His Royal Charges," by Jim Kelly, *Morning Call*, March 13, 1998; "Prince Albert of Monaco" (no byline), *Hello*, April 4, 1998; "Royal Christmas Truce," by Alec Marr, *New Idea*, December 2000; "Those Wacky Grimaldis," by Julie Dam, *People*, October 29, 2001.

Videos reviewed: *E! True Hollywood Story: The Curse of the Grimaldis* (E! Channel); *Grace Kelly: A Portrait* (WinStar).

The Troubles of Grace's Brother, John Brendan Kelly, Jr., in 1975

Interviews: Lizanne Kelly LeVine; Elizabeth Motes; Lexie McVay; Brandon Thomas, Jr.; and Charlotte Winston.

Features reviewed: "There Is Much Irony . . ." by Kenneth Reich, *Los Angeles Times*, March 4, 1985; John B. Kelly, Jr. Dead at 57," by Sam Goldaper, *New York Times*, March 4, 1985; "Cause of Jack Kelly's Death Unknown" (no byline), Knight-Ridder News Service, March 4, 1985; "John B. Kelly, Jr. Dies" (no byline), *Washington Post*, March 4, 1985; "Hundreds Pay Last Respects to Jack Kelly" (no byline), Associated Press, March 8, 1985; "Jack Kelly, Jr., Eulogized as a Giver" (no byline), Associated Press, March 9, 1985; "Margaret Kelly, 91: Head of Influential Family," by Tracy Kaplan, *Los Angeles Times*, January 8, 1990.

Volume reviewed: *Those Philadelphia Kellys*, by Arthur H. Lewis.

Grace and Rainier's Later Years Together

Interviews: Lizanne Kelly LeVine; Gary Pudney; Gwen Robyns; Gore Vidal; Charlotte Winston; Alan Selka; Delores Bingham-Hall; Antoinette Brucatto; Robert Dornhelm; and Barbara Tuck Cresci.

Features reviewed: "Life with Grace: An Exclusive Interview with Prince Rainier," by Douglas Keay, *Ladies' Home Journal*, May 1974; "For

Princess Grace, The Press Is a Pain . . ." by Fred Hauptfuhrer, *People*, September 1, 1975; "The Prince and the Paupers," by Don Katz, *Rolling Stone*, March 10, 1977; "Princess Grace Talks about Her Family," by Mah Hayden, *Arkansas Democrat*, May 22, 1977; "Amazing Grace" (no byline), photographs by Howell Conant, *People*, September 21, 1992; "Years of Grace: Part Three," by Hugo Vickers, *Royalty*, vol. 8, no. 10.

Volumes reviewed: *Rainier and Grace: An Intimate Portrait*, by Jeffrey Robinson; *Royal House of Monaco*, by John Glatt; *My Book of Flowers*, by Grace Kelly with Gwen Robyns; *The Flower Game*, by Fleur Cowles; *Grace*, by Sarah Bradford; *The Bridesmaids: Grace Kelly, Princess of Monaco and Six Intimate Friends*, by Judith Balaban Quine; *Grace Kelly: A Life in Pictures*, by Jenny Curtis; *Grace: The Story of a Princess*, by Phyllida Hart-Davis; *Princess Grace of Monaco*, by Trevor Hall; *Grace*, by Howell Conant.

Videos reviewed: *The Children of Theatre Street* (Kultur).

The Automobile Accident That Claimed Grace's Life, the Funeral Services, and "Life after Grace"

Interviews: Gwen Robyns; Lizanne Kelly LeVine; James Bacon; Barbara Tuck Cresci; Gore Vidal; Yves Phily; Sesto Lequio; Michel Pierre; Roger Bencze; Rita Gam; Charlotte Winston; and Jay Kanter.

Features reviewed: "Portrait of a Lady," by Jack Kroll with Scott Sullivan, *Newsweek*, September 12, 1982; "Death of a Princess," by Clyde Haberman, *Los Angeles Herald Examiner*, September 15, 1982; "Princess Grace's Funeral," by Robert Musel, UPI, September 16, 1982; "A Life of Grace" (no byline), *People*, September 27, 1982; "That Special Grace," by Rita Gam, *McCall's*, January 1983; "The Legacy of Princess Grace," by Richard B. Stolley, *Life*, March 1983; "A Private Conversation with Prince Rainier . . ." by Richard B. Stolley, *Life*, March 1983; "Grace's Girls Go to War," by Darius Sanai, *International Express*, April 14, 1997; "The Truth about My Sister, Grace," by Andrew Wilson, *Daily Mail*, June 27, 1998.

Volumes reviewed: *Grace*, by Robert Lacey; *Palace: My Life in the Royal*

Family of Monaco, by Baron Christian de Massy and Charles Higham; *Rainier and Grace: An Intimate Portrait*, by Jeffrey Robinson.

Videos reviewed: *Primetime Live* (ABC-TV), January 8, 1997 (Diane Sawyer with the Grimaldis); *Grace Kelly: The American Princess* (MPI Video).

Epilogue, and also Material Having to Do with Monaco, after Princess Grace's Death

Interviews: Gary Pudney; Charlotte Winston; Hope Scott; Terry Nation; Addie Murnan; Rose Tobias; Morton Gottlieb; Katherine Archer; Jean Marie Wood; Jackie Levasseur; Leslie Marino; Gwen Robyns; Lizanne Kelly LeVine; James Bacon; Barbara Tuck Cresci; Rita Gam; and Jay Kanter.

Features reviewed: "Grace Kelly of Philadelphia," by Linda R. Marx, *People*, September 15, 1983; "The Ball Is in Prince Rainier's Court," by Jody Jacobs, *Los Angeles Times*, June 13, 1985; "SRO Party Features Reviewed: Monaco Royal Family," by Jody Jacobs, *Los Angeles Times*, November 5, 1985; "Royal Time for Monaco First Family," by Jody Jacobs, *Los Angeles Times*, November 3, 1985; "Attractions of Monaco and Monte Carlo Multiply," by Frank Riley, *Los Angeles Times*, June 2, 1985; "Land of Dreams and Fantasies," by Michael Dobbs, *Washington Post*, May 12, 1985; "Monaco Celebrates the 700th Anniversary of the Grimaldi Family" (no byline), *Hello*, January 1, 1987; "Monaco: No Joke to Loyal Citizenry," by Stanley Meisler, *Los Angeles Times*, February 14, 1987; "Monaco Is a Spin of the Wheel Away," by Beverly Beyer and Ed Rabey, *Los Angeles Times*, June 11, 1989; "Thieves Shake Monaco's Reputation As 'Safe Haven,'" by Penelope Hocking-Vigie, Reuters, May 6, 1990; "Clientele Is Changed, but Monaco's Reputation Is Still Richly Deserved," by Marilyn August, *Los Angeles Times*, November 25, 1990; "Tiny Monaco Requests Full U.N. Membership," Associated Press, May 22, 1993; "Monaco: The Tarnish on the Crown," by William Middleton, *Vancouver Sun*, October 1, 1994; "A Look Back as Monaco Prepares to Celebrate the 700th . . ." (no byline), *Hello*, December 21, 1996; "A Family Affair with the Whole World Watching," by Thomas Sancton,

Time, January 20, 1997; "Monaco's Royal Anniversary," by Marco R. della Cava, *USA Today*, April 29, 1997; "The Prince and the Paupers," by Don Katz, *Rolling Stone*, March 10, 1977; "Monaco's Red Cross Marks Its Half Century" (no byline), *Hello*, August 22, 1998; "First Official Photographs to Mark the Golden Jubilee . . ." by Anne Saint-Jean, *Hello*, January 9, 1999; "In the Company of Sovereign Princes" (no byline), *Financial Times*, May 6, 1999; "Prince Rainier of Monaco Gives a Rare, In-Depth Interview," by Didier Contant, *Hello*, May 25, 1999; "Monaco's Dazzling 1999 Rose Ball" (no byline), *Hello*, April 6, 1999; "Prince Rainier of Monaco" (no byline), *Hello*, February 2000; "Stephanie's Wayward Life Will Cost Her . . ." by Ian Sparks, *Daily Mail*, October 6, 2000; "Lives in the Fast Lane: Young, Rich and Royal" (no byline), *US Weekly*, July 2, 2001; "The Toast of Europe: Charlotte Casiraghi," by John Glatt, *Australian Women's Weekly*, May 2002; "New Law of Succession in Monaco Keeps the Crown in the Family," by Pamela Sampson, Associated Press, May 15, 2002; "Charlotte of Monaco" (no byline), *Hello*, July 2002; "Monte Carlo's Red Cross Ball" (no byline), *Hello*, August 24, 2002; "Fall from Grace" (no byline), *Royalty*, vol. 12, no. 11.

Volumes reviewed: *Princess Grace: An Interpretive Biography*, by Steven Englund; *Royal House of Monaco*, by John Glatt; *Grace*, by Sarah Bradford; *The Bridesmaids: Grace Kelly, Princess of Monaco and Six Intimate Friends*, by Judith Balaban Quine; *Inside Monaco*, by Siri Campbell; *Palace: My Life in the Royal Family of Monaco*, by Baron Christian de Massy and Charles Higham.

Videos reviewed: *Prince Rainier's Fiftieth Jubilee*, May 9, 1999 (privately owned); *Grace Kelly* (Learning Channel); *Grace Kelly: The American Princess* (MPI Video); *E! True Hollywood Story: The Curse of the Grimaldis* (E! Channel).

Index

Index